D0023391

Images of Love and Religion

They never saw piety but in one dresse, that thinke she cannot sute her selfe according to occasions, and put her selfe so farre into the fashion, as may make her the easilier accostable, and yet retaine her dignity and decency

Walter Montague, *Miscellanea Spiritualia*
(sig. G3ᵛ), dedicated to Henrietta Maria

Sir Anthony van Dyck, portrait of Queen Henrietta Maria; the Royal Collection, reproduced by Gracious Permission of Her Majesty The Queen

Images of Love and Religion

Queen Henrietta Maria and court entertainments

ERICA VEEVERS

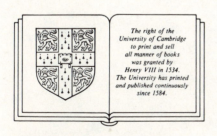

The right of the
University of Cambridge
to print and sell
all manner of books
was granted by
Henry VIII in 1534.
The University has printed
and published continuously
since 1584.

Cambridge University Press

Cambridge

New York   New Rochelle   Melbourne   Sydney

Published by the Press Syndicate of the University of Cambridge
The Pitt Building, Trumpington Street, Cambridge CB2 IRP
32 East 57th Street, New York, NY 10022, USA
10 Stamford Road, Oakleigh, Melbourne 3166, Australia

© Cambridge University Press 1989

First published 1989

Printed in Great Britain by The Bath Press, Avon

British Library cataloguing in publication data

Veevers, Erica
Images of love and religion: Queen
Henrietta Maria and court entertainments.
1. English court drama, 1625–1702.
Critical studies
1. Title
822'.4'09

Library of Congress cataloging in publication data

Veevers, Erica
Images of love and religion: Queen Henrietta Maria and court
entertainments / Erica Veevers.
    p.   cm.
Bibliography
ISBN 0 521 34309 7
1. English drama – 17th century – History and criticism.   2. Great
Britain – Court and courtiers – History – 17th century.   3. Henrietta
Maria, Queen, consort of Charles I, King of England, 1609–1669.
4. Masques – History and criticism.   5. Theater – Great Britain –
History – 17th century.   6. Love in literature.   7. Religion in
literature.   1. Title.
PR678.C7V44 1989
822'.4'09 – dc 19   88–16204
CIP

ISBN 0 521 34309 7

BS

Contents

Illustrations

Inigo Jones's designs for pastoral and masques, from the Devonshire Collection, Chatsworth, are reproduced by permission of the Chatsworth Settlement Trustees; photographs are reproduced by permission of the Courtauld Institute of Art. Bracketed numbers after these designs in the following list refer to catalogue numbers in Stephen Orgel and Roy Strong, *Inigo Jones: The Theatre of the Stuart Court.*

Preface

This book is addressed to readers who are interested in the relations between religion, social fashions, and the arts. Its focus is on the Caroline court, principally from the point of view of Charles's French Queen, and its main concern is with plays and masques presented between 1630 and 1640. It ranges back, however, to the beginning of the seventeenth century for the history of Henrietta Maria's French fashions and religious background, and for the early development of the court stage.

My interest in the topic has extended over a number of years and was stimulated originally by contact with the Warburg Institute, in whose library books on music and magic, art and diplomacy, entertainments and religion, took their places side by side. It seemed to me that that was how these subjects must have existed in a Renaissance mind, and that the 1630s saw the last practical application at an English court of mental habits that made little separation between different areas of knowledge. In recent years of course there have been many outstanding works that have approached the culture of the court in this way. Particularly valuable for interpretation of the masques has been the work of Stephen Orgel and Roy Strong, who brought together texts and designs for the first time. Among earlier writers to whom I am indebted are D. J. Gordon, whose work was crucial to the fresh interest in visual symbolism, and Frances Yates, whose works remain a monument to research on Neoplatonism, religion, and court entertainments.

This study was first completed as a doctoral thesis, and it is a pleasure to acknowledge my thanks to friends and colleagues at Macquarie University, in particular to Professor A. M. Gibbs, who read early drafts of chapters, and to Dr A. D. Cousins, for his counsel in the final stages of writing. I am also very grateful to subsequent readers whose comments added perspective to the study, and from whose criticism I have endeavoured to profit; shortcomings that remain in the work are of course my own. Many of my obligations have been to the libraries in which I have worked from time to time to collect material, and I would like to express thanks for courteous assistance to the staffs of the British Library, London; the Henry E. Huntington Library, California; Stanford University Library; Fisher Library, University of Sydney; the State Library, Sydney; and Macquarie University Library. My thanks to Judy Faulkner for her more than ordinary care in typing.

To family and friends, some of whom have read and given comments on the manuscript or helped in innumerable other ways, my warmest thanks for their helpful interest and their enduring patience.

Table of events in relation to masques, 1630–40

Year	Masques and plays	Artistic events	Anglican and Puritan	Catholic events
1627		Mantua collection purchased	Cosin, *Private Devotions* (1627); tried for innovations in ritual, 1628, 1629; attacked by Smart and Prynne	Queen's French retinue and priests dismissed; her influence greater after Buckingham's death
1628		Honthorst's allegory of the Arts		Caussin, *The Holy Court*, I (1626) translation dedicated to Queen;
1629			Charles's ruling that Church has power to decree ceremony, attacked in Parliament 1629; King begins absolute rule	Capucin Friars arrive Feb. 1630
1630	Miscellaneous	Rubens's allegory of King and Queen and sketches for Banqueting House		Prince Charles born May 1630
1631 Jan. 9 Feb. 22	*Love's Triumph through Callipolis* (K) *Chloridia* (Q)	Commission to Jones for repair of St Paul's (April)	Laud opens St Katherine Kree with conspicuous ceremony	*The Holy Court*, II, dedicated to Earl of Dorset, with new section on 'The Lady'
1632 Jan. 8 Feb. 14	*Albion's Triumph* (K) *Tempe Restored* (Q)	Commission to Jones for Queen's Chapel at Somerset House; Van Dyck settles in England	Star Chamber case over window at Salisbury, Laud defends images (Feb.)	Queen lays foundation stone for Somerset House chapel, dedicated to Virgin, September 1632
1633 Jan. 9 Feb. 2	*The Shepherd's Paradise* performed by Queen 1 repeat performance	Milton's *Arcades* Rebuilding of St Paul's begins	Prynne, *Histriomastix* Laud, appointed Archbishop of Canterbury Charles, Coronation in Scotland; approves Laud's reforms Controversy over Church ceremony	Opening negotiations with Cardinal Barberini for exchange of Agents with Vatican, October 1633; Hawkins, *Parthenia Sacra* written for English Sodality of the Virgin
1634 Jan. Feb. 3 Feb. 13 Feb. 18	*The Faithful Shepherdess* (2 performances) *The Triumph of Peace* 1 repeat performance *Coelum Britannicum* (K)	Milton's *Comus*	Laud enforces Visitation Articles (1633–36) to ensure uniformity throughout Kingdom	Queen's Agent chosen for Rome; Panzani appointed as Papal envoy, visits Paris (Apr.); Davenport's *Deus, Natura, Gratia* argues conformity of 39 Articles with Rome (July); Caussin, *The Holy Court*, III, dedicated to Countess of Portland; Panzani arrives at court (12 Dec.)
1635 Feb. 10	*The Temple of Love* (Q) (repeated on 11, 12, and possibly 14 Feb.)	Rubens's ceiling panels installed in Banqueting House; Somerset Chapel nearing complete...	Violent opposition to Laud's Church policies	Stafford, *The Female Glory* (published with official permission); N. N., *Maria Triumphans* (dedicated to Queen...

Date	Court masques and plays	Paintings and chapel	Political and religious events	Catholic affairs at court
1636 Feb. 24	*Triumphs of the Prince d'Amour*		Arrival of Charles Louis, Count Palatine (Nov.)	Montague converted to Catholicism (Easter), followed by Sir K. Digby (Oct.)
Aug. 30	*The Royal Slave* at Oxford	Valuable gift of paintings from Barberini to King	Arrival of Prince Rupert (Feb.); entertainment of Palatine Princes. Oxford, reformed by Laud's building and artistic programmes, visited by King and Queen (Aug.)	Montague received in Rome by Pope, becomes Oratorian priest (Feb.) Sir Wm. Hamilton arrives in Rome as Queen's Agent (June) George Conn arrives at court to replace Panzani, opens public Oratory (July) Arch-Confraternity of Holy Rosary established in Queen's chapel
1637 Jan. 12	*The Royal Slave* repeated for Queen at Hampton Court	Queen's chapel opens with spectacular services (Dec.) Queen holds public viewing of all paintings from Rome	Burton, *For God, and the King* (Nov.) (criticises *The Female Glory*) Burton arrested; Star Chamber trial of Burton, Bastwick, and Prynne (Feb.) Controversy over position of altars Laud defends images again Rebellion in Scotland Laud issues proclamation against resorting to Mass (Dec.)	Montague back at court, shares Conn's Chapel which becomes centre for Catholic events attended by Queen Wedding of Viscount Montague (July) Conversion of Lady Newport (Oct.) Pontifical Mass for late Duke of Savoy (Nov.) Queen holds Midnight Mass at Somerset House chapel for all recent converts, in defiance of Laud's Proclamation (Dec.)
1638 Jan. 17	*Britannia Triumphans* (K)	St Paul's shown in opening scene of *Britannia Triumphans*	Scottish National Covenant and The First Bishops' War (Feb.)	Lenton, verses on Queen in *Luminalia* entitled *The Female Glory*; *The Holy Court*, IV, dedicated to Duchess of Buckingham; Marie de Medici arrives at court (Oct.)
Feb. 6	*Luminalia* (Q)			
1640 Jan. 21	*Salmacida Spolia* (K and Q) Marie de Medici present		The Root and Branch Petition	Conn dies; replaced by Rossetti, who urges Charles to closer alliance with Catholic powers
Feb. 16, 17	2 repeat performances			

K King;   Q Queen

Introduction

The decade 1630 to 1640, immediately preceding the Civil War, marks the transition in English social and political life from one set of ideas and values to another. The culture of the Caroline court used to be regarded as an aristocratic escape from the tensions of that transition, and only recently have the court and its entertainments been receiving fresh critical attention, after many years of comparative neglect. Stephen Orgel and Roy Strong's studies of court culture, especially the two-volume work *Inigo Jones: The Theatre of the Stuart Court* (1973), put masque studies on a new footing. Graham Parry's *The Golden Age Restor'd: The Culture of the Stuart Court, 1603–42* (1981) has provided a valuable overview, and *The Court Masque* (1984), edited by David Lindley, offers many promising avenues for masque exploration. The many studies of Milton's works, John Demaray's *Milton's Theatrical Epic* (1980) and Maryann McGuire's *Milton's Puritan Masque* (1983) among them, depend on a close understanding of Caroline court conventions and ideas. Martin Butler's *Theatre and Crisis 1632–1642* (1984) has revived the study of Caroline drama, which had received little attention since Alfred Harbage's original study some fifty years ago; Margot Heinemann's *Puritanism and Theatre* (1980) has taken a fresh view of opposition responses to drama under the Stuarts; and Jonathan Goldberg's *James I and the Politics of Literature* (1983) has studied the relationship between authority and its visual and verbal representations. Books by David Norbrook, *Poetry and Politics in the English Renaissance* (1984), Annabel Patterson, *Censorship and Interpretation: The Conditions of Writing and Reading in Early Modern England* (1985), and Douglas Brooks-Davies, *The Mercurian Monarch: Magical Politics from Spenser to Pope* (1983), all include the Caroline period in their explorations of literature in the context of social, political, and religious ideas.

The Caroline court, however, has been seen generally from the point of view of the King, of Parliament, or of public affairs. This study looks at it from the point of view of Charles's Queen, Henrietta Maria, with her French background, her interest in people rather than politics, and her absorption in religion. Its initial concern is with an area that has received very little critical attention, the relationship between the Queen's Catholicism and the fashions of *préciosité* and Platonic love that she fostered at the English court. These fashions are generally acknowledged to have had considerable influence on Caroline court life and literature, but they are in need of reassessment: little work has been done on them since the early years of this century, when J. B. Fletcher traced their origin to the Hôtel de Rambouillet and to the influence of Honoré d'Urfé's romance *L'Astrée*. Subsequent studies, notably of Cavalier and Restoration drama, have relied basically on Fletcher's work. There has been very little attempt to examine French *préciosité* in more detail, or to take into account factors that might have helped to form or change Henrietta's version of the fashion after it arrived in England.

In discussions of Henrietta's influence on literature, moreover, scarcely any attention has been paid to her Catholicism. If it is mentioned at all it tends to be treated as an unfortunate aspect of her character that probably hastened Charles's downfall, but that had little to do with her otherwise light-hearted devotion to pleasure. There has been only one critic to my knowledge (G. F. Sensabaugh, whose work will be discussed later) who makes a serious connection between Henrietta's love fashions and her religion, and he makes it in a context that presents uncritically the Puritan charge of sexual immorality (which Puritans often equate with the Queen's 'idolatry' or Catholicism) amongst Henrietta's circle, a charge that cannot be taken at face value. On the whole Henrietta's fashions have not attracted sympathetic consideration, either from contemporaries outside the court or from later critics. Her fashions were French, feminist, and Catholic, qualities that were unlikely to win sympathy in England at the time, and that were regarded with suspicion long after the Civil War. Even the Stuart propaganda that idealised Charles was not anxious to revive connections with a French Catholic wife. In the 1630s, however, Henrietta was an important figure in the cultural life of the court, and this study, in attempting to look afresh at her social fashions and the arts they influenced, makes new connections between them and her Catholicism. The two were connected in France, and Henrietta herself made no great distinction between entertainments and 'devotions'.

Henrietta's version of *préciosité* is generally taken to be a more or less exact copy of that in vogue in France in the early seventeenth century and practised by the *salons*. Certainly she helped to introduce this type of *préciosité* to the English court in the 1620s, and it continued to exert its influence throughout the 1630s and beyond. *Préciosité*, however, was not a static set of ideas. Like most fashions it tended to move fairly rapidly through different phases, and to change its character according to its surroundings and the people by whom it was practised. Henrietta's version itself was not acquired directly from the Hôtel de Rambouillet, but from circles at the French court dominated by her mother, Marie de Medici. These circles were influenced by the *salons*, but also by the religious enthusiasms of the Counter-Reformation, in particular the Devout Humanism of St François de Sales. Devout Humanism shared with *L'Astrée* an element of Neoplatonic idealism, and religious writers drew on d'Urfé's popularity to spread the influence of religion, particularly in 'the religious romance'. By the late 1620s the two contemporary influences had combined in a phase of *préciosité* of which *honnêteté* was the distinguishing feature.

The concept of *honnêteté*, which came to prominence from about 1630 in polite circles in France, was especially important for the behaviour of women. It invested women with the Neoplatonic qualities – Beauty, Virtue, and Love – but instead of the extreme 'woman-worship' of *L'Astrée* it recommended a conservative feminism, in which women exercised their beauty and virtue in such a way as to make for cordial relations between the sexes and for a general social harmony governed by religion. Certainly this feminism was much milder than any that developed later in the century (or any that would be recognised as feminism today), and it went on to develop as a *bourgeois* concept in France. At its inception, however, and as it developed in the 1630s, it was modelled on, and addressed to, an ideal of behaviour at court. At the English court Walter Montague translated the first important book for women in the genre, Jacques Du Bosc's *L'Honneste Femme* (1632), under the title *The Accomplish'd Woman*. The exact date of the translation is not known, but Montague placed it in a courtly setting by dedicating it to the Duchess of Buckingham, who, he says, is a reflection of the ideas in the book. Montague developed his own ideas on the connections between religion and court life in *Miscellanea Spiritualia*, Part 1 of which he dedicated to Henrietta Maria; these 'Devout Essaies' draw on the ideas of Devout Humanists and suggest a religious context for the kind of 'Platonic love' practised by the Queen. From the evidence of poetry and plays it seems probable that it was the *honnête* type of *préciosité* that Henrietta adopted from about 1630, and that the *salon* type (stemming more directly from *L'Astrée*) centred around Lady Carlisle, the Queen's rival in 'beauty' as she was, very often, in politics.

The recognition of two distinct versions of *préciosité*, and of different versions of 'Platonic love' at court, gives a more secure basis for distinguishing between different kinds of play being written in the thirties. Writers such as Jonson and Davenant, for instance, brought up in the older Italian Renaissance tradition of Neoplatonism, seem to have had difficulty in adjusting to the new French fashion, and it seems to me that *The New Inne* and *The Platonic Lovers*, usually thought of as central to a study of Henrietta's fashions, may not reflect (even as criticism) the version favoured by the Queen. On the other hand writers such as Montague, Carlell, and Rutter, who were at home with the Queen's *honnête* fashion, presented a type of drama in which mutual love and marriage were the ideal, not 'Platonic love' in d'Urfé's sense at all. I suggest, in addition, that a distinction between different versions of Platonic love is useful in judging the moral tone of court drama, about which critics have often come to quite opposite conclusions. The Queen's fashion did encourage a 'Platonic' drama, but of a type in which Platonic love was interpreted as Christian charity and was strongly linked with Divine Providence in a tradition similar to that of *commedia grave* in Italy. The extension of the concept of 'Love' beyond the personal, to a principle of universal peace and harmony approved by 'heaven', made a useful political statement in the 1630s in line with the arguments for peace being advocated by Charles.

A clearer idea of the influence of Henrietta's fashions on the drama is useful also in adding to an understanding of the political role of the drama, and the part that Henrietta played in it. Martin Butler's study, *Theatre and Crisis 1632–1642*, has stressed the lively political debate that was possible in plays of the thirties; he has also emphasised (in chapters 3 and 4) the potentially political function of the Queen's doctrine of Platonic love, which he sees as providing a focus for 'Puritan' opposition to the policies of the King. While a Puritan focus is undoubtedly present in certain plays, it seems to me to strengthen Butler's general argument if the debate in thirties drama is seen first in terms of the 'feminism' that was an important element in it, and only indirectly in terms of political comment. In plays influenced by the Queen's fashions the rights and dignity of women, as well as their virtue, are continually defended against the power and abuses of men. For dramatists such a defence could provide, at one remove, an apposite framework in which other repressed rights (for example, of subjects against kings) might be looked at, and in which a whole range of views and attitudes might be debated. To jump directly to the political motives and to impute complex political interests to the Queen seems to me to miss a step in the argument, making the plight of queens in the plays too directly representative of the political plight of the kingdom, and making Charles, moreover, too directly a profligate or a tyrant. The Queen's love fashions set up a useful polarity between men and women, kings and queens, ruler and ruled, so that views expressed in the plays do, as Butler argues, suggest a tension which has broader implications. But it may be truer to see these debates in terms of the Queen's feminism, which provided an analogy for discussion of broader political issues: issues that in the thirties could still be debated within the bounds of 'love' and the bond of marriage, before the political lines between King and Parliament were so firmly drawn.

The 'politicisation' of love to which Butler has drawn attention had, of course, a long history, which David Norbrook has recently recounted in his *Poetry and Politics*. The expression of this tradition in the seventeenth century had its roots in Sidney's *Arcadia*, which, as Norbrook and others have shown, was a basic political text of Elizabeth's reign. The *Arcadia*'s setting is one of 'courtly' love and contemplation, but its theme is a critique of absolutism and inaction, which Sidney sees as turning inward to the private life while ignoring the public good. The critique might have been thought all too apposite to the thirties, yet, as Annabel Patterson points out in *Censorship and Interpretation*, the *Arcadia* enjoyed a renaissance in Charles's reign. How, Patterson asks (p. 25), could Charles so misread the *Arcadia* as to 'incorporate it into his own visions, his own program of English arcadianism, the halcyon days of the 1630s?' That he did so suggests a deliberate effort of 'cultural revisionism', involving Charles's identification of himself with chivalric romance in the St George legend, and Henrietta's of herself with pastoral romance. The full effects of this revisionism Patterson sees reflected in literature of the 1640s, and in the 'Royal romances' which led up to and celebrated the Restoration. But the roots of this later literature lie, I think, even deeper in the court mythology of the 1630s, and depend on a fuller understanding of Henrietta's role in it.

One of Sidney's initial concerns in the *Arcadia* was Elizabeth's French marriage plans, which his sub-text criticises as romantic indulgence, an unchaste turning away from her kingdom, which, contemporaries feared, was likely to be 'swallowed up' by another French marriage (Patterson, pp. 25–33). Spenser's works, as Norbrook's discussion shows (in chapters 3 and 5), had celebrated to a certain extent the failure of such plans; his mythologising of Elizabeth as the 'Virgin' Queen amounted to a Protestant revision of pre-Reformation (and perforce Catholic) religious imagery, knitting together the threads of English patriotism and apocalyptic militant Protestantism. By 1630, however, the marriage between France and England that had been so long deferred had at last taken place, with every appearance of personal happiness. The object of Caroline mythology seems to have been to overturn Sidney's hidden warnings, and to raise personal happiness to a state of social and universal harmony. Plays and poetry attempted to achieve that aim by an emphasis on chastity and an idealisation of married love. It seems to me that the Queen's pastoral *The Shepherd's Paradise* became for the 1630s the new *Arcadia*. The story (as I suggest later) may contain a romantic allusion to the King and Queen's own courtship, perhaps making the pastoral the first of the 'Royal romances', and its theme is in a sense a reworking of Sidney's. The 'foundress' of the paradise is said to be a former Queen, who dedicated herself to chastity because of her unhappy love for a Prince of France; the new Queen is Bellesa, a daughter of Navarre, whose marriage makes her Queen of 'Albion'. The pastoral, with its insistence on moral courtship and married love, seems to create a mirror image of the militant England of the 'Virgin' Queen, an image of conjugal happiness in which the great 'Bel-Liza' becomes the beautiful 'Bellesa', and in which the French–English marriage can at last promote peace, at home and abroad. Such a theme has recognisable political meaning, but it is also connected with a strong undercurrent of religious propaganda in Elizabethan and Stuart literature, in which the links between Henrietta's love fashions and her Catholicism seem to me to become significant.

To understand the role of religion in connection with love, entertainments, and politics in the 1630s it is important, I think, to understand the type of Catholicism which Henrietta practised. Former historians (for example, S. R. Gardiner in *The History of England* and C. V. Wedgwood in *The King's Peace*) tended to see Henrietta as a heretic Queen, leader of crypto-Catholicism and Jesuit subversion at court. In recent criticism there has been a move to enlist her for the Puritan party. Malcolm Smuts in his paper 'The Puritan followers of Henrietta Maria in the 1630s' sees her as the friend of non-Catholics at court, providing a focus for opposition views and helping to plot (perhaps only half-consciously) against the interests of the King. Martin Butler has followed this trend into the drama, both in *Theatre and Crisis* and in his paper 'Entertaining the Palatine Prince: plays on foreign affairs 1635–1637'. He sees the Queen as a supporter of 'opposition' drama, which defended, for example, the rights of the Palatine Princes who visited the court, and which implied the need for military action (and hence the summoning of Parliament) against Spain. The truth may lie, I think, somewhere between these two views. The seeming paradoxes of Henrietta's behaviour can be explained by an understanding of the nature of her Catholicism (one of my concerns in the following study), and of European politics. The latter was complicated in regard to religion, and Henrietta had, indeed, a tangle of conflicting loyalties to deal with that would have given pause to a seasoned statesman: to her husband, to her religion, and to her country of birth. Her loyalty to the latter was further complicated by the intermittent enmity between Cardinal Richelieu and Marie de Medici, whose close correspondence with her daughter in the thirties culminated in Marie's visit to the English court in 1639. Allegiances between Catholic countries were themselves complex, since they by no means presented a common front against Protestantism.[1] Since the Habsburgs of Spain and Austria carried on the crusade against European Protestantism, France found itself aligned for political reasons with countries such as Holland and Sweden; the Vatican, fearing the power of Spain, was drawn to side with France. When Elizabeth was Queen, England's course had been clear, since Protestant nationalism was served by fighting Spanish sea-power and Catholicism at the same time, but the chronic Stuart 'peace' policy took away this clear-cut picture. Those who pressed for a more active military policy from England were allied with France rather than Spain, but their cause was Protestant rather than Catholic. Since no war could be fought without the recalling of Parliament and voting of money, the supporters of war also tended to be aligned with supporters of Parliament. To be on the side of France against Spain, then, meant to be vaguely on the side of Protestant Parliamentarians. Henrietta was certainly friendly with men who held these views, and she was openly antagonistic to Spain; but it seems an exaggeration to say, with Smuts, that she was therefore an 'instrument' of factions at court 'whose ultimate religious and political goals were inimical to her own' (p. 38). Even if she was fully aware of Parliamentary political aims, the lines between Charles and Parliament were not so irreparably damaged in 1636 that, had he called a Parliament with war against Spain and defence of the Palatinate implicitly in mind, it would inevitably have led to the toppling of the throne. It might indeed have been a sensible course, and could have left untouched Henrietta's loyalty to Charles, to France, and to her own form of Catholicism which was inimical to that of Spain.

Henrietta's religion, French Devout Humanism, was in fact recognised by contemporaries as a moderate form of Catholicism, bearing a similar relation to militant, Spanish-influenced Catholicism as Charles's Anglicanism bore to the more extreme forms of Calvinism. Potentially it could act as a mediator between Charles and more moderate Catholics, and it is in this light that Henrietta's activities can perhaps be considered most fruitfully. The role she seems to have filled, and which was a traditionally feminine one required of *honnête* women, was to promote harmonious personal and social relationships; this, in her position as Queen, meant welcoming and entertaining visitors to the court and mediating between opposing factions. She found no difficulty in doing this as long as she found the individual people likeable and attractive. In the mid-thirties she entertained the Palatine princes during the same period that she was receiving and negotiating with the Roman Catholic agents, Gregorio Panzani and George Conn. In fact the method of dealing with both sets of visitors was exactly the same, and typical of the style of diplomacy at Charles's court: both the Catholic agents (as I show later) and the princes (as Butler shows in his paper, p. 323) were received and entertained in the chambers of the Queen. Here they met for discussions with interested parties (which included on many occasions the King), thus avoiding the difficulties of a formal presentation and providing an opportunity for freer communication. Nor, on a theoretical level, was there such a contradiction in Henrietta's patronage of both parties, since the return of the Palatinate was one of the chief conditions that Charles made to the agents for furthering good relations with the Vatican. Henrietta's role in all this may not therefore have been so much political as social. She kept the channels open for discussion through informal meetings centred on the social life and entertainments which she encouraged, and preserved an atmosphere of pleasure and harmony that chimed with Charles's distaste for controversy and his desire for 'peace'. In this role Henrietta would have been doing no more than other queens who had attempted to moderate religious extremes through the influence of 'love' and the use of court entertainments: of these Catherine de Medici was one of the most notable, and it was to the culture of her court in the Valois reign that the Caroline court turned for many of its ideas. It seems to me, therefore, that the Queen's Devout Humanism, the aim of which was to combine piety with pleasure, had a real effect on the social and cultural life of Charles's court, and that it did this in a way that had, but only indirectly, political and religious implications.

There was, however, an area in which the Queen's religion was more directly connected with her love fashions and which I think may have affected court entertainments. This was the strong emphasis on Platonic Beauty and Love in the form of Devout Humanism practised by the Queen's Capucin priests, and evident in the cult of the Virgin Mary which they established at court. The 'religion' of love has been regarded almost universally as a mockery of religion (and so in many cases it was); but in the form in which it was practised by Henrietta it had some actual connections which made the religious overtones in the language of love not only fashionable, but also, in some sense, significant of more fundamental issues. A Platonic language that constantly raises women to the dignity of saints and gives them connections with Heaven, in a country that discouraged 'idol-worship' of any kind, and especially 'woman-worship', has to be taken more seriously when centred around a Catholic Queen. The Capucins who came to serve in the Queen's chapel in 1630 paid special devotion to the Virgin whom they praised as the exemplar of Beauty and Love, so that the language of Platonic love became a common element in Henrietta's love fashions and in her religion. In the mid-thirties she led an Arch-Confraternity of the Rosary which held weekly meetings and public processions, drawing together people sympathetic to her form of Devout Humanism. Contemporary books in praise of the Virgin suggest that the Queen, as the embodiment of ideals of Beauty and Love at court, might have been regarded by at least some Catholics of her circle as the Virgin's champion and representative on earth. It is evident that the Queen enjoyed the shared under-standing of cult groups, both in her social life and in her 'devotions'. Since her inclination was to express her tastes and interests through theatricals, it seems worthwhile to inquire whether the common language of Platonic love in her religion and entertainments made possible any specific connections between them. I would like to explore the possibility that there was such a connection in the Queen's masques, and that in some masques of the thirties the subject of religion had a more specific relation to contemporary questions than generally has been recognised.

The part of my study dealing with masques must, however, be regarded as speculative, since it has very little written evidence to draw on. Masques of the thirties were largely visual rather than poetic productions: Inigo Jones, who was responsible for the prose descriptions, was not as meticulous as Ben Jonson had been in giving sources for his material, or in explaining the significance of his visual images. With the exception of the first two masques, whose texts were by Jonson, and the one by Carew, the 'invention' of the rest was by Jones, and the form in which the written part has reached us is often little more than sketchy descriptions interspersed with songs or poems. Fortunately a great number of Jones's original designs have survived (more complete for this period than for the earlier masques) and, with the intense interest of Charles's court in visual art, it is more than likely that *ut pictura poesis* remained a vital principle in the audience's perception of masque scenes. That perception, however, depended largely on the relevance of the scenes to contemporary interests, and the sympathies of the spectators. We can try to recover what it might have been, but, without external evidence to confirm it, interpretation must remain at a hypothetical level.

There is indeed a scarcity of contemporary comment on what was understood by the symbolism of masques, although it seems certain that masque-makers had more than simple entertainment in mind. The long and detailed account of *The Triumph of Peace* that has survived shows that its meaning was very carefully planned and had a complex political purpose, both in making reparation to the Queen for Prynne's supposed insult, and in reciprocating with some covert criti-cism of its own.[2] Works that depend for their meaning on visual effects, however, are perhaps least likely in their own time to be subjected to explanation and analysis (it might seem to us superfluous or heavy-handed to 'explain' the signifi-cance of a modern political slogan or commercial). Most eye-witness accounts of masques tend accordingly to concentrate on the squabbles of ambassadors, the behaviour of the audience, or the richness of the jewels, rather than on the symbolic meaning.[3] Other descriptions give quite literal accounts of what took place on the stage, and from these it is interesting to note that foreigners took in much more of what they saw than of what they heard. The long report of Orazio Busino on *Pleasure Reconciled to Virtue*, for instance, describes in detail everything that was seen, but the precise significance remained vague: 'Next Mercury appeared before the King and made a speech, and then came a musician with a guitar dressed in a long robe, who played and sang some trills, implying that he was some deity . . .They sang some short pieces that we did not understand . . .' (Orgel and Strong, I, p. 283). Spectators did, however, tend to interpret what they saw in terms of what they already knew: Busino, for instance, who saw the musicians dressed as 'high priests', or the Savoy Agent who described the Queen as being seated beneath a 'baldacchin'.[4] For the Caroline period the descriptions of masques in diplomatic dispatches generally warrant only a few lines, perhaps because the stock-in-trade of imagery, much of which Jones was borrowing from Continental sources, was by that time so well known that it did not seem worth describing. By 1630 what was required by a sophisticated audience with more than a quarter century of masque-viewing behind it were large visual images, the significance of which was easy to grasp from a knowledge of the established ethos of Charles's court, and of the events that led up to the masque.

To connect any work of art with contemporary events is of course a hazardous undertaking which critics have often had occasion to discuss.[5] Few genres, however, have depended so much on a context as the masque, and few of the masques have depended on it more completely than those of the 1630s, which were produced for a court that was itself hedged off from the rest of society by a particular set of beliefs and attitudes. Masques were by their very nature occasional pieces: they were meant to 'mean', and the relevance of the occasion has been recognised increasingly. Many studies of Jonsonian masques have established their significance in terms of the relation between 'occasion' and the 'more remov'd mysteries' of which Jonson wrote. The relationship was not one of simple correspondence but of considerable complexity, and, as Leah Marcus has recently argued, masques were designed to receive and withstand close scrutiny.[6] In Jonson's masques this complexity is controlled by words and ideas, a control lacking in masques dominated by Inigo Jones in the thirties. Jones's masques were no less complex than Jonson's but his means and emphasis differed: he depended not so much on words and literary invention to convey meaning as on a harmony of all the arts working together to create an effect on the spectators. Such works often have an appeal to the imagination and emotions that is given off only in the ambience of performance. To enter fully into the spirit of Jones's masques, therefore, one must take into account not only the words and extant designs, but the colour, the lights, the excitement of the occasion itself, the festive warmth of the midwinter season heightened both by entertainments and increased religious services and ceremony.[7] When, as in the thirties, the masques were performed by the King and Queen themselves, the lines between the fictional context and reality, so essential to keep in mind when dealing with other works, become more blurred. The spectators assist at an event in which the performers are both their real and their ideal selves, and the function of the masque is to keep the spectator aware and involved on both levels. In this sense masque is more like a ceremony or a religious rite than a work of art: it has a meaning which is immediate the compelling, but which is unexplainable except in terms of the cultural climate and intellectual interests of those who perform and those who perceive it.

The principal interpretation of Caroline masques in terms of their political and cultural background has been by Stephen Orgel and Roy Strong in the introductory chapters of *Inigo Jones: The Theatre of the Stuart Court* and other related works (listed in References). In interpreting visual as well as verbal imagery the authors give full weight to Charles's political interests, which, in the doctrine of Divine Right, were inextricably bound up with his religious interests. They stress the political significance of the Queen's Platonic doctrines (especially pp. 54–7) and their importance in supporting the King's assertions of power: in the symbolic language of the masques, the authors suggest, the joining of the King's authority and reason with the Queen's purified beauty and love amounts to an apologia for absolute rule. In dealing with the Queen's Platonic ideals, however, Orgel and Strong base their analysis mainly on the poetic expression of these in Jonson's first two masques of the thirties; the rest of the Queen's masques are seen as more or less spectacular repetitions of the same ideas, or as echoes of the King's masques with which they are paired. While the Queen's masques do complement the King's and serve to support the Doctrine of Divine Right, it seems to me that they have, in addition, a distinctive character and meaning of their own, one that is conveyed through the contrasting sets of images created for the King and Queen on the stage.

In the King's masques, with their emphasis on neoclassical and architectural images, Charles is associated with the ideal qualities of Reason, Truth, and Harmony, qualities that for Charles exemplified the virtues of his political and religious rule. In the Queen's masques, with their emphasis on movement and light, Jones seems to create a contrasting set of images that depend on the effects of contemporary painting and suggest the 'spiritual' qualities of Beauty and Light embodied by the Queen. These images were no doubt for Jones a correlative of the Neoplatonic ideal in the Queen's fashions, but they also harmonised with that ideal in her religion, and blended with the visual expression of it in Counter-Reformation art. This is not to say, of course, that Jones was deliberately creating 'Catholic' images for the Queen. Although he had been born and perhaps remained a Catholic, his first loyalty was undoubtedly to art, which he pursued with an almost religious intensity.[8] But recent research by John Peacock has shown that Henrietta had considerable artistic influence on Jones's stage productions, and that in the pastorals her influence was directed towards the expression of her religious tastes.[9] It seems to me that in her masques also, the images of Beauty and Light that clustered around her on the stage harmonised with the visual forms of her religion, and especially with the traditional emblematic settings for the Virgin made familiar by the cult at court, giving her masques the potential for conveying meaning in terms of her religious interests.

The images created for Henrietta were not, of course, unique to her. They were in fact traditional to the representation of feminine beauty on the stage (much of it itself derived from religious sources) and part of the common stock of European courts from which Jones borrowed many of his designs. They also echoed similar imagery used for Queen Anne in the early masques of the seventeenth century. In the case of European courts, however, a connection between the ruler of the State and the Catholic church could often be taken for granted, or deliberately encouraged. In the case of Queen Anne's masques, Jonson gave classical antecedents for his images, lending respectability to pre-Reformation forms that had survived on the stage but that Jonson's classical learning made acceptable in an Anglican setting. Queen Elizabeth herself had adapted to her own iconography many images with traditional Catholic associations (including images of the Virgin), so that these had already become familiar at court. Clustered around Henrietta, an overtly Catholic Queen, they may well have regained in the thirties some of their original associations. Such associations were not necessarily 'Catholic' in a narrow sense, but they set up a religious ambience that could be interpreted on a number of different levels. For those with an English background they could simply be a continuation of the iconography made familiar by Jonson's masques. For ambassadors and visitors from Catholic countries, however, it would have seemed natural to see the Queen associated with visual images appropriate to her religion; to Henrietta herself such images would have had an affinity with the Catholic culture in which she had grown up; and for Catholics of her own circle, familiar with similar images in the cult of the Virgin, they would have seemed entirely appropriate for a Queen who claimed the Virgin as her Patroness. The Queen's first two masques may have had no more than a general visual appropriateness to her religion, but the two later masques, *The Temple of Love* and *Luminalia*, do, I shall suggest, have a close correlation with Catholic concerns at court, and in the case of *Luminalia* the connection has external written evidence to support it.

Although Henrietta had her own religious interests to follow they were not totally opposed to those of Charles, and I think that her presence in the masques had an important function in providing a focus for all those 'feminine' qualities that complemented the 'masculine' qualities of the King, and that were important in a religious as well as a political context. Religious authority was linked with political authority, and Charles had several closely connected religious concerns in the thirties: quelling religious dissent in Scotland; introducing conformity of religious worship to the Church; and holding a conciliatory attitude towards moderate Catholic countries while maintaining the independence of his own Anglican rule. It seems to me that the Queen's Devout Humanism exemplified certain moderate elements that were in sympathy with Charles's Anglicanism and were important to all these concerns, most notably in its stress on 'beauty' of religious worship, and in the settling of religious disputes through 'love', or peaceful means. If the Queen's embodiment of the ideal qualities of Beauty and Love had a dimension in which they related to her religion, then the symbolic joining of the King and Queen in the masques may have been useful in suggesting those qualities that were vital to Charles in his own ideal of religion, the combining of the beauty of worship with doctrinal truth, and the adoption of a conciliatory attitude towards differences between religions. In the masques the King clearly is shown as the representative of Anglicanism, and his religion is still the dominant and commanding power, maintaining its claim to purity but strong enough to join with its reformed 'feminine' side once more. The harmonious relationship of the King and Queen in the masques may have been intended as a pattern for Christian peace, one in which the twin figure of the 'Mary–Charles' was emblematic of policies originally put forward by James, of joining opposed religions through marriage and promoting peace through love.

It may be argued that, if religious symbolism were indeed an element in the masques, it ought to have provoked more explicit comment from Puritans. In fact, there is no specific criticism of masques until after 1640, and the one lengthy analysis of a particular masque, *Britannia Triumphans*, was made long after the event (by John Ridpath in *The Stage Condemn'd*, 1698). There was, of course a great deal of criticism in the early thirties of court and stage fashions, and much of it centred around Henrietta, but it is likely that the harsh punishment of Burton and Prynne after 1633 was a severe deterrent to too close a scrutiny of court entertainments. In 1643, however, a parody of *The Triumph of Peace* entitled *The Tragedy of the Cruell Warre*, identifies the war with 'popish' conspiracy, suggesting that the issue of religion was indeed linked with the Royalist shows of the mid-thirties.[10] Critics of the court did, moreover, consistently connect stage spectacle with church ritual and condemn both for their links with 'popery'. In the complaints of the Commons against Laud the whole of Laudian ceremony was described in terms that suggest the homage paid to Royalty in the masques.[11] Such complaints were, of course, at least as old as Christianity, and not necessarily indicative of any specific religious content in productions on the court stage; but the prejudice was, I think, given extra substance in the 1630s. The very visibility of the Queen's Catholicism reinforced the many parallels between religious ceremony and the court stage that had survived the Reformation, and must have seemed to give a Catholic colouring to the way in which Charles was presenting his reign. The conspicuous ceremony in the Queen's chapel, which a contemporary likened to Jones's masque scenes, and the Queen's religious processions, which came after the public processions of *The Triumph of Peace*, must have reinforced visual similarities between Catholic ceremony and court spectacle, seeming to make Charles more sympathetic towards the Queen's religion than he actually was, and perhaps encouraging those who followed the Queen's religion to suppose her more influential than was the case.

Historical events often appear to be a reaction, not so much to what is so, as to what, at the time, is perceived to be so. Whether or not the 'Catholic' associations of imagery in the masques had a polemical intent is perhaps less important in the end than the way in which the perception of outsiders was coloured by the links between Henrietta's love fashions and her religion. Such links suggest that her entertainments were far more vitally concerned in events of the 1630s than generally has been recognised.

1   The Queen's fashions

Préciosité and Platonic love

Henrietta Maria has never quite lived down the impression she made on her arrival in England: that of a lively but temperamental princess, whose mind was probably as light as her dancing or the feather in her hat. When she married Charles early in 1625 she was in fact only fifteen, pretty and somewhat spoilt. Her first years at court did little to change the impression, or to suggest that she was interested in much more than entertaining herself and her followers with play-acting and dancing. It was not until about 1630, following the death of the Duke of Buckingham, whose influence clashed with her own, that she and Charles settled down to a mutually happy marriage, and that she took a central place in the cultural life of the court. Her influence on that culture generally has been judged rather unfavourably, since it encouraged a taste in the drama for windy pastoral or 'Platonic' plays, and in the masque for balletic display and spectacle, seemingly at the expense of meaning.

The fashions of *préciosité* and Platonic love that Henrietta brought with her to the English court are probably better known today for the witty poems that mocked them than for the works that praised them; for instance Cleveland's 'Antiplatonick' verses:

> For shame, thou everlasting Wooer,
> Still saying grace, and never falling to her!

are more familiar than Suckling's solemn 'Letters' to Aglaura on the subject. In the 1630s, however, there were those (including, in other moods, the mockers) who took them very seriously indeed. Her fashions influenced court life and culture throughout Charles's reign, and beyond it to the Restoration.[1] The term *préciosité*, in its simplest sense, refers to the set of manners and literary tastes that had developed in France during the opening years of the seventeenth century. The fashion grew up in Parisian *salons*, which formed a world outside the court though with connections to it, and it influenced French culture throughout the century.[2] The *salons* came into being partly in reaction to the coarse manners and morals of Henri IV's court: some were led by people who were unreconciled to Henri's rule and who still remembered the more sophisticated culture of the Valois court; most were concerned with cultivating the personal interests and social life that the comparative peace and stability of Henri's reign had, after the French religious wars, once more made possible. The *salons*, or large rooms of private houses, became the meeting places for informal assemblies of people who shared similar interests. The assemblies were generally led by outstanding women, of whom Mme de Rambouillet became the best known, and were dominated by feminine tastes; the groups were usually small, and exclusive not solely on the grounds of social rank, but on personal qualities of manners, wit, or learning as well. The emphasis in these assemblies was on elegant yet easy manners which avoided the formality and showy luxury of the court, as well as whatever was thought to be common or coarse in behaviour or expression. They existed for the sake of conversation, which was regarded as an art; learning and knowledge were valued, but pedantry of any kind was laughed to scorn.

The *salons* brought together men and women who had a common interest in social diversion and rational discussion. Relations between the sexes were governed by an ideal of *honnête amitié*, founded on mutual respect, from which passion was excluded. Sexual attraction played its part within the group, adding interest to its relationships, but was firmly governed by a rigid code of courtship. Women were to be venerated for their beauty and virtue and men were expected to compliment and admire such women, calling them their 'mistresses', but not to hope for any return except the continued company and conversation of the beloved. Such 'lovers' were expected to overcome passion by exercising their wit in ways which might interest or entertain virtuous women, and, since all 'honest' courtship was open to the inspection of the group, their efforts became public offerings, often in the form of poems, plays, and romances. From these works the group learnt artistically refined forms of expression, which it adopted as its own language, but this in turn involved writers in finding ever more intricate and *recherché* ways of handling familiar subject matter. From such refinement and inbreeding of language and expression developed the characteristics of *précieux* style: a search for recondite and ingenious comparisons, which at the same time avoided archaic, pedantic, or vulgar expressions; and a dependence on antithesis, allegory, and abstraction, the aim of which was to communicate wittily with the group in ways which avoided obviousness and which often veiled the meaning from outsiders.[3] At its best the style had distinction, at its worst it fell into affectation.

The best known and most influential of the *salons* was that led by Catherine de Vivonne, who had retired from the court soon after her marriage in 1600 to live at the Hôtel de Rambouillet where she gathered around her a group of cultivated people who shared her tastes and interests.[4] At the Hôtel de Rambouillet these people found a peaceful refuge where they could occupy themselves in conversation, writing, painting, and play-acting, and amuse each other with poetry, protracted wooing, and even with practical jokes. It should not be imagined, however, that it was a refuge in which to practise 'natural' manners or loose morals. On the contrary, the group saw itself as setting a high standard of moral conduct. Although *précieux* groups usually require a protected atmosphere in which to flourish, they do not grow out of a surfeit of peace or an over-refined society: as Odette de Mourgues has pointed out (in *Metaphysical Baroque and Précieux Poetry*, p. 116), they tend to appear at times and in places where established values and 'civilized' standards are under threat. They are generally characterised by a desire to improve manners and refine the arts, and they are governed, at least in their inception, by strict codes of moral conduct. The Hôtel de Rambouillet could hardly have functioned for so long as a group if such codes had not been observed. It continued to flourish from the early 1620s, through the 1630s and on into the 1640s, at first under the leadership of Catherine de Vivonne, and later under her daughter Julie; in the middle years of the century it continued as a conservative and aristocratic influence amongst the bourgeois *salons* that had sprung up in its wake.

The group at Rambouillet found a model on which to base their lives and behaviour in *L'Astrée*, the pastoral romance by Honoré d'Urfé.[5] The first volume of this enormously long work was published in 1607, and the last (posthumously) in 1627, so that it developed side by side with the fashion of *préciosité*, and each acted on the other. In the romance, Catherine de Vivonne's group seemed to see a reflection of themselves; it not only provided them with a model of behaviour, but began to incorporate in its stories romantic versions of their own lives, so that it is possible to say of that period 'la société précieuse est la réalité dont *L'Astrée* donne le roman' (Lanson, *Histoire*, p. 375). Part of the appeal of *L'Astrée* was the way in which it wove fact into fiction, and the present into a romantic past. It was a compendium of the materials of Greek, Spanish, Italian, and French romance, distanced in time to the fifth century and set in the mythological kingdom of Forez, ruled in the time of the Celts by Queen Amasis; the pastoral setting was recognizable, however, as the countryside on the banks of the Lignon around d'Urfé's native home. The whole is put together with a lightness of touch and a story-telling ease that appealed to polite society, and contemporaries credited its elegant form of expression with being able to teach manners to men, and philosophy even to women (*L'Astrée*, Préface. xxiii).

Probably the most important feature of *L'Astrée* was d'Urfé's doctrine of Platonic love.[6] In his version d'Urfé managed to bring Renaissance idealism down to a human scale, and to place it in a social setting where it could exercise an influence on the the everyday life of society. Plato's ideas had gone through many transformations in the Renaissance, gathering Christian significance in the Florentine Academy,[7] and being given widespread influence in Europe and England by Castiglione's *Book of the Courtier*.[8] Castiglione in Book 4 had retraced Plato's steps in the *Symposium*, leading the true lover from the experience (through the senses) of beauty and love in particular forms, to experience (through the understanding) of the universal Forms of Beauty and Love, and eventually to the direct perception (shared with the angels) of the heavenly vision of Beauty and Love, which is God. D'Urfé gives a similar background of Neoplatonic theory to his romance.[9] In his discussion of religion, he has Adamas, the High Priest of the 'Druids', explain to the hero Céladon that all beauty proceeds from that sovereign goodness which we call God, a ray of which springs forth from him on all things created. Just as the earthly sun which we see illumines the air, the water and the earth with the same ray, so the eternal sun beautifies the angelic intelligences, the reasonable soul, and matter.   (II, 78)[10]

Adamas goes on to explain that the heavenly intelligences partake of this beauty as direct experience, whereas man must use his 'reasonable soul,' by which he is linked to the intelligences, to extract the principle of beauty from created matter. Through perfecting his intellectual and moral faculties, man may perceive a higher unity, in which spirit and form, soul and body, are one; out of the attraction of this unity grows love, which leads men back to its source in God.

Whereas *The Courtier* more or less ends with this vision, however, d'Urfé uses it as a background, and turns it in practice into much more courtly and human terms. Céladon not unreasonably complains that he cannot understand matters too abstract; but he need not be concerned for God has fortunately provided for human weakness by creating beautiful women, in whom corporeal beauty and human reason are joined. Sylvandre, the Platonist of the romance, explains that women are a link between the angelic intelligences and man, and that 'God has placed them on earth to draw us by them' to Heaven (III, 512–13). Adamas can therefore assure Céladon that, although he may not understand the high mysteries of religion, he can take comfort from knowing that he is instinctively performing a religious duty by worshipping his mistress Astrée: 'fear not ... my child, of falling short towards God, providing that you there honour this Astrée as one of the most perfect works that He has ever made visible to man' (II, 327). This is not to say that beautiful women are perfect – Astrée herself is rather imperious and vain – but that man, in devoting himself to a higher principle, especially one which he can never quite hope to attain, refines his own moral nature. Critics have pointed out that d'Urfé's maxim for the true Platonic lover, 'mourir en soy, pour revivre en autruy' (I, 290) is an echo of the New Testament (Romans 6), the resurrection of the new man in Christ, and that the ideal of love in *L'Astrée* 'has as its end the moral elevation of the soul rather than the hope of physical reward'.[11] Not all the views of love put forward in the romance are, of course, so serious, but a Christian Neoplatonism is the ideal against which other kinds of love are measured, and by which the ideal lover measures himself.

The theory of Platonic love led in practice to certain conventions which the stories of d'Urfé's romance illustrate in almost endless variety. Since beauty in a woman was a sign of her moral virtue as well as of her connection with Heaven, a beautiful woman might have any number of 'servants' whose allegiance to her could result only in the acquisition by them of self-discipline, self-knowledge, and social grace. Strict moral restraints and the lady's own virtue guarded her from any improper advances, although within these restraints a high degree of social intimacy was permitted between men and women.[12] Among the lady's servants there might, of course, be one whose soul had an affinity with her own, and whose service was therefore destined to result in her one day favouring him with a sign that she approved his suit – but not until he had undergone untold suffering and hardships, all borne in secrecy and with admirable fortitude. Marriage is not the aim of these courtships: it is the *nuances* of love, the self-improvement of the hero, his adventures (some not strictly moral) on the way to his ideal love, in which the interest lies. Possession of the beloved, passion and its fruition, are the death of ideal love; marriage can result only, at best, in friendship.

The attractive feature of d'Urfé's version of Platonic love for contemporaries was perhaps the way in which it related Neoplatonic ideals to everyday life without being either too solemn or too cynical. His ideas come from many sources: his idealism from Renaissance Neoplatonism, his veneration for women and the ideal of 'service' for men from courtly love and chivalry (or the reflection of these in the romances), his association of human with divine love from Petrarch and the poets of the *Pléiade*,[13] but he places them all in a romantic pastoral setting which the members of Mme de Rambouillet's circle could any day recreate in their country outings.[14] He minimized the tensions between sense and spirit in the ideal of love. Plato had compared the ascent to God by means of beauty to a ladder or a stair, on which the original steps (the particular objects of love) drop out of sight as one ascends. Ficino and the writers of the Academy accepted the idea of the ladder, but made Platonic love also an intellectual bond between friends, based on the individual's love of God.[15] Even when heterosexual love had entered the notion of Platonic love (partly through the influence of Dante and Petrarch), a distinction was generally made between procreative and spiritual love.[16] *The Courtier*, for instance, insisted that for the former, marriage is the proper goal; for the latter, the lover must follow Plato, that is

take this love for a stayre (as it were) to climbe up to another farre higher than it ... And thus shall he beholde no more the particular beautie of one woman, but an universall, that decketh out all bodies.   (Castiglione, pp. 317–18)

D'Urfé's innovation was to allow the lover to linger on the stair. Rather than leave his lady behind or marry her, he preferred to keep her before him as a constant reminder of his ideal, and a spur to virtuous behaviour. To the role of the saint or the knight he preferred the more humble role of the gentleman: if there were no longer dragons to be slain, there were still the passions of anger and jealousy to be subdued. Paradoxically, d'Urfé's version of Platonic love neutralised love by dwelling on it so much: by making it into an object to be talked about, written about, played with, he succeeded in drawing from love the thorn of passion; by bringing Platonic idealism into everyday life he turned mysticism into manners.

Préciosité, and Platonic love of the type described above, were flourishing in France by the time Henrietta left for England in 1625. The fashion was already known in England, and part of *L'Astrée* had already been translated, but Henrietta's arrival hastened the adoption of its ideas by court poets. J. B. Fletcher in *The Religion of Beauty in Woman* (pp. 181 ff.) traced the fashion back to France, and distinguished between three different types of Platonic love at the English court in the 1620s and 1630s: the *salon* type in which a great lady dispenses her beneficent influence to a *côterie* of 'servants,' who in turn praise her in verse; a more personal type between two people; and a 'troubadour' type which imposes on the lover the obligation of constancy, humility, purity, and secrecy. All these types were treated, sometimes in serious and sometimes in mocking vein, by poets and dramatists of the thirties. The observations of Fletcher were confirmed by A. H. Upham,[17] who gives an instance of Henrietta's probable contact with members of the Hôtel de Rambouillet, and traces the influence of *préciosité* in English literature through to the Restoration. The work of Fletcher and Upham has been supplemented by studies on related aspects of literature in the period: notably by Kathleen Lynch,[18] who gives an extensive analysis of *L'Astrée* and of *précieux* conventions in Caroline court literature as the background for her study of Restoration comedy; and by Alfred Harbage,[19] who gives an important place to Henrietta's influence and *précieux* fashions in his discussion of Cavalier and Commonwealth drama. These works have given a sound basis for considering the influence of Henrietta's fashions on the court and its literature from 1630 to 1640, but they have also given rise to some questions and contradictions.

Most critics, for instance, have distinguished different degrees of seriousness with which the fashion for Platonic love was taken at the English court, but they have not agreed about the seriousness with which it was taken by the Queen, nor about the moral tone of the works to which the fashion gave rise. Fletcher ('Précieuses at the court of King Charles I', p. 139) concluded that 'the literature on the theme [of Platonic love] ranges in mood all the way from exalted mysticism through mere gallantry to mocking cynicism', and Upham (*The French Influence*, p. 331) distinguished between the presence at court of the Platonic Pretender, the Pure Platonic, the Court Platonic, and the Anti-Platonic. These categories can, however, end by making nonsense of the term 'Platonic love', which comes to cover almost every mention of love in literature of the period; both Fletcher and Upham, for example, class William Habington as a 'Pure Platonic', but both agree that he breaks every law of the code. What then is left of the notion of Platonic love? The difficulty has arisen partly because of uncertainty as to whether Henrietta's own attitude to the fashion was serious or not. Fletcher thought that the phase of Platonic love she brought to England 'seems to incline ... rather to the silly and dangerous side than to the sublime' ('Précieuses at the Court', p. 128), and most critics have implicitly agreed. Kathleen Lynch is almost alone among earlier writers in implying a favourable judgment of the Queen's influence, which could encourage, 'within a fashion so artificial and so dangerous as that of Platonic love, the not infrequent illustration of genuine idealism' (*The Social Mode*, p. 62). Kenneth Richards adds that 'her enthusiasm for the Platonic love cult ... may not necessarily be indicative of a shallow and frivolous mind'.[20]

Related to this uncertainty about Henrietta's attitude is the uncertainty about the moral tone of the drama produced under her influence. This is a question on which critics, basing their judgment on the same court plays, have come to diametrically opposed conclusions. Harbage's study of Cavalier drama insisted on the characteristically moral tone of court plays, which he calls 'decorous, indeed very solemn things' (p. 28), and 'astonishingly innocent productions' (p. 45). Another critic, G. F. Sensabaugh, has consistently maintained in a series of articles that the Queen's cult of Platonic love encouraged deeply immoral attitudes at court, and that these attitudes are reflected in the moral decadence of court drama, which, Sensabaugh says, 'codifying cult standards of hollow compliment, worship of beauty, and promiscuity in marriage and love, brought into even sharper relief court behaviour'.[21]

These differences of opinion have arisen partly through the failure to distinguish between different phases of *préciosité* in France, and to determine exactly which phase was adopted by the Queen at the time when she came to have a decisive influence at court, from about 1629 onward. Such a failure is hardly surprising, since *préciosité*, even in France, has proved notoriously difficult for critics to pin down and discuss. The latest study, by Roger Lathuillère,[22] was begun as a study of the language of the *précieuses*, but has grown to a volume of nearly seven hundred pages without going farther than defining the problem and tracing the origins of *préciosité*: the author promises another two parts, which will study the history of *préciosité* proper, and examine the characteristics of *précieux* language (see Avant-Propos). The difficulty of defining *préciosité* arises from the fact that the word, with its somewhat unfavourable connotations of affectation and over-refinement, has commonly been used to cover all the phases of *préciosité*, from its rise at the beginning of the seventeenth century to its development and decadence at the end, and to cover all the characteristics of its literary productions, from *L'Astrée* to *Le Grand Cyrus*. The favourable and the unfavourable senses of the term, and hence its inherent ambiguity, are summed up in the contemporary definition of a *précieuse* given by Furetière (1620–88) in his *Dictionnaire*:

... épithète qu'on donnoit autrefois à des filles de grand mérite et de grande vertu, qui sçavoient bien le monde, et la langue: mais parce que d'autres ont affecté, et outré leurs manières, cela a décrié le nom, et on les a appellées *fausses Précieuses*, ou *Précieuses ridicules*: Molière en a fait une Comédie, et de Pures un Roman, pour faire sentir le faux mérite des *Précieuses*.

(*La Préciosité*, quoted by Lathuillère, p. 18)

In fact the term *préciosité* and its derivatives did not come into use to describe the social and literary fashions to which it refers until about the middle of the seventeenth century.[23] To apply it with its later connotations to French fashions of the first half of the century is therefore something of an anachronism, and tends to set those fashions in a false perspective. In English criticism there has been a similar tendency to judge *préciosité* of the 1630s by looking at it, as it were, through the wrong end of a telescope, and reaching conclusions about it coloured by the ridicule of Molière, or the cynicism of the Restoration. In the present study, which applies to the development of *préciosité* before 1640, the word will be used without the value judgments (of affectation, over-refinement of manners and language, or even of 'advanced' views on morals) which have been imposed on it by its development later in the century. Some of these qualities do apply to *préciosité* of the 1630s, but they are related to the social and historical circumstances of that period, and can only be judged by reference to them.

Allied to the difficulty of defining the word in general terms is the second difficulty in defining *préciosité* itself: namely, that it refers to a social fashion, and social fashions (with their attendant influence on manners, morals, and art) will be different for each individual group, and for each period under study. As Lathuillère writes (p. 14):

la préciosité, telle qu'elle a été, ne peut se comprendre qu'à partir des circonstances historiques dont elle est issue, à un moment précis, et qui ne se retrouvent identiques nulle part ailleurs: l'histoire ne se répète pas.

Thus *préciosité* in England is not likely to be identical with *préciosité* in France, although critics have tended to assume that it was. J. B. Fletcher called Henrietta 'full alumna of the French school' (*The Religion of Beauty*, p 27), and implied that her *préciosité* was a more or less exact copy of that at the Hôtel de Rambouillet; Kathleen Lynch (*The Social Mode*, p. 45) added that to Henrietta, as to her French contemporaries, Platonic love meant 'quite simply the social fashion interpreted with such elaborate fullness in D'Urfé's *Astrée*'. But a social fashion transported from France by a fifteen year old girl, and practised in another country, culture, and court, is unlikely to be quite like the fashion from which it originated. While *L'Astrée* and the Hôtel de Rambouillet unquestionably influenced Henrietta, it may be asked whether they were the only, or even the main, influences on her view of *préciosité* and Platonic love in the 1630s. Even in France *préciosité* was, by 1630, no longer simply dependent on *L'Astrée*. It had been influenced by Devout Humanism, a religious movement which left its mark on most of French society, including the cultural life of the Hôtel de Rambouillet and the court. By 1630 the intermingling of devout and *précieux* ideas in fashionable literature had produced the concept of *honnêteté*, a standard of virtuous yet civilised behaviour advocated for men, and particularly for women. The *honnête* phase of *préciosité* in France was extremely popular in the thirties, and literature connected with it flourished. The principal works on the subject were introduced to the English court and, I believe, influenced the type of *préciosité* practised by the Queen.

Piety and pleasure

Devout Humanism (a term which was given currency by Henri Bremond)[24] developed from the religious teaching of St François de Sales, who, with d'Urfé, had a decisive influence on French culture in the first quarter of the seventeenth century. The influences of the two men were, in a sense, complementary. While d'Urfé's romance occupied the *précieux* groups of the *salons*, Sales's gentle brand of religion governed the spiritual life of circles which, largely through Marie de Medici, were connected with the court. Sales (1567–1622) and d'Urfé (1568–1625) were contemporaries and friends, and they shared many of the same ideas. Both were interested in improving the manners and morals of society, and both addressed their work primarily to women. Sales was an admirer of *L'Astrée*, and, sharing the Counter-Reformation desire to turn whatever was popular in contemporary culture to devotional use, he approved of writers who drew on the attractions of the romance to help popularise the ideals of religion.

Sales's Devout Humanism was based on an optimistic belief in the essential goodness of human nature, and the amenability of the human spirit to the will of God.[25] While Devout Humanism contributed to the spiritual fervour of the Counter-Reformation it placed less emphasis on the strenuous side of religion, the *Combat Spirituel* pursued by the Jesuits, and more on the *Via Affirmativa* of the spiritual life, the way of gentleness, beauty, and love pursued by Orders like the Franciscans and Capucins. It inherited from Christian Humanism the desire to synthesise the spiritual values of Christianity with the intellectual and material achievements of the Renaissance, and it shared with other Counter-Reformation movements the ideal of consecrating the objects of this world by devoting them to God. But whereas Christian Humanism emphasised reason and intellect as ways to God, Devout Humanism placed more emphasis on the senses, the imagination, and the emotions. Sales's ambition, and to a greater extent the ambition of those who followed him and popularised his ideas, was to bring religion into everyday life by making it simpler, and to extend its influence through society and the court by making it attractive.

The early years of the seventeenth century were notable for their religious enthusiasms, all contributing to the stream of Devout Humanism. Paris was stirred by the Counter-Reformation zeal of Spain and Italy: women mystics like Mme Acarie became disciples of St Teresa, setting up the first Carmelite convent in Paris in 1603; Pierre de Bérulle founded the French Oratory (1611) in imitation of the Oratory of Divine Love of Philip Neri in Italy. Cardinal Bérulle was the confessor and confidant of Marie de Medici (Henrietta's mother) who was the Patroness of the Carmelite convent, of which Bérulle was also the Director, and all these people were connected in various ways with St François de Sales. Marie de Medici sent one of the first editions of Sales's *Introduction à la vie dévote* (1609) as a present to James I,[26] and in England a translator, John Yakesley, declared that no other book had been so many times reprinted in so short a time, or been so greatly valued by all types of men (*Introduction to a Devovte Life*, 1614, sig. A2). Sales's personal influence dominated the spiritual life of the period, going far beyond the two religious works that he wrote. He came to Paris in 1602 where his preaching became famous, and he was credited with making countless conversions by private interview. A biographer, Pedro de Ribadeneira, wrote of him:

His way was to draw Soules to God by loue, and sweetnesse, not that he did winke at vice, but that he knew, that where he could caste in, one sparke of the loue of God, thence he could soone cast out sinne.

(*The Lives of the Saints*, trans. W[illiam] P[etre] (St Omers, 1669), sig. B2)

Sales impressed Henri IV, who offered him the coadjutorship of Paris, which he refused; but he remained attached to the court, and did not hesitate to criticise its morals.

Sales was influential in the French culture that centred in the *salons* and the court, particularly as he addressed his teaching in the first instance to women. He placed great reliance on women because, he said, they 'are more easily drawne to piety and devotion than men' (Ribadeneira, sig. E2v), and are often the means of drawing men to God. Much of the advice in his writings was worked out from his experience with women disciples like Jeanne de Chantal, or in response to particular situations where women sought his help. His best-known work, *Introduction to the Devout Life* (I quote here from the translation by Michael Day, Everyman's Library) was written at the request of a lady, Mme de Charmoisy, who wished to know how it was possible to live a devout life at court. Sales's response, with its clear and simple conversational style, became an instant success. Sales leads his heroine Philothée (the soul) gently through the stages of private devotion, as well as through the snares of public life. He does not advise retirement from the world or self-mortification, but rather participation in the normal activities of society. He emphasises the inner devotion that can be practised even in the midst of daily affairs, and his chapters on 'The Practice of Virtue' (part 3) and 'Overcoming Temptations' (part 4) deal with the recognising of small as well as great temptations. His advice comes down to specific items, all of moment to the court lady: true and false friendships, flirtations, proper attire, lawful recreations (which include walking, conversation, singing, music, hunting, and sports – all in moderation), respect in conversation, fidelity, and chastity. The one indispensable condition of virtue is the presence of God in the heart, from which all else flows. With the practice of inner devotion, there was no social activity in which a virtuous woman could not take part. Sales's ideas on women were liberal for a Churchman of his time, and the *Introduction* complemented the influence of *L'Astrée* in raising the social status of women, contributing to the rise of feminism in seventeenth-century France.[27]

Sales's was a religion of love, and he placed love squarely at the centre of his social and religious concerns, saying, in the *Introduction*, 'Love is the soul's dominant passion; it rules all the movements of the heart, making them its own, and making us like that which we love' (p. 135). His thinking, like d'Urfé's, was based on Renaissance Neoplatonism, and ideals of Beauty and Love form the basis of his mystical work *Le Traité de l'amour de Dieu* (1616) (quotations are from Vincent Kerns's translation, *The Love of God: A Treatise*).[28] He begins the work with a discussion of beauty, which appeals to the intellect, attracts the senses, and arouses desire. When this desire is attracted by true beauty, which is associated with true goodness, it becomes love (p. 17), the cause of all our actions. God, however, is the true object of our love, as He is the unique source of all that is good and beautiful. He, like the sun,

the Father of all that gives light ... in his beauty leads our minds to contemplate him, in his goodness leads our wills to love him. His beauty, delighting our minds, brings to birth in our wills a love for him; his goodness, filling our wills with love for him, stimulates our minds to contemplate him, love prompting contemplation, contemplation prompting love.

(p. 284)

Sales states unequivocally that 'one spark of this love [of God] is worth more, is stronger, more to be prized, than any other love a human heart can know' (p. 408), and in all choices the 'uncommitted man' will choose the harder (for example, will choose celibacy before marriage). But Sales recognised that most have not chosen the uncommitted life, and he not only accepted but placed a high value on chaste human love as a means of approaching the love of God.

Sales's ideas, based in the Neoplatonism of contemporary Church teaching and concerned with the interests of women, had much in common with those of d'Urfé, as Sister McMahon (in *Aesthetics and Art*) has shown. Sales recognised the attractions of *L'Astrée*, and his own writing, with its emphasis on the connection between human and divine love, made it easy for their influences to combine. In describing mystical experience in the *Traité*, Sales often uses the language of the love treatises and images of the sonneteers – of melting souls, wounded hearts, and dying lovers – as analogies for religious experience, stating confidently that 'all the terms I am using to describe love are derived from the similarity that exists between our spiritual emotions and our physical passions' (p. 253). He makes Christ sometimes a knight, more often a shepherd, and he makes frequent references to the Canticles, in which, he says, Solomon,

with the idyllic love of a chaste shepherd and modest shepherdess for his theme ... gently lifts our minds to the spiritual romance [*cet amour spirituel*] between ourselves and God.   (p. 22)

Such imagery gives his work a pastoral air in keeping with the pastoral images of love in *L'Astrée*.[29]

In the Preface to his *Treatise* (p. xxix) Sales praised other saintly writings on love, hoping they would become 'a stream of eloquence which will flow throughout France in Sermons and belles-lettres' and he encouraged other Church writers to use the popularity of *L'Astrée* to help spread the influence of Devout Humanism. The most successful was Sales's disciple and friend, Jean-Pierre Camus (1584–1652), Bishop of Belley, who determined to combine the good influences of d'Urfé and Sales in his own writing. In the early 1620s he inaugurated the religious romance, which enjoyed an enormous popular success.[30] Camus's works number over two hundred volumes, and between 1620 and 1630 alone he wrote over thirty novels and collections of short stories. In everything he wrote his aim was to combine an interest in love and adventure with a moral elevation that would insensibly lift the heart towards God. In the Preface to *Les Evénements singuliers* (1628)[31] he shows a good knowledge of romance writers (Belleforest, Giraldi, and Cervantes amongst others), but criticises them for their extravagances and their lack of moral aim. In their place he offers his own stories as being based on truth rather than art,

mettant des Relations chrétiennes, véritables et utiles en la place de celles qui sont profanes, fabuleuses et non seulement inutiles, mais pour la plus grande part pernicieuses.   (p. 51)

In fact Camus based some of his stories on romance sources, and all contain in plenty the ingredients of romance (disguises, love, horror, death), but Camus believed them to be edifying because true. One of the most popular, *La Pieuse Julie* (1625), was based on the story of a girl to whom Camus was confessor, and was dedicated to the real person whose identity, Camus says, was concealed from the eyes of the curious, 'but in such a wise as to be revealed to those who know as much as I do' (see Bremond, *A Literary History*, I, pp. 232–6). Camus's stories therefore were quite in the popular vein of d'Urfé in placing topical events in a romance setting, but, according to Camus's intention, with the addition of an explicit moral aim which was supported by religion.

Camus's romances are not readily available to English readers, but his ideas have been discussed at length by Bremond (from whose work *A Literary History* the following quotations are taken) to show that for Camus, as for Sales, love was the central principle of Christian belief. Almost all the romances are concerned with love, religion, and women's virtue, and their subjects can be glimpsed from some of the titles: *Agathonphile ... histoire devote, où se descouvre l'art de bien aymer, pour antidote aux deshonnestes affections* (1621); *Parthénice, ou peinture d'une invincible chastete* (1621); *Palombe, ou la femme honorable* (1625); *L'Hiacinte ... où se voit la difference d'entre l'amour et l'amitié* (1627); *Casilde, ou le bon-heur de l'honnesteté* (1628). In his stories all kinds of love are good: love of God, love between friends, and married love were rungs of the same ladder, and he does not hesitate to claim the highest religious ideal as love's end:

It is for shameful affections to seek the dark and to hide themselves, but for the pure to walk in the light of day and the radiance of holiness. Why should any blush to love? There is nought so holy, nought so beautiful, when it is pursued in lawful ways. The Christian law is all love and for love; not to love is death.

(*Les Evénements singuliers*, quoted by Bremond, I, 241)

Although love of God is the ultimate goal, Camus is also interested in the effects of love farther down the human scale. In *Palombe* he counsels moderation in love, for then it

awakes the soul, imparting to it an agreeable glow which is not without radiance, for, as says Plato, pure love is mother of comely behaviour, of delicacy, courtesy, and such-like virtues; whereas, when carried to excess, it becomes frenzy ... Pure love has not its eyes bandaged as has Passion, but like that other it too has its torch, its bow and arrows, and its quiver.

(quoted by Bremond, I, 240–1)

'Such-like virtues' were those cultivated by the *salons*, and it is not surprising to find that Camus was a visitor at the Hôtel de Rambouillet, or that *Parthénice* was dedicated to Marie de Medici (Storer, 'Jean-Pierre Camus', p. 733).

Camus' writing brought Sales's morality more fully into the elegant social circles to which, by birth and temperament, Camus himself belonged. He delighted, in what he called his 'historical meditations' (usually set in the Valois reign of the previous century), in creating idylls of court life where virtue and pleasure went hand in hand, and 'the fashionable piety was delightful' (*Hellénin*, quoted by Bremond, I, 220). This picture of the court was taken up by other writers in the 1620s. The ideal is best summed up in a quotation by Bremond from Father Alexis de Jésus, *Miroir de toute sainteté* (1627) in which Grace shows Theopneste a palace where the inhabitants excercise themselves in divers virtues and occupations, all under the sway of religion. Since these people are

gay and happy in an earthly paradise of the good things of this life, while in expectation of a better life above, Grace asks her disciple 'Is not a devout world better than a non-devout?' 'As a pearl surpasses a grain of sand', returned he, 'but to me the best is that it is the same world in all but sin, that the Court, the Parlements, the Army, every lawful recreation and conversation are gilded by grace . . . so much can a will conformed to the will of God do'.

(quoted by Bremond, I, 282–83)

Such a picture of a devout society is concerned as much with manners as with romance, and the ideal of a virtuous urbanity, in which pleasures were governed by religion, helped give rise to the concept of *honnêteté* which was coming to maturity throughout the 1620s, influencing the *salons* and the court.

The classic study of *honnêteté* in France, *La Politesse mondaine* by Maurice Magendie, has shown that the origins of the fashion went back to the influence of *The Courtier* and to earlier writings of the century, but that its more immediate impetus was the current interest in manners and morals of a polite society under the influence of both d'Urfé and Sales.[32] *Honnêteté* was an attempt to make piety and virtue compatible with pleasure and social grace, by placing society under the guidance of religion. From 1630 onwards it became one of the most significant social trends of the period. In 1630 Nicolas Faret published *L'Honneste Homme, ou l'art de plaire à la cour*, and in 1632 Jacques Du Bosc published *L'Honneste Femme*, both books having an immediate success. *L'Honneste Homme* was republished four times to 1640, and was translated into English as *The Honest Man, Or the Art to Please in Court*, by E[dward] G[rimstone] (London, 1632). *L'Honneste Femme* was considerably augmented and republished in 1633, just one year after its initial publication, and second and third volumes were added in 1634 and 1636. In testimony to the importance of these two books in the 1630s François de Grenaille added a whole family between 1639 and 1642: *L'Honneste Fille* (1639–40), *L'Honneste Mariage* (1640); *L'Honneste Garçon* (1642), and even *L'Honneste Veuve* (1640). These exemplary personages were provided for by books like le sieur Bardin's *Le Lycée . . . d'un honneste homme* (1632–34), and Grenaille's *La*

Bibliothèque des dames (1640), *Les Plaisirs des dames* (1641), *La Mode, ou charactère de la religion, de la vie, de la conversation, etc.* (1642) and *La Galerie des dames illustres* (1643), all of which had a pious as well as a courtly purpose.

The writers of these books were bourgeois, but their works are addressed to the court (*L'Honneste Garçon* was dedicated to the Dauphin) which they still regarded as 'the world' rather than as 'worldly'. Magendie says of them:

ils participent tous à ce courant de moralité, qui avec François de Sales, Camus, Nervèze ... traverse le siècle naissant; ils donnent tous à la vertu, à la religion, une place préponderante ... Dans leur conception, honnête homme est vraiment synonyme d'homme de bien.

(p. 384)

Honnêteté later in the century developed as a bourgeois concept of morality, while the ideal courtier became more of an *homme du monde*, but at its inception in the 1630s the ideal was one in which religion and virtue were made to underpin the refinement and polish of the court, and in which the idea of a 'courtisan vertueux' (Magendie, p. 368) was not a contradiction in terms. The ideal had its effect on the court of Louis XIII (Henrietta's brother), which in Magendie's description (part 3, chapter 1) is not unlike that of the Cavaliers, having a 'je ne sais quoi' of qualities comprising gallantry, elegance, learning without specialisation, distinction and ease; these were combined with a certain priggishness, exemplified by an attempt to 'purify' the theatre by banning farce and excluding from tragedy all 'obscene' language, just as Charles's court was credited with 'purifying' drama and the stage.

The concept of *honnêteté* was important for men, but possibly even more important for women. Magendie discussed *honnêteté* mainly from the point of view of men (reference to Du Bosc's *L'Honneste Femme* for example, is confined to a brief mention and a footnote), although he did give full weight to the contribution of women and of the *salons* to its development. Ian Maclean has since focused attention on the importance of the ideal for women in *Woman Triumphant: Feminism in French Literature, 1610–1652*. In the important chapter 'Honnêteté and the Salons' (chapter 5), Maclean sees Du Bosc's book as summing up a new image of woman, and the 1630s as representing a distinct phase of feminism in France, mid-way between the older moralists' notions of women and the more emancipated views of feminists later in the century. The *honnête* ideal for women stressed the traditionally feminine qualities of piety, chastity, compassion, beauty, and modesty, but at the same time insisted that women take a lively part in the activities of society, helping to influence it by displaying both virtue and attractive grace. Moderation was its key note: it admired women for their good qualities, but took a more critical and rational attitude towards their behaviour than romances like *L'Astrée*. On the other hand it counselled women against too austere a virtue, or a piety that was frighteningly dull: ideally women should be religious without austerity, amiable without lightness, elegant without affectation. Women had a special responsibility for the smooth running of society, and one of their main functions, according to Du Bosc, was to set an attractive example of virtue to men; Grenaille even went so far as to say that 'l'honnête fille est une des principales causes de la perfection de l'honnête homme' (Magendie, p. 382). In every way *l'honnête femme* was to be the companion and inspiration of *l'honnête homme*, but her responsibility was even greater than his for keeping the relationship chaste, while doing everything in her power to make it agreeable. The qualities that enabled her to do this were her beauty, which Du Bosc connects in Neoplatonic terms with virtue, and love, but love understood in such a way as to include the moral and religious principles connected with it by writers like Sales and Camus.

Du Bosc's book *L'Honneste Femme* is important for the present study because the first edition of 1632 was translated into English by Walter Montague (see my note 'The Source of Walter Montague's *The Accomplish'd Woman*' in *Notes and Queries*). In view of the influence of *L'Honneste Femme* on the history of *préciosité* and feminism in France, Montague's translation of it would seem to be significant in helping to define the type of *préciosité* adopted by Henrietta in the 1630s. Montague himself was a leading figure in Henrietta's *précieux* circle, and he linked the interests she had left behind in France with those she developed in England. He had first met her at the time of the marriage negotiations in 1624, when he won the confidence of both Henrietta and her mother, Marie de Medici. After her marriage he spent a great deal of time travelling on confidential missions between the two courts, and when, in 1632, the Queen wanted a pastoral to act in herself, it was to Montague that she entrusted the task of writing *The Shepherd's Paradise*. The pastoral was acted in 1633, but not published until 1659, and evidence suggests that *The Accomplish'd Woman*, published in 1656, may, like the pastoral, have been completed at a much earlier date. Certainly Montague's dedication to the Duchess of Buckingham was inappropriate by 1656, since the Duchess died in 1648. Montague was at the French court in 1631, when he would certainly have heard of Faret's *L'Honneste Homme*, and when the ideas for *L'Honneste Femme* (part 1) may have been in the air (it received its 'Privilège du Roy' on 28th July 1632: see Prefatory matter to *L'Honneste Femme*, first edition).[33] Montague based his translation on this first, 1632 edition, even though Du Bosc published an amended and expanded version in 1633. The expanded version was itself translated into English as *The Compleat Woman*, by N.N., in 1639. Montague makes no mention of this translation, nor of the other two parts of *L'Honneste Femme* that Du Bosc added in the middle of the thirties. It would seem then, that his interest in the book, and possibly the translation itself, goes back to the time of its first publication, a time when Montague was also busy formulating the ideas of *The Shepherd's Paradise* (which reads, as Harbage commented in *Cavalier Drama* (p. 37), like 'a conduct book in verse', and whose moralisings are not unlike those of Du Bosc). It seems probable that a book so immediately popular in France would have been known either in French or in translation amongst Henrietta's group, and that it had an influence in shaping the ideal of feminine conduct at the English court.

Du Bosc dedicated his book of 1632 to Mme de Combalet, Richelieu's niece, who was a regular guest at the Hôtel de Rambouillet (Maland, *Culture and Society*, p. 46). Since Montague dedicated his translation to the Duchess of Buckingham, thereby transferring Du Bosc's ideas to an English setting, Montague's translation may conveniently be used here to discuss the concept of *honnêteté*, which will apply both to Du Bosc's *L'Honneste Femme* and to Montague's *The Accomplish'd Woman* (to which page numbers in the following quotations refer). The book is a manual of virtue for aristocratic women, and Du Bosc writes in his preface to the reader (not translated by Montague) that his object is not to make rules for women, but to praise those qualities that will bring them success in society, and at the same time allow them the name of 'honneste femme'. Du Bosc derived his principle of virtue for women from St François de Sales, suggesting in a foreword to the second edition (1633) that the book may be read as 'L'Introduction de l'introduction à la vie déuote'. Like Sales, he makes 'devotion' the key to a virtuous life. There is no activity or condition of life that is not made the better for it:

It makes the professed Religious more cheerfull and Lay men less insolent, moderating pleasures, and sweetning austerities; it makes Marriage the comlier, Warre the iuster, Commerce the faithfuller, and the Court the fuller of honour.

(Montague's translation, *The Accomplish'd Woman*, p. 34)

There is therefore every inducement to make devotion compatible with court life, and a section entitled 'Of inclination to vertue, chiefly to the devotion of the times' implies that, at the time of which he is writing, this has already been accomplished, at least as an ideal: 'We have no need now adayes to seek in Cloysters precepts for a Christian life; 'tis enough now to be a good Courtier, to be devout' (p. 31). The implication is not simple flattery, but the high ideal implicit in the term 'a good Courtier'.

If, as Du Bosc implies, the practice of devotion is already a reality at court, he is left free to concentrate on the social rather than the religious aspects of Sales's advice to women, and to help them make piety agreeable. Accordingly his work is largely an expansion of Sales's discussion of 'The Practice of Virtue' and 'Overcoming Temptations' (parts 3 and 4 respectively of the *Introduction*). Most of the topics touched on by Sales are discussed in full by Du Bosc under the headings of: Cheerfulness and Melancholy, Reputation, Chastity and Complacency, Courage, Constancy and Fidelity, Curiosity and Censure, Cloathes and Ornaments, Beauty, Gracefulness, and Jealousy. A bias toward the happy mean in virtue is reflected by the pairing of qualities in the headings: too much society leads to levity, but too much solitude leads to dullness; there must be a balance between complacency and austerity, between chattering and silence, between gallantry and modesty. He is at pains, however, to show that his ideal of woman is not the common domestic one. In a section headed 'Of Knowledge and Ignorance' he warns that in speaking of this 'accomplished woman' he does not mean merely the mother of a family who 'can governe well her maids, and takes care to combe her children. Musick, History, Philosophy, and other such exercises, are more sutable to our designe' (p. 67). Moreover the study of such subjects is justified on moral grounds, for 'since dishonest love is the trade of those who do not spend their time in some commendable imployment', there is good reason to believe that 'Chastity is preserved by occupation' (p. 47).

Du Bosc relies on the premise that although there are certainly devout women who are not 'accomplished', there is no accomplished woman who is not devout. His main concern therefore is to prescribe rules of conduct for court ladies that will help them to make religion pleasant and attractive, not drive men away from virtue by too much dullness and austerity. With perhaps a side look at Jansenists (and Montague at Puritans) he declares:

I doe not approve of those that put their devotion upon the racke to make it scoul, as if one could not be saved without being ugly. When the grace of God is in the soul, the face is touch't over with the sweetness of it.   (p. 33)

He emphasises the so-called feminine qualities of 'complacency', pity and grace, warning darkly that those who 'think women cannot be vertuous and obliging, understand little the nature of Vertue' (p. 38). To the subject of Beauty he devotes a whole section, defining it in Platonic terms:

In the opinion of *Plato*, it is a humane splendor, amiable in its own nature, that has the power to ravish the mind with the eyes ... it must be the mark of our inclination to good, since we seldome find beauty without vertue, as uglinesse without mischief.   (p. 102)

At the same time, beauty is linked with religion by ascribing it to its divine source, so that 'those that adore or despise Beauty, either offer too much or too little to the image of God'. This lovely quality, he says, may challenge a command everywhere, and those that complain of it being the occasion of ill 'do as idly, as if one should accuse the Sun for dazling his sight when he looks too fixedly on that glorious body' (pp. 103–4). When handsome women are accused of being scornful 'we shall find that their disdain proceeds rather from conscience then vanity' (p. 104). He warns that all beauty has need of 'wit and vertue' to defend it, but beauty properly used is a valuable possession that can only lead to good, for it is given 'on purpose to please our eyes, and elevate our spirits to the love of him that is the head of all humane perfection' (pp. 106–7).

The theoretical basis for this type of Christian Neoplatonism is set out in another work by Walter Montague, *Miscellanea Spiritualia, or Devout Essaies* (part 1, London, 1648), dedicated to the Queen.[34] The book was published just after Montague had been released from the Tower, where he spent the years from 1643 to 1647 convicted of carrying letters from France (*DNB*). The years in prison may have been a convenient time for putting the material together, but since the essays concern the conduct of court life under the rule of devotion, they must refer to the happier days before 1640 when there was still a court in which to put them into practice. Montague had been converted to Catholicism in 1635 and taken Orders in 1636, so that in these 'devout essaies' he writes from the point of view of both courtier and priest, drawing on the ideas of Devout Humanists like Sales and Du Bosc. He addresses the work to Henrietta Maria, 'Daughter of France, and Queen of Great Britain', and in it he places Neoplatonic ideas of beauty and love within a Christian framework, showing how religion and social grace complement each other to make possible a devout life at court.

Montague begins with treatises on Religion and Devotion, which he makes the foundation of court life, and in Treatise 5 takes up the question 'Whether sensible pleasures may consort with devotion'. Treatise 9 discusses 'The condition of courts, princes, and courtiers', and Treatise 10 deals at length with the question of 'How a good conscience, and a good courtier are consortable with one another'. Montague has some reservations on this issue, but he relies confidently on religion to regulate the pleasures, and overcome the temptations, of court life. He insists on the priority of religion, but at the same time calls for 'an allowance of decent civilities in exchanges of Courtship'. He writes, he says, as one who knows courts and the ways of courts, and he knows that piety must wear a smiling face:

If Devotion comming to Court, should declare such a war to the world, as to prohibit our senses commerce with pleasures; which are the natives of this world, she would find but a small party, upon such a breach to follow her.   (sig. F4v)

He commends a piety that is suited to her surroundings, neither light nor frighteningly dull:

They never saw piety but in one dresse, that thinke she cannot sute her selfe according to occasions, and put her selfe so farre into the fashion, as may make her the easilier accostable, and yet retaine her dignity and decency.   (sig. G3v)

To show how this may be done Montague draws on Neoplatonic ideas of beauty and love. The first section of Treatise 5 deals with 'Rectifying our affections, chiefly our love in the sense of beauty', and, like St François de Sales in the *Traité*, he uses the language of human love for religion. Speaking of devotion as a 'Divine passion', he says he will 'put it into the vulgar tongue of the Court, and so make it more familiar for apprehension', and he goes on to

propose the being devout, under the tearmes of being in love with Heaven, because it is the likeliest way of perswasion to the world, to propose not the putting away, but the preferring of their loves, and to transferre them to a fairer object, not extinguish the fervency of their act.   (sig. E4–E4v)

It is his serious belief, he says, that

hearts wrought into a tendernesse by the lighter flame of nature, are like mettals already running, easilier cast into Devotion then others of a hard and lesse impressive temper.   (sig. E4v)

Conversely, piety helps to make human love virtuous and joyful. In writing of love Montague, like Sales, stresses the over-riding importance of religion, which

doth but reduce the wild multitude of humane affections and passions, under the Monarchall
Government of the love of God, under which they may enjoy a more convenient freedome,
then let loose in their owne confused Anarchy.   (sig. F2)

Yet piety, he says, does not desire the death of the affections, but rather that
they 'may turne from their perversions and live' (sig. F3). To achieve this, Platonic
ideas of beauty and love are of the utmost importance. Beauty is 'the readiest
note our sense acknowledges of Divinity' (sig. F4), and when love is guided by
devotion,

then is it so farre from being restrain'd, as it is continued in the command of all the power
of our pieties, and is trusted so much, as it is allowed to hold faire correspondence with
beauty, though that were the party, love had served under against grace.   (sig. F4)

He concludes that 'by these lights we see how the love of God is not only compatible, but requisite with our love of creatures' (sig. Gv). In arguing thus, Montague
defends not only his use of the language of love for religious purposes, but the
efficacy of human love in making the soul more responsive to divine love, and
of divine love in freeing the affections for a fuller life on earth.

The 'convenient freedome' allowed to the followers of Platonic love was one
of the stumbling blocks to acceptance of the doctrine by those English courtiers
and writers who were not raised on the ideas of Sales, nor reconciled to the
attractions of the Queen's religion. Montague himself realises some of the possible
abuses of the position he has been putting, and his Treatise 13 (very like Sales's
section in the *Introduction* on recognising temptations in friendship) is devoted
to the question 'Whether to be in love, and to be devout, are consistent'. Under
this heading he deals with such matters as 'The nature of love and devotion
compared' (section 1); 'Some subtle temptations detected, and liberties reproved'
(section 2); 'The faultiness of flattery to women discovered, and disswaded' (section
5); 'Some scruples resolved about the esteeme of beauty, and the friendship of
women' (section 7). One can see that here was material in plenty for the involved
discussions of love in *The Shepherd's Paradise*, for the debates on points of moral
etiquette in court drama, and the opportunity for subtle distinctions in more
private conversations between the ladies of Henrietta's circle and their Platonic
admirers. Montague himself gets over the difficulties he has raised by recommend-
ing the 'sober passion' of friendship, which 'hath all the spirit and cordiality
of the wine of love, without the offensive fumes and vapours of it, and so doth
the office of exhilarating the heart, without intoxicating the braine' (sig. Aa).

Montague's exposition of this 'sober passion' has the characteristics associated
with the idealistic side of Henrietta's doctrine of Platonic love. Placing beauty
and love under the protection of religion, Montague praises a 'spiritual' friendship
with women, which, he says,

may find a sensible as well as a lawfull delight in the beauty and lovelynesse of the person

... whom we may love so spiritually, as to consider nothing in the person, severed from the whole consistence and virtuous integrity of soul and body.   (sig. Aa–Aav)

This 'high Spirituall point of friendship with Women' is not without its dangers, and he admits that 'many loves have stray'd that pretended to set out towards it', but the dangers may be avoided by the cultivation of a pious love, which always remembers that noble beauty is a reflection of the splendour of the Creator; and by the help of Grace, 'which we may call in to our succour in all the violencies of our nature' (sig. z4v). Above all, Montague depends in his treatment of love on the same kind of Christian interpretation that the followers of Devout Humanism gave to Platonic ideas: that

if God be rightly apprehended as the supreame good, and our Loves primarily directed to that union, then all our affections descend from that due elevation ... and repasse again upon the same gradations up to the Creator.   (sig. v3v)

Montague's application of a Christian Neoplatonism to the conduct of court life sums up, I believe, the theoretical basis of Henrietta Maria's practice of Platonic love. Under the influence of Devout Humanism, Platonic love no longer depended on the extremes of courtly love (worship without hope of reward at one end of the scale, and appetite at the other), nor on the more traditional Platonism of, for example, Castiglione, that left the human beloved behind in passing to the more perfect love of God. Montague followed the Devout Humanists in arguing that religion embraced and validated all forms of virtuous human love, which depended on the practice of piety to keep it within the bounds of moderation, modesty, and chastity. Like Sales he placed religion at the centre of court life, but like Du Bosc he insisted that religion should 'wear a smiling face', that pleasure and piety were not only compatible, but that each was necessary to the proper functioning of the other. It was this version of 'Platonic love' that, I believe, Henrietta found sympathetic, and that was reflected in poetry and plays with which she was connected in the 1630s.

The Queen's ideal of love

To Henrietta it must have seemed natural that her social and religious interests should be combined in the life she led at court.[35] She had been brought up by her mother, Marie de Medici, to whom entertainments and devotion were the two essentials of court life. Marie was interested in the *précieux* activities of the group at Rambouillet (d'Urfé dedicated volume 3 of *L'Astrée* to her) and she received the group at court before Henrietta left for England (Upham, *The French Influence*, p. 319). Henrietta witnessed the elaborate ballets and entertainments staged under the Regency of her mother, and she herself learnt to sing, dance, and act in court theatricals at an early age.[36] When she first arrived in England, in June 1625, she undoubtedly brought with her a taste for the romantic ideas fostered by *L'Astrée*, and for the kind of activities that formed the pastimes of the Hôtel de Rambouillet and the French court. In the first years there are constant references to her amusing herself with her maids in plays and pastorals; she played the leading role in Racan's *Artenice* in 1626, and Gervais d'Amblainville dedicated a pastoral to her under the title of *La Princesse, ou l'heureuse bergère* in 1627.[37] The first two years she spent mainly in the company of her French followers, maids-of-honour, and dancing masters, and when in 1627 most of her French retinue was dismissed, she took refuge in the activities she knew best – dancing, singing, and play-acting – to attract to her a group who could share her tastes and interests. To this group, the latest French fashions must have seemed a way of encouraging a higher (or at least more fashionable) standard for the arts, of improving the uncouth manners that had been acceptable under James, and of raising the status of women, which had sunk particularly low during the former reign.[38]

Marie de Medici had attached a devout purpose to her pleasures, and she took an active interest, which she endeavoured to encourage in those around her, in religion. Henrietta was sent with other young ladies from the French court to the Carmelite convent of which Marie was the patroness and Cardinal Bérulle the director.[39] Henrietta's religious instruction, which was probably the most concerted part of her otherwise rather haphazard education, was intrusted to the Prioress, Mother Madeleine de Saint-Joseph, who was a *protegée* of Bérulle and famed for her sweetness as well as her piety. A description of Mother Madeleine by the Abbé Houssaye, couched as it is in romantic language and with its touch of Platonism, suggests the kind of example to which Henrietta might have responded at an impressionable age, and which may have suggested a model for her own behaviour when she became Queen. Mother Madeleine was said to be

firm without being rigid, and dignified without being proud; sweetness tempered her vivacity; her face was a faithful index of her soul; truly Heaven had bestowed upon her one of those rare natures in which delicacy is wedded to strength, and which seem born to rule, and to be beloved in ruling.   (quoted by Bremond, II, 239)

The description looks forward to Du Bosc's belief that 'when the grace of God is in the soul, the face is touch't over with the sweetness of it', and to the *honnête* ideal of a happy mean in qualities for women. Tributes in similar terms were paid to Henrietta by Platonic admirers in the 1630s.

The influence of Marie's personal and pious interests followed Henrietta to the English court with Cardinal Bérulle, who headed her large company of priests. They supervised the Queen's spiritual welfare, and she spent a great deal of time in private devotion, as well as in the more public exercise of her religion. Beside the more commonly quoted reports of her acting and dancing in the early years of her arrival at court, we should therefore put the reports of the Tuscan representative Salvetti:[40] of her hearing Mass and sermons in her Oratory every day (p. 25);

of walking a mile to her chapel at St James (p. 57); and of going into seclusion for a week at a time at Denmark House, where a long gallery was divided and fitted up with cells, a refectory, and an oratory, and she and her ladies 'sang the Hours of the Virgin, and lived together like nuns' (p. 77). Contemporaries often mention her entertainments and devotions in the same breath,[41] and when it is reported that she retired for 'the religious observances of Christmas, and then returned to Whitehall where she is preparing the ballet' (Salvetti, p. 103), it must have seemed to her English subjects evidence of a naturally frivolous mind. To Henrietta it was all part of leading a virtuous court life.

Henrietta was not, therefore, a typically sophisticated *précieuse* of the Parisian *salons*. Although she helped introduce the interests of the Hôtel de Rambouillet she cannot have had a very deep understanding of the cultural ideals on which they were based; nor, if she had understood them, did she have much English in which to communicate them. In fact her education, apart from its social and religious aspects, had been rather neglected. No one had expected a very important marriage for the youngest daughter of Henri IV, and instead of receiving the kind of education that befitted a future Queen, she had been allowed to grow up with the rest of Henri's legitimate and illegitimate brood. She had not been taught languages, and she herself regretted later in life her lack of formal knowledge in matters like history.[42] Henrietta did not, therefore, have the background of culture that could lend some foundation to the 'games' played at the Hôtel de Rambouillet with language and ideas; and, being so young, it is not surprising that she lacked the maturity of a Catherine de Vivonne, who could attract to her circle people of real wit and intellect. In place of the gracefully turned phrases of a Voiture or Desportes, Henrietta attracted the leaden conceits of a Walter Montague or the ingenious similitudes of William Cartwright. Her own wit seems to have been of the kind associated with vivacity and native quickness of mind, rather than with depth of understanding or with learning.

Henrietta lacked, moreover, the sophistication that could turn love into a game. She was far more affectionate and demonstrative than the cold-hearted shepherdesses of the romances, and the poets represent her as giving, as well as receiving, virtuous love. Edmund Waller summed up her attitude in his poem 'Of the Queen' (ll. 39–44):

> All her affections are to one inclined;
> Her bounty and compassion to mankind;
> To whom, while she so far extends her grace,
> She makes but good the promise of her face.
> For Mercy has, could Mercy's self be seen,
> No sweeter look than this propitious queen.
>
> (*The Poems*, edited by G. Thorn Drury, I, 77–8)

Davenant, one of 'the Queen's poets', consistently represents her beauty, not as dazzling and disdainful, but soft and 'Sweet, as the Altars smoake ... Kind, as the willing Saints, and calmer farre, / Than in their sleepes forgiven Hermits are', yet always attentive to virtue:

> For through the casements of her eyes
> Her soul is ever looking out.
> And with its beams she does survey
> Our growth in virtue or decay,
> Still lighting us in Honour's way.

(The Shorter Poems, edited by A. M. Gibbs, pp. 28 and 241)

Her happy marriage (after 1630) brought in a fashion for married love, and the ideal of love she inspired was the ideal recommended to women by moralists: chaste and domestic rather than coquettish or severe. It is summed up in Carew's poem 'To the Queen' in which he hails her as

> great Commandresse, that doest move
> Thy Scepter o're the Crowne of Love,
> And through his Empire with the Awe
> Of thy chaste beames, doest give the Law,
> From his prophaner Altars, we
> Turne to adore Thy Deitie: ...
>
> Thy sacred Lore shewes us the path
> Of modestie, and constant faith,
> Which makes the rude Male satisfied
> With one faire Female by his side.

(The Poems, edited by Rhodes Dunlap, p. 90)

Such poems are addressed, not to a Platonic mistress, but to a goddess of chaste love and marital fidelity, and they reflect a view of love closer to that of St François de Sales than of d'Urfé.

If Henrietta did not have the qualities of a *salon précieuse*, she did have in abundance the qualities recommended for women by writers on *honnêteté*: she was devout, but without being severe; she knew how to be gay and obliging in company without being immodest; and she had the quality of *complaisance* so essential to the *honnête femme* in her role of a creator of social harmony, of being able to put people at their ease and make social occasions run smoothly. A contemporary described her as being

rare company, and that, not only active, but passive. For besides that she speaks gently and sweetly, and replies readily, and aptly knows how to hold up a discourse, she hath a very patient ear to entertain and countenance anything which is well said by anybody else, and not to let it die in her hands.[43]

Her obliging manner was invaluable in helping the more reserved Charles to create those appearances of social harmony by which he set so much store. Charles himself had many of the qualities of an *honnête homme*, being 'temperate, chaste, and serious', and insisting on at least the appearance of moral virtue in those around him.[44] Charles, however, lacked the ease which according to writers on *honnêteté* should accompany these qualities. A contemporary reported in 1625 that the new King

> shows himself in every way very gracious and affable; but the Court is kept more strait and private than in the former time. He is very attentive and devout at prayers and sermons, gracing the preachers and assembly with amiable, cheerful countenance, which gives much satisfaction.[45]

No doubt it also gave much discomfiture, but fortunately the court did not turn out to be quite such a devout and cheerless place as the portrait seemed to portend. Charles's natural taste in art and the serious attention he gave to court entertainments were enlivened by Henrietta's less discriminating taste, but more spontaneous enjoyment. She brought to Charles's morality the social graces which, in the concept of *honnêteté*, were able to combine piety with pleasure. In the early years of the marriage, Charles had disapproved of the frivolity of Henrietta's pastimes. Although she did not completely change her tastes in the 1630s, she did adapt them to a style more befitting her position as Queen, and in keeping with the moralistic tone of Charles's court. Although Henrietta helped to introduce the fashion for Platonic love as it was known from *L'Astrée*, it would seem that her own practice after about 1629 turned to a side of the fashion that had more in common with the concept of *honnêteté* than with the exaggerated woman-worship of the romances.

The original version of Platonic love developed by the *salons*, in which a witty and beautiful woman attracts a number of followers in an essentially passionless relationship, did, of course, continue to influence the English court in the 1630s. It may, however, have been Lady Carlisle rather than Henrietta who was the central figure of such a cult. Lady Carlisle has been described by J. B. Fletcher as the typical 'salon' *précieuse*: the beauty who dispenses her beneficent influence to a *côterie* of admirers, who in turn immortalize her in verse ('Précieuses at the court', p. 130). This description is borne out by the poetic tributes addressed to Lady Carlisle by contemporaries. Waller, for instance, may have intended an allusion to the *Chambre bleue* at Rambouillet in a poem entitled 'of her Chamber', and a comparison with Catherine de Vivonne when he declares that in her presence

> No worthy mind but finds in hers there is
> Something proportioned to the rule of his;
> While she with cheerful, but impartial grace,
> (Born for no one, but to delight the race
> Of men) like Phoebus so divides her light,
> And warms us, that she stoops not from her height.
>
> (*Poems*, I, 26)

William Cartwright's 'Panegyrick to the most Noble Lucy Countess of Carlisle' (*The Plays and Poems*, edited by G. Blakemore Evans, pp. 441–5) describes her physical and spiritual beauty in Neoplatonic terms, but is more exaggerated in its praise and impersonal in its tone than similar poems addressed to the Queen.

Her physical beauty is nothing but the reflection of her 'proportion'd Soul'; and the light 'which we find / Streams in your Eye, is knowledge in your Mind' (ll. 39–40). Wherever her virtues print Love, 'they print Joy, and Religion too; / Hence in your great Endowments Church and Court / Find what t'admire' (ll. 98–100). Lady Carlisle evidently had (also in contrast to the Queen) a quality that was indispensable to the *salon précieuse*, that of taking an intellectual rather than an emotional attitude towards love. According to Sir Toby Matthew's 'portrait' of her, she could not love in earnest, 'contenting herself to play with *Love*, as with a child. Naturally she hath no passion at all' (*DNB*, see under Hay, Lucy). This immunity from passion allowed the true *précieuse* very free manners, but (at least to believers) placed her morals above suspicion.

Ben Jonson may have had Lady Carlisle in mind in *The New Inne* (1629) when he mocks this kind of *préciosité* in the person of Lady Frampul. Jonson implies that Lady Frampul's ideas of love are the new 'in' fashion. Instead of citing classical or humanist authorities for the genealogy of Platonic love, as Jonson himself would have done, Lady Frampul makes up her own list of successors to Plato with Greek, English, and French romance writers, '*Heliodore*, or *Tatius*, / *Sydney*, *D'Urfé*, or all Loves *Fathers*, like him' (III. ii. 204–5). Her use of the exaggerated language of the romances –

> Where haue I liu'd, in heresie so long
> Out o' the Congregation of Loue,
> And stood irregular, by all his Canons?   (III. ii. 211–13)

perverts Lovell's original exposition of Platonic love, and her egocentricity makes a mockery of both love and religion. Early in the play Jonson refers to the 'toyes' of French romance, which are sent out to 'poison Courts, and infest manners' (I. vi. 128), and his final judgment seems to be, in the words of Pru, that Lady Frampul is one 'runne mad with pride, wild with selfe-loue' (V. ii. 30). In this judgment, however, it should be noted that Lady Frampul is not accused of immorality. Jonson, satirically bent as he is, makes her only independent and eccentric,

> of so bent a phant'sie,
> As she thinks nought a happinesse, but to have
> A multitude of servants! and, to get them,
> (Though she be very honest) yet she venters
> Upon these precipices, that would make her
> Not seeme so, to some prying, narrow natures.   (I. v. 51–6)

Like the true *précieuse*, Lady Frampul scorns such narrow natures, and is both 'peevish' (derived from the word 'frampul') and spirited in living to 'no other *scale*, then what's my own' (II. i. 59).

A similar independence of spirit in real life seems to have characterised Lady Carlisle, and in fact she conforms closely to the description given by Ian Maclean of the typical French *précieuse* as one who has 'a quality of wit, of levity, of delight in intrigue' (*Woman Triumphant*, p. 152). She was admired for her wit as well as for her beauty, and she was constantly at the centre of intrigue. Whether her political intrigue also involved her in amorous intrigue can only be guessed, but poetic tributes in the form of Platonic gallantry, like Cartwright's, involved 'gallantry' in its other sense as well. In the poem 'Upon my Lady Carliles walking in Hampton-Court garden', Suckling conducts a dialogue with Carew, who sees 'danger and divinity' in the Lady's face, while the other mentally undresses her.[46] Such debates became the basis for a literary game, adding a spice of gallantry (in its double sense) which was not inimical to the *salons* (*honnêteté* and *galanterie* grew up side by side) and which is certainly an ingredient in 'Cavalier' poetry.[47] It would, however, have been unthinkable in relation to the Queen. The difference between the two women and between the two types of *préciosité* may be seen from the fact that, after the Civil War when both Lady Carlisle and the Queen were in France, Lady Carlisle became a member of the fashionable Parisian *salons* (her name appears in Somaize's *Grand Dictionnaire des précieuses*, published in 1661[48]), whereas Henrietta did not; she founded a convent where she took part in the religious observances of the nuns (Hamilton, *Henrietta Maria*, pp. 136–7).

The ideas on love encouraged by the Queen, and a pattern for the kind of conduct acceptable amongst her group at court may perhaps be best seen in *The Shepherd's Paradise*, the pastoral written by Walter Montague in which the Queen and her ladies took all the principal parts. It was performed in January 1633, probably repeated in February, had been in rehearsal since the preceding September, and took eight hours to perform![49] It is generally credited with setting the tone for subsequent *précieux* and Platonic drama of the thirties, but it was too undramatic to have direct imitators, and little explanation has ever been offered either of its meaning, or of its importance for the Queen. I suggest that Montague drew on the current fashion for 'true' romance to include in the pastoral an allusion to the King and Queen's courtship, and that it was meant to expound to the court an ideal of chaste courtship and marriage. In this context Suckling's jibe in 'A Session of the Poets' as to whether Montague understood his own pastoral (ll. 83–4) refers, I think, not to the content so much as the contorted expression, which led Patrick Carey to write

> tell me pray, if ever you
> Read th'English of Watt Montague,
> Isn't it more hard than French?   (*Trivial Poems* (1651), p. 7)

Montague in writing at such appalling length presumably had some subject matter in mind, even if it was only, as Suckling implied, 'fooling' to please the Queen.

In France, as Jean Jacquot has observed ('La Reine Henriette-Marie', p. 133), a *roman* on the subject of Charles's and Henrietta's courtship had already been published in 1625 by A. Remy, entitled *La Galatée et les adventures du Prince Astigès. Histoire de nostre temps où sous noms feints sont représentez les amours du roy et de la reyne d'Angleterre. Avec tous les voyages qu'il a fait, tant en France qu'en Espagne*. The *roman* was offered to Henrietta Maria as a wedding present, and it may have served as a convenient source of allusion for masques and entertainments during the 1630s (for instance, Jacquot (pp. 159–60) compares a ballet in the *roman* with the opening scene of *Salmacida Spolia*). An English precedent (though different in moral tone) for this kind of treatment existed in the prose romance written about 1627 by Sir Kenelm Digby, in which, under the assumed name of Theagenes, he recounts the highly coloured version of events leading up to his secret marriage with 'Stelliana', Venetia Stanley, in 1625.[50] The fact that Digby had attended Charles in Madrid (as had Montague's elder brother Edward) on his visit to the Infanta Isabella Maria, and had also been part of the embassy to France for the hand of Henrietta, would have given him a special interest in the subject of the King's two courtships, and he may have suggested to Montague the idea of a romantic treatment of the subject in a pastoral written for the Queen. Montague, in fact, knew the events of the French courtship better than Charles, for he had been one of the courteirs who had conveyed Charles's overtures to the young Henrietta in 1624. His long-lasting friendship with Henrietta and her mother dated from this time, and he formed a close attachment to the French court which continued to the end of his life.

Charles had never in real life courted Henrietta for himself (they were married by proxy), and his only glimpse of her before she arrived in England had been when he was on his romantic escapade with the Duke of Buckingham to woo the Spanish Infanta, a sufficiently unconventional episode in itself to figure in romance, and one which had already been made the subject of a ballet in France by Outre-Manche (Jacquot, p. 133). Travelling *incognito* on the way to Spain, the pair had looked in at the French court where they saw a rehearsal for a masque, with Henrietta, amongst others, practising the dancing (Hamilton, pp. 30 and 41). It is doubtful whether Charles had taken much notice of the youthful Henrietta, since she must have been eclipsed by the finery of the Queen Mother and the young Queen of France, who was sister to the Infanta, with whom Charles professed himself romantically in love. Later, however, this moment was represented as the beginning of his love for Henrietta. Remy inserted the episode in *La Galatée*, and Boisrobert perpetuated the myth in an ode 'présentée à la Reine d'Angleterre, par Monsieur le Comte de Carlile, de la part du Roy son Espous' (Jacquot, p. 133). It was then taken over by English writers. Waller, in a poem of compliment 'To the Queen', writes that her eyes could enslave the gods, and calls to witness 'our Jove, prevented by their flame / In his swift passage to the Hesperian dame' (ll. 39–40). He goes on to picture Charles as the Royal youth who

> pursuing the report
> Of beauty, found it in the Gallic court;
> There public care with private passion fought
> A doubtful conflict in his noble thought:
> Should he confess his greatness, and his love . . .
> Or on his journey o'er the mountains ride?

(*Poems*, pp. 8–9, ll. 43–7, 53)

In a separate poem to the King (*Poems*, pp. 1–7), Waller pictures Charles on his journey back from Spain, braving the storm like a hero, oblivious of danger, harbouring only the 'dear remembrance of that fatal glance, / For which he lately pawned his heart in France' (ll. 101–3). The fact that by 1633 the Royal couple were romantically in love would have been enough to make them want to relive what had been, at the time, a necessarily impersonal courtship, and to give Montague an easy choice of subject.

Besides drawing on French romance Montague might have felt it desirable to place his pastoral in an English tradition, relating it to the Elizabethan past. Sidney's *Arcadia* was the outstanding example of pastoral romance, currently known in France as well as in England (Gervais d'Amblainville, for example, referred to it in dedicating his pastoral to Henrietta in 1627).[51] As it happened, the first episode in the *Arcadia* fitted neatly with the romantic episode of Charles's visit to Spain, which James himself had said was 'worthy to be put in a new Romanso' (Bone, *Henrietta Maria*, p. 18). There is little doubt that contemporaries would have compared the friendship between the young Prince Charles and the dashing favourite Buckingham with the ideal friendship between Pyrocles and Musidorus. In the opening of the *Arcadia* the two princes are on a journey home, but looking for adventure and 'taking Arcadia in their way' they are 'distracted from their main purpose' by falling in love with Pamela and Philoclea (p. 11), just as Basilino and Agenor are distracted from their journey by calling in at the Shepherd's Paradise, where they fall in love, and just as the two actual princes, Charles and Buckingham, had called *incognito* at the French court on their journey to Spain. It may be merely coincidence that Katherine Manners, who married Buckingham in 1620, had copied this particular episode from the *Arcadia* into her 'notebook',[52] but her doing so suggests that it was for contemporaries a commonplace. Montague's name Basilino for the Prince is close to the first proper name mentioned in the *Arcadia*, Basilius the Duke. Agenor (and Genorio, as Agenor becomes in disguise) both contain the letters GEORGE, the first name of the Duke of Buckingham (George Villiers). In the pastoral the Prince has chosen Agenor as his companion and 'the only partner of his thoughts' (sig. B7), as Charles had chosen Buckingham at the time of their journey.

When *The Shepherd's Paradise* opens the Prince has just renounced his love for Fidamira, a lady of the 'Castilian court'. He and Agenor set out in disguise to find the Princess of Navarre, whom the Prince's father has decided he should marry, ostensibly to ask her forgiveness for having loved another. On the way they decide to take in the 'Shepherd's Paradise', where the Prince is entirely captivated by the beauty of the newly elected Queen. This Queen is said to have come from some part of France, bringing with her marks of noble birth; though she came to the Paradise as a stranger, she 'hath lived here ever since with so winning a modesty, as it hath so reconciled the plurality of the sisters to the strangenesse of her birth and beauty as her choice [as Queen] may be ascribed to an inspiration from above, rather than her aspiring thither' (sig. c6v). She later turns out to be the 'real' Princess of Navarre whom the Prince was seeking, and whom he was destined to marry all the time. Bellesa (played by Henrietta, daughter of the former Henri de Navarre) is later reported to have married the King of Albion, at whose court her beauty has 'raised her to the public eminence of a Queen' (sig. F3). In the pastoral, Basilino (disguised as Moramente) and Bellesa discuss the question of having loved twice. To Bellesa's question: 'You think heaven doth allow of love's twice?' Moramente replies: 'As it doth intend, Madam, all good should arise to its perfection, our minds are but love's pupils at the first.' They debate the question, and she taxes him with inconstancy, which concerns her less than that he 'should strive to prove it a virtue', but he defends it with obscure, but winning, logic: 'Had I thought inconstancy a virtue, Madam, I ne'er had been blest with this so great joy of seeing you' (sig. E8–E8v). He declares that he has been reserved by Heaven for this greater love, which is willed by fate, and Bellesa is won to his suit.

Fidamira, a lady of the Castilian court who, when the play opens, is just parting from Basilino, may fit the role of the Infanta, a suggestion that seems to be supported by the visual evidence of the costumes. The editors of Inigo Jones's designs point out that the drawing of Fidamira (figure 1) is a copy of a portrait of the Infanta which is presumed to have entered the Royal Collection during the negotiations for the Spanish match (Orgel and Strong, II, p. 522; no. 261 and figure 91). Stephen Orgel has remarked in a subsequent article[53] that 'it is difficult to believe he [Inigo Jones] did not mean something by alluding to the painting', since it is the only known instance of Jones copying a portrait. The costume would, moreover, have drawn attention to itself by being so different from the other women's costumes in the play: by the standards of the 1630s it is stiff and old-fashioned, quite the opposite of the flowing, feminine lines of the dress worn by Bellesa (figure 2; Orgel and Strong, no. 256). Orgel concludes that the basis of the allusion was probably some Caroline 'in-group joke', but that 'the function of the plagiarism is utterly obscure' (p. 479). If, however, the subject of the pastoral concerned the King's two courtships, the visual reference to the Spanish court and the Infanta would have been easily picked out by the audience (and the unattractiveness of the costume would have compensated Henrietta for the presence of a 'rival' on stage). A design for the King of Castile (figure 3; Orgel and Strong, no. 264) has the same stiff lines and padded shoulders as the Infanta's dress, and another drawing of Fidamira (Orgel and Strong, no. 262) has 'this with the King' written on it, perhaps indicating that Jones had intended the costumes to form part of a 'Spanish' group; it was probably discarded as being too masculine, and a compromise made with the high waist, wide collar, and coronet more typical of the English costumes (figure 4; Orgel and Strong, no. 265 and p. 532). An additional source of allusion to the Spanish court existed in the account by Andres Mendoza of *Two Royall Entertainments Lately Given to Charles, Prince of Great Britaine, by Philip IV of Spaine*, translated from the

1 Inigo Jones, costume design for Fidamira
   in *The Shepherd's Paradise*

2 Inigo Jones, costume design for the Queen
   as Bellesa in *The Shepherd's Paradise*

Spanish (London 1623), which would have added to Montague's ideas. It recorded that in one of these entertainments the nobility went out 'for the enjoying of the rurall Delights of the morning, with long staues in their hands, cloathed after the Pastòrall manner' (p. 25), and the subject defended at tilts was 'that in the rusticity of the Country, there is found the Courtly vrbanity of Loue' (p. 15), a fair description of *The Shepherd's Paradise*.

Whether or not the pastoral holds an allusion to these events, the rules of the society over which the Queen is elected to govern are likely to have had some relation to the rules of the group over which Henrietta presided at court. These rules, which are concisely set out in the pastoral (sig. c3v–c4), are those of a tightly organized group, not unlike those of a religious order. Members are admitted at the discretion of the Queen, upon a vow of chastity 'which is not ever to be dispenced with', and the breach of which is punishable by death; they are to have community of riches and possessions; there is to be no detraction of a sister without proof; they may retire only 'upon designe of Marriage'. Moramente comments 'this order seems a match betweene love, and honour, and chastity, which you are happy sir in being Priest to' (sig. c6). The activities of the

3 Inigo Jones, costume design for the King of Valentia or Castile (first version) in *The Shepherd's Paradise*

4 Inigo Jones, costume design for the King of Valentia or Castile (second version) in *The Shepherd's Paradise*

society, with its vows, ceremonies, priests, altar, temple, and prayers, are carried out with a religious solemnity, and when Bellesa is installed as Queen she vows to keep the laws 'even as I hope to rise / From this, into another Paradise' (sig. C3). After the arrival of Basilino and Agenor, the pastoral consists mainly of high-minded conversations between the inhabitants of the paradise, at the end of which the Prince wins Bellesa's consent to marriage.

In the course of these conversations almost every aspect of courtship and love is discussed, and it is rather a surprise to find that the commonly accepted ideal of 'Platonic love' (that is, love without hope of reward, as in *L'Astrée*) is put forward, but only to be dismissed, and is in fact gently laughed at. D'Urfé's first 'law' of love stated 'Qui veut estre parfaict amant, / Il faut qu'il ayme infini-ment' (*L'Astrée*, II, 181), which is interpreted to mean that the ideal lover must love without any hope of reward, certainly without hope of possession (II, 670), and his love may even be more perfect in absence (II, 201). In *The Shepherd's Paradise*, Martiro is the only spokesman for this kind of love, arguing that impossi-bility makes love rarer and more spiritual; he declares that his adoration of Bellesa never had 'so low a thought as hope' (sig. G8v), and he refuses to consider her suggestion that love should have an object level with itself. He exercises his wit, and bores the others, by producing a long poem on 'impossibility' (sig. G7v–G8). Camena comments (sig. G6) that Martiro's love must live by its wits, for it has nothing else to live on. Martiro's views are used as a foil in several of the discussions on love, but always in order to defeat them. Bellesa, for example, expresses the fear that if a woman admits her love, the man will think himself master, and she asks Moramente how he reconciles his argument for mutual love with Martiro's belief that love between souls rules out physical union? Moramente replies that in true love, hearts are not made subject, but are exalted by physical (as well as spiritual) union, and he dismisses Martiro's theory as 'darke visions' engendered by privation (sig. F7v). This is a turning point in Moramente's courtship, for Bellesa acknowledges herself from now on his 'pupil' in love. No one in the play shares Martiro's view, and he comes to admit by the end that he has wronged Bellesa in trying to part body and soul. 'Platonic love' of the type advocated in *L'Astrée* would not seem to be highly favoured in this group.

D'Urfé's first law of love had as its corollary that all 'médiocrité' in love is betrayal, but the ideal of love in *The Shepherd's Paradise* comes very close to the 'mediocrity' that d'Urfé rejected. Montague's version of love does not reach d'Urfé's extreme of spirituality, but nor does it have his sly humour. In *L'Astrée*, d'Urfé allows a certain amount of human weakness to characters like the worldly Lycidas and Stelle, to the inconstant Hylas who is the constant foil to idealism, and even to the hero Céladon, whose disguise as a girl allows him a good deal of voyeurism and illicit freedom. Montague is much more moralistic. Misbehaviour in the company of the opposite sex is not given the slightest scope: Moramente's greatest misdemeanour is to kiss Bellesa's hand once while she is asleep, for which he is severely reproved; Agenor's wandering eye is rebuked, and every character firmly paired off or placed in his right moral niche by the end of the play. There is not even a satyr to enliven the action, and Agenor, who comes closest to being 'inconstant', is certainly not humorous. Montague's emphasis is, first, on chastity, and then on the ability of true love to refine, not extinguish, the senses, so that the 'undarken'd soul' (sig. H6v–H7) may shine through them. Since pure love is 'a Spirit extracted out of the whole mass of virtue' (sig. F7) it cannot rise to an excess, as does passion, and it finds its proper satisfaction in the union of body and soul.

For all the high-flown words, the ideal of love in *The Shepherd's Paradise* is a domestic one. One of the main debates, between Camena and Melidoro, is on the compatibility of pure love with marriage. Camena expresses the fear that love's flame may be put out by possession, and that marriage will end love. Melidoro replies that spiritual love is preserved by physical union. Pure love, he explains, enters through the senses and is preferred up into our thoughts, where 'it is inthroned higher, than any mortall joy can reach up to depose it;' from this transcendent height 'it may seem to look down on all things, and despise even enjoying'. But when our thoughts, growing dizzy, begin to fall from such elevation, 'then possession is a foundation to maintain Love at that height' (sig. E2). Far from ending love 'Hymen's torches do imply ... love's flame is nourished, not put out: and may not love blaze as well in them, as Cupid's wild fires?' (sig. E2v). In the love of Camena and Melidoro, which has passed through a stormy region, but has now arrived 'at Love's supreamest region, where there is all serenity' (sig. G5), there is perhaps a reference to the frequently stormy relations between the King and Queen in the first years of their marriage. To Camena's question, whether some might not arrive at this peaceful region without the preceding storms, Melidoro answers that opposition is a necessary prelude to noble love:

There is a lower region *Camena*, where common unrefined lovers stay, and joy in flat security, whose pleasure is but an acquiescence. But all aspiring love that seeks to pitch it selfe in this sublimity of joy and glory, must passe through this middle region, where it findes a stormy opposition. (sig. G5–G5v)

The love of Bellesa and Moramente, which in the pastoral passes from the sparring of courtship, to respect for each other's views, to mutual love, and finally to the prospect of marriage which 'fate itself' (sig. L7v) has worked to achieve, looks forward to the sublime region at which the King and Queen presumably had, by 1633, themselves arrived.

Such a view of love and marriage echoed the sentiments of Charles and Henrietta concerning their own marriage, as well as of historians like Clarendon, who described the King's love for the Queen as a combination of 'all those noble affections which raise the passion to the greatest height ... so that they were the true idea of conjugal affection, in the age in which they lived' (quoted by Pickel, *Charles I*, p. 28). It was certainly not a view typical of the 'Platonic' ideal in *L'Astrée*, any more than it was of the views of *précieuses* a decade or so later in the century, who looked on marriage as 'un esclavage.'[54] It was, however, typical of the views of Devout Humanists, and of the concept of *honnêteté* in the 1630s. St François de Sales had been influential in the early seventeenth century in heightening the prestige of marriage by devoting a section to it in his *Introduction*, insisting that 'marriage, in every way, must be held in honour' (p. 184), and that 'mutual love should be altogether holy, sacred and divine' (p. 185). For Sales, love was the basis of happy marriage, just as it was the basis of all successful personal and social relationships, and he did not shrink from approving those physical expressions of affection which are 'so necessary to the preservation of mutual love, for though they do not create this bond they are a delightful means of augmenting it' (p. 188). A similar view seems to be summed up in the concluding couplet addressed to Bellesa in the pastoral: 'May you have all the joyes of innocence / Injoying too all the delights of sence'. The King and Queen's marriage was held up as an ideal for the rest of the court to follow, as Montague suggests in the concluding address:

> your example doth to all declare
> None innocent that love not, nay not faire.
> For they can neither handsome be, nor true,
> That may and yet refuse to be as you.   (sig. M7v)

This ideal of mutual love and marriage was not the only aspect of the love fashions associated with the Queen, but it does help to make sense of some of the literature connected with the court. William Habington's poems 'To Castara', for instance, were published (in March 1634) a year after the performance of the Queen's pastoral, and his poem 'Vpon the mutuall love of their Majesties' refers to the Royal example which would make even barbarians

> by this precedent correct their life,
> Each wisely chuse, and chastely love a wife.
> Princes example is a law. Then we
> If loyal subjects, must true lovers be.
>   (*The Poems*, edited by Kenneth Allot, p. 57)

His poems celebrate, as he says, those 'rites Love offers up to Chastity' ('To Castara, *A Sacrifice*', p. 11), and he follows his portrait of 'A Mistris' with that of 'A Wife'. Habington is usually credited with following a 'serious' side of the fashion for Platonic love, but if, as his editor says, he 'breaks its laws by marrying, and its spiritualization by celebrating married love' (*The Poems*, Introduction, pp. liii–liv), surely he is no longer following the code. His poetry is, rather, a criticism of the code of love in *L'Astrée*, of poets who make an 'Idoll' of woman, and of poetry that 'wantons too much according to the French garbe' (Author's Preface, p. 5). His Castara, on the other hand, is very much an *honnête femme*; his prose portrait of 'A Mistris' (pp. 8–10) could be read almost as a summary of *The Accomplish'd Woman*, both in the topics it deals with (ornament, modesty, 'servants,' conversation, dancing, singing, dignified behaviour), and in the characteristic pairing of qualities to suggest moderation. Habington perhaps leaned more to the sombre and religious side of *honnêteté* than the Queen, but his work makes far more sense if regarded in the light of *honnêteté*, than it does if regarded as an aberrant kind of 'Platonic love'.

It is in dealing with court drama, however, that a distinction between different ideals of love becomes most useful, and where the influence of the Queen's *honnête* fashion can be seen in plays associated with her at court.

2   The tone of court drama

Stage convention and court fashion

Critics have agreed, in general terms, that much of the drama written for the court in the 1630s shows the influence of *préciosité* and Platonic love.[1] There has been little agreement, however, as to the moral tone of this drama, on the basis of which generalisations about the Queen's love cult have been made. The confusion arises partly because the playwrights themselves often seem undecided about whether to take 'Platonic love' seriously or not. William Cartwright, for instance, who could employ the exalted language of Platonic love in his poem on Lady Carlisle, or engage in the involved 'Platonic' dialogues of *The Royal Slave*, in another mood could write in the poem 'No Platonique Love', 'I was that silly thing that once was wrought / To practise this thin love ...' (*Plays and Poems*, p. 494). William Habington uses the religious language of love in sad earnest when addressing his 'Castara':

> O divine
> And purest beauty, let me thee inshrine
> In my devoted soule.   ('To Castara, *Praying*', *Poems*, p. 11)

However, a song from *The Queen of Aragon* shows him in another mood:

> When I sigh and kisse your hande,
> Cross my Armes and wondring stand:
> Holding parley with your eye,
> Then dilate on my desires,
> Sweare the sunne nere shot such fires,
> All is but a handsome lye.   (*Poems*, p. 152)

Habington's court lady who thinks her face 'streight some murder doth commit', and whose virtue 'doth begin / To grow scrupulous of my sinne, / When I talke to shew my wit', is very like the lady in Suckling's *Aglaura*, who no sooner had love named to her than she 'began to talk of flames, and flames / Neither devouring, nor devour'd, of aire / and of cameleons'. The courtiers who mock her label her as one of 'the Platonics ... Those of the new religion in love!' which they consider to be 'a mere trick to enhance the price of kisses' (*The Poems, Plays and other Remains*, ed. Hazlitt, I, 111). These criticisms generally are taken to be directed at Henrietta's fashion, but the fact that the sillier side of Platonic

48

love was criticised in plays approved by the King and Queen (Habington's and Suckling's both had two performances) suggests that they also approved of the criticism.

Confusion about moral attitudes has also arisen because court plays have been treated too much as an undifferentiated group. Before considering the direct influence of love fashions in the thirties, therefore, it might be as well to look briefly at the different conventions of love already in place on the stage. One was French pastoral, which Henrietta helped introduce in the twenties and whose popularity continued into the thirties. The court saw French plays acted when troupes visited London in 1629 and again in 1635, the latter under the protection of the Queen. She herself supervised her maids-of-honour in a performance of *Florimène* in 1635. *Florimène*, for which a summary of the plot has survived,[2] seems to conform to the type described by H. C. Lancaster (*A History of French Dramatic Literature*, pp. 25–6) in which shepherds and shepherdesses pursue each other offering unrequited love; at last, by the intervention of a deity or by some other conventional means, the direction of half the lovers is reversed and love can be satisfied in a series of marriages. The treatment of love in these plays is romantic rather than Platonic, and the closest to the form in English is probably Thomas Randolph's *Amyntas: or The Impossible Dowry* (1638), written about 1630. Here Laurinda is 'a wavering nymph' who loves both Damon and Alexis, but will choose neither since marriage seems to have such dire results: 'Nothing but fears,/Jars, discontents, suspicions, jealousies' (*Works*, ed. Hazlitt, p. 275). The cause of unhappy marriages is an impossible dowry which the 'mad' Amyntas must give for Urania. Some providential wisdom, seemingly against the dictates of reason and custom, keeps everyone virtuous until Echo reveals that 'a husband' is the dowry Amyntas must bring. All this gives the opportunity for long speeches on pastoral happiness, the duties of children, and on married love; the action is accompanied generously by dances, songs, and processions. In the epilogue Randolph wishes 'this blessed isle, / This little world of lovers' the same happiness as the lovers on stage, and ends with an entreaty to the company 'To deign to take part in this public joy'. This pastoral (like *Florimène*, which had elaborately staged *intermedii*) has a singing chorus, temple rites, virgins with candles in procession, a sacrificial altar, and finally the address to the audience to continue the festivities of the play. In pastoral, as in masque, the stage and court worlds overlap.

This simple pastoral form derived from the pastoral of sixteenth-century Italy, of which Guarini's *Il Pastor fido* was a prototype.[3] Guarini established a pattern, with Mirtillo and Amarilli as the ideal pair of lovers, Silvio and Dorinda as less perfect, Corisca and the Satyr as largely corrupt. A similar patterning can be found in *L'Astrée*, with Adamas representing the religious, and Sylvandre the philosophical aspects of Platonism; Diane is the cultivated lady of the *salon*; Céladon, and Astrée herself, have many human failings; and Hylas is the humorous cynic. This characteristic patterning, which gave scope for plot complication and contrasting points of view, was carried over into *commedia grave* and tragi-comedy, in which the ideal of love is contrasted with more worldly, corrupt, or 'satyric' interpretations. The latter are designed to enhance the main theme, and are always defeated in the course of the action. Fletcher's *The Faithful Shepherdess* perhaps comes the closest in English to the form: in this play Chlorin is a virginal nymph who 'cures' the love-sick Thenot by her virtue and wit. Perigot and Amoret are chaste lovers, Chloe and Amaryllis pursue different shepherds in turn, and a sullen shepherd and a satyr are suitably lustful. There is disguising and magic, and a good deal of action. The plot is presided over by a Priest and an Old Shepherd, who, with the help of Chlorin, bring matters to a virtuous conclusion. The play was a failure in Fletcher's lifetime, but was successfully revived in the late 1620s and performed for the court on Twelfth Night 1634, with costumes and sets borrowed from the previous year's production of *The Shepherd's Paradise*. Thomas Goffe's *The Careless Shepherdess*, written some time in the 1620s and revised about 1638, was similar in type, but the action is more fantastic. Two fathers threaten to disinherit their children if they persist in their loves, Apollo utters an oracle, satyrs carry off the women, and the heroes are brought to the point of killing each other. A magician is employed, the women are buried, the men weep, the dead arise, and the oracle is fulfilled, clearing the way for happy marriages. In this type of play there is much talk of chastity, but the plot often depends on ambiguous sexual situations for its interest, and the tone is far from grave.

Tragi-comedies and plays of court intrigue, of which *Aglaura* was one of the more extreme examples, continued to be written and seem to have been enjoyed in the thirties, and one would not want to argue on their basis that court taste was particularly clean or moral. Indeed, much of this drama has an insipid preoccupation with love intrigue that would require a much broader consideration of social and sexual attitudes if it were to be adequately discussed. Presumably dramatists, then as now, were more than willing to titillate audiences by the ambiguities inherent in situations connected with love and sex. If, for instance, there were no rapes on stage, there was often the possibility of one taking place just off stage: in *The Careless Shepherdess*, Arismene and Castarina are carried away no fewer than three times by lustful 'satires', who, when they are not prevented in the nick of time from satisfying their wicked desires, occasionally turn out to be friendly agents in disguise (once Castarina's own father) furthering the convolutions of the plot. In Thomas Randolph's *The Jealous Lovers* the virtuous Evadne is tricked into entering a brothel, where Tyndarus, her jealous lover, tries to rape her to avenge the fancied slight to his honour. Davenant, though not quite so crude, is one of the worst offenders in playing on equivocal situations designed to trade on the expectations of the vulgar, while appealing, in the event, to the 'purity' of the refined. In *Love and Honour* Alvaro has Evandra taken to a secret hiding-place to ensure her safety, and when he confesses his love for her, asks:

Why do you start, as if some jealous thought
Did whisper that my love devis'd this snare?

She denies the thought, but he harps on it: 'Think not I'll use advantage or constraint / Upon thy love ...' (*Works*, III, 121, 123). He protests too much, although his intentions prove to be perfectly honourable. In *The Fair Favourite*, the King insists on visiting Eumena in her bed-chamber late at night, alone, to prove his love is virtuous and chaste. When he urges her several times 'To bed, to bed' (*Works*, IV, 233), she agrees impassively that they should part, so that those who jealously spy on them can get some rest! In *The Platonic Lovers* the same situation is taken to extremes when Theander and Eurithea, the Platonic lovers, indulge in sensuous rhetoric, embrace, and kiss. But *The Platonic Lovers* failed at court, perhaps because, as Davenant has one of his 'Platonic' characters say, it was 'too masculine'. In general, however, playwrights were not shy about sex (a play like Shirley's *The Ball* contains a good deal of frank discussion between men and women on the subject), and doubtless part of the audience enjoyed risqué situations and a more physical approach to love as a foil to 'feminine' sensibilities in plays more directly influenced by the Queen.

The initial reaction of some playwrights, however, seems to have been one of confusion as to what was, exactly, the Queen's idea of Platonic love. It is tempting at this distance to imagine that the concept of Platonic love entered the court fully formed, but writers brought up in an 'English' tradition of Neoplatonism tended, I think, to resist (or not to comprehend) its new French forms, and this resistance may explain some puzzling features of plays in the early thirties. Jonson and Davenant, for instance, inherited Renaissance ideas of Neoplatonism made familiar by Italian writers and transmitted to England in books like *The Courtier*. Jonson based the Neoplatonism of his masques on this tradition, and he defends it in *The New Inne* against the influence of d'Urfé and the romances. His criticism of the French fashion in this play, however, has a rather puzzled air that has led critics to look for other, deeper meanings in it.[4] By 1629 the aging Jonson was growing out of sympathy with the court, and certainly the play was a failure in performance. Whatever Jonson's intentions, however, the play may have doubly misfired, not simply because it appears to criticise the fashion of Platonic love, but also because it was out of touch with the latest phase of that fashion, the type of *honnête* love favoured by the Queen. Another play written in the same year as Jonson's, Lodowick Carlell's *The Deserving Favourite*, gives a much clearer idea of the love conventions that were to influence court plays written in the thirties.

Carlell was a particular favourite of the Queen, whom he claimed later as 'my most gracious Mistress whom I have so long serv'd, and in former plays not displeas'd'.[5] *The Deserving Favourite* was perhaps begun quite early in the 1620s, and it is interesting to see Carlell drawing on Fletcherian materials (crossed loves, chivalrous rivals, the unfolding of identities, and a brother-sister relationship at the end), but also beginning to give the characters attitudes typical of those in plays of the thirties: the admiration of the beautiful heroines for one another (p. 126); the determination of the women to suppress 'Iealousie! the canker / Of true love' (p. 129) when they seem to love the same man; and Clarinda's high-minded agreement when Lysander (apparently about to die) asks pardon

> that I borrow from
> That stream of loue a part to pay the Princesse,
> For which I know thou being wise, canst neuer
> Loue me lesse, knowing that I haue loue enough
> For both, since I can marry neither.   (pp. 147–8)

His love for both is justified in the event, when he is revealed as Clarinda's brother. The feminism in this play is not as strong as it was to become in the plays that followed it: women are not yet *quite* perfect. Clarinda at the beginning of the play still has 'That little portion of wilfulnesse / Which being a woman you are forc'd to have' (p. 84), but she soon becomes very correct in all her actions. Her behaviour contrasts with that of Lady Frampul in *The New Inne*, and perhaps was meant to have a lesson for the ladies at court. Whereas Lady Frampul behaves like a *salon précieuse* in entertaining a 'flock of gallants' and in scorning the gossip that follows, Clarinda takes explicitly the opposite course, much closer to the advice given to the *honnête femme* in, for instance, Du Bosc's chapter on 'Reputation'. She points out that, since others have grown so vicious and quick to slander virtue,

> women are not to satisfie themselues
> Alone with being good; but they must giue the world
> A firm belief of all their actions,
> That they are so.   (p. 98)

Carlell's play, like Jonson's, criticises the exaggerated compliment of the romances, but it is significant that he places the criticism in the mouth of a woman. The heroine Clarinda is wooed by the Duke, who uses just the kind of devotional language of love that Jonson satirized in the speeches of Lady Frampul. The Duke is perfect in the code of the romances, declaring that he will lay his 'bleeding heart' on the altar, 'which now in thought, / And then in act, shall be a reall Sacrifice' (p. 89). Clarinda undercuts his rhetoric, telling him in plain terms

> if you will speake
> Only what in reason is likely to be true,
> I am no Infidell, I shall believe,   (p. 86)

and to his compliments she replies 'I hate flattery, though a woman' (p. 88). When he declares 'I offer up my life and Fortunes, / With a truer deuotion than ever lover did', she replies resignedly

> I see I must allow you the Louers Phrases,
> Which is to call their Mistris St. and their affection
> Deuotion,   (p. 86)

and she reflects that 'there are many false ones here in Loues Religion' (p. 94). The different views of 'Platonic love' in Jonson's and Carlell's plays seem to support the idea that, even as early as 1629, a distinction was being made at court between the *salon* type with its exaggerated compliment, and the *honnête* type favoured by the Queen. By the end of the thirties the former was even more out of fashion and openly scorned. Cleantha, in *The Queen of Aragon*, echoes Clarinda when she tells the posturing Sanmartino, who practises the 'Platonic' conventions for his own ends, to practise if he must 'in suburbs', where 'ladies wait / To be deliver'd by your mighty hand' (p. 332), but at court to 'learn virtue' (p. 379). She herself is tired of a love worn 'so threadbare out of fashion' (p. 329).

Davenant, like Jonson, seems to have had trouble in adjusting to the Queen's tastes. In 1635 he was asked to write the masque *The Temple of Love*, which purports to celebrate the introduction of the Queen's Platonic love to England, but a few months later he followed it with a seemingly tongue-in-cheek treatment of the subject in *The Platonic Lovers*. This play, like *The New Inne*, has been difficult for critics to fit into the pattern of Cavalier drama. By its title it seems to promise clarification of the fashion of Platonic love, and by its dedication to Henry Jermyn, a friend of Davenant's and a favourite of the Queen, it might have been expected to win favour. Yet the play failed in performance both at Blackfriar's and the court, and its treatment of Platonic love is unlike that in Davenant's later plays. I believe that Davenant was at first a rather unwilling convert to the influence of French fashions and to the Queen's version of Platonic love. His whipped-up enthusiasm can be detected in the strained philosophising and mechanical verse of the play *Love and Honour* (1635), and, even in *The Temple of Love* (1635), doubts about the new doctrine far outweigh its praise in the written part (a disproportion that probably went unnoticed amid the visual splendour). Davenant made no use of French *salon* or romance material in the masque, and the nearest he came to a positive exposition of Platonic love is to say that the Queen and the beauties of her train 'raise new doctrines, and new sects of love: / Which must not woo or court the person, but / The mind'. For this view, he needed to go no further than the book that had been the traditional English source of ideas on Platonic love, Castiglione's *The Courtier*, and I believe that this was the source for *The Platonic Lovers*, written only a few months after the masque.

The plot of *The Platonic Lovers* seems to be based on Bembo's distinction in Book 4 between the reasonable (or 'Platonic') lover and the sensual lover: Bembo contrasts his kind of love (the reasonable) with that of Lord Julian (the sensual), and describes the way in which each kind should be received. The reasonable lover 'coveteth but honest matters, and therefore may the woman graunt him them all without blame. But my Lorde Julians woman that is not so assured of the modestie of the yong man, ought to graunt him the honest matters onely, and deny him the dishonest' (Castiglione, pp. 314–15). It is the intention that decides whether these matters are honest or dishonest, and the 'selfe same thinges' that reasonable lovers may happily and freely grant, sensual lovers must be denied. Bembo elaborates on the liberties the woman may allow to her reasonable lover: 'beside the graunting him mery countenances, familiar and secret talke, jeasting, dalying, hand in hand, may also lawfully and without blame come to kissing: which in sensual love according to the Lorde Julians rules, is not lawfull'. A kiss, he explains, 'is a knitting together both of bodie and soule', but a sensual love will take the body's part. A reasonable lover, on the other hand, knows that the mouth may be an issue for the soul, or for words, the interpreters of the soul, and 'for this doe all chaste lovers covet a kisse, as a coupling of soules together' (p. 315).

Davenant's two pairs of lovers follow these rules precisely. In *The Platonic Lovers* Davenant allows his Platonic pair, Eurithea and Theander, all the liberties that Bembo allows to his 'reasonable' lovers, and he limits Ariola and Phylomont, who contemplate marriage, to a cool and formal courtship, which Bembo insists is all that can be allowed the 'sensual' lover. Theander and Eurithea only woo 'the spirit, face, / And heart', and therefore 'their conversation is / More safe to fame' (*Works*, II, 17). They freely embrace on meeting and talk on intimate terms; he visits her in her chamber where they kiss and converse, until they are 'entangled with chaste courtesies of love' (p. 34). Their love, it has been explained, 'is only mutual wonder and applause' and 'therefore can stir no jealousy / In the severest thought' (p. 31). Ariola, on the other hand, can allow her lover no such liberties, since she and Phylomont 'still affect / For natural ends' such as 'libertines call lust, / But peaceful politicks and cold divines / Name matrimony' (p. 17). She is bashful and cool towards her suitor, not allowing him even to kiss her hand. With these two pairs of lovers, therefore, Davenant gives a practical demonstration of Bembo's distinctions, and measures 'Platonic' idealism against the real world. He cannot, of course, resist showing the absurdities of the situation, and he sends his Platonic theorists off to the Friar for some sensible earthly advice. The Platonic pair are, to outside eyes, overstepping the bounds of decency as well as of common sense. The play was not well received, perhaps because Davenant's forthright treatment of the subject was not in tune with the times. Court audiences of 1635 required something more French, more feminine, an art of talking about love moulded by Platonic idealism or the niceties of pastoral and romance. Once again Lodowick Carlell was nearer the mark: he achieved the right mixture in *The Passionate Lovers*, written like Davenant's play in 1635 and treating a similar theme, but in a manner, as Carlell hints in the Prologue and Epilogue to Part I, inspired by the King and Queen. In his subsequent plays, Davenant, too, adopted the new forms and became as good a Platonic lover as the rest. By 1638 he was writing *The Fair Favourite* and *The Unfortunate Lovers*, and by 1639 *The Distresses*, in which none too virtuous men constantly are reformed by women's superior virtue, and in which there is much discussion of women's wrongs, their steadfastness, and their superiority to male passions.

Writers more willing to follow the tastes of the Queen had no trouble in adopting an attitude to love and courtship that conformed more closely to that of Montague in *The Shepherd's Paradise*. In Joseph Rutter's *The Shepheard's Holyday* (*c.* 1635; reprinted by Dodsley, XII) these ideas are fully developed. The play has a special air of royal approval: it was performed before the King and Queen, whose lives, Rutter says in his Epilogue, have brought 'Virtue in fashion, and the world have taught, / That chaste innocuous sports become the stage, / No less than civil manners do the age' (p. 444). Rutter based the play on Jean de Mairet's *Silvanire* (Paris 1631), which was based in turn on the *Silvanire* of d'Urfé, a play which d'Urfé had addressed in 1625 to Marie de Medici.[6] It is probably no accident that a text of Mairet's version found its way to Rutter, who was closely associated with people in the Queen's circle. He was living in Sir Kenelm Digby's house when he wrote his play, and was also tutor to the sons of the Earl of Dorset, the Queen's Lord Chamberlain, who was responsible for arranging her entertainments. Significantly, both Mairet and Rutter adapt d'Urfé by leaving out his indecent lines, presenting, as Rutter says in the Prologue, a piece 'purged from lighter airs', in which 'A shepherd's muse gently of love does sing, / And with it mingles no impurer thing'.

The Shepheard's Holyday, even more than *The Shepherd's Paradise*, reads like a guidebook, full of precepts and cautions, to conducting a virtuous love affair. Men and women must both stick to the rules in wooing. For the man, 'love one' is the rule, for 'one is the only centre / The line of love is drawn to', provided that the one chosen has 'all / Perfections in her, all that's good and fair' (p. 383). The lover must be careful of his lady's honour, guarding it against 'the malicious world, the censuring people, / That haste to caste dirt on the fairest things' (p. 419). When Sylvia generously admits her love to Thyrsis, who seems to be of lower birth (and hence unsuitable in the eyes of society), he reminds her that her name and state 'must needs / Receive a certain scandal and foul blot / If we be seen together' (p. 416), and he high-mindedly refuses her offer to elope (p. 418). A woman should never be too forward in love, even when, like Sylvia, she believes it 'the greatest good' the gods can bestow (p. 417). When she does admit her love she must be careful to hedge the engagement about with conditions that safeguard her honour and 'virgin chastity' (p. 398); if the woman admits her love first the wooer may fall off in his affections, or think only of more 'possession' (p. 374). It is women's virtue that keeps men pure; even Mirtillus (the only vaguely libertine character in the play), who dreams of 'a heavenly life of love' at court, cannot find any lady who will indulge his fantasy (p. 433). The ideal of love presented by Rutter, however, is not 'Platonic'. Although the hero and heroine resolve to gaze their souls out in each other's eyes when their love seems crossed by Fate (p. 418), it is their marriage which is praised in the end as 'the happiest knot that e'er / Knit two such equal hearts and loves together'. Marriage, if founded on true love, is superior to virginity: it is the greater good, 'Perfection and womanhood' (p. 441). Such careful hedging about of love, and its perfection in marriage, owes more to the concept of *honnêteté* than to the freer behaviour of the *salons*.

Platonic love and morality

Side by side with the ideal of married love, the Queen did encourage an ideal of Platonic love which was reflected in the drama, and which has sometimes been used to show that the Platonic fashion, far from being moral or *honnête*, was deeply immoral. G. F. Sensabaugh, in particular, has maintained in a number of studies (backed up by much 'Puritan' criticism of the period) that the Queen's cult encouraged immoral sexual practices at court, and that these are reflected in the moral decadence of the drama.[7] I would not want to argue that Henrietta was a paragon, nor that all the plays influenced by her fashion were particularly wholesome. The ambiguities inherent in situations where heroines virtuously love the same man (as Aglaura and Orithie do in *Aglaura*), or men vie with one another to woo the beauties of the same mistress's mind (as Ascoli and Altophil in *The Unfortunate Lovers*), gave the solemnities of these plays a *frisson* of interest that was to be fully exploited later by Restoration playwrights. But in the 1630s, as Davenant says in *The Unfortunate Lovers*, 'Such rivalship is noble, though 'tis new' (p. 47), and could be interesting for its own sake. The idea of rising superior to physical passion, while enjoying the 'dalliances' of love, may well have appealed to the aristocratic sense of those who, like Theander and Eurithea at the end of *The Platonic Lovers*,

> have a while
> So rul'd each other with nice fears, that none
> Hereafter will in civil kindness doubt
> There are Platonic-lovers, though but few.

It has been thought that Davenant may even have intended an allusion to Henry Jermyn and the Queen, whose familiarity (to the extent of his being seen once with his arm about her neck) had found its way into a piece of court gossip (Carew, *Poems*, p. xxxv). Henrietta was no prude, she certainly enjoyed the company of men, and her behaviour, by English standards of the time, was comparatively free. Nevertheless, I think Sensabaugh is wrong in attributing wholesale immorality to court fashions and plays. I intend to follow up his arguments here, partly because they have not been answered in detail before,[8] partly because the subject of court morality has a wider bearing on literary criticism. Sensabaugh, for instance, used his conclusions about the Platonic cult as a basis for study of John Ford's plays, the moral tone of which has been the subject of much discussion. While these broader aspects cannot be pursued here, a clearer idea of court fashions seems desirable for understanding exactly what writers outside the court were being influenced by, or what they were reacting against.

The Queen's Platonic ideal lies behind the treatment of love in plays already mentioned (for example, in *The Deserving Favourite* and *The Shepheard's Holyday*), but it is also a chief element in plays like Cartwright's *The Royal Slave* (1636) and Davenant's *The Fair Favourite* (1638), both of which had repeat performances. Its principles are most clearly set out in *The Royal Slave*, a play especially commended by the Queen. In this play the hero Cratander is the 'slave' who has been captured by the Persians; according to an old custom he is allowed a brief reign of freedom before being put to death. The nobility of his actions, however, attracts the attention of Queen Atossa, who is the virtuous wife of Arsamnes. She recognises in the 'slave' a noble spirit, which 'dares preserve his own / Honour, and others too' (ll. 271–2). She takes his part, even at the risk of her own reputation, and gradually wins the King and the rest of the court to her view. Cratander and the Queen exchange exalted 'Platonic' compliments, but they go to great trouble to make clear the kind of love that is regarded as truly Platonic. Cratander is inspired by the 'cleare streames of Beauty' which he sees shining in the Queen, but would never presume 'To trouble them with quenching of my thirst' (ll. 917–19). When she informs him that her pure Affections are 'but an Engine of / The carefull Pow'rs, invented for the safety / And preservation of afflicted goodnesse' (ll. 934–6), he assures her in return that he 'can distinguish betwixt Love, and Love'; if her affections, which belong to the realm of 'refin'd Ideas', should 'from the Circle of their chaster Glories / Dart out a beame', it is not his desert but their own goodness that makes them so 'diffusive' (ll. 955–9). Atossa defends this 'diffusive' light of love. When her husband, Arsamnes, is jealous of her attention to Cratander, she asks if the sun does not 'send beames to others than your selfe?' (ll. 1003–5). Love, she goes on, 'is as free as Fountaine, Aire, or Flower', yet like streams in nature that nourish different plants, it always runs 'In a most faithfull course toward the bosome / Of the lov'd Ocean' (ll. 1013–15). The Queen's long speech is the centre of the play (the entire passage is quoted by Kathleen Lynch (pp. 67–9) as one of the best examples of the *précieux* habit of arguing by similitudes) and the King, though somewhat rueful, is convinced:

> Thou are still vertuous my *Atossa*, still
> Transparent as thy Crystall, but more spotless.
> Fooles that we are, to thinke the Eye of Love
> Must alwayes looke on us.   (ll. 1045–8)

He is satisfied that her actions prove 'Not the Offence, but Charity of Love' (1052). The views expressed by the Queen and Cratander in the play come very close to Montague's exposition of the 'sober passion' of friendship, which, if governed by a virtuous piety, is allowed to 'hold faire correspondence with beauty', and to enjoy a convenient freedom which helps to serve the Divine plan.

The arguments in *The Royal Slave*, and passages like it from other plays, were used by Sensabaugh in his paper 'Love ethics in Platonic court drama' (the first of a series which drew on the conclusions reached in that study) to deduce the court code of Platonic love. According to Sensabaugh this code includes, principally, the ideas that fate rules all lovers (p. 282); beauty and goodness are one (pp. 282–6); beautiful women are saints to be worshipped (pp. 286–8); and true love seeks a spiritual union, which is approved by religion. So far, so good. Sensabaugh goes on, however, to show what he considers to be the twisted ethics that arise from these principles (pp. 291–9): that the laws of love, which according to him include individual whim, inconstancy, and a sexual freedom that verges on promiscuity, were more important than society's laws and the sanctity of marriage; and that Platonic lovers put 'a halo of purity around mental adultery and incest' (p. 291).

In reaching these conclusions, however, Sensabaugh tends to take passages out of context, ignoring both the dramatic situation and the characterisation. In another paper, 'Platonic love and the Puritan rebellion', he uses the passage quoted above from *The Royal Slave*, in which the King exonerates his wife, to show that

love, should it be true and Platonic, must seek satisfaction wherever passion may lead … Has Atossa sinned by letting her love be 'communative', by allowing her love to wander outside the conjugal bed? No, she is sure she has not. Even her husband condones.

('Platonic love and the Puritan rebellion', p. 459)

In the first place, Atossa has not allowed her love 'to wander outside the conjugal bed'; in the second, she makes it clear that the kind of love they are talking about is not passion, but charity. Why, the Queen asks, should not such a feeling be shown publicly? If it were hidden, it might be presumed guilty, but 'Who would stifle / An honest Fire? That flame's to be suspected / That hides it selfe' (ll. 1029–31). In another passage from the same play, an attempted rape is excused by Leocrates as

A little Love-sport only; we were arguing
Pro, and *Con* out of *Plato*, and are now
Going to practice his Philosophy.   (ll. 511–13)

Sensabaugh suggests that this passage shows how 'any kind of love may be argued on Platonic grounds' ('Love ethics', p. 281). But Leocrates and his swaggering companions are Ephesian captives pretending to be court gallants, and the ladies are rescued by Cratander, the Platonic hero of the play. Cratander's ability to see through the deception, to protect the ladies, and punish the offenders, is one of the actions that draws the sympathetic attention of the Queen, and the incident is clearly designed to show what does *not* pass as Platonic love, in the play or, presumably, at court.

Dramatic patterning, in which pairs of 'good' lovers show up the 'bad', is particularly important in this type of play, as noted earlier; Sensabaugh however, in the quotations brought to support his conclusions, often draws on the cynical or witty attitudes of minor characters, whose opinions in the play are far outweighed by the elevated presentation of constancy and love which is the main theme. In the plays under discussion here, one pair of lovers (or sometimes the heroine alone) is idealistic, while other pairs play variations on the ideal, with attitudes ranging from the conventional and modest to the frivolous and debased. Thus, in Rutter's *The Shepheard's Holyday*, Thyrsis and Sylvia are the 'purest pair'; others such as Hylas and Nerina are modest; Dorinda is shameless in pressing her love where it is not returned; Daphnis is a 'rich shepherd' who thinks any lady can be won with gifts, and Mirtillus is the 'common lover' whose dreams of a 'free' life of love at court are pure wish fulfilment. In William Berkeley's *The Lost Lady*, Lysicles and Milesia demonstrate an ideal of devotion religious in its form and intensity. On a less exalted level, Hermione finds herself swayed from her absent lover, but fortifies herself with 'some sad tale' which convinces her that the gods punish inconstancy. This high-minded love is relieved by sprightly pairs of minor characters. Ergasto and Cleon make fun of love compliment and declare that there are 'no greater libertines than married men' (p. 549). Phillida and Irene wittily discuss beauty and honour, and ask 'What is to be got by this / Whining constancy?' (p. 586). But Irene finally falls in love with Ergasto, and he ends by being constant to his sharp-tongued mistress. In *The Queen of Aragon*, the Queen's elevated and dignified attitude to her suitors is contrasted with that of the teasing and flirtatious Cleantha. But Cleantha is undoubtedly virtuous, and is won in the end, not by the ridiculous Sanmartino, but by Oniate, a sober courtier. In *The Royal Slave*, the Queen and Cratander take the positive ideals of Platonic love very seriously indeed, while other characters show the way in which the term can be abused. Sensabaugh, however, in the plays mentioned above, gives weight ('Love ethics', p. 298) to the opinions of the libertine dreamer Mirtillus; to Ergasto (p. 293), whose cynical flattery is easy to see through; to Sanmartino (p. 293), a 'half-witted Lord'; and to Fredeline (p. 300), an old *roué* in *The Platonic Lovers*. To say that minor characters express the true motives behind Platonic love in these plays is like saying that the Nurse in *Romeo and Juliet* expresses all that young love is 'really' about.

One of Sensabaugh's chief examples of sexual immorality comes from Davenant's *The Fair Favourite*, which was twice presented at court. In this play the Queen seems to excuse her husband's love for another woman when she declares

> If it were low, and sinful love, I should
> Not think it worth my envy or my fear;
> If pure and noble, as my strictest faith
> Believes, it is too great a treasure to
> Be made particular and own'd by me
> Alone, since what is good doth still encrease
> In merit of that name, by being most
> Communative.   (p. 264)

Sensabaugh claims that in this speech the Queen 'not only exonerates but glorifies' the King's love outside the marital tie ('Love ethics', p. 294). But the King's love for Eumena is not simply 'Platonic dalliance', as Harbage (p. 167) described it. The whole plot rests on the fact that Eumena had long been the object of the King's honourable love; his politicians, wanting a rich marriage, hid her away for two years on pretence that she was dead, releasing her only on the day of the King's marriage to the equally beautiful Queen, whereupon the King refuses to consummate the marriage and returns his affections to Eumena. The Queen, realising that the King has been tricked, magnanimously recognises the claims of a prior attachment (p. 264). She refuses to be jealous of the King's love for Eumena, and Eumena, equally virtuous and magnanimous, refuses to usurp the Queen's marriage. Sensabaugh is ignoring the plot when he uses the speech as one of the key passages in his argument for immorality. The word 'communative', moreover, he takes to imply adultery when he applies it to Atossa's speech in *The Royal Slave* (quoted above), or promiscuity which he equates with 'th' Platonick Law' when he quotes from the satire *Lady Alimony*: 'Is this th' Platonick Law; all things in common?' (*Tragic Muse*, p. 139). But the predominant associations of the word 'communative' in examples given by the *OED* are with religion, and none have a physical connotation. As used in this passage from *The Fair Favourite* it is obviously intended to denote the same kind of religious and charitable love that Atossa describes in *The Royal Slave*.

For contemporary audiences, of course, it is evident that stopping short of physical union (outside marriage) was the crudely mechanical test of 'virtue'. The crux of discussions on the morality or otherwise of this kind of drama will therefore often depend on how we interpret words like 'lover' and 'mistress'. Although they are sometimes deliberately ambiguous, we are by no means justified in always taking them to imply physical intimacy, as Sensabaugh tends to do. For example, a conversation from Brome's *The Northern Lasse* is quoted by Sensabaugh ('Love ethics', p. 292), to show the obviously carnal connotations of the word 'mistress', as we should expect in a conversation between characters with the names of Howdee and Squelch. But Sensabaugh implies that the word in other contexts has the same pejorative sense: for example, he uses it ambiguously when he says the King in *The Fair Favourite* wonders how his wife will react 'when she learns of his mistress Eumena' (*Tragic Muse*, p. 125), when it is quite clear from the context that Eumena has not become the King's mistress in any physical sense. Again, dramatists usually distinguish between spiritual and physical love by the verbs 'love' and 'enjoy'. In Fletcher's *The Faithful Shepherdess*, Perigot, on meeting the false Amoret, who insists that they embrace and kiss, asks in dismay 'What meanes my love?' and she replies 'To do as lovers shud, / That are to bee injoyed not to bee woed' (p. 540, ll. 288–9). Thus Sensabaugh is using the word 'enjoy' equivocally when he says Platonic lovers believed 'beauty should be enjoyed by all' ('Love ethics', p. 296). The plays make it clear that while beauty and virtue may be *loved* by all, individual beauties are to be *enjoyed* only in marriage.

The Fair Favourite is also taken as a principal example of the claim that 'true love' in these plays made 'the institution of marriage a sort of convenience less sacred than individual desire' ('Love ethics', pp. 294–5). While it is true that in these plays love is said to originate in heaven, to be ordained by Fate, and hence superior to man-made laws, it is not true to say that it is incompatible with marriage (and it usually leads to it). The point of *The Fair Favourite* is not to devalue marriage, but to praise both 'mistress' and wife for making virtue and love, not public or political expediency, the proper basis for it. Sensabaugh (p. 293) does quote a passage that seems, out of context, to raise individual desire above the institution of marriage. Pamphilus, in Randolph's *The Jealous Lovers*, declares in front of a statue of Hymen:

> If out of spite thou cross me, know, weak godhead,
> I'll teach mankind a custom that shall bring
> Thy altars to neglect. Lovers shall couple
> (As other creatures) freely, and ne'er stand
> Upon the tedious ceremony, marriage.
> (The Jealous Lovers, p. 165)

In fact the action of the play reveals that the god is not acting 'out of spite': the statue has turned aside when presented with the original pairs of lovers, whose seemingly irrational jealousies have kept the plot turning. Tyndarus proves to be Evadne's brother, and Pamphilus, Techmessa's, so that both unions would have been incestuous, and the cause of the jealousies is explained:

> Nature, abhorring from so foul a sin,
> Infus'd those doubts into us.
> (p. 168)

The couples are rearranged, Hymen is honoured, and heaven obeyed.

In all the other cases of resistance to marriage cited by Sensabaugh, it is enforced marriage that these plays condemn.[9] Forced marriage had been a theme in the drama from the beginning of the seventeenth century, and, as Glenn Blaney pointed out when relating it to the plays of Ford, its treatment in Caroline plays seems to reflect 'a shift of popular sentiment from marriage of convenience to marriage for love'.[10] To judge from social history, one might think that the institution of marriage was in need of the injection of criticism and idealism (particularly in the interests of women) given by these playwrights.[11] In seventeenth-century practice, parental tyranny and marriages of interest were still too often the rule, and not uncommonly resulted in situations such as that in Shakerly Marmion's *A Fine Companion* (1633); here Littlegood wants to make rich matches for his daughters, Valeria to the lascivious Spruce, and Aemilia to Dotario who is 'pickt to the very bones with age and diseases' (Marmion, *Dramatic Works*, p. 129). Aurelio, Valeria's true lover, has been disinherited by his father for loving her, and he makes a time-honoured protest against the power of age and money to stifle youth and love:

> why should I be stay'd from going to her?
> Why should a covetous eye watch o'er that wealth
> That is my right? I will go claim my due,
> And justify the seizure. Why should parents,
> That can give to their children neither minds
> Nor yet affections, strive to govern both?
> 'Tis not justice: yet where should I complain?

> Love has no bar to plead at, nor no laws
> To rule us by, nor Court to judge our cause.   (p. 152)

Sensabaugh says this passage 'sounds the keynote of lawless Platonic love' ('Love ethics', p. 301). Rather it sounds a note much older, and more familiar to comedy: old men and misers are gulled, girls are both virtuous and spirited in getting the husbands they choose, and young men get the girls and the fortunes.

Even the satire *Lady Alimony*,[12] which Sensabaugh takes as exposing the 'real' motives behind Platonic love, exposes rather the real evils of enforced marriage and its consequences. It is possible that the satirised court ladies in this play complain of realities when they plead their causes: one was married to a boy, others to a fool, a coward, a deformity, an impotent, a libertine, and a profligate. Madame Medlar recalls how she had begged her parents

> With sighs and tears, that this unequal match
> Might be diverted, but it might not be.
> The fulness of his fortune winged them
> To consummate the match.   (Dodsley, p. 309)

Tillyvally, one of the Platonic 'servants', asks what wonder if these women

> soon engage
> Their honour to th'embraces of a servant
> Of brave deportment, sprightly eyes, neat limbs:
> A virile presence and a countenance
> 'Twixt Ajax and Adonis; neither fierce
> Nor too effeminate, but mix'd 'twixt both.   (p. 302)

The women demand divorce from their 'disrelish'd beds' (p. 314), but with proper maintenance, and the husbands make it clear that it is the loss of the money, not the women, they resent (p. 317). In this play, husbands, wives, and Platonic admirers are all satirized, and contrasted with the stern Duke who commands the wives to return to their husbands, or else accept a monastic life, and the idle 'Platonic' youth to become soldiers, or else be sentenced to hard labour. The sound values of the citizenry with regard to love and marriage are held up against the supposed abuse of love and marriage in high circles. But court drama too condemns enforced marriage and the adultery that might well be its consequence. Both Nerina in *The Shepheard's Holyday*, and Hermione in *The Lost Lady*, protest that the grave would be a fitter bed than marriage to a man they do not love. Nerina's plea, that such a marriage can bind only her body, not her will, that it would lead only to 'impure delights' (p. 389) and violate her former vows to Charinus, is surely evidence of a moral, rather than an immoral view of marriage. Such pleas are given tragic point by Ford in *The Broken Heart*, where Penthea pays with her life for the paradox that her forced marriage is 'known adultery', and she 'a spotted whore'. On the score of enforced marriage and its attendant abuses, court drama and *Lady Alimony* were at one.

Contemporary playwrights did, of course, criticise the love fashions at court, but not in the way, or for the reasons, that Sensabaugh suggests. Habington's treatment of love in *The Queen of Aragon* is interesting, since the play, though popular with the court, seems not to have been entirely sympathetic to it (its political implications will be discussed later). Here Habington demonstrates three different attitudes to love: that of the Queen in the play, who holds an exalted view of love as a heaven-directed choice; that of Cleantha, the witty court lady, lively but virtuous; and that of the debased courtiers who attempt to use Platonic love to cover immoral conduct. The character of the Queen in the play is of a simplicity and dignity that, together with her beauty, arouse love and admiration in her followers. More interesting dramatically is the character of Cleantha, companion to the Queen. Cleantha is determined to act in the emancipated way of a *précieuse*, careless of appearances but virtuous underneath. Throughout the play she attracts, and mocks, the conventions of 'Platonic love' in its extremes, both the underhand and the over-refined. When Sanmartino offers himself as her 'servant', she makes fun of such a threadbare fashion (p. 329). When she taxes him with being married he argues that 'Platonic' love affairs are much better with a 'married lord' and they debate the point with satiric emphasis (pp. 330, 347). When he makes an assignation with her she promises him kisses, then presents him with his wife, and advises him to 'learn virtue' (p. 379). Cleantha is also wooed by Oniate, 'a sober lord' who represents the other extreme of Platonic love. He offers to serve her, he says, without danger to her chastity, in a way that 'custom approves' (p. 333). Cleantha declares she prefers more lusty lovers. He, however, cannot believe that her outspokenness is any more than a witty mask which she puts on to conceal her true virtue (p. 363), and he undertakes to explain her behaviour to the world as 'some petty venial error' that cunning court ladies choose, to set perfection off (p. 382). Cleantha denies it, but she is won eventually to marry him. Her conduct is rather like that shown in Jonson's summing up of Lady Frampul, taking risks with her reputation though she is 'very honest' underneath. Habington presents in Cleantha an attractive picture of the court lady who, rather like Lady Carlisle, adopts the 'Platonic' fashion of the *salons*, but who, despite leaving herself open to criticism, has wit and vivacity enough to steer her through court life, with both her cheerfulness and her virtue intact. The Countess of Carlisle was, in fact, the cousin of Habington's wife Lucy Herbert (the 'Castara' of the poems), and, since *The Queen of Aragon* seems to have had some Parliamentary backing, Habington's portrait of a court lady in the style of Lady Carlisle may have had some political point. Her 'active' virtue contrasts attractively in dramatic terms with the more passive virtue of Cleodora, the Queen, and by making Cleantha more vividly alive than the Queen, Habington may have been suggesting a more out-going and realistic approach to 'virtue' than that taken by Henrietta.

Habington was a friend and admirer of James Shirley, and their writings express much the same attitudes to Platonic love and court fashions. Shirley's plays, performed at court, were 'well liked' by the King and Queen, and his criticism of the court is valuable because of his intimacy with it (*The Ball* had to be officially censored because its satire of particular people was too pointed). Shirley's play *The Lady of Pleasure* (acted 1635), which looks at the court from the outside, is therefore likely to be a fair presentation of its failings. In it, Shirley echoes Habington's criticism (in his poems 'To Castara') of adopting French fashions, the only purpose of which seems to be to teach a youth to 'wagge his feather ala mode' (C4v), and to teach court ladies to speak French because it is the finest tongue 'to show their teeth in' (F2). He criticises, through the character of Aretina, those silly women who adopt court fashions merely to waste their husbands' revenue in balls, banquets, and plate, who 'study / wayes of pride and costly ceremony' (B2) while 'Praying's forgot ... Tis out of fashion' (C4). On the other hand he gives a not unattractive picture of Celestina, the sprightly young widow, who is also attracted to pleasure, but who keeps her common sense. She is resolved (against the Puritanical strictures of her steward) to 'pay for some delight' while looking for a new husband, and to enjoy her 'sweet freedome' before putting on new marriage fetters. She is lively and witty,

> full of song and dancing,
> Pleasant in language, apt to all delights
> That crown a publike meeting,   (D2v)

but restrained in her favours to those who pay her court. As she confides to Mariana,

> It takes not from the freedom of our mirth
> But seems to advance it, when we can possesse
> Our pleasures with security of our honours.   (D3)

She has need of all her wit and independence to protect herself, not only against the avaricious and the foolish, but against those who profess various forms of Platonic courtship. When Bornewell woos her (to revenge himself on the foolish Aretina) she points out to him that he is already married, and challenges him to 'be virtuous' (E2v). Aretina, on the other hand, is so besotted with the language of Platonism that she sees in Celestina a beauty that 'spreads / Over the soule, and calls up understanding'; she acknowledges Celestina as 'one most worthy / Man's love and wonder' (G4v), and almost recommends adultery to her husband, tempting him afresh. When Celestina does finally meet a nobleman of worth, Lord A., each sets a trap for the other by offering mock 'Platonic' devotion (H2v–H3v). He finds himself untempted by this exchange, still true to the memory of his dead wife, Bella Maria, and she finds he has passed her test. She attributes his noble thought, not to melancholy, but to the example of the King and Queen, those 'two royall luminaries / At court' by whose light 'you cannot lose your way to chastity' (H4).

Lord A., however, returns to offer yet another variation of love 'In the now court, Platonicke way', painting a pastoral idyll of bliss where lovers can 'Embrace and kisse, tell tales, and kisse agen' (I4v). She pretends to take up the theme, describing 'All the delights of *Tempe*', with the graces, fairies, the nymph Echo, a 'wanton river', 'a dying swan', and unexpectedly concludes 'And such love linsey woolsey, to no purpose' (K). She upbraids him and gives a moving defence of her honour, which is not 'worne upon a flagge' but which 'growes and withers with my soule' (Kv). Lord A. is shamed and vows

> ile be a servant to thy goodnesse,
> A Mistris in the wanton sence is common,
> Ile honour you with chaste thoughts, and call you so.   (K2)

The play ends on this note of virtue, with music and mirth in which their souls 'leape into a dance'. While criticising all aspects of the *précieux* and Platonic fashion at court, Shirley does seem to nod in the direction of a more moderate version of it, in which both honour and pleasure can be served by sensible behaviour and a ready wit, whether in town or court. Both town and court have their foolish adherents to fashion, but one can educate the other.

Commentators have tended to make all the abuses of love in plays such as Shirley's synonymous with the court, and the evils they embody synonymous with Henrietta's Platonic love fashion. This is, I think, a one-sided view and leads to some exaggeration in tracing the wider implications of the criticism in such plays. For instance, in Martin Butler's discussion of *The Lady of Pleasure* (*Theatre and Crisis*, pp. 166–72), the 'good' is all equated with the town and the 'bad' with the court. Relating this equation to political criticism, therefore, Butler identifies extravagance at court as 'court tyranny', while Celestina's free spending arises from her true 'generosity' (*Theatre and Crisis*, p. 168). Lord A.'s sins arise from his being 'a platonic in love after the manner fashionable at Henrietta Maria's Whitehall' (p. 169): his presuming on his high position to pursue Celestina is a result of 'the artificialities of courtly platonism' (p. 170), and hence an 'encroachment on her rights' as a subject (p. 171). While the play has these deeper layers of criticism, especially of the tendency of the court to corrupt witless women and presumptuous lords, the lines are not so clearly drawn as Butler's analysis would suggest. Both court and town have their vices, but a steady moral sense and a ready wit are quite sufficient, even in a woman acting alone, to defeat them. Shirley's defence of virtue and of women's honour, in the character of Celestina, does come from the town, but Henrietta's *honnête* version of social conduct encouraged just such a defence of women's honour, and condemnation of corrupt wooing, as Celestina gives here, and is a constant element in court drama. In fact, plays written under the influence of the Queen's fashion cannot be understood properly without taking into account the note of feminism and idealism that gives them their particular character.

Feminism and idealism

An important theme running through plays written for the court is a conservative feminism of the type recommended to women by *honnête* writers, and an ideal conception of love that goes beyond the person to a belief in its connection with divine Providence. In these plays women seek to extend the concept of love beyond its sexual connotations to the whole range of virtuous human actions and relationships. The heroines are neither remote Platonic goddesses nor witty mistresses of the *salon*, but are more like *honnêtes femmes*: they defend beauty and virtue, in themselves and in other women; they argue with husbands and lovers about moral matters, especially those concerned with love, setting them an example of good manners and moral behaviour. They are admired for their personal beauty and goodness, but also for the connection these qualities give them with Heaven. An understanding of *honnêteté* and its contemporary literature is essential to an understanding in these plays of a moderate kind of feminism which is employed, not on the side of 'lawless individualism' as has been maintained by some critics, but on the side of good manners, moderation, and good sense.

Honnêteté attempted to give women a proper sense of self-respect. It did not allow women the haughty manners of d'Urfé's heroines, nor did it allow them the emancipated views of *précieuses* who later in the century rejected marriage and all forms of domination by men. It did, however, expect them to preserve their own dignity and protect their own rights, and court plays reflect these views. It suggested firstly that women should be allowed a freedom of action similar to the freedom enjoyed by men, without having their actions misinterpreted, or being suspected of sexual intentions. It is, after all, a mark of anti-feminism to relate all a woman's actions to a preoccupation with sex, and the Queen in *The Royal Slave* claims for women the same freedom as men in showing an affection for what is noble and good. When rebuked for giving a chain to Cratander, she defends her action by pointing out that when

> a man of valour
> Graceth his Country with a good attempt,
> You give a Sword, an Horse, a Mannoure, nay
> Sometimes a whole Province for reward. We have
> A sense of Vertue too, as well as you:
> And shall we be deny'd the Liberty
> To shew we have that sense?   (ll. 1031–7)

Women express impatience with men's harping on sex, and of double standards for men and women in courtship. When Castarina in Thomas Goffe's *The Careless Shepherdess* tells the importunate Lariscus:

> You men, when you enjoy what you desire,
> Cool in affection, and being married
> We lose our price and value, while we keep
> Our freedome, you poure forth your service to us,   (p. 15)

she is not so much devaluing marriage as evaluating the unequal role of the sexes within it. She goes on to ask, not for Platonic love, but for a little more courtesy and kindness in the wooer:

> Me-thinkes that *Lovers* might content themselves
> Sometimes to meet, and talk, and smile, and kiss,
> Without desire of more *possession*.   (p. 16)

Indeed, one is often struck by the firm and sensible character of the women's speeches in contrast to the men's. They are the sternest critics of 'court eloquence', defending themselves against the exaggerations of false Platonic love, or indulging in its sparring to laugh their suitors into better sense.

Women's sense of virtue sought to extend the ideal of friendship and honour (so important in romance literature between men) to friendship and honour between women. The heroines of these plays are as ready to recognise beauty and support virtue in another woman as they are to honour them in a man, even when the other woman is a rival. In *The Deserving Favourite* Clarinda and Cleonarda admire each other's beauty, and even when Cleonarda falls in love with Lysander, Clarinda's suitor, she tells him that her love would cease instantly if he were to prove inconstant to Clarinda. In *The Lost Lady* Hermione and Acanthe gallantly compliment each other, and Hermione tells Lysicles, who is wooing her, to be true to the memory of his former love. In Carlell's *The Passionate Lovers*, Clorinda, introduced to the woman who has supplanted her in her lover's affections, is moved to declare

> By all the Gods, I never saw a Lady yet
> That I could think each way so excellent,   (p. 68)

and they discuss the disguised Agenor's perfidy in front of him. In *The Fair Favourite* Eumena and the Queen praise each other's beauty and virtue, and comfort each other against the unjust suspicions of men. When Eumena is chided by her brother because of the false position the King has placed her in, she appeals to the Queen:

> Madam, I'll turn me from that cruel man,
> And sigh away my soul, if what he says
> Hath any leave from your consent,

and the Queen counsels magnanimously 'forgive him, fair Eumena' (p. 239).

The heroines of these plays support each other in a high-minded view of love which goes beyond personal interest, and eventually leads to a happy conclusion. In *The Fair Favourite* the Queen, as we saw, recognises in her husband's love for Eumena the claims of a prior attachment, making no other claim herself

> but what my patience and affection can
> Deserve. He that did join our hands did give
> Me but a formal interest, since to Eumena
> You dispos'd your heart before
> We knew those sacred rites.   (p. 264)

She admires Eumena's beauty and virtue, pities her position, and declares that 'True love admits no jealousy' (p. 264). Her husband's fault has been forced on him by circumstance, and she cannot believe that his love is anything but noble: if it were other, it would not be worth her envy. These heroines do not countenance a 'low and sinful love' as being connected with themselves or anyone they admire, and a solution finally is made possible because of honour between the two women. When the King demands of his wife

> a liberty as is not fit
> For me to ask, nor thee to grant. Seal me
> A licence for each choice mine eyes shall make

she calmly replies 'Take, Sir, the freedom you desire' (p. 255). The King, of course, knows that the liberty can do him little good, for it 'never can usurp' upon the virtuous Eumena's heart. Because of the two women's support of one another and 'the care of Heaven' (p. 278), the King's love is at last won by the patient Queen, a happy solution for which Eumena too has prayed. The suggestion is that if all women were virtuous, men would become so too.

The action of *The Fair Favourite* thus confirms a moral principle of *honnête* writers, that good women save men from men's own worst impulses by somewhat passive, but correctly virtuous, behaviour. In *L'Honneste Femme* Du Bosc, for example, advises women against jealousy in love, saying that 'an ingenuous liberty is a better guard than any restraint' (quotations from Montague's translation, *The Accomplish'd Woman*, p. 133). Du Bosc argued that 'freedom extinguishes desire, and interdiction kindles it' (p. 133): the principle on which the Queen acts in *The Fair Favourite* and the argument which Atossa, too, puts to her husband in *The Royal Slave*. Even if appearances are against the person concerned (as they are against the King in *The Fair Favourite*), it may still be better, Du Bosc argues (p. 135), 'to believe a miracle then a sin, and to acknowledge the power of God, rather than the weaknesse of the creature', a policy followed by Davenant's Queen. If wives are deserted by their husbands, according to Du Bosc, they should go on loving them, as Octavia did Anthony, and by this means may win them back, as the King in *The Fair Favourite* is at last overwhelmed by the virtues of his wife. 'Charitable' love of the sort shown by both Davenant's Queen and Atossa is an attribute of virtuous women, says Du Bosc, and can lead only to good. He defends such love against curiosity and slander (*médisance*), saying that 'vertuous Women chase vice out of the world by their charity' (p. 43).

The behaviour of the high-minded heroines of court plays is modelled on that of heroines in Greek romances, as Harbage has shown (*Cavalier Drama*, pp. 39–40), but they are no less *honnêtes femmes* for that. Camus modelled his exemplary heroines on the heroines of romance, and Du Bosc went to the ancient poets and historians, because he says the 'Pagans' stole from the Prophets, and their stories 'contain much excellent morality mixed with superfluous matter'.[13] Throughout *The Accomplish'd Woman* examples from Greek, French, and Roman history are used to illustrate the generous actions taken by women for 'the preservation of their countrey, for love of their husbands, and for the religion of their ancestors' (p. 48). In French literature of the period the *femme forte* developed from sentiments expressed by writers like Du Bosc,[14] and Davenant seems to make a passing bow to her in the play *Love and Honour* (1634). Du Bosc had

written that it is a mistake 'to reject Women from Publick and Particular Government ... Their Wit is apt for more elevated actions: and if one will mark what
they have done, one may easily judge what they are capable of. If men sometimes
took their advice ... it may be they would have a happier success' (pp. 56–7).
In *Love and Honour* Davenant has Leonell admire in Evandra such

> A great example of a female fortitude
> As must undo all men, and blushing make
> Us steal from our unjust advancement o'er
> The world ...
>   let women sway
> Councils and war, whilst feeble men obey.   (*Works*, III, 151–2)

Cartwright's *The Lady Errant* seems to be another essay in the convention, but
this type of feminism did not become popular in England (there are signs of
it just before the Civil War). The heroines of the 1630s preferred a more personal
context for their actions.

Nevertheless these plays go beyond the defence of women's personal dignity
to the wider implications of women's virtue and love. The type of 'Platonic love'
they praise is an ideal of Christian charity, a magnanimous love that is linked
with Heaven, and which links this drama with a similar type on the Continent.
The investiture of Heaven's interests in a beautiful and virtuous woman and
a trust in Providence that amounts to quietism, are distinguishing marks of Italian
commedia grave, as Louise Clubb has pointed out in her paper 'Woman as
wonder'.[15] In sixteenth-century Italy, plays such as *L'amor costante*, *La donna
costante*, and *La Pellegrina*, exalted women to the position of saint, at first only
in metaphor, but later in acknowledgment of love's power, and woman's own
'conscious virtue or unconscious harmony' with Heaven ('Woman as Wonder',
p. 130). The heroine's constancy in love is enhanced by sets of secondary characters
(a pattern similar to that of the plays discussed above), whose less idealistic views
of love are shown to be false by the outcome of the action. The Neoplatonic
identification of love with the first cause of all good enables the protagonists
to celebrate the triumph of love in Christian terms, praising God for the happy
outcome (p. 119). The saintly beauty and virtue of the heroine is used to arouse
moral and religious wonder, and the action typically ends in forgiveness and
reconciliation, presenting a 'theatrical image integrating the secular and religious'
(p. 123).

Such a pattern is very close to the pattern of court drama under discussion
here. Women in these plays become both the custodians of virtuous human love
and the vehicles of Divine Providence, which works through beauty to create
universal harmony. Play after play points out the connection of the heroine's
beauty with the Deity which has 'let downe / Himselfe into those Rayes', and
which would be injured if others should 'Draw nigh without an awfull Adoration'
(*The Royal Slave*, ll. 924–6). In *The Passionate Lovers* Agenor sees divinity in
the 'harmonious composing' of Austella's person, and the 'care of heaven' that

governs her actions (p. 48). These beautiful heroines invariably bring the action
to a happy conclusion, which has been fore-ordained by Fate, and in which virtuous
love has gone hand-in-hand with religion. Sometimes the heroine's role is passive,
as in *The Shepheard's Holyday*, where Sylvia, 'conducted by the power of simple
love' alone, fulfils the oracle by marrying a Prince, to whom she had remained
constant throughout the play when he seemed only a simple shepherd. Those
who had opposed the lovers acknowledge being mistaken, and all repair to the
temple that they may

> With holy sacrifice appease the gods,
> Whose great decrees, though we did strive to hinder,
> Yet are they now fulfill'd. It is in vain
> T'oppose the Fates, whose laws do all constrain.   (p. 444)

Poetic justice works in this type of drama as a divine power to enforce 'moral'
standards, as it does in Mairet's *Silvanire*, the prototype for Rutter's play (see
Perry Gethner, 'Jean de Mairet and poetic justice: a definition of tragicomedy',
Ren. Drama, n.s., 11 (1980), 171–87).

Sometimes the heroine's role is more positive, and the action is given an explicitly
religious dimension by the language used throughout the play. In *The Fair Favourite* the Queen has a religious belief in love that guides all her actions. She knows
that

> peculiar and distinct
> Affections are but small derived parts
> Of what we call the universal love;
> And universal love, undoubtedly,
> Must be the best, since 'tis ascrib'd to heaven.   (p. 255)

The love-plot unfolds as a religious progress: the Queen bears her sorrow with
Christian stoicism; she seeks a nunnery where she may 'expiate' with prayers
her husband's 'unwilling sin'; her patience is such that it seems to come 'From
Heaven, not men'. She is called 'this great type of virtuous love'. Her rival Eumena
also has her 'prayers for the Queen ... observ'd above' (p. 278), and is told
'Thy causeless sufferings have rais'd / Thee to the dignity of Saints' (p. 276).
Religion and love together win back the King to a proper reconciliation with
both women, and he calls on the court to 'celebrate this miracle of love' (p.
278). The Queen intones as a kind of chorus:

> Who is it that will doubt
> The care of Heaven? Or think th'immortal
> Pow'rs are slow, because they take the
> Priviledge to chuse their own time when they
> Will send their blessings down.   (p. 278)

Another play, Berkley's *The Lost Lady*, echoes the language of martyrdom, a
popular theme in Continental drama. In this play the minor characters make
fun of love compliment, but the main characters connect the religious themes
of sacrifice, suffering, and martyrdom with virtuous love and its eventual triumph.

Hermione is a 'martyr' for her love, and regards opposition to her marriage as a field of suffering 'to exercise / My faith and love' upon (p. 582). Milesia, believed dead, is a 'saint'; she returns disguised, is nearly poisoned, but is resurrected because her visible 'divinity' shows through her dark disguise; the language is all of religious suffering, disguise for the faith, and a martyr's crown (see especially pp. 597–8). Such language is suggestive of the mingling of fashionable and religious subjects in Counter-Reformation drama and the popular plays on 'she-saints' discussed by Louise Clubb in an earlier paper, 'The Virgin Martyr and the tragedia sacra'.

As in commedia grave, the heroine's constancy and the triumph of virtuous love evoke a religious sense of wonder. The Royal Slave ends in such a scene: as the priest prepares to sacrifice Cratander at the altar, Heaven intervenes. The sun veils his face, and the sky sheds 'tears' to put out the sacrificial fire. The Queen, who has taken Cratander's part from the beginning, congratulates the priest on his good sense in acknowledging a power greater than his own:

> Thou hast now,
> The voyce and visage of the Gods, good Priest.
> The heav'ns were never more serene. The Gods
> Have justify'd my care, Cratander.

The King declares:

> 'tis not my hand
> That spares thee, blest Cratander, 'tis some God.   (p. 250)

The play ends in mercy, reconciliation, and peace. In Italy such plays served the interests of the Counter-Reformation by presenting, Louise Clubb says, 'tableaux of reconciliation made to radiate suggestions of Christian forgiveness and resurrection' ('Woman as wonder', p. 123). It is not coincidental that plays like The Royal Slave and The Queen of Aragon, both of which end in expressions of reconciliation, had stage sets by Inigo Jones, whose spectacular scenes were designed to evoke just the sense of wonder that is suggested by the text. Theatrical images of reconciliation and forgiveness were very apposite at court in the 1630s, and the Queen's ideal of love made a fitting vehicle for them.

I believe that these broader implications in the ideas of feminism and love made possible the use of Platonic conventions for comment on more general issues in plays of the 1630s. Martin Butler's analysis of drama of this period has suggested that, contrary to established opinion, playwrights were interested in debate on contemporary issues, and that this debate often centred around the Queen and was conducted in terms of the Platonic and romantic interest in the plays (Theatre and Crisis, chapters 3 and 4). I think he is right in seeing the plays as a forum for the discussion of a variety of issues, many of which have political implications, but he has perhaps made the Queen too narrowly a focus for the expression of 'Opposition' views, which were often critical of the King. It seems to me that the argument for political significance is strengthened if the debate is understood first in terms of feminist and moral, rather than specifically political, interests. The transition from one to the other was of course made possible by the fact that romances are often set in courts, and take kings and queens as representatives of their sexes. In plays, therefore, which debate feminist issues and defend women's rights, kings (as they are representative of men) often come off badly, while queens uphold unexceptionable moral principles. But the principles put forward by Henrietta's moderate form of feminism, in which lively and virtuous women worked towards better manners, chaste courtship, and general social harmony, were all ones with which Charles whole-heartedly agreed. It is this, surely, that gave dramatists of the period so much freedom to discuss the dilemmas of kings, to which Butler draws attention in his chapter on 'Lovers and tyrants', and to subject them to a good deal of criticism. If, however, we jump too rapidly to political motives without understanding the feminist position, we miss the step that made such discussion and outspoken criticism possible. If we take the queens in these plays as being too narrowly equivalent to 'the Queen', we run the risk of Charles's having to see himself consistently represented as weak, tyrannous, and lecherous, a position which a sensitive, play-reading king is not likely to have tolerated. In a play such as *The Royal Slave*, for instance, where a weak king is contrasted with a kingly slave, Butler seems to go too far in implying that the Queen's preference for the slave Cratander is a political rebuke to Charles (another critic can argue on the same evidence that it was a compliment to him).[16] Rather it is an exalted defence of the rights of love, and particularly of women's love, to extend beyond sexual preference to a general ideal of the Good, and to uphold it for men, and kings, to follow.

Discussions of love encouraged by the Queen's fashions in court plays did, however, provide a useful background for airing views of an essentially political nature. They gave a framework in which to glance at all kinds of moral questions, including what makes a good man, lover, or king, as well as what makes for a mutually happy relationship with those dependent on him, whether it be in marriage or in the kingdom. The plays question conventional attitudes, debating the relative values of authority and love, power and the law; they raise issues which not only those opposed to the King, but those concerned with compromise, and even the King himself, might have been interested in pursuing into the political field. This seems to have been the case at least in *The Queen of Aragon*, in which Butler convincingly demonstrates a political dimension (*Theatre and Crisis*, pp. 62–74). The play was sponsored by the Earl of Pembroke, Habington's relative and a critic of Royalist policy. It was performed in April 1640, just before Parliament reconvened and at a time when an airing of Opposition views in diplomatic terms was opportune. Habington worked within a convention already familiar to the court, making political comment broadly acceptable through the emphasis on love dilemmas, which in this play are explicitly tied up with dilemmas of State. But within this convention he makes the Queen a rather retiring figure and it is the bustling masculine world of warring factions that dominates the action. His final *coup* is to switch the emphasis on choice from the Queen to the men, so that, near the end of the play, she is given back to her own first love Florentio through the magnanimity of her other two suitors, Ascanio and Decastro. As Butler points out, the choice is finally directed, not by the will of Heaven, but by the generosity of the people, whose champion Decastro is. By drawing on the pattern of feminism and implied 'divine' guidance for part of the play, Habington is able to make his subject acceptable to the court, while, by switching the source of divinity to 'the people', he is able to adapt the political emphasis to the contemporary situation. However, the play may have been less of a direct confrontation than Butler implies, and more part of a debate in which political views could be indirectly canvassed. It was performed twice at court, which suggests that Charles was interested in the message it contained, and indeed Butler (p. 75) quotes him as echoing the words of reconciliation with which Habington ended the play. Habington's 'democratic' sentiments in this play are often quoted to show where his sympathies lay, but it should be noted that his speeches on the equality of men (*The Queen of Aragon*, pp. 170–3) are still put in the mouth of Ascanio, a disguised King. Charles, in the masque *Salmacida Spolia* presented only a few months before the play, had been at pains to represent his own side of the debate through the character of Philogenes, 'Lover' of his people: perhaps Habington's play is part of 'the people's' reply to his claim. Within the conventions of love debate, therefore, the court stage may well have given the opportunity for expressing a diversity of political opinion; it perhaps also provided a means by which ideas might be 'rehearsed' or tried out to see how they would look in practice, before the two sides, King and Parliament, were inalterably opposed.

To sum up, Henrietta's fashions seem to have encouraged debate in the drama that went beyond a simple interest in love. They emphasised the moral questions of personal relationships and the rights of women, which, at one remove, could be extended to the political field. The treatment of love in the plays also went beyond narrowly sexual interests, and I think it is important to recognise that, although contemporaries often criticised both court and drama in terms of 'immorality', their motives for doing so were often based on concerns much wider than sexual morals. Few courts of the time were expected to be beyond reproach on that score, and in fact the courts of James I and Henri IV, although far more immoral in the narrow sense, did not attract the same amount of sexual criticism as Charles's. It seems that for contemporaries the subject of 'love' included the broader political context, and that, just as the court used the language of love to debate its own interests, so critics used the term 'immorality' to symbolise the faults of what seemed a self-absorbed and 'effeminate' court, neglectful of its public duties. For a true obverse of the image of Charles's court as a paradise of love we have to go back to the official imagery of Elizabeth's reign, with its emphasis on a 'Virgin' Queen, 'married' to her people. The reflection of the

Elizabethan images in court entertainments had religious as well as political significance, and it seems to me that the Caroline images, too, take on special significance
in view of the links between love and religion in the type of Catholicism followed
by the Queen.

3   The Queen's religion

Proselytism and *préciosité*

Henrietta's preoccupation with court entertainments might have remained for her contemporaries a harmless whim if it had not been for innate connections between her love fashions and her religion. To my knowledge, the only previous investigation of such a connection has been, once again, by George Sensabaugh. His paper 'Platonic love and the Puritan rebellion' (1940) associated the cult of Platonic love in court drama with devotion to the Virgin Mary, and showed the way in which Puritan attacks connected them. Sensabaugh did not, however, recognise Henrietta's *honnête* fashion of the 1630s as a phase of *préciosité* that was connected in France with Devout Humanism, and which therefore already had an inherent connection with Catholicism. He concluded that the basis for the connection made by Puritans between the Queen's love fashions and her Catholicism was the immorality of both: 'in Puritan eyes the cult's ethics were Rome's ethics; and since Catholics sponsored the cult, advocating its loose morals, Puritans could easily confuse the two and so attack the cult on religious grounds' ('Platonic love', p. 481). If, as I have argued, there were actual links between the Queen's cult of Platonic love and her Catholicism, Puritans had no need to 'confuse' the two, but had sound reasons for attacking the cult on religious grounds. These attacks were often expressed as criticism of sexual morals, but I think they may have been inspired not so much by 'immorality' as by 'irreligion', for which Puritans possibly saw Henrietta's fashions as a cover.

It is unlikely that in her first years at the English court Henrietta made any direct connection between her entertainments and her religion. She obviously delighted in dancing, play-acting, and singing for their own sake, but not to the exclusion of devotion: it was the example of the Queen and her ladies that, according to John Evelyn, prompted a request to John Cosin to compile an Anglican *Collection of Private Devotions* (1627), so that Anglican court ladies '(who spend much time in trifling) might at least appear as devout, and be so too, as the new-come-over *French* Ladys, who tooke occasion to reproch our want of zeale, & Religion'.[1] Catholic interests in France and Rome, however, were anxious to encourage Henrietta not simply to give equal time to devotional and social activities, but to place her social activities under the rule of religion in the way recommended by Devout Humanists. At a French Catholic court such an injunction was unexceptionable, but at an Anglican court it placed her social

75

fashions in a new light, especially in view of the proselytism that was expected of her.

There can be little doubt that Henrietta, from a Catholic point of view, had a duty to proselytise, and that considerable pressure was placed upon her to do so. In Catholic eyes she had left France, when she married, to rule over a country of heretics. Her marriage with Charles was looked upon as not so much a private matter, as a religious vocation, in which nothing less was expected of her than that she should bring Charles, and with him the rest of the country, back to the 'true' religion. Pope Urban VIII, who was her godfather, wrote to her with her marriage dispensation that she was to be the guardian angel of English Catholics, 'the Esther of her oppressed people, the Clotilda who subdued to Christ her victorious husband, the Aldebirga whose nuptials brought religion into Britain'; in expectation of this the eyes of the whole spiritual world were turned on her.[2] She received a parting admonition in a semi-public letter from her mother, Marie de Medici, in similar terms.[3] Marie's letter was written with the help of Cardinal Bérulle, Marie's confidant and confessor, and it admonishes Henrietta on her duty, first to God and her religion, then to her husband, whom she must love 'pour le ciel et non-seulement pour la terre'. The hope that, by this 'sainte affection', Charles will be drawn back into the religion for which his grandmother (Mary, Queen of Scots) died, is Mary's wish, and should be Henrietta's most ardent desire. In fact it is

un des desseins de Dieu sur vous qui veut vous faire en nos jours une autre Berthe, fille de France comme vous et reine d'Angleterre comme vous, laquelle obtint par sa sainte vie et par ses prières le don de la foi en cette île dans laquelle vous allez entrer.
(Leveneur, Comte de Tillières, *Mémoires*, p. 75)

Henrietta was duly impressed, and on setting out for her marriage she reassured the Pope that she would do all in her power to carry out these instructions, 'n'ayant rien au monde qui me soit si cher que la sureté de ma conscience et le bien de ma religion'.[4]

The Catholic Church accordingly sought ways in which Henrietta might further the interests of her religion without alienating the sympathy of Charles, or the court in which she had gone to live. Perhaps with this in mind a book written by Nicolas Caussin, *La Cour sainte* (Paris, 1624) was translated into English under the title *The Holy Court* in 1626.[5] The translator, Thomas Hawkins, was elder brother of the Jesuit priest Henry Hawkins and came of a staunchly Catholic Kentish family. He was skilled in music and poetry, translated Horace, corresponded with James Howell, and was chosen by Edmund Bolton for his projected 'Royal Academy' (*DNB*). Hawkins dedicated the translation to Henrietta Maria, 'a pious Queen' who, he writes:

exemplarly maketh good, what diffusedly is heer handled. Let then lesser lights borow beams of radiance, from your greater Orbs; and persist you (Glorious Example of vertue) to illumine and heat our more Northern Clime, with celestiall ardours. Adde to earthly crownes heauenly diademes of piety.
(*The Holy Court*, I, Dedication)

Caussin (who was a Jesuit priest at the French court until 1637) had written the first volume of *La Cour sainte* in 1624 for Henrietta's brother, Louis XIII, whom Caussin served for a time as confessor. The theme of the book is that the arts and pleasures of court life acquire virtue when practised under the rule of religion.

Caussin was a Devout Humanist who was rather less optimistic about human nature than writers like Sales and Camus: in the first volume of *The Holy Court*, the sub-heading of Book 1, 'That the Court and Deuotion are not incompatible', gives the rather wistful tone of his work. In Book 1 he follows Castiglione in pointing out that the great advantages enjoyed by the nobility (riches, beauty, education, health, courage) should be used with humility and prudence, to help those less fortunate and give an example of virtue to the rest of society. He knows too well, however, the obstacles (ambition, avarice, envy, carnal love, all discussed in Book 2) to such a view. It is only a firm grounding in religion, and the daily practice of devotion according to the forms of the Catholic church, that can reconcile the real and ideal worlds, and Book 3 outlines the virtues that devotion brings: chastity, temperance, modesty, magnanimity. This general discussion is followed by two long 'histories' exemplifying first an impious, and then a pious, court. Caussin followed this volume with three others all translated into English in the 1630s. Volume 2 is devoted to full-length portraits of the Prelate, the Soldier, the Statesman, and the Lady; volume 3 develops maxims of Christianity against the Prophane court. Volume 4 begins with a Treatise entitled 'Of Love', a discussion of love in all its forms from the sensual to the 'Divine'. Like Sales and like Montague (who may have gleaned many of his ideas for *Miscellanea Spiritualia* from Caussin's work), Caussin grounds his religious beliefs on the Neoplatonic view that beauty, goodness, and love join to make 'a perpetuall circle of God to the world, and of the world to God' (IV, 7). Amongst the discussions of love that follow he devotes a section to 'Amity betweene persons of different sexe' (section 4). For himself, he says, he can only speak from experience of 'the sagest and most vertuous women', but he gives it as his opinion that women, as 'they commonly are more deuout, and religious than men, so they observe vertuous amityes with respect, and entertaine them out of conscience, and especially such as are grounded on piety' (p. 18). After discussing the nuances of such 'Amityes', which he warns are only for great natures (section 5), he goes on to a discussion of sensual love, its sources, effects, and remedies. 'Celestial Amityes' are dealt with in the second to last section, where Caussin quotes Plato to the effect that love in the world is a memory of the 'first, fayre, soveraigne, and most pure of all bewtyes, which is the Diuinity' (p. 57), and the Treatise ends with a discussion of the nature of 'Divine Love'.

The elaborate title-page of *The Holy Court*, reproduced from the French editions in the English translations (figure 5), shows blind Cupids being tumbled from their pedestals, allegorical figures of the arts and sciences bearing their appropriate

5 Title-page illustration from Nicolas Caussin, *The Holy Court* (1634)

emblems, and sedate courtiers observing a King whose humble posture puts him in direct communication with Heaven (not unlike the posture in which Charles was to be represented on the title-page of *Eikon Basilike*). In the words of the accompanying verse:

> While Great-ones vertue ioyne to noble birth
> Th'are Petie-Gods, which to the heavens aspire;
> Gods, whom the world adores, Angels admire.

Ideas such as these were of course already familiar at the English court, and were quite compatible with the philosophy developed by James (in a work like *Basilikon Doron*) and carried on by Charles. In *The Holy Court*, however, it seems that they were being promoted in the interests of Catholicism. Hawkins, who translated Caussin's volumes as soon as each appeared, directed them specifically to the court by dedicating the first volume to the Queen, and subsequent volumes to close members of her circle. The translation of the second volume (published in 1631) was dedicated to Edward Sackville, Earl of Dorset, who (though a non-Catholic), as Lord Chamberlain of the Queen's Household, was in charge of arranging her court entertainments. Dorset was patron of dramatists who wrote for the court, and Caussin, himself a writer of *Tragediae sacrae* (published in 1620), perhaps hoped his book would have some influence on English dramatists.[6] Hawkins thanks Dorset for having brought the book 'into the fruition of English ayre', and gratefully acknowledges the many favours he has received from the Earl. The 1634 edition of these translations contains a third volume dedicated to Lady Frances Weston, Countess of Portland, who was companion to the Queen in many of her masques and a notable Catholic. Her 'knowne propension to the reading of pious books', Hawkins says, has encouraged him to bring this new volume into English light. The translation of the fourth volume (1638) was dedicated to the Duchess of Buckingham (Katherine Manners, daughter of the Catholic Earl of Rutland), who had reverted to Catholicism soon after Buckingham's death and who by 1638 was married to the Irish Catholic, Viscount Dunluce (*DNB*, see under Macdonnell, Randal). The relevance of these dedications to the question of religion at court is made clear by Caussin in the first volume. Amongst the obstacles to a holy court life he lists 'Errour in faith and in Religion', and he entitles this section 'Friendly and holesome counsel to the Nobility of the Pretended Religion' (p. 59). He counsels adoption of a peaceful and conciliatory attitude in dealing with such matters, and the advice he gives against wrangling and rebellion would have fallen on many sympathetic ears, Anglican as well as Catholic, at the English court.

Of special interest for the consideration of Henrietta's *préciosité* in its connection with religion is volume two, which contains a new section entitled 'The Lady'. Caussin says at the end of this section (II, 324) that he had been urged to write it by his friend Camus, Bishop of Belley, whose works Caussin praises in fulsome terms. It may be that Camus, whose own works were being translated into English at about the same time with dedications to the Queen and to notable Catholic ladies (the Duchess of Buckingham and the Countess of Arundel),[7] saw a topical application in England of the flourishing French literature that was combining the interests of *préciosité* and piety. Caussin begins the section with an address to ladies, in which he calls them 'the Deuout Sexe', whose 'innocent charmes' are rendered safe to those like himself who look on them 'as the ideas of *Plato*, which haue nothing in them common with matter' (p. 255). He refers to the use made by the evil spirit in Paradise to overthrow Adam by 'the alluring pleasures of an *Eve*' (p. 256); but, he says, if women's innocent charms are so powerful in wicked actions, they have an equal power for good, when directed by a virtuous soul. St Peter judged the good conversation of women 'a singular meane to gaine those to God, who would not submit themselues to the Gospel' (p. 256), and he cites many examples of women who brought Christianity into 'pagan' countries, amongst them Helena to Rome, Clotilda to France, Indegondis to Spain. On the other hand he warns (like Du Bosc) against an austere and forbidding piety in ladies that may drive men (especially courtiers) away from virtue; as an example he cites Catherine, wife of Henry VIII, who was 'infinitely pious, yea without limit', but whose way of life led to Henry's dissipation, and the divisions of Christendom that made 'one tombe of two parts of the world' (p. 92).

In this section it is difficult to escape a parallel with the English court. Caussin begins by observing

that God hath made such vse of the piety of Ladyes for the aduancement of Christianity, that in al the most flourishing Kingdoms of Christendome there are obserued stil some Queenes or Princesses, who haue the very first of al aduanced the standart of the Crosse vpon the ruines of Infidelity.   (p. 256)

Among ancient examples (and one that had been cited to Henrietta by the Pope) is that of Clotilda converting Clodoueus: 'God was willing to winne him to himselfe by the wayes of chast loue, and by the meanes of a wife, who should sanctify his person and house' (p. 278), 'and so many poore Catholikes, as were then in *France*, looked on her as the dawning of the day . . .' (p. 284) (see figure 6). When Clotilda married, she was surrounded by feasts and pomp, but kept her eyes firmly fixed on the benefits of God while taking part in the festivities. She spent time in her Oratory, yet was careful to manage

al her actions with singular discretion, that she might not seem too austere in the eyes of her Court, for weake soules might be diuerted from Christianity . . . But al that which most passed in a common life was done by her and her maydes, with much purity, feruour, maiesty, and constancy. (p. 285)

Caussin relates how Clotilda honoured and loved her husband, took pleasure in his pleasures, and, through her good council and sweetness, 'found the King dayly disposed better and better' towards her religion. She introduces all the virtues at court, but still the King hesitates, 'for Religion and State are two pieces

Sponsus meus inter lilia.

IHS

Amans rosæ

S. CLOTILDE, I. Reine Chrestienne de France.

6 Queen Clotilde, from Nicolas Caussin, *The Holy Court* (1634)

which mutually touch one another very near', but eventually he is converted, bringing many thousands of his countrymen to embrace the Queen's religion.

The story, seen through Catholic eyes, is significant for the position of Henrietta at the English court. Her first attempts after her arrival at showing her religious zeal had been so direct as to be a total failure.[8] Cardinal Bérulle and his Oratorian priests went out of their way to provoke notice, and scandalised Protestants by their ostentatious services in the Queen's chapel at St James. Henrietta drew attention to herself by going in public to visit places of Catholic martyrdom, and refused for religious reasons to take part in Charles's, and her own, Coronation service. These naive attempts at asserting her religion simply had the effect of antagonising Charles and promoting hostility to Catholics. In 1627 most of the French retinue and priests were dismissed from the court, and, partly as a consequence, better relations developed between the King and Queen. Out of mutual understanding grew more toleration for the English Catholics, and the Queen used her influence to such good purpose that in 1629 a French priest was able to write that in England,

the heat of persecution hath ceased, through the dignity of a magnanimous King, and most invincible Prince by the Bourbonian Star, which hangs over these Countries in a most dear Wife; by which Stars, peradventure the Tempest of Persecution will in time be appeased.
(quoted in John Rushworth, *Historical Collections* (1721), II, 15)

The religious influence that Henrietta had failed to gain by assertion and argument she had gained by understanding and love, thus confirming by her own experience the moral of the story spelled out by Caussin in the example of Clotilda.

Other stories, in which a similar pattern emerges of piety and pleasure combining in the interests of religion, were brought to the attention of the Queen in the thirties. The story of Esther, whose intercession with the King of Persia saves her co-religionists, the Jews, from a planned massacre, was particularly popular with poets and dramatists of the Renaissance, and encouraged by Catholic interests (Luther said that he so hated the book that he wished it did not exist). The example of Esther had been cited to Henrietta in their letters on her marriage by both Marie de Medici and the Pope, and Francis Lenton, one of the 'Queen's poets', treated the story in detail in a manuscript poem of 1637, 'Queen Esters Haliluahs' (other MS copies were made in 1638, 1641, and 1649).[9] Lenton stresses Esther's beauty and virtue, her dutiful obedience to the King, combined with her sacred allegiance to her people, the 'Jews'. When she sues to the King for mercy for her people, she decks herself with jewels and beautiful clothes in which 'this holy starre' outshone Diana. She banquets him 'in the feasting roome' (sig. 49r) and wins him to her love. But the King cannot immediately alter 'our grave Persian Law': the best he can do is grant contrary laws, 'And so you have Decree, against Decree' (sig. 65v). Mordecai, with Esther's help, warns the Jews of Hamman's plot against them and they rise and kill their foes. Their victory is ascribed to God and to

> gratious Esther (gratious indeed)
> In God's deare sight, her did he send with speed
> To save his people from that wicked Cain. (sig. 72v)

The poem ends with peace and happiness – and the King levying a tribute.

The moral of these stories is clear: women like Clotilda, Esther, and other exemplary heroines cited by Caussin, used their beauty and chaste love to win men to God. Religion uses the powers of women for its own ends, and those in high places should work for God's will. To Puritans, who were assiduous readers of Catholic literature in the 1630s, the reasoning was equally clear. William Prynne in *The Popish Royall Favourite* (London, 1643) counters Rome's propaganda with biblical parallels of his own:

wee have great cause to fear (if *Adams*, *Solomons*, or *Ahabs* seducements by their wives be duly pondered) that his Majesty ... may ere long be seduced to their Religion, as well as to their Party;

(sig. H2)

and what wonder, he says, when the Catholics 'have *Queen Mary* her selfe in the Kings own bed and bosome' (sig. G4v). In another work by Prynne of the same date, *Romes Master-peece*, he says that the King has so many of the Popish faction about his 'Closet, Bedchamber, if not Bed', that it would be remarkable if the rest of the court, 'with so many enticements to withdraw them, both in their Beds, Bedchambers, Closets, Counsels, Courts, where ever they go or come, should possibly continue long untainted, unseduced' (sig. E2v). Henrietta's role as wife, and the way in which she was thought to subjugate love to religion, may be summed up for the Puritans by Lucy Hutchinson, who wrote after the Civil War:

This lady being by her priests affected with the meritoriousness of advancing her own religion, whose principle it is to subvert all other, applied that way her great wit and parts, and the power her haughty spirit kept over her husband, who was enslaved in his affection only to her, though she had no more passion for him than what served to promote her designs.

(*Memoirs of Colonel Hutchinson*, p. 71)

Puritan fears and Catholic expectations probably both ran ahead of what Henrietta was actually able to accomplish, since it appears that she did not have much power to change Charles's mind once it was made up.[10] Puritans, however, could never be sure how far her power went, and the more extreme Catholic party was always urging her to go farther. Henrietta, following the median line so often advocated by Devout Humanism, saw herself essentially as a moderator: to the promptings from Rome she argued that she did as much as she could, and that the concessions she won in the 1630s went beyond those won by queens in any other court. Certainly she had no inclination to jeopardise her personal happiness and marriage for apparent gains that would only antagonise all parties; antagonising Charles would do no good in any case, since whatever influence she had in promoting her religion depended on his good will. On the whole she seems to have followed her own inclinations, depending on Charles's affection to gain favours for her friends, and combining her interest in *préciosité* and Platonic love with her religious interests. Whether her Catholicism was actually promoted by her love fashions is perhaps not so important as the perception of people such as Prynne that it might have been, a perception which contributed indirectly to the causes of the Civil War. As Robin Clifton has pointed out ('Fear of Popery', p. 150), the seventeenth century was the first time that a Catholic threat was perceived to come from internal conspiracy rather than from external invasion.

Catholicism did in fact prosper at court under the auspices of the Queen from about 1630 on, when communications were re-opened between England and the Vatican. The history of this relationship has been studied in detail by Gordon Albion in *Charles I and the Court of Rome* (1935), and the record of these negotiations published in part as the *Memoirs* of Gregorio Panzani, translated and introduced by Joseph Berington (1793).[11] From these accounts it appears that by 1633 official relations had been re-established with Rome, the first for nearly a century, and negotiations begun for receiving a Papal representative at court. Charles gave his tacit consent to these arrangements as long as Rome did not meddle in State affairs, and all dealings were conducted through the Queen (Albion, pp. 117–54). The negotiations culminated in December 1634 with the arrival of the Papal envoy Gregorio Panzani, who was accredited to the Queen, and welcomed through her by the King. Panzani was impressed by his reception and sent back his reports to Cardinal Barberini who, as 'Protector of England and Scotland', took a close personal interest in the progress of Catholic affairs at the court. Pope Urban VIII (another of the Barberini family) took a special interest in Henrietta, who was his god-daughter; he had been Papal Nuncio at the French court when Henrietta was born, and professed a warm regard for her and for Charles, whom he held in high esteem. Cardinal Barberini relayed the Pope's messages to Henrietta, acknowledging her guardianship of the English Catholics, and telling her that, as St Urban had desired nothing more of St Cecily than the conversion of her husband, this is 'all that the present Pope expects from her Britannic majesty' (Berington, p. 203). From the English court Panzani wrote back, confidently predicting that the British Rose would one day offer honeyed pasture to the bees of Urban (Albion, p. 153). Arrangements were made for an exchange of agents between the English court and the Vatican, and the choice fell on two Scotsmen, William Hamilton, to represent the Queen at the Vatican, and George Conn, to represent the Pope at court.

Panzani realised the importance of choosing an agent whose personal qualities would meet the approval of the Queen and her ladies, and Conn was an ideal choice. Panzani had consulted Father Philip, the Queen's confessor, on the best qualities for an agent, and was told that the man chosen must combine piety with social grace: he should be a man of fine appearance, noble and rich enough to be generous, 'of exemplary life, though of no straight-laced piety'. He should know French well, and take into account the youthful liking of the Queen for perfumes, beautiful clothes, and witty conversation. He must likewise pay homage to all her ladies 'through whom much business had to be done at the English court'; but he added that such attentions must never be open to wrong interpretation, 'as the English, with the irreproachable example of the King and Queen before them, took scandal at the slightest thing' (Albion, p. 152; Berington, p. 188). George Conn fitted the picture exactly. He was a Scot of noble birth, and had published a book on the life of Mary Queen of Scots; he was educated at the English College, Douai, had been in Paris, and now served in Rome as Secretary to Cardinal Barberini (*DNB*, see under Connaeus, George). He was warmly recommended by Walter Montague, who was now in Rome negotiating on the Queen's behalf. He was as welcome to Charles as to Henrietta for his fine taste in art, which matched that of the art-loving Barberini; through him and the other Catholic agents generous gifts of paintings were sent from the treasuries of the Vatican to the King.[12] Charles regarded Conn as a friend and fellow-countryman, with whom he enjoyed discussing both art and religion. Conn, for his part, was always courteous, but also honest in expressing his opinions to the King, particularly in regard to religion, and he won the liking and respect of most people at court.

The task of the Papal agents was to explore the possibility of reconciliation between Catholicism and Anglicanism (a possibility that had its adherents at court in the 1630s), to make converts, and generally to spread as tactfully as possible the influence of the Queen's religion. Following Panzani's advice Conn set himself to win the support of the ladies, a task which he accomplished easily. His obvious success prompted the remark that he 'evidently contemplated subjecting the whole realm through women' (Albion, p. 162); Conn replied that as his mission was to the Queen, not the King, he had necessarily more to do with the ladies than with the men. In this respect the atmosphere that the Queen had built up by her type of *préciosité*, with its mixture of gallantry and high moral tone, was a great advantage to the agents. The relative social freedom of women provided situations in which men and women could meet and talk on equal terms, and the communicative freedom, on which safeguards were put by the elaborate rules of courtship, gave the agents much freer access to the Queen and her ladies than they would have had, for instance, in James's reign. Secondly, the Queen's social independence smoothed over the difficulties of a formal presentation of the agents at court: they were accredited to the Queen, and she simply introduced them to Charles and other important people when the latter visited her apartments at Somerset House. From the evidence of the agents' letters and diplomatic reports (Albion, pp. 174 ff., pp. 234 ff.), discussions of religion were frequent at these informal meetings, and Charles openly discussed theological questions with Conn (Albion, pp. 160–1) in the presence of Anglicans and Catholics alike.

Préciosité was also of use to the agents in having built up around Henrietta a group of people who had a wide range of contacts inside and outside the court. Some of these people were certainly Protestant, for example the Earls of Holland (Henry Rich) and Northumberland (brother of Henry Percy), but many were

Catholic or had strong Catholic connections.[13] Among the latter was Sir Kenelm Digby, a leading figure in the group. A life-long friend of the Queen, he was 'a party in all the royal diversions, which indeed he frequently planned and directed';[14] his Catholicism became doubly conspicuous when, after turning Anglican in 1630 out of loyalty to the King, he publicly returned to Catholicism in 1635. Walter Montague, son of the Puritan Earl of Manchester, was converted in 1635, and he and Digby were both friends of Henry Jermyn, a favourite of the Queen.[15] Digby was connected with Sir John Winter, the Queen's Catholic Secretary; Winter was the friend of Endymion Porter who had strong Catholic sympathies and was the patron of Davenant (who became Catholic in the 1640s). Porter was a business partner of Sir Basil Brooke, who helped Thomas Hawkins with the translation of *The Holy Court* (*DNB*); Hawkins had contact with the Earl of Dorset who, as Lord Chamberlain to the Queen, helped dramatists like Joseph Rutter. William Habington, who was friendly with Davenant, Porter, and James Shirley (the latter a Catholic), had firm Anglican connections, but came of an old Catholic family, was educated at the English Jesuit College of St Omers, and was one of the candidates for representing the Queen at the Vatican.[16] Membership of the Queen's group did not necessarily mean being Catholic, and I would agree with recent critics (for example Malcolm Smuts and Martin Butler), who have found that Henrietta included 'Puritans', or at least Anglicans, among her friends. Part of the group's value, however, was that it provided a middle ground for people who were drawn together by an interest in literary pastimes and by personal liking, but who were of different religious persuasions.

Similarly, among the group of ladies who regularly attended Henrietta in court entertainments (see Table of women masquers, p. 87), there were people of different religious views, but the group included prominent members who had strong Catholic sympathies or connections. As early as 1626 the Countess and Duchess of Buckingham, the Marchioness of Hamilton, the Countesses of Rutland and Denbigh, and 'Mme Sauvage', were listed amongst the ladies permitted to attend Mass with the Queen in her Oratory.[17] These ladies or their relatives all had connections with members of the Queen's *précieux* group. The old Countess of Buckingham was well known for her Catholicism, as was the Duchess, Katherine Manners, daughter of the Countess of Rutland. It was the Countess of Denbigh who in 1627 inspired Cosin's book of *Private Devotions*, regarded as 'Popish' because it revived the tradition of the Primer and the Offices of the Virgin. Her daughter, Mary Feilding, the Marchioness of Hamilton, showed a keen interest in converting to Catholicism in the thirties until her father stopped her almost daily visits to George Conn (Albion, p. 212). Mary was the cousin of Endymion Porter's wife Olivia, an ardent Catholic and the busiest proselytiser at court. Olivia was the daughter of Buckingham's half-sister Elizabeth and John Boteler, a staunch Puritan whom Olivia succeeded in converting shortly before his death. Olivia's sister (Anne Boteler) who became Anne Blount, Countess of Newport, took part with the Queen in every one of her masques, and in 1637 publicly

Table of principal women masquers

	Chloridia	Tempe Restored	Temple of Love	Luminalia	Salmacida Spolia
*The Queen		✓		✓	✓
*Countess of Newport — Anne Boteler, d. Sir John Boteler and Buckingham's half-sister Elizabeth; m. Mountjoy Blount, Earl of Newport. Convert to Catholicism, Oct. 1637 (Albion)		✓		✓	✓
†Countess of Carnarvon — Anna Sophia, d. Sir Philip Herbert; m. Robert Dormer, Earl of Carnarvon who was Catholic (DNB)		✓		✓	✓
*Countess of Portland — Frances, m. Richard Weston, Earl of Portland (Lord Treasurer). Both supported Spanish Catholicism, and the Earl died a professed Catholic (DNB)					
†Marchioness of Hamilton — Mary Feilding, d. Wm Feilding, 1st Earl of Denbigh and Susan Villiers, sister of Duke of Buckingham; m. James, Marquis of Hamilton. Catholic sympathies (Albion)		✓	✓	✓	✓
Countess of Carlisle — Lucy, d. 9th Earl Northumberland (Henry Percy); m. James Hay 1617		✓	✓	✓	
Countess of Oxford — Lady Diana Cecil, d. Earl of Exeter; m. Henry de Vere, Earl of Oxford		✓	✓	✓	
Duchess of Lennox — Lady Mary Villiers, d. of Buckingham; m. James Stuart, Duke of Lennox and Richmond		✓		✓	✓
†Lady Howard — m. Sir Wm Howard (Viscount Stafford), a son of Earl of Arundel. The Arundel family was originally Catholic (DNB)		✓			
*Lady Katherine Howard — m. George Stuart, Lord D'Aubigny, who was brought up Catholic. She converted to Catholicism in 1630s (Albion)		✓	✓	✓	
Lady Frances Howard — d. Earl of Berkshire		✓		✓	
Lady Ann Cavendish — d. Earl of Devonshire; m. Robert, Baron Rich				✓	
Lady Elizabeth Cecil — later Countess of Berkshire				✓	
Lady Elizabeth Feilding — later Lady Kinalmeaky				✓	
†Lady Anne Weston — d. of Catholic sympathisers, the Earl and Countess Portland; m. Lord Basil Feilding, later Earl of Denbigh (DNB)		✓			
*Mistress Porter — Olivia Boteler, sister of Countess of Newport, cousin Marchioness Hamilton; m. Endymion Porter. Catholic (DNB)		✓			

*Catholic, or with strong Catholic sympathies; † possibly Catholic; d. daughter of; m. married to. Names based on lists in masque texts in Orgel and Strong. Family and religious affiliations based on DNB; additional information in Albion, Charles I (especially pp. 200–14).

declared her Catholicism, to the consternation of her Protestant husband. The Countess of Portland, who took part with the Queen in two masques, was Frances Weston, wife of the Lord Treasurer Weston, both well known for their Catholic sympathies. Their daughter Anne Weston, who took part in two masques and the Queen's pastoral, married Basil Feilding, second Earl of Denbigh, and was sympathetic to Catholicism in the 1630s. The Countess of Carnarvon, the other important person to take part in every one of the Queen's masques, was Anna Sophia, daughter of Philip Herbert, the guardian of Robert Dormer, whom she married in 1628. Robert's mother was described as 'an absolute recusant' (*DNB*), and he was brought up and remained a Catholic (his name appears in the list of Catholic lords who fell in Charles's cause). The Catholicism of these people was not all of the same kind or intensity, nor was the Queen sympathetic only to people of her own religious views (the fuller subject of court religion will be discussed in chapter 6). What is important for the moment is that the group who took part in Henrietta's social activities included a significant number of Catholics, especially important Catholic ladies who, like the Queen herself, were in close contact with leading Anglicans. The spate of conversions in the mid-thirties must have given concern to outsiders that Catholics might be taking advantage of the intimacy within the Queen's group to press the claims of her religion.

There was in fact a good deal of optimism among court Catholics in the thirties that some kind of accommodation might be found with Rome, and that even the King might be won over by the persuasions of the Catholic agents. The agents themselves and the Queen's Capucin priests were active proselytisers, and expected an equal zeal from the Queen's Catholic following. For this purpose the rules of a *précieux* group could, in fact, provide an ideal background for the discussion and dissemination of an officially suppressed religion, since the same rules would apply to the Catholic group at court. A *précieux* group preserves its exclusiveness by using a language and set of rules that only its own sect can understand, and its code of ethics enjoins tact and secrecy upon its members.[18] Moreover, the doctrine of Platonic love which played on the language and ideas of religion could, in an atmosphere of proselytising zeal, provide a tactful means of disseminating Catholic ideas, passing from gallantry to religion without the observation of an outsider. That it was sometimes intended to do so seems to be suggested by Walter Montague, who in *Miscellanea Spiritualia* admits to such a tactic as a way of attracting people to religion. Some will accuse him, he says, of sailing under false colours, capturing the heart for religion while talking of love – an interesting variation on the usual accusations against 'Platonic love' of doing the reverse. He points out that:

> when prophane passion seekes to value itselfe, and to possesse the minds of others, it puts on a heavenly habit, and speakes the language of Devotion, in reverence and adoration; thus, as it were, confessing the due interest piety hath in our hearts.   (p. 34)

Montague justifies himself in using the language of love to refer to religion by saying that he has called devotion 'love' so that those he would speak with 'might not fly from piety at first sight' (p. 34). He goes on to explain that putting devotion 'into the vulgar tongue of the court' gives it a 'more convenient conference with our senses', and hope for admittance to our hearts. By this easy way of introduction 'Devotion may come to get possession in some minds, by commerce of a good companion, sooner then by open claims of her owne rights', and he concludes by asking 'May not piety then to recover the easilier her due, without irreverence, be put into the lighter figure of passion?' I am not suggesting, of course, that all court compliment was directed towards religious ends. The Queen's fashions had their social, and no doubt their gallant, or merely silly side. It seems possible, however, that the interminable debates on the religion of love, and the exposition of its doctrines that were a part of the drama and drawing-room could, in a changed atmosphere, become debates on and expositions of religion itself.

In Montague's explanation of his methods we may, perhaps, catch a glimpse of one more phase in that long war fought between religion and courtly love. If courtly or Platonic love had originally stolen the language and images, even perhaps the emotions and ideals, of religion, then Counter-Reformation religion in the seventeenth century was busily stealing them back. For a *précieux* group it could be an added refinement and delicate irony if the language of religion – of altars, vows, prayers, devotion, and worship – which gross men interpreted as a cover for sensual appetites, were in fact restored to its rightful use: if the design of Platonic lovers was, as they declared, to unite not bodies but souls. Such a love could truly be called 'Platonic' for it was directed towards spiritual union, and the service of God. It is at least an intriguing possibility that in the thirties the connection of some members of Henrietta's group with a proselytising form of Catholicism could have made *préciosité* a far more lively pursuit than it has generally been thought, and that Catholic support may have lent substance on occasion to the pastimes – dancing, entertainments, and play-acting – that occupied so much of court life. The 'immorality' which Puritans and moralists saw as inherent in the increased freedom and charity of women's love may have been countered on the idealistic side by the excitement of belonging to a suppressed but still attractive religion, the satisfaction of 'saving men's souls' outweighing the temptation to amorous intrigue among devotees of the cult. If, by the same token, the idealistic view of love argued by court Platonics was backed by religion, the fact that the religion was Catholicism would have been a greater sin in Puritan eyes than immorality itself.

A fear that women, using the arts of love, might be capable of 'seducing' men to an alien religion does in fact seem to underlie the attacks of a propagandist like William Prynne. His *Histriomastix* (1633) was theoretically a comprehensive attack on the immorality of the stage, but, examined closely, it is not so much an attack on drama itself, as an attack on the arts associated with the stage at court, on women as a corrupting influence, and on the connection of both with Catholicism. Approximately the first three hundred pages of *Histriomastix* are taken up with a condemnation of court activities which Prynne associates with effeminacy and illicit sexual attraction. He barely discusses stage plays themselves, but rather those things which accompany them: 'effeminate mixt Dancing, lascivious Pictures, wanton Fashions, Face painting ... amorous Pastoralls, lascivious effeminate Musicke' (Prynne's Introduction, no page numbers). It should be noted, however, that in Prynne's later detailed discussion of each of these items they are condemned, not simply because they are 'immoral', but because they tend to 'seduce' Christians from their own religion by exhibiting Popish practices. Thus the stage is immoral because Popish priests and Jesuits prophane the Old Testament by putting passages from it on the stage (p. 112); English actors are 'professed Papists' (p. 142), whose dissolute lives lead them to a dissolute religion; fashionable women cut their hair in imitation of 'shameless' Papish nuns, to signify that they are 'freed from all subiection to men, or to their husbands', and both are whores (p. 203); dancing [the chapter is one of the longest, and contains the famous reference to 'Queenes themselves ... who are commonly most addicted to it' (p. 236)] is compared to a church service, or Devil's Mass, in which 'the Devill tempteth men and women ... and he that danceth, maintaineth his pompe, and singeth his Masse' to the accompaniment of fiddles and bells, while the 'Parishioners' look on (p. 230); amorous songs, and obscene, lascivious poems, which were formerly heard in churches, are now heard in pastorals (p. 261); in church 'delicate, lust-provoking Musicke' turns the oratory into a theatre (p. 288). For Prynne, all the current court arts end in effeminacy or seduction, and all seductions end in Catholicism. It seems that the arts were 'immoral' because Prynne suspected that women were using them to seduce men to an 'immoral' religion.

Puritan criticism of the court was, of course, based on a long tradition of antagonism to 'feminine seducements', and to the stage,[19] but in the Queen's love fashions of the 1630s people like Prynne may have sensed a new danger. In *préciosité* they disapproved of women being given an exalted position, and of men becoming 'effeminate' in their service; in Platonic love they disapproved of what they assumed to be an equivocal moral attitude. But to the old fear of woman as sexual temptress was perhaps added a new, and what may in the circumstances have been a well-grounded fear, of women tempting men to a hostile religion. The Queen's fashions obviously made an easy target for moral attack because of the social intimacy among men and women in the group, the increased freedom of women, and the fact that *préciosité* was based on the idea of love. To outsiders the whole idea of Platonic love was ridiculous: men do not kneel in adoration at the shrines of their ladies and visit them in their bedchambers without some ulterior motive. Moralists and Puritans assumed that such practices must lead to sexual intrigue, but their attacks may often have been motivated as much by religious as by moral interest. Attacks on religion couched in sexual terms are familiar in paper warfare: the same allegations of promiscuity were being made against contemporary sects like the Quakers and Ranters, and most minority religious groups have been accused of immorality, including the early Christians, and counter-culture groups of our own day.

Fashions in love have often played a part in social and religious change, and Christopher Hill has pointed out that sexual revolution was connected with the introduction of the Protestant ethic in the seventeenth century.[20] Conversely the Queen's cult of love, its exaltation of women, and its connection with Catholicism, may be seen as the defiant gesture of a minority group – élitist, feminist, and Catholic – whose existence in the 1630s was being threatened by forces outside the court. For this reason we should be cautious of taking all Puritan charges of immorality at face value. Whatever abuses of the Queen's love cult there may have been, it is clear that many of the Puritan charges of immorality against members of her group have a religious rather than a sexual basis. When Lady Newport became Catholic, for instance, she complained to Conn that when she was going to Mass, those who wished to discredit her, spread stories that she was keeping assignations with lovers (Albion, *Charles I*, p. 213). When we hear from Prynne of George Conn that 'two houres before day (In Winter) his manner was to visit Ladyes and Gentlewomen, and to enquire of them how they slept that night' it is taken as evidence of Conn's scandalous behaviour (quoted as such by Sensabaugh, 'Platonic love and the Puritan rebellion', p. 460). When we read of Conn's activities in Catholic reports, it is evidence of the large numbers of people he visited daily in his often successful attempts at converting them. When Prynne writes, in describing the activities of Olivia Porter and other Catholic women at court, that 'the Jesuite learn of the Serpent to seduce men by female Instruments to their ruine' (*Romes Master-peece*, sig. C4v), Conn writes proudly to Cardinal Barberini that 'amid all the temptations of Court life there were people like Olive Porter capable of heroic action' (Albion, p. 209). In each case it is clear that the moral judgment, though put in sexual terms, has a religious basis.

Prynne often implies immoral behaviour when all he means is Catholic behaviour. When he writes about seductions, beds, and bed chambers, for example, in the passage quoted above, he is not referring to intrigue or adultery – he is referring to Catholic wives, Olivia Porter, the Countess of Arundel, and the Queen. When he complains of '*Queen Mary* her selfe in the Kings own bed and bosome', he is not referring to the impropriety of the Queen, but to the impropriety of a Catholic Queen. The crime is not that these women are behaving immorally, but that they are behaving 'irreligiously', and using their sex to seduce men to Catholicism. Catholics were capable of even deeper cunning in Puritan eyes: worse than using sex for religious ends, Prynne suggests, they *counterfeit* sex and immorality to cover religious ends. Speaking again of George Conn, he says

Hee had a palace adorned with lascivious pictures, which counterfeited prophaneness in the house, but with them was palliated a Monastery, wherein forty Nunnes were maintained, hid in so great a Palace. It is situated in Queenes-street, which the statue of a Golden Queene adornes. (*Romes Master-peece*, sig. Dv)

We are reminded of Dr Johnson's address to the Thames lighterman: 'Sir, your

wife under pretence of keeping a bawdy house, is a receiver of stolen goods.'
Sexual licence has not always had a monopoly on the word immorality.

Maria Triumphans

The function of the Queen's *préciosité* in the cultural life of the court was no
doubt basically social rather than religious, although it had sufficient links with
her Catholicism to arouse the suspicions of those who were opposed to it. The
ideal of Platonic Love had, however, a more specific connection with Catholicism
which seems significant in the culture of the court. The Counter-Reformation
in the seventeenth century had adapted Neoplatonic ideals of Beauty and Love
to the cult of the Virgin Mary, and in the thirties Henrietta led such a cult at
court. The Queen's association with this side of Neoplatonism began, or was
strengthened, when in February 1630 Capucin Friars arrived from France to
serve in her chapel. The Friars were assigned to the Queen's Household, and
a first-hand account (published in Thomas Birch, *The Court and Times of Charles
I*, II) by Father Cyprien de Gamaches gives an enthusiastic report of their activities.[21] The Capucins were a missionary Order and one of the most successful
in the seventeenth century in reclaiming territories lost to Catholicism at the
Reformation. They placed themselves under the direction of *The Congregation
for the Propagation of the Faith* (founded 1622), and by 1625 they had provinces
in all the principal countries of Europe. Their mission in England was like that
to any other 'heretic' country, and under the auspices of the Queen they worked
tirelessly to win back those who had been lost to the faith, or to convert others
who were attracted to it.

Capucins had been chosen to serve the Queen because they were acceptable
to both the English and French courts. They were acceptable to Charles because,
unlike some of those who originally had accompanied Henrietta, they were known
for their courtly tact and gentle piety; five of their number were said to have
been born Englishmen (Birch, II, 298–9). They were acceptable to the French
because Capucins were influential at that court, and one of those who led the
English mission, Father Joseph (Francis le Clerc du Tremblay) was in the confidence of Louis XIII, Marie de Medici, and the Pope.[22] Henrietta herself had
always held them in esteem, and 'desired them for her service', while in Rome
Pope Urban VIII, who had a brother in the Capucin Order, was the special
patron of the Friars. The Pope expressed satisfaction on this occasion that the
Order had been chosen for the 'noble and profitable office' of England (Birch,
II, 296–7). The Capucins were a reformed branch of the Franciscan Order, founded
in the sixteenth century in an attempt to return to the basic principles of Christianity that had inspired St Francis of Assisi. They had been influential in helping
to form the ideals of French Devout Humanism in the early years of the seventeenth
century, when a group of Capucins, who included the English writers Father
Archangel and Father Benedict of Canfield, joined the religious circle of Mme

Acarie, St François de Sales, and Pierre de Bérulle.[23] As the century progressed, the Capucins adopted Sales's teaching as the inspiration of their movement. Sales's stress on gentleness and love was thoroughly compatible with their teaching, and the basis of Neoplatonism in his work was valuable to them in their writings.[24] Capucin books became popular throughout Europe, and around 1630, France, in particular, became the centre of Capucin activity. Two of the most important writers of the period were Zacharie de Lysieux and Yves de Paris, whose ideas were certainly current amongst the Capucins at Henrietta's court. Zacharie de Lysieux served for a time as one of Henrietta's chaplains, and in 1637 dedicated a book to her entitled *La Philosophie chrestienne*.[25] Zacharie was a close friend of Yves de Paris,[26] whose writings in the early 1630s summed up contemporary Capucin thinking.

Yves de Paris' major work, *La Théologie naturelle* (4 volumes, Paris, 1633–6), thoroughly mingled Neoplatonism and Christianity. His ideas have been discussed at length by Bremond (*A Literary History*, I, 370–96) and by Father Cuthbert (*The Capuchins*, II, 415–70), both of whom quote extensively from his work, and I have depended on them for the following discussion. Bremond calls Yves 'a Marsilio Ficino who could have written *L'Introduction à la vie dévote*' (I, 331). In *La Théologie naturelle* Yves elevates Platonic theory into a universal social and religious system, a 'cordial union' which unites the world with God, and in his chapter entitled 'De la beauté et de l'amour' he argues that human perfectibility comes from those sympathies which draw us to the divine. The steps of the argument are similar to those outlined by Castiglione, by Sales, or by d'Urfé: the divine ray shining through the beauty of visible objects gains our senses, and forces the reason to seek beauty in its source, thus involving the soul. The soul's involvement is proof that 'corporeal beauty is no more than a shadow, a sketch of that divine beauty which is the true object of our love, and which, being of infinite perfection, can satisfy to the full our whole capacity' (quoted by Bremond, p. 386). When reason is joined by love, the soul has need only of a small ray of divine Faith to complete this 'lovely circle of light' that reunites the world with its origin, and man with God; love as a way of coming to God is superior to reason itself, for whereas reason can progress only by degrees, love is unitive: 'one impulse of the heart fuses all the soul, and with it all the world, with its original source' ('un élan du coeur rejoint toute l'âme et avec elle tout le monde à son principe': quoted by Cuthbert, p. 417). Yves warns against being misled by beauty, but, approached in the right spirit, beauty is a force for good, and should not be shunned: 'it is not asked of you to be blind to the beauties of the court', he wrote, 'it is allowable to regard them as closely as the gems of a cabinet, with admiration but without touching, as things which are not, nor ought to be at your disposition nor even at your choice' (quoted by Bremond, p. 388). Human love is an image of the real object of our desire, and even the language familiar to lovers, of altars, vows, and prayers, is a warning that love is seeking a higher object than possession, for the progress of true love is 'a flight from earth to heaven'. In this combination of Christian teaching with humanist interests, the fashionable cult of Platonic love, rightly conceived, was not only compatible with Capucin spirituality, but complemented it. In place of a human object of adoration, however, the Capucins put the supreme feminine object of religious veneration, the Blessed Virgin Mary.

In the early seventeenth century, Mary had become one of the most important figures of the Counter-Reformation, although her cult was, of course, far older. In the twelfth century it had grown out of the mystical interpretation of the Canticles by St Bernard of Clairvaux, and historically it had never been far removed from secular cults of love. It had developed side by side with the cult of courtly love, had later gathered elements from troubadour poetry and the romances of chivalry, had contributed to Dante's vision in the *Paradiso*, and was even hinted at as a central ideal by d'Urfé in *L'Astrée*.[27] Devotion to Mary was one of the subjects of particular deliberation at the Council of Trent (1545–63), which defended Mary against the attacks of Reformers, and specifically recommended her praise. Marian literature flourished as a result, and to the religious Orders who had already devoted themselves to her service (the Cistercians, Dominicans, and Franciscans) were added Orders like the Capucins, who found her cult of great value in their stress on the *Via Affirmativa* of the spiritual life, the way of gentleness and love. Like St François de Sales, who had dedicated his life to the Virgin, the Capucins adopted Mary as their patroness. In Mary they found a perfect focus for the Neoplatonism that inspired the thinking of Sales and Yves de Paris, and at the same time a figure that helped humanise Neoplatonic ideals. The Blessed Virgin summed up and raised to an ideal plane the virtues of Goodness, Beauty, and Love: the description of the Bride in the Canticles, '*tota pulchra es, amica mea, et macula non est in te*', was taken as a proof and consequence of her total virtue, and beauty and virtue together aroused love and drew souls to God. All the tensions and contradictions inherent in placing the ideal of love in a mortal woman were reconciled in devotion to Mary: she is beautiful, supreme among women; she is both Virgin and Mother; she can be adored completely because devotion to her leads to love of heaven. In the Capucin view there need be no conflict between earthly and heavenly love. By emulating the Virgin, virtuous women could awaken souls to divine love, which was a continuation and ideal end of the love inspired by beauty and virtue on earth, and they could thus, like Mary, lead men to God.

The Queen's group of Capucins at the English court dedicated their chapel and devoted their services to the Virgin, who was the patroness of both the Friars and of the Queen herself. Henrietta, as her mother reminded her in the letter written on her marriage, owed 'une dévotion particulière' to Mary, whose name she bears, and who is 'mère de votre âme' (Leveneur, Comte de Tillières, *Mémoires*, pp. 73 and 76). When Henrietta practised her devotions in her Oratory after arriving in England, she and her ladies 'sang the Hours of the Virgin' (HMC, *Salvetti*, p. 77), and Father Cyprien wrote that the Queen 'had always regarded the Blessed Virgin as her good mistress and her dear mother' (Birch, p. 316). When therefore, in 1632, a new chapel was begun for the Capucins in the grounds of the Queen's Palace at Somerset House, a commemorative plate recorded that the Queen laid the foundation stone 'sub felicibus Beatissimae Virginis Mariae auspiciis Patronae suae' (Birch, pp. 308–9). This chapel was a significant step in the progress of Catholicism, and its opening was celebrated with Masses and ceremonies that lasted for days.[28] In the mid-thirties it became the centre for an Arch-Confraternity of the Holy Rosary, for the establishment of which the Capucins had obtained permission from the Pope, and which was led by the Queen (Birch, p. 316).

Fraternities and Sodalities in honour of the Virgin had become very popular on the Continent, following the establishment of the first Sodality by the Jesuits in 1563.[29] Their members bound themselves to the practice of piety and to the service of the Virgin, with special emphasis on her help in leading souls to God. According to a book on *The Societie of the Rosarie* by Luca Pinelli (1624), among the duties of the members was to pray 'for the concord & vnion of Christian Princes, extirpation of heresies, & exaltation of our holy mother the Church' (sig. M8v, p. 208). An Arch-Confraternity also had the power to affiliate other societies of a similar kind, and it is possible that there were already Sodalities of the Virgin in England: there was a prayer for admittance into 'The Sodality or Association of the little Chaplet of our Blessed Lady' found among papers in 1628,[30] and the English emblem book *Partheneia Sacra*, published in 1633, was addressed to 'The Parthenian Sodality' (Dedicatory Epistle). The Queen was the first to be inscribed in the Arch-Confraternity at court, and Father Cyprien describes how all the Catholics of her court,

gentlemen and ladies, small and great, and innumerable people with them, followed her in this devotion. Every Saturday in the year, the litanies of the Blessed Virgin and other reverential services were sung with great solemnity in that chapel dedicated to the glory of that celestial lady who was held in such veneration by the Catholics, French and English.   (Birch, p. 316)

An Arch-Confraternity was given the duty of holding public religious observances – group recitations of the Rosary, singing of the Litanies, and staging of outdoor processions – to attract attention and make converts; thus Father Cyprien reports that when the brothers and sisters of the Rosary met to confess and communicate on the first Sunday of each month, they 'held celebrated processions, which were attended out of curiosity by many secretaries' (Birch, p. 316). Capucin processions had been a feature of the Valois reign in France (from which the Caroline court borrowed ideas for entertainments to be discussed later), and illustrations of these may give some idea of Henrietta's processions (figures 7 and 8; the French illustrations are discussed by Frances Yates in *Astraea*, 'Religious processions in Paris, 1583–4', pp. 173–207 and illustrations 24–39).

There was no shortage of books giving guidance on all aspects of Marian devotion, which was of course (as George Herbert appears to remind himself[31])

7 'Procession de Louise de Lorraine' (1584)

8 'Procession de Henri III' (1579)

officially forbidden in England. Despite the Reformation, however, Mary had never been completely neglected. Books of private devotion had kept her memory alive in the sixteenth and seventeenth centuries, either by means of foreign books smuggled into the country by ambassadors, or by English books printed secretly in England or on presses in the English Catholic Colleges abroad.[32] A survey of the titles listed by Allison and Rogers in their *Catalogue of Catholic Books* indicates that publication of Marian books in English increased after Henrietta came to the throne in 1625, and increased markedly between 1630 and 1635. For instance, an English version of *The Primer, or Office of the Blessed Virgin Marie*, which had editions in 1615 and 1617, had another edition in 1630, another with a re-issue in 1631, and two editions in 1632 (A&R, nos. 688–94). The English translation of an extremely popular book by Pedro de Ribadeneira, *The Liues of the Saints* (incorporated in Alfonso de Villegas, *Flos sanctorum*) went through six re-issues and editions between 1621 and 1638 (A&R, nos. 854–60). *The Arch-Confraternity of the Holy Rosary* (A&R, no. 36) was printed secretly in England in 1636, the date suggesting that it may have been printed for the use of the Arch-Confraternity in the Queen's Chapel. Besides these books aimed directly at assisting devotion to Mary, there were many others that took such devotion as given, and played on various aspects of her praise. For example, Sabine Chambers was one of many who treated the theme of *The Garden of our Blessed Lady* (A&R 230); John Falconer treated Mary as *The Mirrour of Created Perfection* (A&R 302), and many others treated the methods of devotion to her service (see titles in A&R under numbers listed in note 32 above). Of the books printed I would like to look closely at three of the most important published in the 1630s, all of which are relevant to the present subject: *Partheneia Sacra* (1633), *The Female Glory* (1635), and *Maria Triumphans* (1635). The first two seem to relate, through style and treatment of subject matter, to the ideas of Platonic Beauty and Love made current by Henrietta's *précieux* fashions, and the third explicitly links the name of the Queen with the name of Mary.

Partheneia Sacra, or The Mysterious and Delicious Garden of the Sacred Parthenes (Rouen, John Cousturier, 1633) was written by 'H.A.' (Henry Hawkins) for a Parthenian Sodality, to assist devotion to Mary.[33] It stands out from other emblem books of the period both in form and style: it is more elegantly produced than its contemporaries, the writing is more urbane, and it seems to appeal to knowledge of the court. When the author wishes to contrast the Virgin's beauty with worldly beauty, for instance, it is the 'magasin of Feminin riches' familiar to the court that he describes: the 'Vermilion or Ceruse in the face, bracelets of Oriental-pearles on her wrist, Rubie-carknets on the neck, rich pendants in the eares, and a delicious fan of most exquisit feathers in her hand' ('The Proëme to his Genius', sig. A iiij). A passage introducing a meditation on the symbol of the star begins by asking 'Haue you seen a statelie Mask in Court, al set round, and taken vp with a world of beautiful Ladies, to behold the sports and reuels there?' (pp. 114–15). Hawkins's references to the music of Dowland, to Sidney's *Arcadia*, to a poem

by Robert Southwell, and other references to literature and legend, were all originally pointed out by Rosemary Freeman (*English Emblem Books*, p. 194). In
addition, Hawkins has a passage on 'the architect' that suggests he may have
taken an interest in contemporary affairs at court. In it he says that 'The good
Architect should linck his spirit with his hand, and the compas with his reason,
setting his hand to work, as wel as the brayne. The first do frame but bodies
without a soule, the second, soules without a bodie, the third do build the whole,
and are men of note and reputation indeed' (pp. 168–9). The wording of the
passage is similar to that in Vitruvius's book *On Architecture* (book 1, chapter
1, p. 2), to which Inigo Jones alluded in two masques (*Albion's Triumph* and
Tempe Restored, performed the year before *Partheneia Sacra* was published) making visual reference to the quarrel between himself and Ben Jonson.[34] Jones would
have been gratified particularly by the opening of Hawkins's passage, which calls
Architecture 'A soveraigne Mistris', and says 'We recurre then to the Architect,
for direction in al.' Hawkins was the younger brother of Sir Thomas Hawkins,
who has already been noticed as the translator of *The Holy Court*, and a protegé
of Sir Basil Brooke (for whom see *DNB*), whose surname he took when he entered
the English College at Rome to train as a Jesuit priest.[35] Brooke translated Caussin's
The Penitent, or Entertainments for Lent (1643), with a dedication to Henrietta
Maria, and was connected with Endymion Porter, Montague, and Digby. With
so many avenues open to the court it would be strange if so elegant and courtly
a book as *Partheneia Sacra* did not play a part in the Marian revival being fostered
in the 1630s by the Queen.

   The book appears, moreover, to follow the fashions of Devout Humanism
being recommended to the court. It is very sophisticated in the variety of devices
it uses to entertain the reader, being intended for both 'pleasure and deuotion',
and set out with 'Pious Devises and Emblemes for the Entertainement of Devovt
Sovles' (title-page). In 'The Preface to the Reader' the author explains that he
has endeavoured to appeal to the natural delight in change and variety, but to
make 'Varietie the hand-mayd to Pietie'. He excuses the 'instruments' he uses,
such as 'Impreses, and Mottoes ... Emblemes, and Poesies', by saying that,
though they may seem prophane, 'yet they may be like that Panthaeon, once
sacred to the feigned Deities, and piously since sanctified, conuerted, and consecrated to the honour of the glorious Queene, and al the blessed Saints of Heauen'.
He addresses a feminine audience, and says that his book consecrates the ideals
of Beauty and Love, directed by poets to the objects of human love, by raising
them to a heavenly object, the Virgin. In 'The Proëme to his Genius' he writes
in Neoplatonic terms, basing his praise of Mary on her beauty and purity, and
connecting the beauty of her soul with the beauty of her form. He imagines
God as the supreme artist or sculptor, who, 'with his most exquisit fingars',
has bestowed 'much art and industrie in her delineation'; he describes her physical
features, 'black and archie browes' with 'bright lamps' of eyes, 'a countenance,
graceful without softnes or leuitie, graue without statelines', through which 'a

certain Diuinitie of beautie dazeled the aspects of men.'[36] Mary is the ideal object of praise because she not only brings to human beauty a spiritual perfection, but to spiritual perfection a human reality, in which there is no danger to the soul. Hence, he says,

If thou needs must praise, extol and magnify Beautie, Vertue, Honor; not in the ayr only of *Ideas*, or abstract from sense, but in a subject really, subsisting: I say, if thou needs must dignify and eternize a pure creature aboue the skyes ... Behold she is even now at hand, whom worthily thou mayst, and whom thou canst not prayse enough.

Hawkins uses all the traditional visual symbols of Mary's cult, the enclosed garden with its emblems (compare figure 25, below), and the sun, moon, and star (Frontispiece illustration, figure 9) as starting points for meditations in her honour. His style has many of the characteristics that Odette de Mourgues has described in relation to French baroque writers, full of comparisons, correspondences and sometimes strained conceits, and although Latin sources have been suggested for the material, it would not be surprising to find that the book was closely related to contemporary books of devotion in France, as Mario Praz has suggested.[37]

Another book that elaborated Neoplatonic ideas of Beauty and Love was *The Female Glory: or The Life, and Death of our Blessed Lady, the Holy Virgin Mary* (1635) by Anthony Stafford. Stafford devotes whole sections to the discussion of Mary's beauty of body and soul, imagining God as a painter who bestowed the beauty of earth and heaven in 'the limming of this rare Piece' (sig. BV), and describing Mary as a statue 'carved by God's own hand' (sig. B2). Her external beauty is surpassed by her inner purity: she is the most beautiful because the most virtuous of women, and he quotes a description in which the sun, the earth, and the whole of the vegetable and animal kingdom pay homage to her (sig. B7v). Stafford is careful to give Mary a place 'above all Angels, but below thy Sonne' (sig. A8), but his book draws on all the traditional Catholic sources of Marian devotion. The poems prefixed to the text include 'A Panegyricke on the blessed Virgin MARY' (sig. D4v–D6), in which she is praised under all her titles in the Litanies, and other poems describe her as 'The Morning-star, whose light our Fal hath stay'd' (sig. C8), the 'Throne of Glory, beauteous as the Moone, / The rosie Morning, or the rising Sun' (sig.C8v). Stafford himself describes Mary's assumption in traditional images (compare the frontispiece of *Partheneia Sacra*):

the orbes bowed and bended themselves to make her a triumphant Arch ... The Sunne with his brightest beames imbrac't her, that it might be said. A woman cloathed with the Sunne. The Moone stooped to her, that it might be divulg'd the Moone was under her feet. The brightest of the Starres interwove themselves to make her a radiant crowne.   (sig. P3)

Stafford concludes his praise with the words 'O Thou bashful Morne that didst precede and produce our Sunne ... Thou deserv'st a Quire of Queenes here, and another of Angels in Heaven, to sing thy praises' (sig. R3v–R4).

Stafford's book is addressed principally to women, and he seems to echo the

9 Frontispiece illustration of the Virgin from Henry Hawkins, *Partheneia Sacra* (1633)

ideal of feminine virtue put forward by writers on *honnêteté*. He dedicates his book to one who, he says, is notable for her religion, virtue, beauty, and modesty, but whose demeanour is not

froward [i.e. contrary, perverse], and formall, but gentle, free and communicative. You show the world that there is a Christian freedome, of which we may lawfully partake. By your faire Demeanour you cleerly demonstrate, that sanctity may be without Austerity, and vertue securely sociable. (sig. A6v–A7)

This is reminiscent of the happy mean in feminine behaviour recommended for *honnêtes femmes*, who have no need to 'put their devotion upon the racke to make it scoul'; of Montague's opinion that piety may 'sute her selfe so farre into the fashion, as may make her the easilier accostable, and yet retaine her dignity and decency'; and of Caussin's advice to the virtuous woman not to seem 'too austere in the eyes of her court, for weake soules might be diverted from Christianity' (quoted above). In Stafford's book, however, the ideal is linked with devotion to Mary, and he says he will use simple language acceptable to women, so as to help them 'to beautifie their lives, and to kindle in their faire bosomes an holy ambition to aspire to the perfections of that devout life, which this our incomparable Lady led' (sig. Ev). This devotion he explicitly links with proselytism. In his 'Address to the Feminine Reader' he calls Mary 'the Mirrour of Female Perfection', whom to adore is to strive to imitate, and whom to imitate is to convert others:

Al her Visitants were but so many converts, whose bad affections, and erroneous opinions, the sweetness of her discourse had rectified. The leprosy of sinne was her dayly cure, and they (whom vice had blinded) were by her restored to their inward sight, and their prostrate soules adored divine, Majesticall vertues residing in this Sacred Temple. The conference with her rais'd them above themselves, and enfranchis'd their soules till then, chained to their bodies. (sig. B4v–B5)

He concludes 'On this, ground your beliefe, that shee amongst you who shall constantly tread in her paths, shall at length arrive at the Celestiall Paradice' (sig. B5–B5v).

The Female Glory was one of the most controversial books to be published in the 1630s, because it was licensed by authority of the Anglican Church and published openly in London.[38] Nothing like it had happened since the publication in 1627 of John Cosin's *Collection of Private Devotions* which had revived the tradition of the Primer and its associations with the Office of the Virgin, causing an outcry from Burton and Prynne. *The Female Glory* was published just before the establishment of the Arch-Confraternity in the Queen's Chapel, which opened at the end of 1636, and perhaps was written in an attempt to make devotion to Mary acceptable to the moderate Anglicans at court. Stafford said that he endeavoured to keep 'the meane', and claimed that his book contained nothing contrary to the teaching of the Anglican Church. He assured Puritans and other detractors that 'till they are good *Marians*, they shall never be good *Christians*, while they derogate from the dignity of the *Mother*, they cannot truly honour the *Sonne*' (sig. P8). My suggestion that it may have been connected with the Queen's Confraternity is strengthened by the fact that another book published in the same year (1635), *Maria Triumphans*, makes explicit the connection between Mary and the Queen.

Maria Triumphans, by N.N., takes the form of 'A Discourse, wherein ... the *B. Virgin Mary* Mother of God, is defended, and vindicated, from all such Dishonours and Indignities, with which the *Precisians* of these our dayes, are accustomed vniustly to charge her.' The dialogue is between Mariadulus, imagined to be an imprisoned English priest, and Mariamastix, 'a *Precisian* imagined to have preached ... against our B. Lady' (sig. A5). By this, the author says, he does not wish to stir up controversy amongst learned Catholics nor the 'more sober Protestants,' but only to write against 'the fiery *Puritans*, who ... disgorge their poyson against the said most blessed Virgin' (sig. A5v). The author dedicates the book to Queen Henrietta Maria, whom he addresses as 'Most renowned Princesse, and Mirrour of Vertue', in the hope that the book may, 'with the Wings of your gracious Patronage ... more freely, and vnrestraynedly flye abroad' (sig. A2). In the dedication he explicitly associates the Queen's name with that of the Virgin, saying that by her protecting the book:

She, whom it cheefely concernes, will a new become your Patronesse: And thus will *Mary* intercede for *Mary*, the Queene of Heauen for a great Queene vpon earth; the Mother of our *Celestiall King*, for the mother of our future terrene King. And finally, by your protecting and pleading for it, the Immaculate Virgin will (in a more full manner) become an Aduocate for you, her *Aduocate*.

He praises the Queen for her 'more than manly' resolution in defending the ancient faith, 'For which your immouable Constancy, all good Catholikes do most ioyfully sound forth your due Panegyricks, and Laudes.' His own praises, he says, 'do but coment your owne daily Deuotions towards the Intemerate Virgin'. There can be little doubt that there is a double reference in the *Maria* of the title, to the Virgin in heaven, and to the Queen who is her champion and defender on earth.

The initials 'N.N.' were often used pseudonymously by authors of controversial books on religion, and *Maria Triumphans* may have been written by John Brereley, alias Laurence Anderton. In 1632 Brereley had written a sonnet sequence *Virginalia, or Spirituall Sonnets in prayse of the most glorious Virgin Marie*, in which prose passages linking the sonnets contain wording almost identical with passages in *Maria Triumphans*.[39] In the sonnets, devoted to each of Mary's titles in the Litanies, Mary is made to sound more like an object of Platonic love than an object of religious veneration. Some sonnets sound as though they could be addressed as well to the Queen as to the Virgin, when the author says that Mary's 'graces do inflame / Each vertuous hart' with sacred love (Sonnet 10), and asks:

Who but an Atheist will refuse to serue

> So great a Mistresse? who doth euery way
> Such supreme honour worthily deserue.
> O let vs then, great Virgin, while we stay
> In this frayle world, thy humble agents be,
> To moue thy greatest foes to honour thee.

(Sonnet 15)

Having written in praise of the Virgin in 1632 Brereley may well have come to her defence again in 1635 on the founding of an Arch-Confraternity in her honour, linking her name with the Queen's as a double triumph for the name of Mary.

The Queen and devotion to Mary

An association of the name of the Queen with that of the Virgin would not have seemed out of place to contemporaries. For Catholics, the Queen's roles, of mediatrix, mother, and bride must have seemed to parallel those of Mary. As mother and bride she won Charles to mercy and love; as intercessor on behalf of her Catholic subjects she protected the Catholic Faith in England. Indeed a comparison between Mary's power to intercede, for those who dedicate themselves to her, with the same power of a great Queen on earth, is made in a book by Alexis de Salo, *An Admirable Method to Love, Serve and Honour the B. Virgin Mary* (trans. R.F., 1639). This book was written for those in 'the Confraternity of the Rosary', and in the *Introduction* the author pictures Mary as a Queen honoured by heavenly courtiers. Such a Queen protects those who truly serve her, and if one of her loyal servants should fall from favour, or even be banished from the court, she 'would vndertake his defence & reconcile him with his Prince ... obtain his repeale if he was banished from the Court, and not only restore him to his former estate again, but aduance him higher' (Introduction, no sig.). There are many examples of Henrietta doing this: a topical instance for Catholics was that of Walter Montague who, after he was converted (1635), was banished temporarily from the court by Charles, but not from the Queen's favour, and was soon back enjoying a more influential position than before. 'What a felicity is it then', as de Salo says of the Virgin, 'to have so powerful a friend as she' (p. 41).

Alexis de Salo was a Capucin priest, and he praises the Virgin in 'Platonic' terms, often in words that echo the kind of poetic compliment addressed to the Queen. Mary is described as 'the Mother of beauteous love' (p. 20), who affects her servants with pure love, requiring of them in return chastity, cleanness of mind and purity of heart. She wins followers by love, for 'shee is very sweetnes, meeknes itself, and there is nothing, in earth or heauen more affable, more courteous, then shee' (p. 23). Her beauty streams from her in 'beames and rayes of light', and her eyes are 'two continual fires burning with Divine Love, al who beheld her, and yet in an admirable manner quenching al carnal loue the whilst'

(p. 562). Similar virtues are ascribed to the Queen throughout the masques, and may be summed up in the passage by Davenant from *Salmacida Spolia*:

> All those who can her virtue doubt
> Her mind will in her face advise;
> For through the casements of her eyes
> Her soul is ever looking out.
> And with its beams she does survey
> Our growth in virtue or decay,
> Still lighting us in Honour's way.
> All that are good she did inspire.
> Lovers are chaste, because they know
> It is her will they should be so.
> The valiant take from her their fire.
>
> (ll. 415–25)

The comparison can, of course, work either way, with the language of religion being borrowed to enhance the compliment to the Queen. One meaning did not rule out another, but simply added another level to it.

The Queen's role as mother also connected her with Mary. On her bearing of a son, and winning Charles to her love, the future of the Catholics, and of the Catholic faith in England, depended. This seems to be the implication of a French print by Abraham Bosse, which shows the King and Queen offering their first-born son to the Virgin (figure 10).[40] The Virgin is seated on a throne surrounded by a glory; the French emblem, the fleur-de-lis, covers the baby's robe and the cloak of the Queen, and from the Virgin's mouth comes a scroll with the words 'Pro omnibus floribus elegi mihi lilium'. She speaks as though to Charles, who is represented as saying 'je combats pour la gloire / De vostre Fils et de Vous'. In England great store was set by Henrietta's bearing of a son, and her success as a mother was celebrated in court poetry in almost religious terms. In contrast to Elizabeth, celebrated as 'the Virgin Queen', Henrietta became the Fruitful Queen, from whom stems

> A Golden Harvest of crown'd heads, that meet
> And crowd for kisses from the LAMB's white feet.
>
> (Crashaw, *Poems*, p. 261)

Crashaw revelled in such comparisons. Even before he became Catholic, he hardly distinguishes between poems written for the Queen and poems for the Virgin. A Latin poem 'Ad Reginam' written in 1633 is religious in tone:

> *O salve! Nam te Nato, puer aurëe, natus*
> *Et* Carolo & Mariae *tertius est oculus.*
>
> (*Poems*, p. 187)

A poem to Mary on 'The Assumption' seems more secular in tone, and could be addressed equally well to the Queen:

> *Mary*, men and Angels sing,
> *Maria*, Mother of our King.
> Live rarest Princess, and may the bright

10 Abraham Bosse, French engraving of King Charles and Queen Henrietta Maria presenting their first-born to the Virgin

Crown of an incomparable Light
Embrace thy radiant browes, o may the best
Of everlasting joyes bath thy white brest.

(*Poems*, p. 141)

Francis Quarles wrote in a lighter vein:

Foure Marye's are eterniz'd for their worth;
Our Saviour found out *three*, our *Charles* the fourth.

(*Divine Fancies*, sig. Y3v)

Charles himself was said to prefer for his wife the name of Marie, which he 'rather chose to have her called by than her other, Henrietta, because the land should find a blessing in that name' (Lucy Hutchinson, *Memoirs*, p. 71). It was perhaps because of associations with this aspect of the Queen's religion that statues of the Virgin, broken or defaced after the Reformation (figure 11), began returning to public prominence in the 1630s (figure 12).

The other important attribute of Mary, dwelt on at length by Stafford in *The Female Glory*, was her power to convert others and lead them to follow her. This aspect of the cult seems to take on significance in view of the Catholic literature that was urging pious women to follow Mary's example in leading men, by the attraction of beauty and the practice of virtuous love, to the 'true' love of God. Whether or not the members of the Catholic circle ever put these ideas into practice cannot be known for certain. What is important is that the connection of Neoplatonic ideas with Catholicism may suddenly have placed the Queen's social fashion of 'Platonic love' in a new and, for many, a disturbing light. If court Platonists spoke of the religion of beauty in woman, and of women leading men to love of God, Puritans asked: which religion, and whose God? They could soon discover that Devout Humanists as well as court poets spoke the language of Platonic love, and, under the stimulus of Catholic agents, the proselytising zeal of the Capucins, and the evident attraction of Catholicism to many members of the court, they may have suspected that court ladies were using their beauty or even risking their virtue, to lead men back to the 'old Religion'. Henry Burton's criticism of *The Female Glory* in his sermons *For God, and the King* (the masculine emphasis as opposed to the feminine is implicit in his title), singles out for particular mention Stafford's insistence on Mary's power to convert others, and the way in which she has appeared at court as a new goddess, and a Queen. He quotes in full the epistle 'To the Feminine Reader', which speaks of converting others from 'bad affections, and erroneous opinions' (quoted above). He objects to Stafford 'magnifying the Virgin Mary, as considered, not as a meere woman, but as a type and Idea of an accomplished piety' (sig. Q2v, p. 124), and to his calling her 'a glorious Empresse', and 'Empresse of this lower world' (sig. Q3); he quotes ironically the passage 'Thou deservest a Quire of Queenes here', and comments in the margin 'Lo here the new great Goddesse, Diana, whom the whole Pontifician world worshippeth'. He mentions the chapels and temples

12 Church of St Mary the Virgin, Oxford, with south porch by Nicholas Stone (1637)

11 Ely Cathedral, Lady Chapel with mutilated statue of the Virgin

erected in honour of Mary, and the numbers registered in the Sodality of the Rosary, and concludes

Loe therefore what a metamorphosis of our Religion is here. Here is a new goddesse brought in amongst us. The author glorifieth, that he is the first who hath written (as he saith) in our vulgar tongue, on this our Blessed Virgin. And God grant he be the last.   (sig. Q3v, p. 126)

It seems clear that Puritans recognised the association Catholic writers made between the Queen and Mary. What angered them most was the parallel way in which devotion to the Virgin derogated from the power of God, and devotion to the Queen derogated from the power of Charles, while both strengthened the power of Catholicism. Prynne, who was an assiduous reader of Catholic books, points out how the Queen's role at court parallelled that of the Virgin's role, as represented in Catholic books, in Heaven. He quotes particularly from Pedro de Ribadeneira, *The Lives of the Saints*, in which the Virgin is pictured in courtly terms, dazzling all by her beauty and adored by heavenly courtiers. In this court, Christ is Lord and universal Prince of Justice, while Mary intercedes for Mercy. She is

treasuress, and dispensatrix, and neck of this mystical body, by whose hands are distributed, and through whom, as through a conduit pipe, are derived all the graces and gifts of God.
(Ribadeneira, p. 617)

Ribadeneira describes her seated beside her Son,

aboue all the Quires and Hierarchys of the celestial Spirits, and aboue all the Saints. Then came those diuine Courtiers to do reuence [sic], and to render obedience to her as to their Queen and Lady, admiring at her beauty, her grace and her Sanctity.   (p. 618)

Prynne, in *The Popish Royall Favourite*, identifies Henrietta Maria with the Virgin in Ribadeneira's context, repeating the image of the conduit pipe, and paraphrasing the Catholic text to fit the court situation. The Catholics, he says, had

Queen Mary her selfe in the Kings own bed and bosome for their most powerful *Mediatrix*, of whom they might really affirme in reference to his *Majesty*, what some of their popish Doctors have most blasphemously written of the Virgin *Mary* in relation to *God and Christ*, *That all things are subject to the command of Mary, even God himselfe: That She is the Empresse and Queen of Heaven, and of greatest Authority in the Kingdome of Heaven, where shee may not only impetrate but command whatsoever Shee pleaseth;* ... *That she is the Fountain, Treasurer and Dispenser of all Gods Graces, Favours; the very neck and conduit-pipe through which they are all conveyed: That God hath freely bestowed on her the better halfe of his Kingdome, to wit, all his mercy, reserving only his Justice to himselfe, yet so subject to her restaints [sic]; That if any* (Roman Catholike) *doth finde himselfe aggrieved in the Court of Gods* (or the Kings) *Justice,* (for being prosecuted for his Recusancy or seducing the Kings people) *he may safely appeale to Maries Court of mercy for reliefe, shee being the Throne of Grace, of which the Apostle speakes,* Hebr. 4. 16. *Let us goe boldly unto the Throne of Grace, that wee* (Catholiques) *may recive* (from her) *grace to helpe us in time of need.*   (sig. G4–H, pp. 56–7)

The Queen here plays Mary's role in heaven, and the parallel suggests that Prynne too was aware of the double significance of 'Mary' for Catholics at court. For Puritans, of course, devotion to Mary overturned the most basic tenets of the Reformation, seeming to usurp the supremacy of Christ and to restore idolatry to Church worship. In the parallel influence of the Queen, they saw the danger of the Kingdom being delivered into the hands of Catholic powers through Henrietta as an 'Idol Queen' (as Milton was later to call her in *Eikonoklastes*), under the influence of a new kind of woman-worship at court.

From the side of the court it seems significant that when the Earl of Dorset defended the Queen against the imputations of *Histriomastix* at Prynne's trial, he responded to the implied criticism of the Queen's religion by making her not simply an example of perfection, but an example of *Catholic* perfection. He begins by saying that she 'drinks at the Spring-Head, whilst others take up at the Stream', and that, 'were all such Saints as She, I think the *Roman* Church were not to be condemned'. The language he chooses could be taken from any of the current books on Mary: the Queen sums up all the feminine virtues; she is the redeemer of her sex, the champion of women and friend of men.

Her Heart is full of Honour, Her Soul of Chastity; Majesty, Mildness, and Meekness are so married together, and so impaled in Her, that where the one begetteth Admiration, the other [begetteth] Love.   (Rushworth, *Historical Collections*, II, 240)

This defence suggests that the connection made by Prynne between Catholicism and court arts did not go unnoticed, and that Dorest (although not Catholic himself) was not averse to using the language of Marian devotion in connection with the Queen.

The common element of Platonism in the Queen's love fashions and in her religion thus made it easy for contemporaries to pass from one to the other, and could lend a double significance to works based on its language and imagery. Court masques were the form most deeply indebted to Platonism, and it was in the Queen's masques that, it seems to me, 'Platonic' images of Beauty and Love did on occasion take on additional significance in terms of the Queen's religion.

4   The Queen's masques

Platonic images on the court stage

Of the nine masques presented at court between 1630 and 1640, four were presented by the Queen, four by the King, and the last was a joint masque (see *Table of events* for titles and dates). The Queen's masques, which were once thought to be examples of almost meaningless spectacle, are recognised now as having considerable visual beauty, marking advances by Inigo Jones in stage technique, and contributing, through their symbolism of Platonic Beauty and Love, to the political principles of Charles's rule.[1] However, they have been treated largely as complementing the visual imagery and political significance of the King's masques. I would suggest that the Queen's masques have a distinctive visual character that differentiates them from the King's, and that, while they do complement his, they also have a meaning of their own. In the following discussion I would like to place the Queen's masques in the context of her religion, suggesting ways in which the images of the masques might have been seen through Catholic eyes. When interpreting visual symbols it is, of course, difficult in the absence of written evidence to be certain about what was understood by contemporaries. I have discussed these difficulties in the Introduction, and again it has to be stressed that only in the case of *Luminalia* is there external comment which seems to confirm Catholic significance. My suggestions must remain at the level of inference; yet the parallels between the Queen's masque imagery and Catholic interests seem to make the suggestions worth while.

Since the King and Queen each took part in masques which they themselves presented in the 1630s, we can be fairly certain that they took an interest in planning them. We know from the evidence of the drama that Charles read the texts of plays, and that he was accustomed also to looking over masque designs with Inigo Jones.[2] He certainly used the masques to canvas political issues such as Ship Money, and it has been said that after 1630 the King himself became Jones's chief collaborator.[3] There is no reason to think, however, that the Queen did not have an independent say in organising her own masques, and her personal experience of the stage may have made her an even more active participant than Charles. She had more time to spend on such matters, and, besides the main masques and pastorals which she took part in or supervised at court, there were many less formal occasions when she took charge of the arrangements; in 1632, for instance, we read of her dancing in a masque which she herself had 'arranged and studied' to celebrate the birth of her sister's son, the Prince of Savoy.[4] The contemporary habit of ambassadors' crediting Queens with the authorship of their own productions (as Queen Anne was credited with *The Masque of Beauty* and Henrietta with *Artenice*)[5] presumably would have ensured that these Queens paid attention to the subject matter. Jones was accustomed to working for Henrietta, for example, in designing paintings for her house at Greenwich and building the Capucin chapel at Somerset House. She was a connoisseur of costume and stage design, as her recorded comments (for example on *Coelum Britannicum* and *The Royal Slave*) show, and we know that Jones was obliged to consult her on the design of her costumes for masques.

It is only recently, however, that the full extent of Henrietta's influence on Jones has been recognised. John Peacock's study, 'The French element in Inigo Jones's masque designs' (in *The Court Masque*, ed. David Lindley), demonstrates her influence on stage design, and sees her as 'an exigent mediatrix of her native culture' (p. 155). He traces many designs for the Queen's masques and pastorals to French artists (notably Léonard Thiry and Daniel Rabel) through whom, in Jones's adaptation of them to his own purposes, can be seen 'a new upsurge of French influence, with the Queen as the moving spirit' in Caroline masques (p. 159). Jones of course reworked the borrowings in his own idiom, but the French element in the Queen's entertainments gives them a visual flavour distinct from the King's, which drew predominantly on Italian sources. Peacock interestingly has followed Jones's coming to terms with this French influence (and by inference with the Queen's taste) in the proscenium arches for her three pastorals. In *Artenice* (1626) he comments on Jones's (not altogether successful) attempt at a design in which Peacock sees him trying to capture the '*dévot* quality of the play's ethical and religious atmosphere'. It is, Peacock says, an atmosphere which is recognisably and peculiarly Catholic, 'not with the extroverted Catholicism of baroque Italy but with the spirituality of St François de Sales' (p. 156). In *The Shepherd's Paradise* (1633) Peacock shows (pp. 156–7) that Jones has come to terms with this quality; Jones uses church imagery to match the religious tone of devotions and processions, and modifies the rather severe Doric order of *Artenice* with an 'enriched Doric', a method which he also followed for the Doric order in the screen for the Queen's chapel (compare figures 26, 27, and 28 below). By the time of *Florimène*, which also has a quasi-religious air of devotions and processions, Jones is thoroughly at home in this stage idiom, which carries with it visual overtones of the Queen's religion. If the Queen was able to influence so indomitable an artist as Jones in the direction of her tastes and interests in the pastoral, she was no doubt able to do the same in her masques. I suggest that a religious tone similar to that in the pastorals is present in the Queen's masques, and that Jones creates it in part by the visual images that he chooses to associate with the Queen on the stage.

In masques of the thirties Jones seems to have built up around the King and Queen separate but complementary sets of images that reflected different sides of his own artistic temperament, his love of architecture and of painting. In the King's masques the 'Roman' buildings of *Albion's Triumph*, St Paul's Cathedral in *Britannia Triumphans*, the Piazza in *The Triumph of Peace*, and the vision of a great city in *Salmacida Spolia* all take on, as Orgel and Strong have pointed out (p. 39), the role of Platonic ideas. The classical proportions of Palladian architecture, with increasing emphasis on its adaptation to the English genius, symbolise the order and harmony that Charles is represented as having restored to the realm. In the Queen's masques, however, Jones faced a challenge which he makes explicit in *Tempe Restored*, of finding for the Queen a visual equivalent of the Platonic ideal of Beauty, so that 'corporeal beauty, consisting in symmetry, colour, and certain inexpressable graces shining in the Queen's majesty, may draw us to the contemplation of the beauty of the soul, unto which it hath analogy' (ll. 361–4). Symmetry, colour, graces that shine, all suggest a painter's approach, and, in responding to the aesthetic element in the Queen's Platonic ideal, I believe that Jones explored the painterly qualities of his scenes. He was interested in painting long before be became an architect, and during the thirties he worked with painters like Gentileschi in the Queen's House at Greenwich, and with Rubens in the Banqueting House, to decorate the walls and ceilings of buildings he had designed.[6] His instructions to Jacob Jordaens for panels to be painted for the Queen have been preserved, and they show the care he took for composition and lighting.[7]

These were paintings on a grand scale, and must have influenced the way Jones conceived the main scenes of his masques. During the 1630s he seems to have been thinking as an artist about the grouping of masque figures, consciously making them less stiff and formal (for example, in *Albion's Triumph*, ll. 262–4, and *The Triumph of Peace*, l. 632); in *Salmacida Spolia* he is interested in chiaroscuro effects, when light from above the Queen illuminated her throne so that 'all the ladies about her participated more or less of that light, as they sat near or further off' (ll. 387–8). Many painterly effects were recreated in the culminating spectacles of these masques, which often recall *trompe-l'œil* painting: living figures blended with others that were not real at all, but *feinto*, painted on a backdrop; or *in relievo*, modelled and cut out to look real in the distance, blurring the distinction between painting, sculpture, and actual living figures, in the way admired by contemporary baroque artists.[8] These qualities were enhanced in the thirties by Jones's advances in stage technique, most of which were made in the Queen's masques. In *Chloridia* he used a fly-gallery for the first time, making possible the extensive aerial motions which became increasingly complex in succeeding masques.[9] In *Tempe Restored* he produced a spectacle of outstanding brilliance for the Queen's appearance as Divine Beauty, a spectacle that, as Jones tells us in his description, 'was for the difficulty of the engining and number of the persons the greatest that hath been seen here in our time' (ll. 204–6). *Luminalia* ends with a daring aerial ballet which Jones again comments on, saying that this apparition 'for the newness of the invention, greatness of the machine, and the difficulty of the engining was much admired, being a thing not before attempted in the air' (ll. 409–11). This greater technical freedom gives the scenes a fluidity of line that allowed Jones to experiment with the qualities of colour, composition, and light, qualities which he associates especially with the Queen. Indeed, in order to express the 'inexpressable', he seems to have turned to a style of baroque painting made particularly popular at court from about 1630 by the painting of Rubens.

Rubens and Jones were near contemporaries, both had spent their formative years in Italy, and both admired the great Venetian painters. During his visit to the court (from June 1629 to March 1630) Rubens discussed with Jones and the King plans for the panels in the Banqueting House, and it has been suggested that Jones himself supplied the 'programme' for the ceiling.[10] Jones's arrangement of the panels was similar to that of churches in Venice, and the central panel of James's *Apotheosis* (figure 13) derived from Veronese's *Coronation of the Virgin* in the Sacristy of San Sebastiano, a painting which Rubens had already adapted for his own *Coronation of the Virgin* in the ceiling of the Jesuit church at Antwerp (completed 1620).[11] Rubens's paintings with their flamboyant colours recreated in the Banqueting House something of the atmosphere of Renaissance and Baroque churches, bringing a style of painting associated with Catholic religious art into the heart of the English court. Jones could hardly have remained unimpressed by Rubens's style in these paintings: he certainly showed his admiration for them by copying their details for the border of his scene in *Salmacida Spolia*,[12] thus recalling to the audience the allegory of the ceiling and implying that, like Rubens's painting, his border consists 'of picture qualified with moral philosophy' (l. 67), so tempering delight with profit. Jones may, I believe, have borrowed from Rubens even before the panels were fixed in place in 1635. In *Tempe Restored* (1632) the final spectacle consists of 'a new heaven ... in the midst of which, Jove, sitting on an eagle, is seen hovering in the air with a glory behind him' (ll. 260–2) (figure 14). The scene has a general likeness to scenes in Italian entertainments and no doubt Jones took the idea from them, but it may also have held a topical allusion to a preliminary painting by Rubens for the central panel of the Banqueting House, showing James seated on an eagle (figure 15). The masque scene, in performance, would have been similar to the sketch, when 'Cupid from another part of the heaven comes flying forth, and having passed the scene, turns soaring about like a bird', like the figures in Rubens's painting, while Pallas and other figures, with the 'great chorus', stand below (ll. 263–7). Such a conflation of sources would have appealed to the audience, pleased the King by alluding to James (as Jove), and reminded everyone of the paintings that were soon to make a 'new heaven' of the ceiling overhead in the Banqueting House, where the masque was being performed.

Rubens made several allegorical paintings during his visit, including one of the King and Queen (figure 41 below), and several showing the 'Apotheosis' of the Duke of Buckingham in a baroque style that was obviously attractive to the court. His treatment of his subjects, whom he presents as ideal yet sensuously

13 Sir Peter Paul Rubens, *Apotheosis of James I*, central panel in ceiling of Banqueting House, Whitehall

15 Sir Peter Paul Rubens, oil sketch for Banqueting House panel of James on an eagle (1629–30); reproduced by courtesy of the Trustees of the Glynde Endowment Settlement, and the Trustees of the National Gallery, London

14 Inigo Jones, Jove on an eagle with a glory behind him in *Tempe Restored*

beautiful, mythological yet paradoxically real, was similar to the treatment of the King and Queen in masque, and the qualities of his painting, full of rich colour, luminosity, and a sense of space and movement, must all have made a deep impression on Jones in the thirties. The qualities of Rubens's painting seem indeed to become particularly important in the images of beauty and light which Jones associated with the Queen, and which complemented the images of reason, order, and proportion associated with the King. *Tempe Restored* was the masque in which Jones speaks of his scenes as being 'nothing else but pictures with light and motion' (ll. 49–50). The phrase may have been put in as a wry comment on the criticism of people like Ben Jonson, but there is enough truth in it to make it an apt description of masques such as *Tempe Restored* and *Luminalia*. The main scene of *Tempe Restored* is remarkable for both these qualities. It opens with eight musicians, representing the spheres, seated on a cloud. To the music of these spheres two other clouds containing eight stars descend to the middle region of the sky, and another greater cloud, containing six stars, descends from above them; above all, in a chariot richly adorned with precious gems, sits Divine Beauty (the Queen) 'over whose head appeared a brightness full of stars . . . striking a light round about it' (see ll. 186–97). The scene is accompanied by a wealth of music and singing, but, not surprisingly, the words of the songs all direct the attention back to the sight. The verse explicitly renounces its claim to attention: 'I cannot blame ye if ye gaze, / And give small ear to what I say', sings the Highest Sphere (ll. 226–7), and 'How are we ravished with delight / That see the best!' sings the Chorus (ll. 256–7). The verse compliment to the Queen becomes, indeed, a compliment to Jones's art:

> The music that ye hear is dull,
> But that ye see is sweet indeed,
> In every part exact and full,
> From whence there doth an air proceed,
> On which th'intelligences feed,
> Where fair and good, inseparably conjoined,
> Create a Cupid that is never blind.   (ll. 230–6)

The Platonic mingling of beauty, goodness, and love in the Queen is indistinguishable from those qualities in the image of Divine Beauty which Jones has created for her on the stage.

In *Luminalia* Jones concentrated on the symbolic properties of light. He had, of course, from the beginning of his career, been interested in light, and he used hundreds of torches and lights to illuminate his scenes;[13] in *Luminalia*, however, the whole 'invention' was based on it (l. 13). The opening scene (figure 16) shows:

a scene all of darkness, the nearer part woody, and further off more open, with a calm river, that took the shadows of the trees by the light of the moon, that appeared shining in the river, there being no more light to lighten the whole scene than served to distinguish the several grounds that seemed to run far in from the eye.   (ll. 57–62)

16 Inigo Jones, night scene for opening of *Luminalia*

17 Inigo Jones, clouds for transformation scene, *Luminalia*

The action of the masque proceeds, through scenes of night and sleep, to dawn, and the promise of a new light in which 'intellectual and corporeal brightness are joined' (l. 256). This was, of course, the Queen, and she appears resplendent with light: 'behind all was a bright sky, and in the midst, about the Queen's majesty's seat, was a glory with rays, expressing her to be the queen of brightness' (ll. 255–7). The gradual lightening of the stage is a superb theatrical effect, but (as will be shown later) also an essential part of the masque's meaning. In the concluding spectacle Jones goes on to create an image of 'lightness' in terms of movement: a heavenly vision in which 'a bright and transparent cloud came forth far into the scene', upon which many *zephyri* began a sprightly dance (ll. 403–7). This airy vision joins with the images of light to suggest that in this masque corporeal beauty had indeed achieved a transcendent form.

Jones's images for the Queen, depending on 'light and motion', were harder to represent as drawings than were his architectural images for the King, which depended on line and proportion. A series of sketches for *Luminalia* and for the discovery of the Queen in *Salmacida Spolia* does, however, give some impression of the qualities which Jones was trying to reproduce on the stage. The scene for the opening of *Luminalia* (see figure 16) was based on detail of a painting after Adam Elsheimer, and is the most 'painterly' of Jones's masque designs.[14] Elsheimer's effects of light and shadow were admired by Rubens, who has a painting *The Carters* (in The Hermitage, Leningrad) which shows a similar detail of the moon reflected in water. Another sketch for the 'new and strange prospect of chimeras' in the masque (ll. 170–1) (figure 17) is based on cloud effects in Parigi's Intermedium for *The Return of Astraea* (O&S, figure 115), which shows the general effect that Jones intended. Two other sketches for the final scene, the 'heaven full of deities ... with instruments and voices' (ll. 386–8) in detail (figure 18), and in the whole scene (figure 19), show how Jones imagined it on the stage. The dance of the '*zephyri* and gentle breasts' in the upper part of the heaven was suggested to Jones by the figures in another scene from Parigi, *The Temple of Peace* (see O&S, figure 70). These 'heavenly' scenes in connection with the Queen are continued in Jones's sketches for *Salmacida Spolia*. The 'huge cloud of various colours' (l. 381) is shown (O&S, no. 407), and then the vision which it opened to reveal (figure 20). In a 'transparent brightness of thin exhalations, such as the gods are feigned to descend in' (ll. 383–4) sat the Queen, over whose head darted 'lightsome rays that illuminated her seat' (ll. 386–7). Jones's sketch for this scene attempts to suggest some of the airiness and luminosity of the stage vision, which he calls 'this brightness' (l. 388), and which descended to the stage 'with many streaks of thin vapours about it, such as are seen in a fair evening sky'. In these scenes for the Queen, Jones plays on the imagination and the emotions, demonstrating the power of Beauty to appeal through the eye to the soul, and creating for the Queen a Platonic image of great visual force.

The two sets of images for the King and Queen, although they seem confused in the written version of the masques, would have been quite distinct visually

18 Inigo Jones, a heaven full of deities, *Luminalia*

on the stage. In the King's masques, the discovery of the masquers is associated with images of civic order, or with the rugged 'earthy' aspects of nature: the 'stately temple' in *Albion's Triumph*, a cave in the Mountain of the Three Kingdoms in *Coelum Britannicum*, the Palace of Fame in *Britannia Triumphans*, and the throne in *Salmacida Spolia*, which is placed in a setting of 'craggy rocks and inaccessible mountains' representing 'the difficult way which heroes are to pass ere they come to the Throne of Honour' (ll. 292–300, 345). In the Queen's masques the discovery is associated with pleasant aspects of nature or with 'heavenly' scenes: the fragrant bower in *Chloridia*, the heavenly chariot in *Tempe Restored*, a richly adorned maritime chariot in *The Temple of Love*, a garden set against a 'bright sky' in *Luminalia*, and a luminescent cloud in *Salmacida Spolia*. The King always makes his entry from the ground, while the Queen on two occasions makes her appearance from the 'heavens'. These paired sets of images were appropriate representations of the 'masculine' and 'feminine' principles symbolised by the King and Queen in the masques: of military courage and chaste love (*Albion's Triumph*), of Heroick Virtue and Divine Beauty (*Tempe Restored*), of Understanding and Will (*Temple of Love*), of Reason and Intellectual Light (*Salmacida Spolia*). Jones's complementary sets of stage images reinforced visually the basic dualities of Neoplatonism, of masculine and feminine, body and spirit, earth and heaven. The uniting of these complementary qualities at the end of each masque represented an ideal unity, which was reinforced by the harmonious union of the King and Queen.

19 Inigo Jones, a sketch for the whole scene, *Luminalia*

'Spiritual' painting

Jones's two sets of images, however, were appropriate not only to the Neoplatonic roles of the King and Queen in the masques but also to their roles as representatives of their respective religions. Jones's creation of 'Roman' images for the King (for example in *Albion's Triumph*), with increasing emphasis in later masques on images of modern Britain, harmonised with the Imperial tradition of which England was supposedly the inheritor. These images had strong political implications, as modern critics have shown.[15] They also had religious significance, and there can be little doubt that the masques were intended to show Charles

20 Inigo Jones, the great cloud in which the Queen descended, *Salmacida Spolia*

in his role as Head of Church as well as State. The 'Roman' and 'British' themes closely reflected the twin ideals of Roman Imperialism and early British Christianity to which the Doctrine of Divine Right appealed for authority. The allegorical figure of 'Religion' herself appears in the concluding spectacle of two of the King's masques: in *Albion's Triumph* her companions are Peace, Justice, and Concord; in *Coelum Britannicum*, Truth, Wisdom, and Good Government. These qualities are associated with the King, and certainly represented for Charles the virtues that grew out of the *via media* of the Anglican Church. At the end of *Coelum Britannicum* Charles is shown in his role as Head of the Church when he is represented as the brightest star in the crown of Eternity, and Eternity herself is enthroned over Windsor Castle, which was for Charles a chief centre of Anglican ceremony. Jones's architectural images, moreover, drawn from classical tradition and modern British practice, themselves translated into visible form the qualities of Reason, Proportion, and Harmony which Charles, following Anglican theologians, regarded as the fundamental principles of Reformed religion. They showed the best of ancient traditions reinvigorated by new moral values, and the rebuilding (symbolised in the picture of St Paul's in *Britannia Triumphans*) of a renewed and purified British Church.

The contrasting stage images for the Queen were equally appropriate in visual terms to her religion. 'Heavenly' images of beauty and love were familiar in art of the Counter-Reformation, and stage 'pictures with light and motion' were accepted as part of the religious fervour and artistic enthusiasm in which autocratic courts on the Continent were closely allied with the Catholic Church. Such art drew for its inspiration on the element of Neoplatonism in Renaissance culture, in which the visible world was an image of the divine, an element which was present not only in the Queen's cult of Platonic love, but also in the cult of the Virgin with which she was associated at court. The Marian cult was accompanied, moreover, by a strong visual tradition in which the images of Beauty and Love associated with Mary blended easily with the same images in the Queen's Platonic cult. The tradition derived from an identification of Mary with the Bride in the Song of Solomon, from which came her attributes of beauty: 'Thou art all fair ... and no spot is in thee' (4:7); of purity: 'a garden enclosed, a spring shut up, a fountain sealed' (4:12); and her exaltation: 'fair as the moon, clear as the sun, and terrible as an army with banners' (4:10). She was identified also with the figure pictured by St John of the Apocalypse as 'a woman clothed with the sun, and the moon under her feet, and upon her head a crown of twelve stars' (Revelation 12:1; compare the frontispiece of *Partheneia Sacra*, figure 9). These images were translated into visual form in the Middle Ages, when they appeared in church windows, tapestries, emblem books, and paintings, and were passed down almost unchanged to the seventeenth century.[16] They could be arranged statically, or take their place in a small scene where they were placed within the garden against the background of the heavens, as in the illustration to *Partheneia Sacra* (figure 24 below), or in the sixteenth-century print from the Breviary of Cardinal Grimani (figure 21). In these scenes the moon, sun and stars, fountain and flowers, ship, temple, tower, and rocky mount all have spiritual significance. They were emblematic of the many names (*stella maris, hortus conclusus, porta coeli*, etc.) under which Mary was hailed in the Litanies, and they were gathered, with many more, in the sixteenth-century Litany of Loreto (the form that has survived today). Their significance must have been familiar to those at court who belonged to the Arch-Confraternity of the Rosary, and who joined each week in singing the Litanies with the Queen.

In masques of the thirties the main scenes in which the Queen appeared on the stage were settings that in visual terms were also appropriate as emblematic settings for the Virgin: in *Chloridia*, *Tempe Restored*, and *Luminalia* she is associated with gardens, fountains, and flowers; in *The Temple of Love* with shell, ship, and haven; in *Tempe Restored* and *Luminalia* with light, moon, and stars. These settings were not, of course, specially created for Henrietta. They were in fact part of the established stage imagery (itself partly derived from associations with the Virgin in religious drama) for presenting feminine beauty and virtue. Female masquers regularly appeared in some variant of a bower, ship, or shell, or enthroned in heaven, and every one of the masque settings in the 1630s had been used in masques written by Ben Jonson in the previous reign. In *The Masque of Blackness*, for instance, Queen Anne had appeared in a concave shell with lights atop (ll. 51–5), or in *Tethys' Festival* in an aquatic throne, with a 'great scallop of silver' (ll. 185–6) decorated with jewels above her head. In *Hymenaei*,

21 Illuminated scene from the *Grimani Breviary* (*c.* 1520), showing the Virgin's emblems
in an allegorical setting

the scene of Juno enthroned in a cloudy heaven, attired like a Queen, above her the region of fire and below her the rainbow, sided by ladies dressed in celestial colours (ll. 200–11), sounds quite as magnificent (and as potentially symbolic of religion) as the scene for Divine Beauty in *Tempe Restored*. Many of Jonson's descriptions of scenes rival Jones's later descriptions for splendour; however, Jonson's are always much more sharp-edged in their symbolism. The masquers appear in shells because the sea is part of the masque's setting; the gods in *Hymenaei* are firmly related by their attributes to classical antecedents, and Jonson's masque world is divided, not into a vague heaven and earth, but into the elemental regions of water, earth, air, and fire. In these early masques, moreover, it is doubtful whether Jones's scenes had achieved the technical perfection which later gives them an air of almost mystical splendour. In *Tethys' Festival*, for instance, the 'heavens' open at the same time that the masquers are discovered in their cavern, but the 'three circles of lights and glasses' (ll. 165–70) that move about in the heavens are there to distract attention from the change of scene rather than as an integral part of the symbolism. In *The Masque of Blackness* the appearance of the Moon enthroned in the upper part of the stage, dressed in white and silver and crowned with a sphere of light (ll. 193–200), does not have the same imaginative appeal as the impressionistic scene (itself based on a religious painting) with which *Luminalia* opens; here the moon suffuses the whole masque with light which gradually gathers to a point with the appearance of the Queen. It may, however, have been no accident that this kind of imagery dominated the early masques of the century, at a time when Jonson and Jones, both born Catholic, were working for Queen Anne, who was secretly Catholic herself;[17] that it drops out of the masques in the period when James and Buckingham dictated the taste of the masques (from about 1610–18); and that it reappears after 1630 in masques for Henrietta, this time in association with an overtly Catholic Queen.

The very universality of this imagery meant that it could be interpreted on a number of different levels. For part of the audience it was no doubt simply a continuation of the Christian Neoplatonism made familiar by Jonson. For another part, however, it could take on the additional interest of an association with the Queen's religion. For the Queen and for Catholics of her circle there was, indeed, considerable inducement to find religious significance in visual imagery. The recommendation to do so was a commonplace of Counter-Reformation teaching; Catholic writers were eager to point out how pictures, images, external objects, or even the circumstances of daily life, should be turned to spiritual reflection. The practice had been widely disseminated throughout Europe by the spread of Jesuit methods of meditation, and it was adopted with gentler emphasis by Orders like the Capucins, who translated spiritual truths into graceful or witty conceits.[18] One of the most popular products of this teaching in the seventeenth century was the religious emblem, which had systematically turned the images of profane love to images of sacred love, often with very little change in the visual content of the emblem.[19]

Henrietta herself had grown up in a court where the interpretation of 'picture' in terms of religion was actively encouraged. The most influential emblematist at the French court was Louis Richeome, who had dedicated his *Peinture spirituelle* (1611) to Marie de Medici. He was concerned with the education of Henrietta's brother, Louis XIII, for whom he designed the *Catechisme royal* (1607), a book of pictures, emblems and devices that were to be given a spiritual interpretation.[20] Henrietta could hardly have escaped something of the same kind of education. Some of Richeome's books were translated into English and may have helped bring similar habits of religious interpretation to the English court. In *Holy Pictures of the Mysticall Figures . . . of the Eucharist* (1619), translated into English by C.A. 'for the benefit of those of that Nation, as well Protestants as Catholikes', Richeome points out that it is the spirit brought to the viewing of pictures or images that determines whether their significance is sacred or not (sig. B2), and that everywhere 'God teacheth vs celestiall things by terrestriall, and spirituall, by those that are corporall' (sig. C4v). Another work, translated by C.A. in 1618, *The Interiour Occupation of the Soule* by Pierre Coton (A&R no. 263), shows how every external object or circumstance of daily life may be turned to spiritual reflection. There are, for instance, sections entitled 'In seeing the magnificency of the Court' (no. 32), 'When we admire the beauty of any building' (no. 37), 'In putting on Jewels, and other ornaments' (no. 40), 'When you use your Fanne' (no. 43), all of which are turned to meditation on God or his Saints. In the Preface the translator recommends this practice as a method acceptable even to Protestants, who may regard it simply as a way of apostrophe, 'For in such figurative senses, the most learned Doctors of thine owne religion, do understand those innumerable prayers to Saincts, which every where they reade in the Holy Fathers', and he illustrates with prayers made to the Blessed Virgin (sigs. *5v–*6v).

The Counter-Reformation, in addition, placed great emphasis on the Joyful Mysteries of the Virgin, of which her Assumption and Coronation were favourite themes for description and painting. Contemporary books of devotion to Mary recommended that the reader should behold in the imagination this celestial Queen 'most beautifully adorned with all perfections both of mind and body, all the blessed inhabitants of Heauen attending her, & reioycing at the increase of her glory' (Sabine Chambers, *The Garden of our B. Lady*, sig. 14v). Alexis de Salo advised that in praying to her it is desirable to 'represent her to the eies of thy mind, Inthroned in a most glorious manner aboue al the rest . . . encompassed round about with innumerable Saints and Angels' (*An Admirable Manner*, p. 417). These were the visions that had been captured by Renaissance painters, and writers urged Mary's devotees to 'procure som Picture both deuout and faire, before which we are to do our reuerences . . . I say faire, for faire obiects do soonest stirr vp the affections of the mind' (de Salo, p. 435). Such paintings were in fact available, and they became quite familiar at court after the great influx of art during the 1620s and 1630s. A glance at Abraham Van der Doort's 'Catalogue of the Collections of Charles I'[21] shows that amongst the paintings on biblical subjects there were, in particular, a great number by Titian and Tintoretto on the Virgin and Christ. Tintoretto's 'our lady & Christ in the Clouds a half moone below. placed for the present tyme in the Cabbienett rom at St James' (p. 182), for instance, took its place among many others on similar subjects in the King's collection. Amongst the Titians in the Queen's Palace at Somerset House were 'our Lady, Christ and St Catherine'; in the Queen's bedchamber a 'madonna with Christ and St John'; in the Queen's withdrawing room 'de gret ourladi' (pp. 183–4). In her collection at Nonesuch was an 'our Lady with Christ and St John', and an 'our Lady in the Clouds, below sepulchre of flowers and disciples kneeling' (p. 186). In the Queen's apartments these subjects tended to be interspersed with paintings of Venus, Cupid, and Psyche, in the King's apartments with paintings on 'classical' subjects, echoing the characteristic images associated with the King and Queen. For art lovers, of course, these paintings were expressions of Renaissance artistic talent, but for those who had Catholic interests they also had unavoidable associations with religion. At Nonesuch House, for instance, the placing of 'an Aulter peece conteyning 4 entire figures almost soe big as the life of our Lady and another St kneeling . . . in the Queenes Chappell roome' (p. 185) could hardly have been accidental.

That the Queen liked to find religious significance in 'picture' is suggested by an incident recounted in Panzani's *Memoirs* (ed. Berington, p. 251) concerning the reception of paintings sent by Cardinal Barberini to the Queen in 1635. It contained 'several excellent pieces of painting of the best hands of the present and last century'; when the present arrived, the King and Inigo Jones were delighted with the rich gifts. The paintings represented various stories, but the Queen 'finding that none of them had any relation to devotion, seemed a little displeased'. Cardinal Barberini had to send special explanations of their religious significance through his next agent, George Conn, whose persuasive talking to the Queen 'satisfied her curiosity that way.' In this we may glimpse a habit of mind important in interpreting the arts, especially those in which the visual sense was involved: the pleasure in mysteries and puzzle-solving that was strong in the seventeenth-century sense of religion. This interest had been institutionalised by the Jesuits, who taught it in their Colleges by producing painted 'enigmas', biblical or mythological scenes from which a hidden meaning was to be uncovered.[22] The enigma, which had to contain human figures, was not unlike a static masque scene, and it became a regular feature of religious and public festive occasions. Its meaning might not at first be obvious. The most valued conceit was one which fulfilled the requisites of wit by having propriety, novelty, ingenious allusion, and which required admirable reflection; indeed it was the more greatly valued if its full meaning was not discernible to all, but was revealed to the initiated and the witty.

I suggest that something of this spirit was brought by a section of the audience to viewing the main scenes of the Queen's masques, which show her in settings appropriate to emblematic settings for the Virgin and thus emphasise the Queen's connection with the cult. The Queen's first masque, *Chloridia* (1631), may contain no more than a hint of such allusion, but it set up a pattern in which it was easy to pass from images of love to images of religion. In keeping with the Ovidian myth on which it is based (ll. 7–8) *Chloridia* is a masque about natural beauty and fertility, 'purified' by moral and spiritual aspiration. On one level Henrietta represents Chloris, the nymph who transforms the earth to the beauties of the Spring. This theme is in harmony with the Queen's youth: she is the young bride and lover,

> The sweetness of all showers,
> The ornament of bowers,
> The top of paramours.   (ll. 270–3)

She is also a mother, who not long before had produced a healthy male heir to the throne. But love, which is at the centre of such fertility, fancies a slight, and Cupid has gone to Hell, bringing back Jealousy, Disdain, Fear, and Dissimulation to trouble the gods (l. 135). These figures appear in the anti-masques, but are dispersed by the appearance of Chloris in her bower, which in turn gives place to the throne of Juno, Queen of Heaven, love, and marriage, and her messenger Iris. On this level, the masque is a delicate compliment from the Queen to the King on their reconciliation after the early years of marriage, which were disturbed by Jealousy and Disdain, and on their present love and fruitful union. Jonson, in keeping with his Ovidian myth, gives these events a cosmic setting. Chloris is a nymph of earth, associated with Spring in the rites of fertility and regeneration. The masque opens with a reference to the fructifying powers of the sun and the generative powers of water, drawing from the earth new beauty and new birth. Thus the lovely bower in which Chloris appears enthroned is also a bower of love, reminiscent of the many other bowers and gardens over which Venus presides.

The masque naturally superimposes a moral interpretation on the pagan myth. Venus teaches her mischievous son to leave his evil companions, Juno sanctifies love by marriage, and Jove sanctifies the 'flowers' of natural union by giving heavenly approval, turning them into stars on earth. The theme, that the powers of natural beauty and love have to be guided by Heaven, is echoed in the symbolism of the scenes. The scene of nature with which the masque opens, of pleasant hills planted with young trees, of banks adorned with flowers, and fountains which flow into a river (ll. 17–20), is changed, with the appearance of the masquers, into a civilised garden, 'a delicious place figuring the bower of Chloris' (ll. 163–4). Chloris sits enthroned in an arbour 'feigned of goldsmiths' work,' ornamented with garlands and fragrant flowers, while 'beyond all this in the sky afar off appeared a rainbow' (ll. 164–7). The Queen, the bower, and the rainbow make the connection between heaven and earth, for, after the Queen has danced and impressed the earth with flowers, the heavens open to reveal Juno and Iris 'and above them many airy spirits, sitting in the clouds' (l. 210). Thus the bower of Chloris is more than a bower of natural beauty and love: it is natural beauty civilised by art, a garden of love, but of love transformed by spiritual grace.

Chloridia is based on the same passage in Ovid as Botticelli's *Primavera*, which itself was based on a Neoplatonic programme.[23] The painting belonged to Medici circles from the early sixteenth century (Gombrich, 'Botticelli's mythologies', pp. 14–15) and it haunted the Renaissance imagination. Its presence has been suggested behind Milton's pastoral vision,[24] and Jones's costume for Chloris (figure 22) bears a resemblance to that of Flora in the painting. Both masque and painting may have a generally similar meaning. In the Neoplatonic allegory of the painting, as Edgar Wind points out (*Pagan Mysteries of the Renaissance*, p. 119), the central figure of Venus is a goddess of moderation and harmony; her companions are the Graces, whose movement towards the upward-pointing figure of Mercury leads out of the picture and back to the upper world, completing the connection between heaven and earth, and the movement of love and generation with which the painting began. But Venus here belongs iconologically with figures of the Virgin: her tilted head and raised hand are similar to poses of the Virgin in other paintings; her place in this garden of love is reminiscent of her place in sacred gardens, and behind her head the branches form a circle which frame her figure in an aureole of light. Her presence in a setting of natural beauty, love, and fertility makes of the garden a Paradise, but a Paradise in which pagan nature is transformed to Christian spirituality, and in which beauty is designed to awaken a feeling akin to religious enthusiasm. *Chloridia* has a similar upward movement, beginning in natural love and ending with the scene of the gods in heaven. The Virgin/Venus in the painting and the Queen in the masque are each the pivot on which this movement turns.

The transformation of passion to love was, of course, an ancient theme, and its representation in the symbolism of the garden was deeply embedded both in classical and Christian literature.[25] In classical literature the garden was associated with Venus, both as a lovely place, and a place for love. Its prototype, which summed up much ancient garden poetry, was described by Claudian (in the fourth century AD) as a place in Cyprus where Venus lived, where the mountain sloped down to a lovely plain, always bright with flowers, and where the country round was enclosed with a hedge of gold. But this garden also became Mary's garden. The elements of the walled garden and Venus' bower were syncretised by Christianity with the imagery of the Song of Solomon, and the verse 'A garden inclosed is my sister, my spouse; a spring shut up, a fountain sealed' (4.12) was indefinitely allegorised in relation to God and the Church, to the Virgin Mary, and to Divine Love. The enclosed garden or bower became not only one of Mary's attributes, but an actual place in which she is seen, as in paintings of the Annunciation. For the Middle Ages the garden helped to bring Mary closer to human experience, and her gardens were often imagined as actual places, 'not so different iconologically from the haunts of more earthly goddesses like Ceres and Flora' (Comito, *The Idea of the Garden*, p. 13). The associations between

This designe I conceaue to bee fit for the invention onlif it please hir ma.
to add or alter any thing I desir to receaue hir ma. comand and tho.
designe againe by this bearer.   The collors allso are in hir ma.
choise; but my opinion is that seuerall sorts of greenes mixt with gould and
siluer will be most propper./

22 Inigo Jones, the Queen as Chloris goddess of flowers in *Chloridia*

Venus and the Virgin, between profane and sacred love, became a continuing theme in literature and art, and by the seventeenth century the garden, and its association with love, was being reappropriated for religion by the Counter-Reformation cult of the Virgin. Louis Richeome's *Holy Pictures*, for instance, begins with a description of the 'first garden', with its plains and little hills, its fountains forming rivers, where trees and plants, flowers and fresh colours make the air sweet with predominant Spring (sig. C3), not very different from the description of the garden in the opening of *Chloridia*. Hawkins's *Partheneia Sacra* was only the latest of many books based on the idea of the 'mysterious and delicious garden' in which Mary is imagined as a 'Paradise of flowers' or 'celestiall earth all starred with flowers' (p. 9), and in which all the objects of nature become starting points for meditations in her honour.

Tempe Restored (1632) begins in a sense where *Chloridia* left off. Again, the masque opens with the scene of a garden, in which the Naiades and Dryads, the good powers of nature, are the companions of Circe, as before they were of Chloris. But Circe represents natural beauty and desire unredeemed by reason and beauty of soul; her garden is a place of danger because it also contains sensual desire, which makes men lose their virtue and valour, turning them to beasts (ll. 336–8). To live by nature and the attraction of beauty is not enough: reason must govern sense, and desire be attracted by a vision of spiritual beauty, so that man becomes 'only a mind using the body and affections as instruments' (ll. 352–3). Divine Beauty is not detached from bodily beauty, however, but shines through it, drawing us 'to the contemplation of the beauty of the soul, unto which it hath analogy' (ll. 363–4). *Tempe Restored* borrowed the 'allegory' of the story from the *Balet comique de la reine*, which will be discussed later. In performance, however, the story was probably less important than the broader visual symbolism of the two great forces, Circe and Divine Beauty, who opposed each other at the beginning and the end of the masque. The myth of Circe was a common symbol for the false attraction of the beauty and pleasures of this world as opposed to the true beauty and harmony of the ideal world, and in religious literature the image of the passions as wild beasts was often opposed to the image of Divine Love, which redeems man from his merely 'natural' state. In a contemporary book like *The Devout Hart* (translated by Henry Hawkins from the French emblem book *Le Coeur dévot*), for instance, the author likens the heart to 'a sty for Swine' filled with pernicious beasts and vices (p. 68). The heart, which vehemently desires beauty and can be led astray with what is false, can be restored to true knowledge only by the aid of Divine Love. After the heart is set in order by Jesus it is compared to a flourishing garden, and the author invokes Mary: 'of whom I will craue the meanes first to keep chastity, and then earnestly beg her help and patronage, to vanquish easily all the temptations of the flesh' (*The Colloquy*, sig. H1ᵛ, p. 170). Mary was traditionally thought of in this context as the anti-type of Eve. As Eve was our first and 'natural' mother, so Mary was 'our second *Eve*, our spiritual and celestial Mother'

(*Partheneia Sacra*, p. 68), and her garden became 'the second Adam's Paradise.'[26] In *Partheneia Sacra* (p. 6) Hawkins described the garden of Mary in terms not very different from those used for the garden of Circe in *Tempe Restored*: 'It is a Paradice of pleasures, whose open walks are Tarrases, the Close, the Galleries, the Arbours, the Pavillions, the flowerie Bancks, the easie and soft couches'. The different attitude to these attractions lies simply in the purity of heart of those who follow Mary. According to Anthony Stafford she is the support of virtue and the redeemer of her sex, a 'terrestrial Paradice, whereunto serpent never entered' (*The Female Glory*, sig. R3). There was thus in Catholic literature an implicit contrast between gardens of worldly pleasure and Mary's garden, between the sensual allurements of a Circe or an Eve, and Mary as an ideal of heavenly beauty and love. In *Tempe Restored* a similar contrast between the false beauty of Circe and the 'Divine Beauty' of the Queen may have been suggested through the visual imagery accompanying the Queen.

23 Inigo Jones, the Queen as Divine Beauty in *Tempe Restored*

After the opening scene and the brutish gambolling of the anti-masques, Circe's palace is swept away by the wealth of music that announces and accompanies the appearance of Divine Beauty (figure 23). The scene in which the Queen appears this time transcends the garden: she is enthroned in the heavens themselves, against the background of a fair sky and a calm sea, environed with stars and accompanied by the music of the spheres. Only the background for this scene is shown in Jones's designs (figure 24), but it has features in common with the buildings, tower and rocky mount, ships and haven which are shown, in figures 21 and 25, and all of which had symbolic significance in emblematic settings

25 Illustration of 'The Garden' showing the Virgin's emblems, from Henry Hawkins, *Partheneia Sacra* (1633)

24 Inigo Jones, a haven with a citadel in *Tempe Restored*

for the Virgin.[27] Against this background must be imagined the scene for the appearance of Divine Beauty. Like the scene from *Partheneia Sacra* with its striking chain of stars, the masque describes how, against a 'calm sea' and a sky 'such as appears at the sun rising' (ll. 182–5), the spheres are suspended in the air on a cloud 'which in a circular form was on each side continued unto the highest part of the heaven, and seemed to have let them down as in a chain' (ll. 186–9). Other clouds bearing stars take their place to either side and in the centre of the heavens, framing the figure of the Queen, over whose head was 'a brightness full of small stars that environed the top of the chariot, striking a light about it' (ll. 195–7). The whole scene is filled with reference to stars. The Queen is dressed in 'a garment of watchet [pale blue] satin with stars of silver embroidered and embossed from the ground, and on her head a crown of stars' (ll. 212–15) (see figure 23). Her companions are stars, and she herself is 'the brightest star / That shines in heaven', for whom it is fitting that

> the heavenly spheres
> Should be her music, and the starry troupe
> Shine round about her like the crown she wears.   (ll. 219–21)

In *Partheneia Sacra*, Hawkins explains in relation to Mary that the stars that surround her are her court, 'among whom, as a choice *Hester*', she shines for the King of Heaven 'to cast his most amorous glances and fayrest influence upon' (p. 119). So is she styled also *Venus*, 'not as the Goddesse of Love, which the Poets feigne, but for that she disposes them to love, whom she swayes, and exercises her vertues on', and 'enflames mens harts with Divine love' (p. 120). Through her steadfastness and brightness, 'Marie our Starre ... directs the Marriners through the vast sea of the world ... to the Haven of the Heavenlie countrie' (p. 122). The latter was a traditional image and is echoed in *The Temple of Love* when the Queen, arriving in a maritime chariot seated beneath a 'great scallop shell' is hailed as

> More welcome than the wand'ring seaman's star
> When in the night the winds make causeless war.   (ll. 428–9)

Such imagery, appropriate both to the cult of Mary and to the cult of love, suggests that the Queen's masques (like her pastorals) reflected her religious tastes. *Chloridia* and *Tempe Restored* may have given no more than a suggestion of Catholic interests, but two later masques, *The Temple of Love* and *Luminalia*, seem to allude in a much more specific way to Catholic affairs at court.

Temple of Love, Festival of Light

Masques were intended for public show as well as for private pleasure, and the Queen may well have wished to impress on visitors from abroad the efforts she was making on behalf of her religion. Ambassadors took note of such signs: in

Queen Anne's time, for instance, the French Ambassador reported it as a hopeful sign of a more favourable attitude towards Catholics that for *The Masque of Beauty*, 'presque toutes les Dames que la Reine a appellées pour en être sont Catholiques' (Ben Jonson, *Works*, X, 458, quoting from La Boderie, *Ambassades*, II, 490). Henrietta likewise was accompanied by notable Catholic ladies in her masques, but she was always being urged by French ambassadors and Papal agents to take an even more active part in promoting her religion. While the sincerity of her own devotion was never in doubt, she was sometimes thought to be slow in pressing her influence. Her confessor Father Philip reported that she had no sins but of omission, and George Conn considered that she should work harder to gain the ministers;[28] in Rome it was thought that, although she had great influence with the King and could probably secure his conversion, she and her ladies were fully occupied with dances and court entertainments.[29] Henrietta, however, believed that piety was more effective when accompanied by pleasure, and that the influence of love was preferable to argument or political intrigue. Her masques may have been an opportunity to make a semi-public demonstration of her views, and to show, not that she was fully occupied with a personal cult of Platonic love and court theatricals, but that she was active in the interests of Catholicism, and that her sponsorship of Platonic love was a means by which her religion was made acceptable at court. Her next two masques seem designed to convey such a meaning.

The Temple of Love was presented on three successive occasions (10, 11, 12 February) in 1635, a year in which interest in both Platonic love and Catholicism reached a high point. James Howell's letter reporting the 'news' of Platonic love at court has often been quoted:

> The Court affords little News at present, but that there is a Love call'd Platonick Love, which much sways there of late; it is a Love abstracted from all corporeal gross Impressions and sensual Appetite, but consists in Contemplation and Ideas of the Mind, not in any carnal Fruition. This Love sets the Wits of the Town on work; and they say there will be a Mask shortly of it, whereof Her Majesty and her Maids of Honour will be part.
>
> (*Epistolae Ho-Elianae*, ed. Joseph Jacobs, I, 317–18)

Most commentators agree that the masque referred to was Davenant's *The Temple of Love*, in which the Queen takes the part of Indamora, who, 'by the influence of her beauty', re-establishes the temple of Chaste Love in the island of Britain. Divine Poesie had hidden the temple because certain Magicians (enemies to Chaste Love) had sought to use it for their own base ends, by which 'many Noble Knights and Ladies had been tempted and misled'.[30] Certain noble Persian youths hear of it, are almost seduced by the magicians, but are warned by Divine Poesie to wait for the appearance of the Queen, 'at whose sight they, being inspired with chaste flames, might be permitted by their faithful observance and legitimate affections to enter and enjoy the privileges of that sacred temple' (ll. 1–29). The Magicians scoff at the notion of Platonic love:

Indamora, the delight of destiny!
She and the beauties of her train, who sure,
Though they discover summer in their looks,
Still carry frozen winter in their blood.
They raise strange doctrines and new sects of love,
Which must not woo or court the person, but
The mind, and practice generation not
Of bodies, but of souls.   (ll. 186–93)

The magicians attempt to seduce the youths, but the appearance of the Queen and her masquers rescues them and confirms them in seeking chaste love:

At first they were your beauties' prize,
Now offer willing sacrifice
Unto the virtues of the mind;
And each shall wear when they depart
A lawful though a loving heart,
And wish you still both strict and kind.   (ll. 450–5)

The Temple appears, and Amianteros invokes 'Indamora's royall Lover' to witness its consecration, thus making

all our thoughts and actions pure;
When perfect will and strengthened reason meet,
Then love's created to endure.   (ll. 484–5)

Thus the masque praises the chaste version of Platonic love favoured by the Queen. One might be inclined to ask, however, why Platonic love should have been causing so much comment and excitement at court at this time, since neither the subject, nor masques treating it, were particularly new by 1635. What may have been particularly interesting was the connection of Platonic love with the Queen's religion.

From the point of view of the Queen and the Catholic circle, the subject that might well be regarded as 'news' was the arrival of Gregorio Panzani, the first accredited representative of the Pope. Panzani arrived in England in December 1634, travelling from Paris (whence Walter Montague arrived at the same time), bringing letters for the Queen, and charged with negotiating the formal exchange of agents.[31] *The Temple of Love* was the first official court function after his arrival, and an appropriate occasion for the Queen to impress on him the part she was playing in advancing her religion. It may also have been an opportunity to make a semi-public presentation of Panzani's embassage to the King. Panzani and the succeeding Papal agents were never formally presented to Charles (although they were privately introduced in the Queen's apartments). Officially they were accredited to the Queen, and all communication with Charles had to be carried on through her. On his arrival Panzani had thanked the Queen for her efforts on behalf of English Catholics, who, he said, the Pope always desired to show a loyal obedience to the King. This the Queen relayed to Charles, who said he was pleased at Panzani's coming, and merely asked him to work quietly, without meddling in state affairs (Albion, *Charles I*, pp. 149–53). Panzani was encouraged by his reception, and the masque may have provided the Queen with a further opportunity of showing her influence. It opens with 'Divine Poesy' leading an embassy of the reformed ancient poets up to the State, to make known a 'great affair' (l. 116) to the King:

> The monarch of men's hearts, rejoice!
> So much thou art beloved in heaven
> That Fate hath made thy reign her choice,
> In which Love's blessings shall be given.
> (ll. 120–3)

The exact nature of the 'great affair' is left vague, but 'Love's blessings' consist, it seems, in the rule of Truth and the appearance of the true Temple of love which 'Indamora with her beauty's light' (l. 131) will restore. The full significance of this temple becomes clearer, it seems to me, in the presence of the Papal agent, and in the light of a Catholic chapel which Jones was building for the Queen.

It had seemed a turning point for the fortunes of Catholicism when (about 1630) the Queen obtained permission from Charles to build a new chapel for the Capucins at Somerset House.[32] The Queen laid the foundation stone in September 1632 (the same year that *Tempe Restored* was presented); a French description shows how capital could be made of the event, not only to the glory of the Catholic Church, but to the Queen herself as the champion of it.[33] The writer describes how, following the will of God, the Queen had begged Charles 'avec tant de respect, d'amour et de larmes' (p. 7) for permission to build the 'temple', and how, against all expectation, permission had been granted. It was regarded as a personal triumph for Henrietta, and, in France at least, aroused the hope that the King 'par quelque bonne influence celeste', would come to desire one and the same religion for the two countries (p. 15). The Capucins in London were delighted, and Father Cyprien gave credit to the Queen who, as a champion of the Catholic Church, had once more 'planted the cross upon the mount of Somerset House, the first place from which heresy hurled it when the religion was changed in this unhappy Kingdom' (Birch, *Court and Times*, II, 308). The laying of the foundation stone was watched by more than two thousand people, and in Catholic quarters was hailed as the return of true religion to the country. In this ceremony the Queen appeared in what must have resembled one of the 'enclosed garden' settings appropriate to the Virgin, to whose service the Queen dedicated the chapel. The plot of ground on which the chapel was to stand was closed around with rich tapestries and roofed with costly stuffs; the floor was strewn with flowers 'which diffused an agreeable odour', while at one end was an altar garnished with such magnificent ornaments that it might be compared with 'Solomon's Temple' (Birch, *Court and Times*, II, 308). For the King and the others who witnessed it (including, no doubt, Inigo Jones, who was the architect) the scene perhaps recalled the stage images of the Queen, as a goddess of flowers in *Chloridia*, and as the personification of Divine Beauty in *Tempe Restored*, sanctifying beauty and bringing it to earth. When *The Temple of Love* was presented in 1635 the chapel (which opened at the end of 1636) must have been well on its way to completion.

In visual terms the main subject of this masque is, in fact, a 'Temple', which is first glimpsed through mists and clouds (l. 150), and which in the final scene comes to occupy the whole stage, concluding the masque with a magnificent image of unity and love. The Temple had, of course, symbolic significance (which I shall discuss later), but purely as a visual image in the masque it may have referred to the Queen's chapel. Jones's habit of referring to buildings in which he had an interest has been noted in the King's masques: the new Banqueting House in a masque of 1621 (a year before the building's completion), and again in *Albion's Triumph* (l. 339); St Paul's Cathedral (on which Jones was working currently) in *Britannia Triumphans*.[34] For the Queen's performance in *Artenice* (1626), Jones had produced a concluding masque scene of Somerset House, the actual building of the Queen's Palace in which the play was being performed (O&S, I, 385). The word 'temple' (often used by contemporaries in connection with Catholic worship)[35] was appropriate for the Queen's chapel, since the inscription on the foundation stone refers to it as *Templum hoc* (Birch, *Court and Times*, II, 308), and the French description calls it *un temple* (p. 8). In the masque the appearance of the Temple is undoubtedly the climax of the performance, being given a scene to itself after the Queen has danced and is seated under the State by the King. Jones wrote an elaborate description of it:

this temple instead of columns had terms of young satyrs bearing up the returns of architraves, frieze, and cornice, all enriched with goldsmiths' work; the further part of the temple running far from the eye was designed of another kind of architecture, with pilasters, niches and statues, and in the midst a stately gate adorned with columns and their ornaments, and a frontispiece on the top, all which seemed to be of burnished gold. (ll. 458–65)

When the masque was produced in 1635 Jones must have been thinking about the interior design of the chapel, and it would be interesting to know if any of the details in the masque description correspond with his designs. His design for the screen to the Queen's closet in the chapel (figure 26) has terms supporting a decorative architrave, and Jones had already used the same 'enriched Doric' for the proscenium arch of *The Shepherd's Paradise*. He had also used terms to support the architrave in another design for the pastoral, 'Love's Cabinet' (figure 27), and the rest of his description of 'another kind of architecture, with pilasters, niches and statues' is reminiscent of a second scene, the 'Interior of a Temple with Tombs' (figure 28). Jones never minded using 'twice conceyud, thrice payd for Imagery' (as Jonson called it in his *Expostulation with Inigo Jones*, l. 90), and a conflation of these two scenes with an interior view of the chapel, as well as a reference back to the pastoral that had helped introduce the Queen's idea of love to the court, would have been an appropriate visual image for the two themes of the masque, a new Catholic chapel for the Queen, and the introduction of the Queen's version of Platonic love to the court. This double theme, of love and religion, seems to be carried through in the rest of the masque's imagery.

26 Inigo Jones, screen in the French style for the Queen's chapel, Somerset House
(1630–5)

Jones designed the border of his scene as 'a new invention agreeable to the
subject' (ll. 43–4), one side representing the Indian monarchy, the other the
monarchy of Asia or an 'Indian borderer' (ll. 48–9), whose countries include
Persia.[36] In the masque the 'Indian' side, ruled over by Indamora 'the glorious
Indian Queen' (Henrietta), represents England and the 'Persian' side those who
arrive on the English shore. Indamora helps to reconcile the two sides by the
influence of her beauty and her doctrine of Platonic love. If a religious context
was intended, it seems appropriate that the main scenes of the masque should
be remarkable for the number of 'priests' and 'musicians' who take part: 'Brachmani', high-born Indian (English?) priests, and 'Magi' or Magicians, a religious
sect of Persia (perhaps a reference to Jesuit priests who were suspected of harming
Panzani's mission). It is appropriate that the 'priests of the Temple of Love'
(l. 380) should be the Queen's priests, the Capucin friars for whom the 'temple'
was being built, and who, according to their own principles, practised a religion
of love. These 'priests that burn Love's sacrifice / Our Orpheus greet with ravished
eyes' (ll. 397–8), and the arrival of 'Orpheus' would have been appropriate as

27 Inigo Jones, Love's Cabinet in *The Shepherd's Paradise*

a reference to Panzani, who was a priest of the Oratory, an Order noted for its music.[37] His arrival and the harmony of his music bring with them an atmosphere of calm and conciliation:

> No winds of late have rudely blown,
> Nor waves their troubled heads advance!
> His harp has made the winds so mild,
> They whisper now as reconciled,
> The waves are soothed into a dance.
>
> (ll. 386–90)

A quite complex musical dialogue, perhaps intended as a propitious omen, is played out on the stage in the exchange between Orpheus and his companions in their barque, and the chorus of musicians or priests on the shore: Orpheus plays his harp, and 'he playing one strain was answered with the voices and

28 Inigo Jones, interior of a temple with tombs in *The Shepherd's Paradise*

instruments of the brachmani joined with the priests of the Temple of Love'
(ll. 379–80). The calmness produced by Orpheus' arrival prepares the way for
the appearance of the Queen and the accomplishment of her purpose: the introduction of 'Love's true temple' (l. 404) to England. Thus the masque would have
presented Jones's 'temple' in a context that welcomed the first Papal agent to
England, and that paid a compliment to the Queen on her patronage of both
love and religion at court. It also gave an opportunity to display to Rome the
sophistication of English art and architecture, a sophistication which Jones claims
at the end of the masque (ll. 522–5), and which of course reflected credit on
himself.

There may, indeed, have been personal reasons for Jones to bring his work
to public attention before such an audience. He had been criticised by Catholic
authorities for taking so long to build the chapel, a delay which they thought

might have been owing to 'Puritan' sympathies in Jones.[38] Jones turns the charge from himself by including among the anti-masques various bad influences that at first delay the appearance of the temple: one is of 'a sect of modern devils ... sworn enemy of poesy, music, and all ingenious arts, but a great friend to murmuring, libelling, and all seeds of discord' (ll. 273, and 300–3). Those witnessing the magnificent scenes of the masque could hardly accuse Jones of being sympathetic to any such devils. The unfavourable influences are dispersed by the arrival of Orpheus and the good graces of the Queen. With the appearance of the Temple at the end of the masque, the grand chorus go up to the State, where the Queen too is now seated, 'to invoke the last and living hero, Indamora's royal lover, that he may help and witness the consecration of it' (ll. 39–41). In Catholic eyes the King's approval was the crowning triumph in building the Capucin chapel, and hence in restoring a 'true' temple to England.

The near completion of a Catholic chapel was of interest (either as a good omen or a bad) to everyone at court, and there was good reason why the masque should present it in connection with the Queen's love cult. On one level the controversial nature of the chapel was cloaked by its being put on the stage under the protection of Chaste Love, an unexceptional virtue and one that could be turned to compliment of the King and Queen. On another level the chapel had significance for Catholics in relation to the Queen's devotion to Mary, and the application by the Capucins to establish in it an Arch-Confraternity on its completion. The verses describing the Queen in the masque develop a version of Platonic love close to that which books such as *The Female Glory* do in relation to the Virgin. Stafford, in urging his feminine readers to follow the example of Mary, declared that 'Al her visitants were but so many converts' whom 'the sweetness of her discourse had rectified ... and enfranchis'd their souls till then, chained to their bodies' (sig. B4v–B5). In praising the beauty of Mary he repeated St Bonaventure's affirmation that had become traditional:

That her chaste eyes sent forth such divine beames that (though her Lovelinesse moved not only all mindes to honour her, and all Eyes to gaze on hers) yet they never kindled an unholy fire in the most adulterate bosom.   (sig. Q7, p. 237)

Similarly when the Queen appears she and her train have all

> That wise enamoured poets beauty call!
> So fit and ready to subdue
> That had they not kind hearts which take a care
> To free and counsel whom their eyes ensnare,
> Poor lovers would have cause to rue.   (ll. 422–6)

The lovers however are safe, for although they came

> Seduced at first by false desire,
> You'll kindle in their breasts a fire
> Shall keep love warm, yet not inflame.   (ll. 447–9)

Non-Catholics might have cause to fear that those who received the 'counsel'

of such beauties might also become 'so many converts'. If such were the case,
Indamora and the beauties of her train, who

> raise strange doctrines and new sects of love,
> Which must not woo or court the person, but
> The mind,

could truly be said to 'practice generation not / Of bodies, but of souls' (ll.
190–3), thus mocking the mockers of the opening scenes. In this light the 'true
temple' of Love that the Queen was about to introduce was, quite literally, a
place

> Where noble virgins still shall meet
> And breathe their orisons, more sweet
> Than is the spring's ungathered flower.   (ll. 406–8)

The two themes of religion and love come together in the visual and verbal images
of the masques.

The Queen's next masque, *Luminalia, or The Festival of Light* (1638), may
also have a specific 'Catholic' context which in this case seems to be confirmed
by external evidence. The years from 1635 to 1638 marked a period of optimism
for the Catholic party at court. Important people in the Queen's circle – Walter
Montague, Sir Kenelm Digby, Lady Newport – made public declarations of their
conversions, and others who had been Catholic before began to practise their
religion openly.[39] The Capucins gave enthusiastic accounts of the people converted
each week, and of the numbers attending their services. The King took an interest
in the arrangements of their chapel, and sometimes looked on, 'by his silence
approving of their devotion', at the crowds flocking to it (Birch, II, 343). The
Queen kept two chapels open, and George Conn another in his own house, which
became a centre of Catholic revival. Walter Montague shared Conn's chapel after
he became a priest, and other well-known priests visited it every week to hear
Confession. Daily Masses held there increased to the number of eight, and Conn,
writing in February 1638, said he had never had to postpone any service in response
to threats, or for any other reason.[40] The chapel became a fashionable place for
court ceremonies, such as the wedding of Viscount Montagu in July 1637. In
November of the same year the Queen held a full Pontifical Requiem (celebrated
by her Almoner Duperron who was now Bishop of Angoulême) for her late brother-
in-law the Duke of Savoy. Many Catholics tended to take this new-won freedom
for granted, drawing the attention of Puritans to the Court. Archbishop Laud
(for one) saw the damage done to Anglicanism by Charles's apparent sympathy
with his wife's religion, and in December 1637 Laud published a Proclamation
warning that the laws against English Catholics were in future to be strictly
enforced. Five days after its publication the Queen 'staged' a reply which made
the Proclamation virtually ineffective. She held a Midnight Mass in her Chapel,
to which all the recent converts were especially invited; her own tribune was

filled with ladies, including the Countess of Newport (on her first public appearance after the commotion caused by her conversion), who received Holy Communion with the Queen.[41] Conn had questioned the wisdom of this display, but Henrietta insisted, afterwards saying triumphantly to Conn that now he might see the effect of the Proclamation. The year 1637 was therefore one in which court Catholicism attained an increasing confidence under the protection of the Queen, and *Luminalia*, presented early in 1638, seems to take its place in this series of events.

Luminalia has been agreed generally by critics to have very little meaning apart from the beauty of its scenes. The stated subject seems to have nothing to do with the action, and the large number of entries and anti-masques give the text a chaotic appearance. To find the meaning, however, it is necessary, as Jones says in the description, to go to 'the main masque of light' (l. 15), and to regard the introductory scenes as 'a foil to set off more nobler representations' (ll. 72–3). Thus the opening scenes, ruled by Night and her attendants, and the fantastic visions that spill out of 'the City of Sleep' merely lead up to (and vanish before) the Queen, the climax of a meaning that has been developing from the beginning. It seems to me that *Luminalia*, like *The Temple of Love*, makes specific reference to its subject in the title. The masque was, quite literally, a 'Festival of Light' as its subtitle states. Everything in its performance contributes to this theme, from the lighted lamps that ornamented the frontispiece (l. 49), to the 'bright sky' and glory with rays that frame the Queen's appearance as 'the queen of brightness' (l. 357) in the discovery scene. But a 'Festival of Light' also had contemporary religious significance, especially in relation to the Feasts of Mary. Stafford had drawn particular attention in *The Female Glory* to the Feast of the Purification, or Candlemas, as a ceremony dedicated to Mary. He calls it 'the *Day of Lights*', and explains that it is celebrated in the church by the singing of Mass and the burning of 'very many Tapours' so that 'that which was performed by superstitious Idolaters in honour of *Ceres* and *Proserpina*, may be turned into the praise and glory of the Virgin Mary' (sigs. L5–L5v). The Feast of the Purification is celebrated on 2 February, and *Luminalia* was presented on 6 February (Shrove Tuesday night), just four days after Catholics at court would have seen Candlemas celebrated, no doubt with a good deal of elaboration, in the Queen's chapel. A visual connection between it and a masque on the theme of light would have been hard to ignore.

The connection takes on further meaning because of current controversy over ceremonies such as Candlemas, which for Puritans were the very essence of 'Popery'. After the Reformation, Elizabeth's injunctions had condemned 'all Candlesticks, Trendals, Rolls of Wax, and setting up of Tapers, for that they be things tending to Idolatry and Superstition'.[42] Under Charles, however, such practices had begun to creep back into the church, and as early as 1628 William Prynne, in condemning John Cosin's *Private Devotions* for containing Marian material, cites as evidence of Cosin's 'Popery' his causing 280 Lights and Tapers ... besides Torches, to bee lighted ... on Candlemas day last past, after the Popish custome, as if the God of Light had needed Light and Tapers to behold his blind and dark Devotions.

(*A Briefe Survay and Censure of Mr Cozens his Couzening Devotions*, p. 95)

Such practices discover him to be, not only a 'Papist', but 'a Pagan rather: who were addicted to this Ceremonie, of lighting Tapers to their Idoll Gods'. Stafford had renewed the controversy in 1635 by his description in *The Female Glory*, and especially by his explanation, that on this day

the Church used to pray, that as the visible Lights chased away the darkenesse of the night: so the hearts of the Faithfull might be illuminated by the Invisible flames of the holy Spirit, & (being cured of their blindnesse brought upon them by vice) might with pure and cleare eyes discerne those things which are pleasing to God, and having pass'd through the sad, darke, and dismall accidents of this world might at length arrive at Heaven, where they shall behold a Light everlasting.   (sig. L5v–L6)

This was one of the passages that Henry Burton had picked out for special comment in the sermons *For God, and the King* in November 1636, saying that new rites on Candlemas day 'with their hundreds of capers, and candles', instead of bringing spiritual light bring 'spirituall darknesse upon mens soules, by shutting out the ancient morning Prayers' (p. 161). At the beginning of 1638, when the masque was presented, this controversy was still very much alive. Burton had been brought to trial in June 1637 for his criticism of the court in these sermons, for which he was condemned and imprisoned. During 1637 Peter Heylin and Christopher Dow both wrote against Burton, and included a defence of Stafford's book. Stafford himself wrote a long vindication (unpublished at the time) dedicated to the Archbishop of Canterbury and to the Bishop of London, the latter having granted the licence for *The Female Glory*.[43] The controversy was therefore well known at court, and a masque by the Queen on the theme of light suggests a celebration of the victory of Mary over her Puritan detractors, as well as the victory of light over spiritual darkness.

To suggest such a connection is not arbitrary, because the scene in which the Queen and her masquers appear is filled with Marian imagery, some of it seeming to echo the language of Stafford's book. To introduce the masquers the heavens begin to be enlightened as before the sun rising, and the scene changes to a 'delicious prospect', the beautiful garden of the Britanides (ll. 244–98). Aurora and Hesperus appear in the Heavens, and reveal that 'the sun hath for this time given up his charge of lightening the hemisphere to a terrestrial beauty, in whom intellectual and corporeal brightness are joined'. Hesperus, the Morning Star, is bid descend from heaven and summon 'the arch-flamens and flamens to celebrate with divine hymns this goddess of brightness' who is about to appear. The imagery is appropriate in Platonic compliment to the Queen, but it is even more appropriate in books on Mary. The Morning-Star, with the Sun and Moon, was Mary's chief emblem, whose special attribute was to sing her praises.[44] It is also representative of Mary: Brereley's sonnet *Stella Matvtina* hails her by this name, saying

> The sky's most glorious star cannot compare
> In glitt'ring clearnes with the morning star.   (*Virginalia*, p. 36)

Ribadeneira expands the words of the Canticles: 'who is that which ascends, and goes increasing with light like the dawning of the day', and says of Mary 'the day did break, and the true morning star appeared to the world, and gave us notice of the coming of eternal day' (*Lives of the Saints*, p. 689). In the description of this scene in the masque there are several apparent echoes of *The Female Glory*. The Morning Star, for instance, is accompanied by Aurora, who appears 'in a chariot touched with gold', her arms bare, 'her hair dishevelled' (ll. 247–51). The picture was a common one in literature,[45] but Stafford had used it recently in comparing Aurora to the appearance of the Virgin on Candlemas Day; although he says he hesitates to show her thus, 'in the stile of the stage', he describes her as 'sitting in a golden Chariot, her yellow hair spread over her milky shoulders' (sig. L7v). Again, the Queen's beauty is said to outshine the light of the sun (ll. 277–87) and the image is another common literary device, but also traditional to Mary, being derived from the Canticles. The author of *Maria Triumphans*, for instance, interprets Mary to mean 'Lady, and one, that giueth light' (sig. F), because she is 'purer then the beames and brightnes of the sunne' (sig. F2). In the masque, the sun knows that were he to appear he would be eclipsed by a brighter star (l. 285), the goddess of brightness, who is the Queen. Stafford had used the conceit in a similar way in connection with Mary:

the Sunne ... this day burnish't his face, the better to illustrate the world and to appear gracious in her sight, who carried in her breast a fire purer, and clearer than his own Rayes.
                                                                 (sig. B7v)

When the Queen finally appears it is in a setting appropriate to Mary. The further part of the garden opens and the Queen sat enthroned above the fair nymphs 'dependents on her splendour', on a seat in the form of a half oval; she was dressed in star-like garments, and crowned with jewels and stars (ll. 350–68); behind all was 'a bright sky, and in the midst, about the Queen's majesty's seat, was a glory with rayes' (ll. 355–6). Stafford had given a similar picture of the Virgin 'accompanied with a bevy of Shee-saints', describing how

the orbes bowed and bended themselves to make her a triumphant Arch ... the Sunne with his brightest beames imbrac't her ... the Moone was under her feet ... and the brightest of the stars interwove themselves to make her a radiant crown,   (sig. P3)

a picture which Burton had attacked as making Mary into a 'new great goddesse, Diana', and 'Empresse of this lower world' (*For God, and the King*, sig. Q3). The echoes of Marian imagery in the scene, and the all-pervasive theme of the triumph of Light, seem to give religious significance to the whole masque, for which Stafford's passage on the significance of Candlemas might serve as a text. Stafford had said that Candlemas is celebrated to show that spiritual light chases away the darkness of the night, and that the hearts of the faithful, after passing through the dark and dismal accidents of the world, at length arrive at Heaven where they behold a light everlasting. Similarly, the masque, which begins with a scene copied from a painting on the subject of the Virgin (*The Flight into Egypt*), progresses through scenes of Night, Sleep, and fantastic dreams, opens out into a vision of the world enlightened by a power superior to the sun, and ends with heavenly rejoicing, the 'heaven full of deities' and figures dancing in the clouds. The Marian imagery connected with the Queen may show that the masque celebrates, not only Candlemas, but the triumph of spiritual illumination over the forces of darkness and superstition, a triumph of 'true' religion over false.

The interpretation of the masque offered above is reinforced by independent contemporary evidence, Francis Lenton's *Great Britains Beauties, or The Female Glory ... Encomiastick anagrams and acrostiches, upon the highly honoured names of the Queenes most gracious Majestie, and the gallant Lady-Masquers in her Graces glorious Grand-Masque* [i.e. *Luminalia*] (London 1638). Lenton's use of so controversial a title as *The Female Glory* in connection with the Queen's masque cannot have been accidental. He signed himself on the title-page 'the Queenes Poet', and he would hardly have used *The Female Glory* in the title if the reference would have embarrassed the Queen. On the contrary, the title points to *Luminalia*'s having been designed to support Stafford's book and devotion to Mary, and to Lenton's taking his place on the side of the Queen. Lenton's verses in praise of the Queen in the masque seem to confirm this, for they echo the language and imagery of Marian devotion. He dedicates his book to 'the Most Graciovs, most Candide *Queene* of all Christendome, our Magnificent *Queene* MARY' (sig. A), whom his prostrate Muse adores as a 'Mirrour of goodnes'. The anagram upon the Queen's name, MARIA STVART, is I AM A TRV STAR, followed by the Distichon:

> A Royall, Sacred, bright, tru *fixed* Star,
> In whose compare, all other Comets are.   (sig. BV)

The second Anagram is again based on the name of Mary, this time belonging to the Duchess of Lennox:[46] MARYE STVART, A TRVSTY ARME (emblem of love, courtesy, and loyalty). This time the language is more moderate, but the acrostic again makes play on the name of Mary:

> MARYES *blest Name you have, and* Maryes *Grace*,
> And Maryes Vertues decke both Soule, and Face.   (sig. B2v)

Other poems do not make use of the Marian language, but the tone remains one of respectful obeisance to women, angelic in brightness and beauty of character, at whose 'high Altars' Lenton offers his poem. Each lady is praised in terms appropriate to her state, whether married or single, but the 'golden Ball' for which they all strive is virtue, to which they are led by the Queen:

> Of these great Ladies, you the Leader are,
> Who (like the Wisemen) follow you, their Star.   (sig. A2v)

In the poem that follows the Distichon on the Queen, the 'Illustration', the language of the Litanies is used in reference to the Queen, and gives verbal meaning to the imagery of light in the masque, making the Stuart court a replica of the heavenly one. The Queen is

> A Morning *Star*, whose Rose at blush and smile,
> Shewes the dayes solace, and the nights exile;
> A radiant *Star*, whose lustre, more Divine,
> By *Charles* (our Sun) doth gloriously shine:
> No wandring Planet, that moves circular,
> But *a tru*, constant, loyall, fixed *Star*:
> *A Star* whose influence, and sacred light,
> Doth beautifie the day, and blesse the night;
> Which shining brightly in the highest Sphaere,
> Adornes those smaller Stars, which now appeare
> Before her presence; by whose gracious sight,
> Their numerous feet now pace with rich delight:
> O happy they approach unto that Throne,
> Where vertues are the constellation.
> > And let it be proclaimed nigh, and far,
> > That our illustrious queene, is *a tru Star*.   (sig. BV)

The verse could serve as a text to accompany the appearance of the Queen and her ladies in *Luminalia* (ll. 350–7), a scene on which the poetry in the masque is silent. The language of Marian devotion applied to the Queen by Lenton, and specifically related to this masque, could hardly be more explicit.

Once *Luminalia* is placed in the context of the Queen's religion, Jones's statement of his 'Subject' at the beginning of the masque takes on more meaning. One part of the meaning concerns the return of the Muses to Great Britain, which is confirmed by the picture of the Queen in the garden of the Britanides. But the Muses are not the only subject of the opening lines. The reason that formerly they 'wandered here and there indecently without their ornaments and instruments' was that 'the arch-flamens and flamens, their prophetic priests', had been constrained 'either to live in disguises or hide their heads in caves' (ll. 19–22). There is a good deal of evidence in the literature of the thirties that the terms 'flamen' and 'arch-flamen' were being used to refer to Catholic priests. The terms of course belonged to Roman antiquity, but in the seventeenth century they had become familiar in pastoral: *L'Astrée* (II, 324–6), for instance, has an elaborate description of the way in which Roman rites became Christianised, flamines and vestal virgins becoming priests and priestesses in the 'Gaulish' religion. Similarly in England the terms had been used semi-historically to denote two grades of priests in the old religion, alleged to have been replaced, on the conversion of the country to Christianity, by Bishops and Arch-Bishops (*OED*, under Flamen). The terms 'flamen' and 'arch-flamen' thus came to have both a literary association in relation to their familiar presence on the stage in pastoral and masque, and a religious meaning. The terms became polemical, however, when the Puritans used them in their attack on Bishops, saying that the heathen Britons had their Archflamins and Flamins: the Archflamins of London, York, and Chester became Archbishops; the Flamins, Bishops (Albion, *Charles I*, p. 406). The connection with ancient Rome suggested a connection with modern Rome and contemporary Catholicism. Prynne, writing in *The Popish Royall Favourite*, which uncovered the Romish 'plots' of the 1630s, says that the chief Catholics at court all had code names, the Pope himself being 'the great Arch-Flamin' (sig. FV, p. 42).

In masques connected with the King, such as *Albion's Triumph*, the flamens retain their classical appearance (see Orgel and Strong, II, no. 199, p. 467), but in pastorals under the influence of the Queen they may have taken on some of the attributes of Catholic priests. Thomas Randolph's *Amyntas*, for instance, has a Chorus of priests, and an 'Archiflamen' who is the High-Priest of Ceres (p. 295). The action is divided between the pastoral setting and the Temple of Ceres, to which Vestal Virgins come in procession, and 'pass over the stage with wax candles in their hands' (p. 337), as in a procession for Candlemas. In *Florimène* (see description Orgel and Strong, II, 632–7) the pastoral action is set in a more solemn frame by the scenes at the beginning and the end which take place around a 'stately temple' (l. 19) sacred to Diana. The pastoral opens with a procession in which 'the priests of Diana, with the arch-flamen and sacrificers' enter, with music and singing; while the priests sing, 'the high-priest passeth between them and goeth into the temple', and the shepherds and shepherdesses present their offerings (ll. 19–30). The procession of the priests and the singing and music in the pastoral must have called to the mind of many at court the elaborate services held by the Capucins in chapels for the Queen, and the connections between 'arch-flamens', priests and musicians on the stage.[47]

In *Luminalia* it is the flamens and arch-flamens who join with Hesperus in singing praises to the King and Queen, and who 'celebrate with divine hymns' the goddess of brightness (ll. 257–9). Jones is non-committal about their appearance, saying they were 'habited in rich habits of several colours, as they are described by the ancients' (ll. 302–4). In the lengthy opening description, however, it is difficult not to see in them a reference to the Catholic priests who were dispersed from England, and who now return once more under the protection of the King and Queen. The arts, Jones writes, had suffered because the flamins and arch-flamins had been forced to live in disguise or hide in caves:

and in some places, whensoever they [the flamins] begin to appear, they were, together with peace, driven out by war; and in the more civilised parts, where they hoped to have taken some rest, Envy and Avarice by clipping the wings of Fame drave them into a perpetual storm, till by the divine minds of these incomparable pair, the muses and they were received into protection and established in this monarchy ... making this happy island a pattern to all nations, as Greece was amongst the ancients.   (ll. 20–38)

In this light, the deferential songs addressed by Hesperus and the flamens to the King, and their praises of the Queen, become more than perfunctory compliment; they are a grateful tribute to the King and Queen for their protection, part of the religious subject-matter and the Catholic slant of the masque. *Luminalia*, therefore, which in terms of poetry and literary ideas is the most incoherent and meaningless of the masques, is perhaps, in terms of its images and the connection between the Queen's Platonic love and her religion, the most significant, an optimistic assertion of the Catholic interests of the Queen.

Religious ceremony and the masques

Church and stage

If on one level the Queen's masques reflected her own interests, on another level they seem to me to relate to two aspects of her religion that were sympathetic to Charles – the ideal aspects of Beauty and of Love. The latter summed up in part that desire for peace and civilised life reflected in the Arcadianism of the 1630s, the expression of which in the masques will be the subject of the next chapter. The former, the ideal of Beauty, was connected with the aesthetic, artistic, and liturgical tastes of the King. These tastes were closely related, and all three aspects were reflected, I believe, in a constant theme of masques in the thirties, the 'reformation' of the arts and their restoration to England.

These themes in the masques were presaged near the beginning of the period, in 1628, in a painting by Gerard Honthorst (figure 29a). Its subject, the Liberal Arts being presented to the King and Queen by the Duke of Buckingham, had a solid basis in fact, the purchase and arrival in England during the 1620s of the great collections of the Earl of Arundel, the Duke of Buckingham, and the King.[1] The painting is conceived in masque-like terms and could stand as an introduction to masques of the thirties. The King and Queen are crowned with the symbols of the sun and the moon, and the King as Apollo, father of the Muses, leans forward to welcome the Arts; the Queen as Diana, goddess of chastity, ensures that they are purified and reformed (figure 29b). The vices, like the figures of an anti-masque, are tumbled into the darkness below the throne, and the play of light in the painting connects the central group of the Arts with the Royal group, which reflects light to the heavenly figures above. These themes, of restoration and reformation, are repeated in masques throughout the thirties. In the first two masques, *Love's Triumph through Callipolis* and *Chloridia*, the King and Queen purify the actual qualities of Love and Beauty. In *Tempe Restored* the Queen reforms the arts and muses, and in *The Temple of Love* the ancient poets. In the King's masque, *Coelum Britannicum* (1634), the heavens themselves are reformed on the pattern of the English court. In this masque the arts and civilised pleasures go through an elaborate process of 'purification'. This, it is made clear, is no puritanical Reformation, austere and iconoclastic, but a 'new Reformation', conservative and aristocratic, in which beauty, morality, and pleasure go hand in hand. In ideal terms these masques seem, in fact, to refer to an English Counter-Reformation, calling on values that have their roots in British tradition, but

29a Gerard Honthorst, *The Liberal Arts Presented to King Charles and Queen Henrietta Maria* (1628); the Royal Collection, reproduced by Gracious Permission of Her Majesty The Queen

29b Detail of above, showing the King as Apollo and the Queen as Diana

sympathetic to the tastes of the Continental Counter-Reformation. In this chapter I would like to explore the ways in which the masque stage, together with its spectacle and ritual, may have lent itself to the expression not only of Charles's artistic tastes, but of his liturgical tastes as well, and to suggest that masques themselves played a part in the contemporary debate over 'beauty' in church worship.

Charles's loyalty to his ideal of Anglicanism was never (as events abundantly proved) in question, but it was in the area of aesthetics that Anglicanism and Counter-Reformation Catholicism most nearly approached one another. Charles's own view of his religion was summed up (characteristically in an image from the arts) in some of his last words:

Not but that (the draught being excellent as to the main, both for doctrine and government, in the Church of England) some lines, as in very good figures, may haply need some sweetening and polishing, which might here easily have been done by a safe and gentle hand, if some men's precipitancy had not violently demanded such rude alterations, as would have quite destroyed all the beauty and proportions of the world.[2]

To Charles and the leading members of his clergy, Anglicanism was not alone a religion of Reason and Truth, but a religion of Beauty, in which the traditional liturgical forms of the Church were of the utmost importance. The issue became one of increasing urgency in the 1630s as Archbishop Laud, backed by the King, attempted to enforce uniformity in liturgical matters in churches throughout the Kingdom, and as the attempt came under increasingly bitter attack. It seems possible that something of Charles's heartfelt desire for 'beauty and proportion' in his religion is reflected in the emphasis on spectacle in the masques, and in the ritual and ceremony of the court stage, much of which centres around the Queen.

Masques were indeed a fitting vehicle for referring to the questions of ritual and ceremony, since the masque stage provided a setting that was in many ways analogous to the setting for religious ceremony in churches. Inigo Jones was influenced in the development of his stage by theatre spectacle in countries like Italy where the Reformation had made no clear break between the established church and the state, and in which many of the forms of religious ceremony had been absorbed into court ceremony and entertainments.[3] In Italy, the Medici *sacre rappresentazione* of the fifteenth century had grown out of the *Laudesi* and *Divozione* of the church, and were adapted to the secular stage for pastoral melo-drama such as *Orfeo* (performed 1472) with very little alteration. The *intermedii* that accompanied them were later adapted to convey political messages and compli-ment in court festivities of the seventeenth century.[4] In France, religious plays were performed for Royal entries in Paris in the fifteenth century, and continued to be performed on these occasions as *tableaux vivants*, simply by suppression of the text. Many elements which later became characteristic of the baroque stage were already present in the French *mystères* which were adapted to the entertain-ment of Royalty: the *gloire* or luminous halo around the head of a saint, the clouds on which the gods were seated, the canvas-covered platform on which figures could perform or sing, the *ciel* with angels, Mary and Child, or God the Father, were familiar among other spectacles at Royal progresses.[5] *Tableaux vivants*, originating in church festivals, were taken over for Royal entries and often only the names of deities were changed, Jupiter or Jove taking the place of God in the throne of Heaven, nymphs and goddesses taking the place of the religious virtues, without causing any special change in dramatic or pictorial form.[6] When, as happened in the later Renaissance and the Counter-Reformation, autocratic rulers wished to emphasise their connections with the Church, the classical deities were simply changed back into the Christian virtues, or the angel-like spirits, from which they had originally developed. These associations were reinforced from the beginning of the seventeenth century by the adaptation of the secular stage for religious spectacle and propaganda. Counter-Reformation Orders such as the Oratorians, Theatines, and especially the Jesuits adopted all the spectacular devices of the court stage: interludes, musical chorus, ballet, and theatrical machines.[7] Their stage developed during the same period as the perspective stage that influenced Jones, and by the 1630s they were amongst the foremost practitioners of stage-craft, vying with the opera in popularity. Jesuit theatre was certainly familiar to English courtiers (and perhaps even to Jones) through the English Colleges at Rome, Douai, and St Omers, where English visitors were entertained and plays frequently performed.[8] In France, where Marie de Medici was a regular attendant at their productions, they influenced the development of ballet.[9]

Before the Reformation in countries such as England, the process of adapting religious subjects and ceremony to Royal celebrations had been similar to that on the Continent.[10] The Reformation interrupted this process, but it did not by any means destroy associations between court iconology and religion. Frances Yates and Roy Strong have shown how, when the monarch became head of Church and State, court ceremony itself took on added significance by absorbing into itself many pre-Reformation religious forms.[11] Catholic ritual was banned from the Church, but liturgical processions, festivals, and Saints' days found their way into civic processions, Royal progresses, and national celebrations, serving the purposes of a new nationalism and symbolising the concentration of religious as well as political power in the monarch. Even the older forms of religious drama, banned from public display, went underground to emerge again in the service of a Protestant State. A scheme organized by Thomas Cromwell under Henry VIII recommended turning plays, processions, bonfires, and sports, all associated with 'Popery', into propaganda against the Pope, and there were attempts to substitute Protestant open-air plays for the Catholic cycles, the latter not being suppressed finally until between 1570 and 1600.[12] The Morality play and Interlude were similarly adapted to anti-Catholic propaganda, which grew to such proportions that the authorities had to take steps to suppress it. It is obvious that, right up to the seventeenth century, the stage and other para-theatrical activities were still vitally connected both in the public mind and that of the authorities with the expression of religious belief, whether on the Catholic or the Protestant side.

These connections were suppressed on the public stage, but seem to have resurfaced on the court stage, largely through the development of the masque. The masque form owed a good deal to the native tradition of Morality and Interlude: Jonson and Jones's *Hymenaei* (1606), for instance, with its microcosm 'figuring man', a dance of humours and affections, the action directed by Reason, and its vision of 'heaven' at the end, can easily be seen as a sophisticated staging and complex reworking of Morality themes. Similarly in *The Masque of Queens* (1609), where Jonson first formulated his ideas for the anti-masque, his hags or witches come from an ugly Hell smoking and flaming to the roof, and disappear to the infernal regions at the appearance of Virtue, or a vision of Heaven at the end. The authority Jonson gives is classical, but the scene might come from the religious stage. The aim of these early masques was not, of course, to emphasise, but to play down any associations they may have had with pre-Reformation Catholicism. Jonson achieved this by setting his masques in a Humanist framework, thus giving respectability to the formal elements adopted from a discredited religion. In the masques of the early seventeenth century he is relentless in citing 'classical' authorities for his practice and ideas; he is careful to assign stage properties to his abstract or allegorical figures according to the 'ancient poets' or emblembook writers (for example in *The Masque of Queens*), and his 'Heaven' is populated usually by gods and goddesses with strictly classical names. Even the altar that occupies the centre of the stage in *Hymenaei* is made respectable by relating it to ancient Roman marriage customs, presumably avoiding by this means the suspicions of people like Busy in *Bartholomew Fair* who could detect the 'peeping out of Popery' in places far less obvious than the court stage. Any suspicion of a Catholic bias in the elements of these early masques was met by taking a stand on the principles of Renaissance Humanism, which, by relating them to ancient Rome, avoided the imputation of a connection with modern Rome. Jonson's classical learning helped to clothe with poetic invention and imperial imagery James's claim for himself as God's representative on earth, while his careful reference to classical sources helped adapt elements of the old religious stage to a new English usage.

Although Jonson succeeded in neutralising the inherently religious elements in the literary content of masque, he had less influence over the parts of masque that were unaccompanied by words, the stage settings and other properties which retained strong visual links with pre-Reformation theatre. The measures taken in the sixteenth century to control the religious content of plays did not suppress the stage-craft associated with it, and Glynne Wickham (in *Early English Stages*, II, 39) considers these visible reminders to be a basic ingredient in the continuing Puritan opposition to the stage, since in costume and setting could still be seen the 'three-dimensional enactment of Catholicism'. The continued use of these visual reminders of a religious stage seems to have come about originally through laxness or expediency on the part of the authorities rather than by deliberate design, since after the Reformation the actual vestments of the Catholic Church were hired or sold to the players, and the monuments, tombs, and sculptures which were common props of the Miracle plays continued to be used on the stage (*EES*, II, 57–9). Court masques, with their strong ceremonial qualities, found a particular use for scenery and costume of this kind, and the older religious associations were by no means always explained away. Figures in 'priest-like habit' (*Masque of Beauty*, ll. 216–17) were regular participants in Jonsonian masques, as they were later in Jones's, and became no less priest-like to the eye because they were sometimes called Muses or Musicians. For instance, in *Pleasure Reconciled to Virtue* the chaplain to the Venetian ambassador saw the 'musicians' as being 'dressed in the long red robes of high priests, with golden mitres' (O&S, I, 283); in Chapman's *Memorable Masque*, the 'Priests' of the Sun (the *Phoebades*) pay homage to James in his role as representative of a Christian, rather than a classical, Heaven (O&S, I, 261, ll. 561–604).

Fundamental to similarities between court and church ceremony was the kind of architecture that Jones developed from the beginning of the seventeenth century as a distinctive setting for Stuart ceremonial occasions. The two halls he built for James (the first in 1606, replaced by the Banqueting House in 1618–22) were both designed on the model of the Roman basilica (that is, in the proportions of a double cube, approximately 110 feet × 55 feet), a form which gave new dignity and discipline to court entertainments by focusing attention on a raised stage at one end of the hall.[13] Jones's introduction of the perspective stage was a natural outcome of the Vitruvian principles perfected in Italy by Buontalenti at the end of the sixteenth century and later by Alfonso and Giulio Parigi, which demanded that building and stage should form a single architectural unit (figure 30).[14] These arrangements contrasted with those of Elizabeth's reign. Halls and raised stages had of course long been used for plays, but the houses and machines were either wheeled on stage, or left as simultaneous settings; more commonly at court entertainments, they were dotted about the hall on the same level as the audience, as in the scene for the French *Balet comique de la Reine*, 1582 (figure 31), considered by E. K. Chambers to have been typical of court stage settings in Elizabeth's reign.[15] Jones's first staging of a masque in 1605 (*The Masque of Blacknesse*) gathered the dispersed settings, placed them behind a proscenium arch and arranged them within the scene of perspective, at once concentrating and controlling the attention of the audience.

At much the same time that the perspective stage was being developed at courts in Italy, the Counter-Reformation adopted the same basilical model for the building of its churches. This was a departure from the central-plan churches built in the High Renaissance,[16] and it answered the needs of the Counter-Reformation for a piety which placed new emphasis on the role of preaching and on the Sacrament of the Mass. When the Jesuits chose the basilical model for Il Gesù (built by Vignola in 1568), they were well aware of its advantages for enhancing the

30 Jacques Callot, etching of a scene by Giulio Parigi showing perspective stage setting
in the Uffizi Theatre, Florence (1617)

31 Frontispiece from *Balet comique de la Reine* (Paris, 1582) showing settings dispersed
about the hall

oratorical quality of the service, and for directing the congregation's attention to an altar which, as the seventeenth century progressed, became increasingly stage-like and ornate. Jones must have been aware of the similarities between contemporary church and court architecture in Italy, and when he came to build his two Catholic chapels, the first at St James (begun in 1623 for the Spanish Infanta) and the second at Somerset House for Henrietta, he designed them in the proportions of a double cube, like the Banqueting House but on a smaller scale.[17] The basic similarities can be seen by comparing the interior of the Banqueting House (figure 32), which was first built with a 'great neeche' or apse occupying the south end to half its height,[18] with an impression later in the century of the interior of the St James chapel (figure 33) fitted out with a perspective scene. Even after the 'neeche' was removed, Jones's scenes for the masques, with the proscenium arch framing the 'picture' and (especially after 1630) with a scene in the 'heavens' or upper stage as well, often closed the view with an effect similar to that produced in many churches of the period.

Jones's setting for the masques was closer in many ways to the setting for worship in Counter-Reformation churches than to that in Reformed churches of Elizabeth's reign. The similarities and differences may be suggested by comparing a sketch of Jones's setting for the *Masque of Blacknesse* (1605) with a sketch of the interior of Palladio's *Il Redentore* (1576–92) (figure 34). The buildings have similar proportions, and the focal point of each, the stage and the altar, is in a similar position. Both settings depend on the laws of perspective for their full effect, and they have other physical similarities. For masque performances the stage was separated from the body of the hall by steps, proscenium arch, and sometimes (as in the case of *Blacknesse*) by a curtain; in Counter-Reformation churches the altar was separated from the nave by steps, a frame with niches and statues, and sometimes a screen or railings. Both settings depend on a sense of distance for their effect, but also on arousing a sense of wonder (hence the importance of spectacle) in order to involve the imagination and the feelings of the participants. These settings, with their similarities, may be contrasted with the setting for court entertainments in Elizabeth's reign, which is similar to the setting for worship in Reformed churches (figure 35). Glynne Wickham's reconstruction from Daniel's description of the setting in *The Vision of the Twelve Goddesses* (1604) shows the typical arrangements for court entertainments before Jones's introduction of the perspective stage; there was a cave of Sleep and a temple of Peace at one end of the hall, and a mountain at the other; the audience surrounded the acting area and the dais was more or less on floor level. Similarly, in the plan for Communion in a Reformed Church of the early seventeenth century there is no separation between the Communion area and the congregation, and there is little distinction between the minister and the participants. In both settings all those present have an equally good, or equally poor, view of what is going on. It is perhaps significant for the history of English theatre that Elizabethan drama (which is believed to have been played 'in the round', and which drew

32 Inigo Jones, interior of the Banqueting House, Whitehall, with Rubens's ceiling
    panels (after 1635)

33 Johannes Kip, engraving showing the Queen's chapel at St James's Palace with a
perspective scene behind the altar (1686–8)

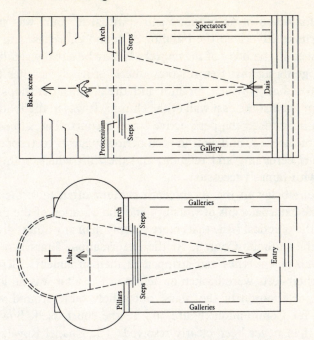

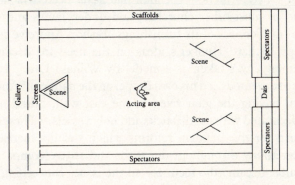

34 Simplified sketch comparing Jones's perspective stage setting for masques with perspective setting of a Counter-Reformation church

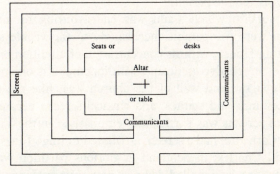

35 Simplified sketch comparing setting of court stage before Jones with setting for Communion in a Reformed English church

on the Reformation for much of its patriotic and spiritual fervour) was staged at a time when Reformers advocated the building of round churches, and altar and minister were placed in the body of the church. It may be equally significant that in 1604, James, going against Reformation edicts, ordered the altar to be put where 'most convenient',[19] which for him and the Anglican Bishops who shared his tastes meant against the east wall of the church. It was in the following year that Inigo Jones introduced the perspective stage at court. The similarities between the position of the stage and altar in each period suggests corresponding attitudes towards court ceremony and religion, and the shift which both these attitudes underwent with James's accession.

Debate over religious belief in the seventeenth century often took the form of controversy over the external signs of worship, and the question of the proper place of the altar was the practical issue that, more sharply than any other, divided the Reformed from the Catholic Church. At the Reformation, altars had been torn from the east wall of churches and stripped of their ornaments. Screens, chancel arches, and choir-lofts were broken or defaced. The altar was no longer to be a stage for the celebration of the Mass, but a holy table around which the faithful gathered for Communion (figure 36). In the court itself, however, the issue of the altar had never been clearly resolved. The Chapel Royal, even in Elizabeth's day, had retained many more of the visual forms of Catholic worship than were allowed by strict Reformers.[20] The altar had never been detached from the east wall, as it had in most other churches, and under James and Charles it steadily increased in the richness of its furnishings. Bishop Andrewe's chapel, which put into practice Richard Hooker's ideas on the need for decency and beauty in church ceremony, was taken as a model by William Laud. Laud, as Dean of Gloucester in 1616, remodelled his own chapel on the pattern of Andrewe's chapel and the King's, having the altar fixed to the east wall, raised on steps and railed, and richly decorated with candlesticks and holy vessels.[21] These chapels then became the pattern for the Laudian reforms which steadily increased the richness of Anglican ceremony throughout the 1620s and 1630s (compare figure 37). In the 1630s the altar became the focus for all the issues concerning images and ceremony that deeply stirred the period.[22]

The visible signs of worship which Laud was endeavouring to introduce throughout the Kingdom were comparable increasingly to the visible signs of ceremony in the Banqueting House, with its concentration of attention on a pro-scenium-arch framing the perspective scene and with its emphasis on spectacle. The altar raised on steps at the end wall of the church was, like the masque stage, often framed by columns and statues, and chancel screens became more ornate. The importance of screens was particularly emphasised in the Visitation Articles, and Winchester Cathedral had a screen, attributed to Inigo Jones, which held statues of James and Charles; in Scotland 'a glorious partition wall with a degree ascending thereto' was later pulled down as being superstitious (Addle-shaw, *Architectural Setting*, pp. 35, 39). To stress the importance of the altar,

36 'The Lord's Supper' from *A Course of Catechizing* (London, 1674), showing the communicants around an altar set table-wise in the body of the church

37 St Paul's Cathedral after the Laudian reforms, showing altar separated from the nave by railing and steps; from J. D. Chambers, *Divine Worship in England*

Laudians were placing it under a stained glass window, with a reredos or tapestry behind, and adorning the chancel roof with paintings or sculptural forms. They erected new galleries on top of the chancel screens for musicians, choir, and organ, just as Jones's stage had its raised musician's gallery behind the scenes (shown in the stage plan for *Florimène*, Orgel and Strong, II, 643, figure 104).[23] Similar justification was advanced for the changes in both hall and church. When, for instance, Laud defended his reasons for replacing the altar at the end wall, the reasons he gave were largely those which made Jones's perspective stage an improvement on the old dispersed settings for court entertainments. Apart from the position being traditional, its advantages are practical: it adds order and convenience to liturgical occasions; it takes up much less room than in the body of the church; and the minister can be seen and heard better than when he is on the same level as a crowd of people.[24] Other defences of the ceremony favoured by Laud were given on analogy with court ceremony. When John Pocklington wrote in defence of bowing, for instance, he says that the Knights of the Garter bow towards the altar at services 'because it is the throne in earth of that great Lord, from whom their honour proceedeth', and that reverence is due to it 'in regard to the presence of our Saviour whose chair of State it is upon earth'.[25]

To those who opposed the increasing elaboration of church ceremony the resemblances between church and stage were obvious, especially as images being displayed in some Anglican churches bore a strong resemblance to those on the masque stage. Peter Smart, for instance, complained in 1628 that John Cosin had set up

> so glittering Angels round the quire of Durham Church, in long scarlet gownes, with golden wings and gilded heads: together with three other Images over the Byshops Throne, one of them beeing the Image of Christ, with a golden beard, a glorious blew cap with rayes like the Sunne beames, which betokens in the Popes School, some Deitie in the head which it coaureth.   (*The Downe-fall and Vanitie of Popish Ceremonies*, sig. *2v)

He goes on to complain of the candles and lights, the 'piping and singing' (p. 8), the old copes 'used in May games' (p. 10), and the ever greater number of images and pictures (p. 11). In his sermons *For God, and the King* Henry Burton preached against innovations in the King's chapel, such as 'a quire of Gentlemen, Singing men, & other Choristers, which dayly sing Service in the Chappell', and in St Paul's he criticised the 'mitred Images and Statues newly erected' and 'winged Angels round about the Quire . . . metamorphosed into a Curtizan-like garbe' (p. 161). These innovations echo court usage and, he says, if holiness stood in outward rites, 'in false shows, and will-worship, in a kind of Courtship, in a complement, in a Congee', then these were very religious men: 'then is Popery piety, and Superstition holinesse' (p. 99).

Underlying the comparison between church and court ceremony was, of course, the suspicion that both were 'Popish'. In the complaint of the Commons against Laud in 1634, the Commons cited as criticism of Laud's practices a homily from Elizabeth's time, in which the whole of Catholic ceremony was compared to court pageantry. The homily, attacking the wearing of copes, says that:

> because the whole Pageant must thoroughly be played, it is not enough thus to deck Images and Idols (with Gold, Silver, Rich, Wanton and Proud Apparel, tempting their Paramours to wantonnesse) but at last come in the Priests themselves, likewise decked with Gold and Pearls, that they may be meet servants for such Lords and Ladies, and fit worshippers of such Gods and Goddesses; and with a solemn pace they pass forth before the Golden Puppets, and fall down to the ground on their Marrow-bones before the honorable Idols (and their gorgeous Altars too).   (John Rushworth, *Historical Collections*, II, 180–1)

From Tyndale on, of course, 'Popish' liturgy had been compared scornfully to theatre,[26] but in the 1630s visual resemblances between Anglican ceremony, the court stage, and Catholic spectacle must have added point to Puritan fears. Those who feared that the outward signs of ceremony were an invitation for the return of Catholicism cannot have been reassured to see the opening services in the Queen's chapel carried out with all the spectacular devices of the court stage.

Catholic spectacle and masque scenes

When Inigo Jones's chapel for the Capucins was completed in December 1636 it was fitted out with a spectacular perspective scene for the celebration of the opening Mass. The scene belonged to an aspect of religion fashionable at the time in Rome, the *quarantore*.[27] These were a kind of *theatrum sacrum* designed for use in churches; they usually consisted of a spectacular scene built around the Eucharist, accompanied by elaborate singing and music, the purpose of which was to uplift the spirit with a display of the splendours of religion. The church served both as stage and auditorium, and it has been pointed out how well the Gesù, which became one of the main centres for these displays, lent itself to theatrical purposes: with its flanking wings enclosing a deep room, and extending towards a light backdrop, it conformed to the scenic principles in use on the court stage.[28] Giulio Parigi built sets in the chapel of the Pitti Palace, and from 1630 the form developed under the particular patronage of the Barberini (Mark Weil, 'The devotion of the Forty Hours', pp. 228–32). In 1633 a *quarantore* for Cardinal Barberini's church at San Lorenzo in Damaso was designed by Pietro da Cortona, and the design for it has been preserved in the collection of Roman drawings at Windsor Castle (figure 38).[29] It is interesting that George Conn, who was Canon of San Lorenzo in Damaso before coming to England (*DNB*), would have witnessed this scene, as well as the scene in the Queen's chapel (he arrived in July 1636). The document referring to Cortona's design describes it as a splendid apparatus for the setting of the Eucharist,

arranged in the form of a Theatre, with columns, niches, and gilded statues of saints, and other ornaments representing at the high altar the rays of the sun, in the midst of which was placed the Holy Sacrament supported by two great Angels, with great abundance of wax lights in silver candle-sticks above this apparatus, and with tapers of silver, and with continual sermons and music.[30]

This description and illustration may serve as a convenient background to the scene in the Queen's chapel, an account of which was written by Father Cyprien (bracketed page numbers that follow refer to his description, taken from Birch, *Court and Times*, Volume 2).

The chapel opened with a full Pontifical Mass, the first to have been celebrated in England for nearly one hundred years. To mark the solemnity of the occasion the Capucins applied to François Dieussart, an eminent sculptor lately come to London from Rome,[31] to design for them a 'scenic machine' about forty feet

38 Pietro da Cortona, *Quarantore* design for Cardinal Barberini's church of San Lorenzo in Damaso, Rome 1633; Windsor Castle, Royal Library © Her Majesty The Queen

in height, to display the Holy Sacrament shining at the centre of a Paradise of glory. Dieussart first erected a great arch supported by two pillars in front of the high altar, leaving a space between the columns and the walls for the priests to pass to and from a portable altar beneath the arch. The ascent to this altar was by six steps, leaving an unobstructed view in front, and by two sets of steps 'in theatrical form' (p. 311) at either side. Over the spaces at each side of the arch were placed the choir, organ, and other instruments, and in front of each space stood the figure of a prophet. Behind the altar, forming the centre of the perspective, a Paraclete was seen above seven ranges of clouds; in these were figures of archangels, cherubin and seraphin 'to the number of two hundred', some adoring the Holy Sacrament, others singing and playing on all sorts of musical instruments, the whole 'painted and placed according to the rules of perspective' (pp. 311–12), so cleverly that the distance and the number of figures appeared to be double what they were. Circles of decreasing size led to the Sacrament at the centre: in the first circle were angels larger than life, singing and playing on instruments; in others deacons with censers, some kneeling, some prostrate, others pointing to the Sacrament; more distant circles contained smaller angels sporting in the clouds, inviting the people to rejoice; and in the last circles were cherubin and seraphin surrounded by luminous rays. The Sacrament itself was aglow with golden light, the whole so skilfully illuminated that 'the painting seemed to vanish, there was left nothing but the brilliancy of the lights, which caused that place to appear all on fire' (p. 312). There were four hundred lights, besides a multitude of tapers ingeniously arranged on the altar to light the first circles. The scene was covered by two curtains. When the Queen and her court came to hear Mass, and the Queen was seated in the place prepared for her, the curtains were drawn back and the scene revealed to the excited admiration of the Catholics:

At the same time, the music, composed of excellent voices, set up an anthem, the harmony of which having no outlet but between the clouds and the figures of Angels, it seemed as if the whole Paradise was full of music, and as if the Angels themselves were the musicians ... thus eye and ear found at the same time gratification in this contrivance of piety and skill.   (p. 313)

The Mass itself was sung in eight parts, and the whole performance repeated at Vespers, 'to the satisfaction of the Queen, and the applause of the whole audience' (p. 313).

The language used by Father Cyprien is unmistakably that of the theatre, and the form of the scene, with its 'stage' and the scene in the 'heavens', has similarities to that set up in the Banqueting House for the masques. The altar is placed beneath a proscenium arch in the centre of a raised stage, and the priests come and go to it by passages at the sides of the scene; in performing the service they use the fore-stage with its setting of the altar, much as the fore-stage is used for the action of a masque. The 'picture' behind the proscenium arch forms the background for this action, and the raised stage is connected with the nave by steps 'in theatrical form'. The Queen in the chapel has a special seat prepared for her, the equivalent of the State prepared for the King or Queen at a masque, so placed that it has a perfect view into the perspective scene. The main scene over the high altar is placed behind the proscenium arch, arranged 'according to the rules of perspective', and ablaze with colour and light, similar to the scenes in the heavens or upper stage of Jones's spectacular masques. The scene is covered initially by two curtains, and the congregation becomes the audience who applaud the magnificent sight. The whole performance is accompanied by a wealth of vocal and instrumental music.

The fame of the scene in the chapel spread throughout the court, and the Queen gave orders that it should remain undisturbed until Christmas (a period of about seventeen days), to satisfy the devotion of the Catholics and the curiosity of the Protestants 'who never ceased coming from all parts to behold this wonder' (p. 314). On the third night the King himself came with a train of gentlemen to the chapel, gazed at the scene for a long time, 'and said aloud, that he had never seen anything more beautiful or more ingeniously designed' (p. 314). Inigo Jones no doubt accompanied the King on this occasion, since he was the architect of the chapel, and Charles's constant adviser on matters of art. He too would have found much to admire, and little to surprise him, as he himself used his stage as a 'scenic machine' in a similar way. In fact the scene suggested to at least one contemporary a comparison with Jones's masques. Garrard wrote in a letter to the Earl of Strafford:

This last Month the Queen's Chapel in *Somerset-House-Yard* was consecrated by her Bishop; the Ceremonies lasted three Days, Massing, Preaching, and Singing of Litanies, and such a glorious Scene built over their Altar, the Glory of Heaven, *Inigo Jones* never presented a more curious Piece in any of the Masks at Whitehall.   (Garrard to Strafford, 8 January 1635)[32]

The comparison with Jones's masque scenes is significant for several reasons: first because it came naturally to the mind of an eye-witness; secondly because Garrard uses the phrase a 'curious Piece', which suggests that Jones's spectacular scenes were singled out from the masque as a whole to be admired for their pictorial qualities; and thirdly because it is rather surprising to find the English court stage being compared to Counter-Reformation church spectacle in its most elaborate form.

Garrard must have been calling to mind scenes from the earlier masques of the thirties, such as that for *Tempe Restored*, for example, in which the spheres suspended on a cloud provide music for the appearance of the stars and the masquers. In later masques, however, Jones may have aimed in turn at producing some of the effects of the scene in the chapel. A notable feature of the scene was the way musicians were concealed behind the proscenium arch in order to produce the magical effect of music issuing from the clouds, seeming to make the painted or relief figures themselves the musicians. Jones already had his raised musicians' gallery behind the scenes (as in the stage design for *Florimène*, O&S, figure 104), but in a masque such as *Luminalia* he seems to exploit this more deliberately. In the concluding spectacle, remarkable for its aerial music and dancing, appeared 'a heaven full of deities or second causes, with instruments and voices' (ll. 386–8). This was made up of a scene on the upper stage (figure 18 above), together with a painted or relief scene of musicians on the lower (figure 19 above; see Orgel and Strong's analysis and diagram of the scene, no. 387). The text states that all these (painted or cardboard) musicians 'join with' the Muses of Great Britain and a chorus of priests (the actual musicians) in singing to the King and Queen. To achieve this effect Jones would have had to have musicians behind the scenes to give the illusion that the painted figures were themselves joining in. These clouds and semi-circles of singing and playing figures form the backdrop to another scene in which 'the upper part of the heavens opened, and a bright and transparent cloud came forth far into the scene' (ll. 403–4). On this cloud figures in rich garments begin a sprightly dance to the music of the violins, joining hands in rounds. This scene was inspired by the *intermedium* for Giulio Parigi's 'Il Giudizio di Paride', but the total effect of the scenes on the stage, and of musicians and dancers, may be compared with that in the chapel, where the first circle of clouds contained angels 'singing and playing on instruments', and more distant circles contained smaller angels 'sporting' in the clouds, 'inviting the people to rejoice'. Jones's technical achievement in the masque gives reality to what in the church could be no more than the illusion of life and movement.

The final scene of *Salmacida Spolia* (1640) is more sombre but equally spectacular, and may have attempted similar effects. In the highest part of the heavens a cloud appeared bearing eight persons representing the spheres; this,

joining with two other clouds which appeared at that instant full of music, covered all the upper part of the scene; and at that instant, beyond all these, a heaven opened full of deities; which celestial prospect, with the chorus below, filled all the whole scene with apparitions and harmony.   (ll. 460–4)

The illustration of this scene (figure 39) shows clearly that the two clouds 'full of music' bore only two and three musicians respectively, a rather small number considering that Jones stresses that the 'whole scene' is filled with harmony. To give the effect of music issuing from the clouds, he may have supplemented the playing of the visible musicians by concealing others behind the wings on the upper stage, where there was ample space since the back shutters formed the back, not of the stage, but of scenery worked on the shutter principle, two-thirds of the way between the front and back of the stage.[33] Beyond these clouds opened the heaven full of deities (figure 40), two semi-circles of painted or relief figures revealed by drawing apart the upper stage back shutters. The most distant group of deities is arranged around the central point of a glory, providing a perspective point similar to that of the luminous rays surrounding the Sacrament in the chapel. Both the masque and the chapel scenes have the characteristics of baroque art, depending as they do on the manipulation of large masses to form a harmonious whole, and on the illusion of infinite space to create a sense of heightened reality. Both suggest, through an appeal to the imagination and the emotions, the spiritual world that lies beyond, but remains linked with, the real world.

It is perhaps significant that Jones in these two masques notes with satisfaction that the spectacular scenes were approved especially by all 'strangers' and 'travellers of judgement' (*Luminalia*, ll. 7–8; *Salmacida Spolia*, l. 486) that were present. On the Continent the interchangeability of stage devices for court and church spectacle was taken for granted. The Jesuit stage designer Jean Dubreuil, summing up practices already in use in his treatise *La Perspective pratique* (Paris 1642–49),[34] says that his stage properties may serve equally 'aux Autels, et Oratoires des Eglises ... aux Alcôves, Théâtres, Ballets'. He restores the *gloire*, which had been adopted by Renaissance courts, to its ecclesiastical function, particularly for celebrations of the Eucharist, but makes it clear that this does not preclude its use on the court stage;

Je dis si c'est pour y mettre le S. Sacrement: car on peut se servir de ces nuées en des Théâtres et des Ballets, où on veut représenter le Paradis, même on peut y faire monter, et descendre des personnes ...   (Traité IV, Pratique ix)

Jones was in no way dependent on foreign influence for new ideas in stage

39 Inigo Jones, final scene for *Salmacida Spolia*

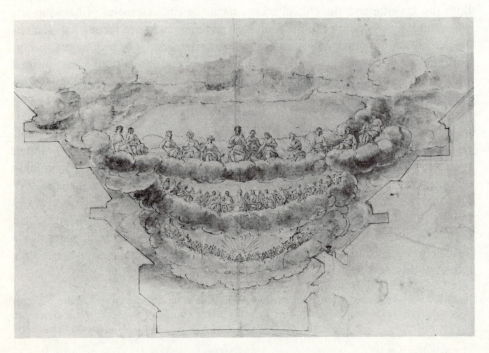

40 Inigo Jones, detail of final scene with gods enthroned in heavens, *Salmacida Spolia*

technique, but he must have been interested in the scene in the chapel, and the admiration expressed by the King and Queen would have been one of the strongest motives for wishing to emulate it. He was always open to new ideas, and aware of his work within a wider tradition. In these masques he particularly appeals to the cosmopolitan members of his audience who were familiar with stage performances abroad, yet who, he says, hold 'our English masques ... to be as noble and ingenious as those of any other nations' (*Luminalia*, ll. 7–9).

Such people, and many at the English court as well, would have been familiar with the similarity between court and religious spectacle in Catholic countries abroad. In Rome the Barberini Palace, which opened in 1632, was a centre of hospitality for people visiting or staying in Rome, especially those with letters of introduction from the Queen: Walter Montague was received there when he went to Rome in the winter of 1635–6, to be ordained as an Oratorian priest.[35] The theatre of the Palace (later in the thirties capable of holding 3,000 people) became a centre for operatic productions.[36] Bernini (who was also a designer of *quarantore* for the Barberini) was theatre-manager, and the opera with which the Palace opened was produced with magnificent scenes ranging from Hell, to a landscape, to a palace, to the final scene in Heaven and the triumphant appearance of Religion.[37] Bernini was at that time engaged in sculpting the bust of Charles from drawings by Van Dyck, and considering the close relations between the Barberini and the English court in the 1630s, it would be unusual if reports of stage spectacle designed by so eminent a person had not found their way to Jones. Another centre of stage production in Rome was the Jesuit English College, and English travellers did not have to be Catholic to be entertained there. One visitor recorded that 'wee Protestants' at that time were very kindly received at the College 'in respect of our Queene', and that 'desiring one day to be admitted unto an Enterlude in *Stilo recitativo* acted before some Cardinals and persons of quallitie ... we were presently bid goe in and had given us very comodious seats'.[38] The writer adds that the hospitality of the College was not without religious motive since: 'These Invitations are done to our Nation certaynely to gayne what they can upon those of our Religion, and soften us as to theirs' (Stoye, p. 182). Certainly to many spectators of the masques the general popularity of the religious stage abroad, and the easy access which members of the court had to its productions, would have made an association between the spectacle of Jones's stage and religious spectacle on the Continent a commonplace. When such spectacle was also witnessed at court in Catholic ceremony sponsored by the Queen, it must have appeared a strong indication not only of the court's artistic tastes, but of its religious tastes as well.

'Divine' beauty and the arts

Although opponents of the court had good reason to associate court spectacle with religious spectacle, and to attack the 'Catholic' bias in both, the issue for

Anglicans was not a simple one. To those who shared the liturgical tastes of Archbishop Laud and the King, beauty and ceremony were not the property of one religion alone: they belonged to a Christian tradition which an English Church, now considered to be thoroughly reformed, could once more safely introduce and practise. The question of beauty in church worship became one of deep personal concern to Charles in the 1630s, and it seems possible that masques themselves, which were resumed on a regular basis in 1631, were used as vehicles to defend it. Disputes concerning innovations in church ritual and decoration had been one of the prominent features leading up to Charles's dissolution of Parliament in 1629 and beginning the period of his personal rule (for a detailed treatment see S. R. Gardiner, *History of England*, VII, and John Phillips, *The Reformation of Images*). In 1629 Parliament had complained of the growing use of pictures, lights, and images in church services, had spoken of the danger of supporting Papist practices and influences at court, and had questioned the clause which had been added to the 20th Article (not contained in the Act of 1571): that 'The Church hath power to decree rites and ceremonies, and authority in controversies of faith.' (Gardiner, VII, 48, and 65–7). These complaints had been precipitated by a series of cases (in 1628 and 1629) against John Cosin at Durham, where the Cathedral was being turned into a centre of High Church ceremony. Cosin was praised at one of his trials for helping to bring 'decencie and order' to God's service, the first of a series of such judgments, backed by the Crown, in favour of Laudian reforms (Phillips, pp. 151–2, and 180). In 1629 there was a celebrated case of a painted window at St Edmund's; in 1630 Laud opened the church of St Katherine Kree with conspicuous ceremony that drew Puritan attack; in 1632 a notorious case about breaking a church window in Salisbury went to trial, and forced Laud to defend images in the Court of Star Chamber (Phillips, p. 163; Gardiner, VII, 242 ff.). Events rose to a climax in 1633 with the appointment of Laud as Archbishop of Canterbury, with jurisdiction over all ecclesiastical matters, and the power to decree the form of liturgical ceremony in the rest of the kingdom. In the same year Charles's visit to Scotland for his Coronation, which was carried out by Laud with full ceremony, aroused in the Scots 'great fear of inbringing of Popery' (Gardiner, VII, 286). In the mid-thirties Laud's enforcement of conformity through the Visitation Articles met with great hostility; although open opposition was stifled, resentment over liturgical matters and the differences in theological beliefs that they symbolised contributed to the outbreak of the Civil War.

The issue of church ceremony was one in which the Royal prerogative was closely involved and, like other issues over which Charles felt deep concern (such as Ship Money), I believe it was referred to in the masques. Masques may already have been used in James's reign to defend Anglican ritual, as Leah Marcus has argued. Among the several forms of 'union' which *Hymenaei* treated was a unified English church, symbolised in the masque by a union of opposing religions in the groom and bride, the Calvinist Essex and the pro-Spanish Howard families.

From such a union was expected to spring a new harmony, including the 'mysterious rites', the ritual (justified by Reason on 'authentic grounds') of the Anglican church.[39] Marcus has pointed out that another masque treats a later phase of the same basic policy, James's attempts to impose order and ceremony on the Scottish 'kirk'. In 1617 James sent to his chapel at Holyrood House paintings and religious figures, organ, choristers from the Chapel Royal, and a carved choir and stalls reputed to be by Inigo Jones.[40] They were accompanied by an admonition to the Scots Presbyterians to distinguish between pictures intended for ornament and images made for worship. The Presbyterians replied that all were Popish, as was William Laud's histrionic vestment and action in kneeling to receive the Sacrament. In the masque of the following season, *Pleasure Reconciled to Virtue* (1618), Marcus shows that the ritual final portion has a strong resemblance to liturgical forms, that Jonson's verses may be read as a defence of the 'comely *via media* of the Anglican Church', and that the figures in long red robes and golden mitres are representations of the Anglican Bishops. In the final scene the Bishops are set tactfully between Daedalus and a white-clad goddess, showing that Religion and the Arts are reconciled by Virtue. Jonson himself had just become 'reconciled' to the Anglican Church, and Jones, in addition to backing up Royal policy, had a vested interest in drawing attention to his own arts (Daedalus is the god of architecture and sculpture), and their part in enhancing the ceremony of church service and court stage. The masque is both a defence and a celebration of James's policies, and of their worthy execution by people like Laud and Jones himself. Neither James's policies nor this masque enjoyed immediate success, but the issues which the latter set out became part of the concerted policy of Charles (who had been the chief masquer in *Pleasure Reconciled to Virtue*) and Laud in the 1630s.

Jones's emphasis on the visual rather than the verbal aspects of masques in the thirties gave them an especially appropriate bearing on the question. A fundamental issue in the debate over Beauty in religion was the question of whether art and images could lead to contemplation of the Divine, as Anglican theologians and Catholics claimed. Traditionally the Church had defended images on the grounds that, if properly used, they served to bring back the memory of their archetypes and hence led to contemplation of the Divine.[41] Anglican clergy, who claimed to walk a 'middle path' in liturgical as well as in theological matters, looked for their models to the practices of the early Church. On the question of ceremony Richard Hooker, who laid the foundation for Anglican practice in his work *Of the Laws of Ecclesiastical Polity* (1594), had strongly defended the external and 'visible signs' of traditional worship. Men are edified, Hooker wrote, either through their understanding or their affections, and for this purpose 'not only speech, but sundry sensible means besides have always been thought necessary'. Especially important are:

those means which being object to the eye, the liveliest and the most apprehensive sense of all other, have in that respect seemed the fittest to make a deep and strong impression: from hence have risen not only a number of prayers … but even of visible signs also; which being used in performance of holy actions, are undoubtedly most effectual to open such matter.

(book 4, chapter 1, p. iii)[42]

He goes on to say that 'words, both because they are common, and do not so strongly move the fancy of men, are for the most part but slightly heard', so that deeds of weight have always been accompanied by sensible actions, 'the memory whereof is far more easy and durable than the memory of speech can be'. Views similar to these were the basis of court as well as church ritual, and such a passage coincides with Jones's view of the masque, and the emphasis on visual forms in the 1630s: when great matters are at stake 'We speak in acts, and scorn words' trifling scenes' (*Albion's Triumph*, l. 99).

Jones himself was closely involved with the return of the arts to the Church. He was busy in the thirties with the building and repair of churches, and in the context of religious debate his defence of the visual arts in the masques may take on added significance. The concluding *tableau* of Fame in *Chloridia* (1631) seems to predict a new importance for the arts when Fame, supported by Poetry and History, Sculpture and Architecture, announces action which is 'virtuous, great and good' (l. 238), and which will be preserved by such arts for eternity. In the following year (1632) Jones made an elaborate defence of his own arts in the border of the scene to *Albion's Triumph* and *Tempe Restored* (see D. J. Gordon, 'Poet and architect' in *The Renaissance Imagination*). This defence was directed at people like Ben Jonson who resented the dominance of the visual arts at court, but it came at a time when the issue of the visual arts was fast becoming a test for the authority of the Church and the King. The case of a church window at Salisbury in February 1632, for instance, was tried in the court of Star Chamber and forced Laud to a public defence of images.[43] Moreover, in *Tempe Restored* Jones's statement that 'corporeal beauty … may draw us to the contemplation of the beauty of the soul, unto which it hath analogy' (ll. 361–4) had a direct relation to religion at a time when some Anglican Bishops were arguing that objects and images were 'the visible signs of invisible graces'.[44] Indeed, the presentation of a whole masque on the subject of 'Divine Beauty' may be seen as a defence against the many people who resented the growing emphasis on visual forms, not only at court but in the Anglican Church.

Jones's statement in *Tempe Restored*, that corporeal beauty has the power to lead to spiritual illumination, becomes even more contentious when he adds that the beauty which has this power consists of 'symmetry, colour, and certain inexpressable graces, shining in the Queen's Majesty' (ll. 361–3). The embodiment of the ideal of 'Divine Beauty' in the Queen seems significant in view of the debate over how far 'Beauty' in Anglican worship meant 'Catholic' beauty. In the thirties this debate centred on whether the Catholic origin of many of the forms of Anglican ceremony was a ground for discarding them, or whether they were part of the common heritage of spiritual beauty which Anglicans and Catholics shared. To theologians like Hooker and Andrewes the traditional liturgical forms of religious worship were not to be discarded simply because they were practised by the Catholic Church. By the 1630s Laud believed that men were sufficiently aware of the right use of images to avoid the dangers of idolatry, and he could therefore lay down the rule for Anglican clergy that 'all such Rites as had been practised in the Church of Rome, and not abolished ... were to continue in the same state in which they found them'.[45] Moreover, to accusations of Arminianism and Popery, he had the precedent of people like Richard Hooker, who had concluded that:

> Where Rome keepeth that which is ancienter and better, others whom we much more affect leaving it for newer, and changing it for worse; we had rather follow the perfections of them whom we like not, than in defects resemble them whom we love.
>
> (*Of the Laws of Ecclesiastical Polity*, book 5, chapter 28, p. i)[46]

To Laud, and especially to Charles, beauty of worship was one of the 'good' parts of Catholicism. A reformed and refined ceremony, freed of pre-Reformation excess and added to the reason and truth of Anglicanism, would result in a religion in which Beauty and Truth were one.

This theme seems to be reflected in the masques under images for the King and Queen, whose union is played out on the stage with strong suggestions of religious ritual. The Queen is the figure around whom conspicuous Catholic ritual revolved at court, and throughout the masques the classical austerity and discipline associated with the King are softened and enlightened by joining with the complementary qualities of beauty and light shining in the Queen. In *Love's Triumph*, Charles is not the 'Heroical Warrior', but the 'Heroical Lover', and the city into which he makes his triumphal entry is Callipolis, 'the city of beauty and goodness' (l. 8). In this masque, as Orgel and Strong have noted (1, 53) there is a formality reminiscent of Laudian Anglicanism in the ceremony with which the Chorus move about swinging censers to purify the approaches to the Queen's 'city of beauty'. Callipolis is the 'seat and region of all beauty' (l. 74), and the Queen herself is its 'temple' (l. 113). Here 'Love in perfection longeth to appear', but cannot do so until the chorus 'make lustration of the place' with 'solemn fires and waters' (ll. 83–4):

> Then will he flow forth like a rich perfume
> Into your nostrils, or some sweeter sound
> Of melting music, that shall not consume
> Within the ear, but run the mazes round.   (ll. 78–82)

The sensuous beauty of religious ritual could hardly be described more richly, and it would, in performance, have been greatly enhanced by the action on the stage. The ceremony of purification leads to that meeting of ideal Beauty, embodied by the Queen, and ideal Love, embodied by the King, which created form from chaos,

> And left imprinted in the air
> Those signatures of good and fair,
> Which since have flowed, flowed forth upon the sense,

> To wonder first, and then to excellence,
> By virtue of divine intelligence!   (ll. 149–53)

The order created by a 'reformed beauty' is part of the divine plan.

In the Queen's companion masque, *Chloridia*, the actual subject is 'adornment' of earth. Jonson's motto for the masque is '*Unius tellus ante coloris erat*' (the earth was formerly one colour), and this, Jonson says, is the hinge upon which 'the whole invention moved' (l. 11). The quotation is from Ovid (*Fasti*, v, l. 222), and Jonson goes on to explain that the subject is to be

> some rites done to the goddess Chloris, who ... was proclaimed goddess of the flowers ... and was to be stellified on earth by an absolute decree from Jupiter, who would have the earth to be adorned with stars as well as the heaven.   (ll. 5–10)

In Ovid's myth the nymph Chloris is loved by Zephyr, whose passionate breath changes her to Flora, the goddess who transforms the earth from 'one colour' to the beauties and variety of the Spring. There is a hint of this part of the story in the opening section, where Jonson tactfully removes the fructifying power from Zephyr to 'the warmth of yonder sun', which is Charles himself:

> Give all to him: his is the dew,
> The heat, the humour –
>
> All
> That wisest nature cause can call
> Of quick'ning anything.   (ll. 55–6, 60–2)

If a compliment to the Queen had been all that was intended, the masque should have ended with the covering of earth with flowers, as in the Medici entertainment on which this part of the masque was surely based.[47] *Chloridia*, however, takes the process of beautification a step further. When the Queen dances, the flowers which she makes grow by 'th'impression of her foot' (l. 206) are not the products of nature alone, but the product of art acting on nature, and her dance is, in the literal and metaphorical sense, a witty 'stamping out' of beauty, creating a beautiful form. Beautiful form, however, has to have heavenly approval, and this is given by Jove to the beauty that springs from the King and Queen's union. The masque is built on a structure of complementary opposites personifying the masculine and feminine principles of the universe – Heaven and Earth, Zephyr and Spring, King and Queen. The masculine is the dominant and commanding power, but the feminine brings to it the beauty and variety which belong to the universal order, as ineluctably as the beauty and variety of the seasons and elements belong to the natural order. Why should there be any enmity between earth and heaven on this point? Enmity has been stirred up by Disdain, Fear, and Dissimulation, but now, through the love and virtuous union of the King and Queen, Earth and Heaven are reunited:

> It is decreed by all the gods
> The heav'n of earth shall have no odds,
> But one shall love another.

> Their glories they shall mutual make,
> Earth look on heaven for heaven's sake;
> Their honours shall be even.   (ll. 40–5)

The result of this union is a beautification of the earth, formerly dull and 'one colour'; now that harmony is established:

> Jove will have earth to have her stars
> And lights, no less than heaven.   (ll. 47–8)

King and Queen, earth and heaven, form and 'beauty' are one.

In the next pair of masques, beauty and ritual are again associated with the Queen, and made perfect by their union with the manly virtues of the King. In *Albion's Triumph* the King is described in heroic terms: his triumph is

> mighty as the man designed
> To wear those bays, heroic as his mind,
> Just as his actions, glorious as his reign,
> And like his virtues, infinite in train.   (ll. 88–91)

But this mighty hero and his companions are themselves conquered by Love and Chastity, qualities enshrined in Alba, the Queen, whose beauty has 'a great affinity with all purity'. The introduction tells us that 'the King's devoting himself to this goddess is but the seeking of the happy union which was preordained by the greatest of the gods' (ll. 10–13). The second part of the masque is dominated by the images of religious ceremony associated with the Queen, just as the first part is dominated by the images of classical heroism associated with the King. The King and his attendants are discovered in a 'stately temple' sacred to Jove (l. 261). Cupid and Diana, appearing in the heavens, shoot at the masquers, 'and Albanactus, yielding to the gods, moves down the steps in a stately pace to music made by the chorus of sacrificers, that sing as the masquers descend' (ll. 296–8). The masquers, subdued by Alba's beauty, become 'Love's sacrifice' and now are 'all divine' (l. 295). The Queen is the centre of this religious ritual. When the masquers have descended, 'the high priests and sacrificers, treading a grave measure, walk up towards the Queen singing' (ll. 317–20), and the hero is presented as a sacrifice to her chaste love:

> Here comes the trophy of thy praise,
> The monarch of these isles,
> The mirror of thy cheerful rays,
> And glory of thy smiles:
> The virtues and the graces all
> Must meet in one when such stars fall.   (ll. 330–5)

The King and the Queen are united, and the virtues that spring from their union are Innocency, Justice, Religion, Affection to the Country, and Concord, 'being all companions of Peace' (l. 344). The classical gods are brought to pay tribute, and, for a conclusion, 'the gods, poets and priests join and sing a valediction to Hymen's twin, the Mary-Charles' (ll. 440–1). In performance, the emphasis on religious ritual in the 'grave measure', the high priests, and the singing of the chorus, would have been unmistakable, and the tribute paid to the King and Queen at the end makes them, together, representative of a higher religious virtue than the classical gods, whom they now transcend.

In *Tempe Restored* the same pairing of opposites is stated in the 'Allegory', where the King possesses the attributes of Heroic Virtue, being 'the prototype of religion, justice, and all the virtues joined together' (ll. 358–60), while the Queen possesses the complementary attribute of beauty, which attracts and elevates the soul. Charles's 'religion and justice' here provide a background for the vision of 'Divine Beauty', whose appearance Jones accompanies with all the adjuncts of material beauty that his stage could command. Jones's scenes, too, make sense of the title, which is meant to convey the fact that 'Tempe, which for a time had been possessed by the voluntary beasts of Circe's court, is restored to the true followers of the Muses' (l. 26). On reading the masque one may be excused for wondering how the Muses come into it, for they do not appear in the rest of the text. In the allegory, however, there is a sudden shift which makes the Dryads and Naiades, whose normal occupation is 'to gather the most exquisite herbs and flowers of the earth for the service of their mistress', into figures for 'the virtues and sciences, by which the desire of man's spirits are prepared and disposed to good' (ll. 332–5). The way in which this transformation is achieved is to turn the affections from false to true beauty, and the way it is achieved in the masque is through the effect on the spectator of the scene in which Jones presents the Queen as Divine Beauty. Having perceived true Beauty, intemperate men who have for a while possessed the Vale of Tempe are converted to love of virtue, and Tempe may once more become 'the happy retreat of the muses and their followers... to whom of right only that place belongs' (ll. 340–4). In *Tempe Restored* the rather defensive air of Jones's scene with Fame and the Arts at the end of *Chloridia* has given place to the confident assertion that the arts have the power to attract, and Beauty to elevate the soul.

Coelum Britannicum, the King's next masque, is a quite explicit statement of a new English 'Reformation' (l. 469) in which morals are purified, and the arts have a prominent place. The masque not only commends the court for the recent practice of commemorating noble acts in 'picture, sculpture, tapestries' and other works of art (ll. 426–31), but laments the despoliation of the Church by the destructive zeal of the Reformation. The text echoes a common accusation (that reform was activated by greed) when 'Wealth' describes how

> your deities
> Are for my sake slighted, despised, abused,
> Your temples, shrines, altars and images
> Uncovered, rifled, robbed and disarrayed
> By sacrilegious hands.   (ll. 520–4)

The masque ends with the appearance of the allegorical figure of Religion, who praises the King and Queen for the 'Religious zeal' and 'Pure adoration' (ll. 1095, 1108) now practised under their combined influence in the newly reformed Heaven of the British court. The Queen's masque *The Temple of Love* is, on a general level, again a treatment of moral and artistic reform, since the ancient poets who once sang of lascivious love are now taught by the Queen's new cult to purify their verse, and the 'Magicians', who once led youth astray in their temples of false beauty, are now reformed by the appearance of the Queen's new Temple, whose true beauty encourages love 'of souls'.

The Queen's last masque, *Luminalia*, like *Tempe Restored*, opens with a long introductory passage which appears to have nothing to do with what follows, and again (as in *Tempe Restored*) Jones makes a remarkable shift from the subject, 'consisting of darkness and light' (l. 13), to yet another discussion of the Muses. This begins as a long lament:

> The muses being long since drawn out of Greece by the fierce Thracians, their groves withered and all their springs dried up, and out of Italy by the barbarous Goths and Vandals, they wandered here and there indecently without their ornaments and instruments, the arch-flamens and flamens, their prophetic priests, being constrained either to live in disguises or hide their heads in caves . . .

> (ll. 16–22)

Jones's words, linking the destruction of the arts first with the Goths and Vandals and then with the persecution of 'their prophetic priests', seem to echo the Introduction to Vasari's *Lives of the Painters*.[48] Vasari's book was one of the most heavily annotated in Jones's library,[49] and Jones may have had in mind the passage in which Vasari describes the destruction of Rome, first by the Goths and Vandals, and then by the fervent but misdirected zeal 'of the new Christian religion', a phrase which could well stand to Jones in a contemporary context for the destructive zeal of the Reformation. This zeal, Vasari says, devoted itself 'with all diligence to driving out and extirpating root and branch every least occasion where error could arise', and in so doing 'not only defaced or threw to the ground all the marvellous statues, sculptures, pictures, mosaics and ornaments of the false gods of the heathens, but even the memorials and the honours of numberless men of rank' (p. xlviii). There was an obvious parallel to be made with more recent examples of such zeal, and the sentiments must have found a sympathetic echo among both Anglicans and Catholics at Charles's court. Jones goes on to say that after the 'perpetual storm' into which both the arts and priests have been driven over many years, they are at last 'by the divine minds of these incomparable pair [the King and Queen] received into protection and established in this monarchy, to the encouragement and security of those well-born wits represented by the Prophetic Priests of the Britanides' (*Luminalia*, ll. 26–9). Charles was, in fact, restoring the arts to the English Church as well as to the country, and his deepest wish was that Anglicanism should be a religion in which Truth and Beauty were one. The action and images of these masques seem to reflect such an ideal, uniting English moral reform with 'divine' beauty, and creating an image, in the union of the King and Queen, of a new and resplendent 'British' heaven.

6   Love and religion

Anglicanism and Devout Humanism

The way in which the King and Queen's love and marriage was presented in the masques had strong political implications (as Stephen Orgel has conclusively shown), symbolising the union of ideal Authority and ideal Love that Charles regarded as the qualities of his absolute rule. But political authority was closely allied to religious authority, and one of the imminent threats to Charles's ideal of Arcadian peace in the 1630s lay in differences between religions. These differences were manifest in the religious wars still being fought in Europe, and in dissidence between militant supporters of Protestantism (notably Puritans and Presbyterians) and of Catholicism (notably the Jesuits) at home. It seems to me that the political symbolism of the King and Queen's marriage has a further level of symbolism applicable to religion, and that the way in which their harmonious relationship is presented in the masques suggests a way in which their respective religions might also exist in harmony. Underlying this question is, of course, the way in which Henrietta's type of Catholicism related to Charles's Anglicanism. Although I have stressed Henrietta's Catholic interests, I do not think it so great a paradox that her religion and Charles's existed more or less peaceably side by side at court. French Devout Humanism, especially as practised by the Capucins in the 1630s, was recognised by contemporaries as a moderate form of Catholicism, a counter to the aggressive Catholicism of the Jesuits who were hated and feared for their connections with Spain. In James's reign crypto-Catholicism at court had been of the latter kind: Queen Anne was under Spanish Catholic influence,[1] other members of the court received pensions from Spain, and James had turned to Spain in his first choice of a bride for Charles. At Charles's court the Spanish influence declined, and friendly contacts were all with Paris and Rome. Marie de Medici was a link between Henrietta and the Pope, who took a special interest in the progress of his god-daughter at the English court, while in Rome Cardinal Barberini went out of his way to entertain and impress English visitors with his hospitality. It was publicly said of him at court that he had 'done more to reclaim the northern nations by his civilities, than Cardinal Bellarmin had ever done by his writings'.[2] Within the Catholic party itself Henrietta represented a moderating influence. She did not choose her friends among the older English Catholics, the Countesses of Buckingham and Arundel, or the King's Secretaries Weston and Cottington, who were considered to be under Jesuit influence. The Catholics of her immediate circle were more typically women companions who had come under her influence, or urbane courtiers who had been at the French court. She stood in the middle of the Catholic party, and in the negotiations with the Papal agents her role essentially was to act as an intermediary between them and the King, keeping good relations on both sides. The more active and proselytising roles were left to people like the Countess of Arundel, who sponsored Conn's activities, or Olivia Porter, who worked publicly at making conversions. To the agents from Rome, who necessarily had to work with the more active Catholics like Sir Francis Windebanke, her neutrality must have seemed like lack of zeal, and hence their complaints about her association with 'Puritan' followers. They had no such complaints about the closest of her confidants, Walter Montague, who was well received by Cardinal Barberini and the Pope, and praised as being of the greatest value in the negotiations with Rome (Berington, *Memoirs*, pp. 190–1, 215).

Henrietta's friendships were not, as I have mentioned earlier, confined to Catholics, and I would agree with Malcolm Smuts's view, in 'The Puritan followers of Henrietta Maria', that some of her followers 'supported moderate policies and divided their loyalties between the crown and its parliamentary and puritan enemies' (p. 27), and his summing up, that English Catholicism was 'split by disputes between an intransigent, Jesuit faction and a secular party seeking accommodation with the crown. The queen strongly supported the latter ...' (p. 34). This does not mean, however, that she was actively engaged against the interests of moderate Catholics, or of Charles. Smuts seems to over-emphasise the political aspects of her friendships by referring to 'the Queen's party' and 'the Queen's faction' (phrases which continually recur), which is then equated with the 'Puritan' party. For contemporaries the term 'Puritan', as Smuts himself points out, really meant no more than those not attached closely to either Catholicism or to the King; to Europeans such as Panzani it was often only a name for non-Catholics, and even amongst Anglicans it might be applied to anyone 'who spoke well of the Reformed religion' (Smuts, pp. 27, 31). As for the Queen's 'party', it turns out, on Smuts's own presentation (pp. 27, 30, 33), to be mainly the Earls of Holland and Northumberland, Walter Montague, and Henry Jermyn. Of these, Montague and Jermyn were certainly not Puritan and both (according to Smuts) had converted to Catholicism by 1636; besides, they were ladies' men and court intriguers rather than politicians, and the same might almost be said for the charming but wavering Holland, who was eventually executed as a Royalist conspirator (*DNB*). For the rest, people like Henry Percy and the Earl of Dorset fought for the Royalists, not for Charles's opponents. Henrietta did not like Charles's chief minister Weston, nor Archbishop Laud, but nor for that matter did most other people, and her dislike was impartial in that it covered both Catholic and Anglican. Although she may at times have lent herself to those who wished to 'win the support of a naive young queen' (Smuts, p. 45), her 'plotting' on the Puritan side does not extend to much more than a liking for agreeable company and a dislike of anything Spanish; on the Catholic side the main complaint of French ambassadors and Catholic agents was that she would *not* engage in intrigue, or do what she was told to exert her political influence one way or the other.[3] Her friends (Smuts does not consider women friends, apart from Lady Carlisle) came from both sides of the political and religious spectrum, and it was for this reason, it seems to me, that her form of religion was a useful middle ground, attracting moderates on both the Catholic and Anglican sides.

Moreover, Henrietta's dissociation of herself from the extremists among the Catholics at court, and her friendship with Protestant lords, was, as Smuts himself brings evidence to show (pp. 33–4), very useful in obtaining favours for the moderate Catholics. John Finch, whose patron was the Earl of Holland, promised the Queen that if he became Chancellor he would do nothing affecting the English Catholics without her consent, and promised to perform favours for all her priests. As Smuts points out, this would seem to be odd behaviour for 'Puritan' followers. It is not so much of an anomaly, however, if it is understood that the Queen's Devout Humanism had elements in it that were sympathetic to many moderate Anglicans, and that during the 1630s there was a good deal of contact and theological debate between moderates on either side, inside and outside the court. One such place was Great Tew, the home of Lucius Cary, where Walter Montague and Sir Kenelm Digby were regular visitors.[4] There they could hear William Chillingworth's 'Disputations' on religion, and Cary himself wrote an answer to the letter, a semi-public declaration, in which Montague announced his conversion to Catholicism. Chillingworth, who wrote *The Religion of Protestants* (1638) at Great Tew, was a noted controversialist who had himself been converted to Catholicism while at Oxford. He had gone to Doway in 1630, but returned to Oxford in 1631, having been led to doubt Catholicism by a series of letters written to him by William Laud (*DNB*). In 1634 he declared again for Protestantism, and published a statement of his reasons for becoming Catholic, together with a confutation of them by himself. His writings show the influence of St François de Sales, whose *Traité* was being translated at Doway during Chillingworth's stay there, and the 'courtesy' of his approach to religious questions appealed to the King.

Charles himself enjoyed debate on theological matters, while remaining deeply committed to his ideal of Anglicanism: in his last letter to Prince Charles before his execution he was able to write with conviction, 'I tell you I have tried it, and, after much search and many disputes, have concluded it to be the best in the world, not only in the community, as Christian, but also in the special notion, as reformed, keeping the middle way betweene the pomp of superstitious tyranny, and the meanness of fantastic anarchy' (*The Letters*, ed. Petrie, p. 269). At some points, however, this 'middle way' in the 1630s touched more closely the views of moderate Catholics than the extreme views on either the Spanish or the Presbyterian side. In the sixteenth century, post-Reformation Protestantism had been unrelentingly hostile to any form of Catholicism, but in the seventeenth century the Anglican position was to recognise the Catholicity of the Christian Church, maintaining that Anglicanism represented the Church in its pure form, while Roman Catholicism did not. Thus James in his first speech to Parliament was able to say 'I acknowledge the Roman church to be our mother church although defiled with some infirmities and corruptions',[5] and Charles to maintain, in his polite discussions with the Papal agents in the 1630s, that he too was a good Catholic, and not a schismatic.[6] Already in James's reign Richard Montagu (who was James's Chaplain and later became Charles's) had traced the history of the English Church back to 'ancient founts' derived from classical and patristic authority, and to early Christianity in England. He established the proposition that 'the present English church is a sound member of the Catholic church', and he believed that the aim of Anglicanism should be to 'stand in the gapp against puritanisme and popery, the Scilla and Charybdis of Ancient Piety'.[7] William Chillingworth, in the dedication of *The Religion of Protestants: A Safe Way to Salvation*, addressed Charles as a 'tender-hearted and compassionate son towards your distressed mother the catholic church', and goes on to stress the moderation of his own writings, which were directed against those of the Catholic Church that make 'the Roman religion much more malignant and turbulent than otherwise it would be' ('Epistle Dedicatory', p. iv). Charles approved of this moderate tone. Whereas James had thrived on controversy and encouraged it in regard to religion, Charles remarked that 'instead of encouraging controversies, we should rather work for union'.[8] On his side he wanted nothing better than peace at home and abroad, and a conciliatory attitude towards moderate Catholics was one of the means by which he hoped to gain it. If he was to continue his experiment of rule without Parliament he had to maintain cordial relations with his Catholic neighbours, something which his cosmopolitan tastes made it easy for him to do.

In the early thirties, moreover, there was open discussion at court of a possible accommodation between England and Rome. Friendly communications were carried on with the Vatican over the exchange of agents between the Pope and the Queen, culminating in Panzani's presence at court from 1634 to 1635, and the arrival of George Conn in 1636. Prominent members of the court were sympathetic to Rome, including two of the King's chief ministers, Cottington and Windebank. Windebank was the most outspoken, discussing with Panzani the Oath of Allegiance, assuring him of the good will of all moderate men, and declaring that 'if we had neither Jesuits nor Puritans in England, I am confident, an union might easily be effected'.[9] The King's chaplain Richard Montagu conferred with Panzani, suggesting that an attempt at settling differences should be made by a meeting of moderates on both sides, preferably in France 'because of the strict affinity between the two crowns', and their likenesses in doctrine and discipline (Albion, p. 179). Lord Arundel talked with Panzani on the subject, offering to go himself to Rome as ambassador.

Charles for his part was interested in an arrangement whereby the Anglican

Church would retain its autonomy while extending toleration to moderate Catholics. His conditions for allowing Papal agents at court were that Rome should reconsider its ban on English Catholics taking the Oath of Allegiance, and should help in the peaceful restoration of the Palatinate.[10] Under these conditions he envisaged Anglicanism enjoying a certain parity with Rome, as part of a reunited Christendom. In 1634 a book was published that seemed to suggest a theological basis for such an idea. Christopher Davenport, the Queen's chaplain, wrote a treatise to prove that the Thirty-nine Articles of the English Church did not differ essentially from Roman doctrine. The treatise was dedicated to Charles, and was published first on its own, then as an appendix to *Deus, Natura, Gratia ... Ubi ad frutinam fidei catholicae examinatur Confessio Anglicana* (Lyons, 1634). Rome did not approve of Davenport's meddling with doctrine, but the moderate party at court appealed to Rome through Panzani not to proceed against it, saying that Davenport was much esteemed by the King and Catholics round the Queen, and that the book contained nothing contrary to the Catholic faith.[11] With the arrival of Conn in 1636 these ideas were dampened. Conn pointed out clearly to Charles that propositions like Davenport's were unacceptable, that the Vatican did not envisage any relaxation on its side of the fundamentals of religious doctrine, nor did it share any idea of parity with the English Church. In the early thirties, however, the support of moderate Catholics must have seemed to Charles a welcome change from the enmity of extremists among Puritans and Jesuits, whose turbulent preaching stirred up controversy and ill will. The preaching of peace and love in the Queen's chapels was, by contrast, a support to Charles's policies, both at home and abroad.

Charles was under constant pressure to take part in the European wars of religion, especially as the death (in 1632) of Gustavus Adolfus of Sweden left the Protestant side without a champion. The enemies of Protestantism were the Habsburgs of Austria and Spain, and the dilemma was presented to Charles in personal as well as political form since the Palatinate had been seized from his brother-in-law Frederick by the Habsburg Emperor Ferdinand II. Charles's widowed sister Elizabeth and her sons were a constant reminder of England's inaction, and the situation was exacerbated with the visit of the popular young Palatine Princes to the court in 1636, seeking military aid to regain their territory.[12] Charles's instinct was to seek settlement by peaceful means, which meant negotiation with European Catholic powers. His general attitude to the religious conflict in Europe was (as James's had been) that England could be more valuable to the Protestant cause as an example than as an active participant; that religious toleration was a sensible course if only all parties would adopt moderation. England with its 'reformed' Christianity had found an independent stance in religion, in which peace and civilised life could flourish; Europe, after the devastation of the religious wars, might do well to follow her example. The emphasis in court culture of the thirties on Arcadian peace, harmony, and love has a polemical insistence that cannot be divorced from religion.

From the early years of the century an implied dialogue had been carried on in literature and court entertainments between the supporters of militant Protestantism and the supporters of 'peace' policies that were thought to be dangerously tolerant of Catholicism. The former looked back to the heady nationalism of Elizabeth's reign and despised the 'effeminate' court of the Stuarts, whose victories lay, at best, in an unprecedented appreciation and cultivation of the arts. In the middle years of James's reign there had seemed great hope of the two sides coming together in the person of the young Prince Henry, who seemed to combine the best qualities of both, and to the forming of whose heroic image Jonson and Jones contributed in masques and court entertainments (see Graham Parry, *The Golden Age Restor'd*, chaps. 3 and 4). His sudden death in 1612 (probably from typhoid fever) dashed these hopes. The marriage of Henry's sister Elizabeth, from whose union with the Count Palatine great hopes were also held for the Protestant cause, almost coincided with his death. When some years later she was dispossessed and left a widow, dissatisfied English nationalism transferred its hopes to her, a second Elizabeth, and later to her sons. Charles, on the other hand, was very much an inheritor of James's 'peace' policies. He was never popular in the way that Henry had been, nor did he have the type of personality that lent itself to heroic myth-making. He did, however, fit the category of 'saintly' Kings, whose personal life was beyond reproach and whose religious interests were internal and spiritual rather than public or military. This kind of spirituality was built up in the religious services of the Order of the Garter, and into the figure of the King as a champion of Anglicanism, a combination of Roman Emperor and chivalrous St George.[13] In the interests of peace, however, it was desirable that the Elizabethan myth be somehow accommodated and incorporated into the myth of the Caroline court. The 'Arcadianism' of the thirties seems in part an attempt by court culture to readopt the Elizabethan myth, and to continue a dialogue that had begun in the previous century. To do this it was necessary to rework, rather than to ignore, the religious implications in Sidneian criticisms of peace, and it is in this respect that Henrietta's presence in the Caroline myth becomes particularly important.

It seems to me that Henrietta's 'Platonic' cult provided a framework in which she might become, not an anti-type of Elizabeth but a 'reformed' Elizabeth, in whom love and religion might now safely combine. As pointed out in connection with the pastoral, Sidney's *Arcadia* had implied a criticism of Elizabeth's marriage plans, and both Spenser's and Sidney's works had become a store of Protestant and apocalyptic imagery, used in Elizabeth's time in patriotic opposition to Catholicism in Europe. Following its pattern, religious propaganda had used the figures of women for a century after the Reformation to symbolise the antagonism between Protestant and Catholic, often in language that had explicitly romantic or sexual overtones.[14] The antagonists were symbolised under the names of Elizabeth and Mary: on the one hand was Queen Elizabeth, the Una of Spenser's *Faery Queen*, the 'Virgin' champion of Protestantism and heroine of pastoral romance; on the other hand was Queen Mary of the martyrs' deaths, followed by Mary Queen of Scots, the Duessa of Spenser, who attracted the apocalyptic imagery of the Whore of Babylon and Harlot of Rome. James I ignored as far as possible the ambiguity of being the latter Mary's son, mainly by creating for himself a myth of Biblical and 'Roman' descent (see Jonathan Goldberg, *James I*, chaps. 1 and 2). In the Caroline court however, France and England, Catholic and Protestant, were at last united in marriage, with another 'Mary' sharing the throne. Now the aim of court literature seems to have been to insist on the purity and chastity of this new Mary (the theme of 'chastity' echoes from one work to another in the early thirties, from *Histriomastix* to *The Shepherd's Paradise*, from *The Faithful Shepherdess* to *Comus*), and on the 'reformation' of old ways: the reformation of arts, love, and morals accomplished throughout the masques in the marriage of the King and Queen. Now this marriage is represented as no longer self-indulgent and shameful, as Sidney had suggested, but chaste and reformed, offering the court an emblem of idyllic peace which extends outward from the personal, to the political and religious spheres.

In this connection the Marian imagery that I have suggested was a feature of the Queen's masques seems to take on added significance. The images of Mary had, paradoxically, already been taken over and adapted to court iconology by Elizabeth, in her role as Virgin Queen (an adaptation first recorded by E. C. Wilson, *England's Eliza* (1939), pp. 200 ff.). The transition from a Catholic to a Protestant significance had been made through the medium of the classics, by a gradual identification of Elizabeth with Virgil's *Astraea*, the just Virgin of the *Aeneid* whose return to earth, accompanied by the prophecy of a new birth, were interpreted by Christian apologists as a prophecy of the birth of Christ. Astraea, the classical Virgin, was seen as a type of Mary, and Elizabeth adapted the Catholic as well as the classical symbols to her own cult: Catholic festivals of Mary were converted to celebrations of Elizabeth's Accession Day and Birthday; pastoral themes, already interwoven with religion, were used by Spenser, Drayton, and Sir John Davies to honour the English Virgin.[15] In these works Elizabeth, like the Virgin Mary, reconciled the opposing principles of Virginity and Love. In poetry and painting she was represented as a chaste Diana as well as a lovely Venus, both as a Bride to her Kingdom and as a mother to her people, a Virgin goddess of Beauty and Love. Her emblems were the rose, the moon, and the star; as Gloriana she was radiant as the sun, a 'stella Britannis' whose light eclipsed Mary's Star and attracted to itself the rich symbolism formerly associated with the iconology of the Virgin.[16] In the masques of the 1630s all these images were returning to the court stage, but this time under a Catholic Queen. It would not have been difficult for the images to revive their former associations with Catholicism, but this time within a 'reformed' context in which the attractive feminine qualities of religion, the beauty and love symbolised by the Queen, might once more be safely entertained at an English court. Just as Edmund Waller made an attempt in poetry to transfer to Henrietta Elizabeth's titles of 'Gloriana' and 'Queen of Love' (*Poems*, 1, 77 and 82), so court iconology seems to be reclaiming for Henrietta the traditional images of religion originally co-opted by Elizabeth. The emphasis of court entertainments on 'chastity' and 'reform' in the thirties seems intended to suggest that these images were themselves reformed, and that the opposition between marriage and militant Protestantism that had been built into Elizabethan imagery had been resolved at the Stuart court. Now peace, including religious peace, might prosper under the reformed love of the King and Queen.

An 'allegory' painted by Rubens while at the court, and which Charles kept in his private collection, seems to echo this meaning. It shows Charles as St George rescuing Henrietta from a slain dragon in the Thames Valley (figure 41).[17] Critics have pointed out the religious symbolism of the King represented as St George, but no one, to my knowledge, has noticed that Henrietta is really the central figure of the painting, and that the allegory may be interpreted in terms of her religion as well as of Charles's. The main purpose of Rubens's visit to England (from 1629 to 1630) was to arrange peace with Spain, the attainment of which would be another step in the long-drawn-out settlement of the European religious wars. Rubens felt a deep personal concern in the subject, and another allegory painted for Charles at the time showed in classical imagery the horrors of war and the blessings of peace.[18] In the painting of Charles and Henrietta, however, the imagery is much more personal and the significance more specific to England. Charles is wearing the armour and insignia of the Order of the Garter, which, by the time of his reign, had been built up to represent all the most serious claims of Anglicanism to represent a 'purified' form of Christianity. In the depiction of Charles is suggested the chivalrous Knight of Christ, a role which was much elaborated in Stuart propaganda. In the dragon, therefore, surrounded by the bones of the dead, is suggested not only the evils of war, but the evils of the Religious Wars, and the surrounding figures, who look towards Charles and Henrietta for succour, are its past and potential victims. Rubens was, of course, Catholic, and he would not have proposed that Anglicanism alone could solve the problem of religious toleration. What he does seem to suggest, through the symbolism of the painting, is that Charles's form of Anglicanism, and Henrietta's form of Catholicism, together may do so. Henrietta is accompanied by the Lamb (traditional to St George's rescued maidens, and St Agnes's symbol of chastity) and she rises, young and beautiful, above the dark ruins of death and destruction. Everything in the painting – the play of light and the placement of the central and surrounding groups of figures – makes her the centre of attention. For Rubens, surely, she represents a vision of what was best in Catholicism, Counter-Reformation religion in all its artistic beauty, freed of fear, war, and death. Charles had already embraced such beauty in its human and artistic form: might he not also, as the chivalrous St George, rescue it in its religious form, to set an example of toleration? To Rubens, who had spent over a decade as a diplomat and painter working for peace, harmony between religions was the only way in which lasting peace could be brought to Europe, and in this painting he seems to show that

41 Sir Peter Paul Rubens, detail from an allegorical painting of King Charles as St
George rescuing Henrietta Maria (1629–30); the Royal Collection, reproduced by
Gracious Permission of Her Majesty The Queen

here, in the peaceful landscape of England, love makes such toleration possible. Angelic forms hovering overhead are about to crown the King and Queen, and present them with the palm of heavenly approval.

An interpretation of this allegory in terms of the King and Queen's religions is reinforced by the way in which the St George legend had been put to use in religious propaganda after the Reformation, and had incorporated into the legend the figure of the Virgin. Rubens's painting may be compared with an engraving (figure 42) of Queen Elizabeth as St George rescuing 'Truth' or 'Religion'

42 Thomas Cecil, engraving of Queen Elizabeth as St George rescuing Truth or Religion (1625)

(the latter commonly represented in emblematic literature with a book) from her cave. The symbolism here is both military and religious: Elizabeth is dressed as a virginal warrior and the scene in the background refers to the Armada and the defeat of Spain.[19] Rubens's painting follows a similar pattern, but it is the very opposite in mood. Where Elizabeth is mounted and imperious, Charles is the chivalrous Knight of romance, courteously stepping forward to the maiden he has rescued. In place of the military encampment and the fleet in the background is the fertile and peaceful valley of the Thames, which is suffused with heavenly light. Henrietta, shining and bare-bosomed like Truth in her cave, takes the part of the rescued maiden. That she is also an aspect of 'Religion' is suggested by the way in which the iconology of the Virgin had become connected with the legend of St George. The symbolic figure of the Virgin as the antitype of Eve, crushing the serpent's head (the 'dragon'), beneath her foot, had been adopted by both the Protestant and the Catholic side after the Reformation.[20] To Catholics it meant the crushing of heresy and schism, to Protestants it meant the destruction of 'Popery' and anti-Christ. Elizabeth, as the new Virgin of Protestantism, adapted it to the cult of St George, taking to herself the attributes both of the Saint and the Virgin. The dragon beneath her horse's feet in the engraving is undoubtedly Anti-Christ, or the Pope. In Rubens's painting Charles has replaced the fierce Protestant St George, and he is no longer armed. The dragon now is no longer the Pope, but, according to Peter Heylin, the official chronicler of the Order of the Garter in 1631, 'that old malicious *Serpent*' the Devil; he goes on to explain that the badge worn by the Knight of St George shows

how bravely he repelled the Devil, how constantly he persevered in the profession of his faith; the whole Church praying with him, and kneeling (like the Virgin) by him.

(quoted by Strong, *Charles I on Horseback*, p. 62)

The Virgin was, in fact, represented accompanying St George in the tapestries which hung over the altar at services of the Garter at Windsor,[21] so that Henrietta in Rubens's painting may take over attributes of the Virgin, just as Charles takes over from Elizabeth the attributes of the Saint. Now, however, again in contrast to Elizabeth, it is the feminine aspects of the Virgin that are emphasised. In Rubens's painting Henrietta's expression and figure are almost motherly, in harmony with the female figures in the foreground and the group behind her who, in happier circumstances, might become the Graces. Her stance suggests the maidens of chivalry who had contributed their own legend to that of Mary, and who had taken on her attributes of beauty and chastity. She is also the rescued maiden Religion whom Elizabeth was shown releasing from her cave, now characterised not as naked Truth, but as the epitome of feminine beauty and love, the new and gentle Virgin of the Counter-Reformation.

Rubens had been concerned with myth-making on a grand scale for the French court in the 1620s, and Henrietta had seen his cycle on *The Life of Marie de Medici* before she left Paris in 1625. He was just as concerned with myth-making for the English court in the 1630s with his panels for the Banqueting House ceiling. In this more personal allegory for Charles and Henrietta, however, with its romantic yet religious tone, Rubens seems to set the mood for the way their marriage was treated in the heightened imagery of the masques. In the following section I would like to explore the suggestion that in the masques to 1635 the King and Queen's marriage was presented not only as an ideal example of personal happiness, but as a 'pattern' for the way in which opposite religions, existing in harmony on the English throne, might also learn to exist in peace and harmony on a universal scale.

Marriage and masques

Two masques of the early thirties were based on works connected with plans for religious peace and reform. *Tempe Restored* (1632) was based on Baltasar de Beaujoyeulx' *Balet comique de la Reine* (1582), and *Coelum Britannicum* (1634) on Giordano Bruno's *Lo Spaccio de la Bestia Trionfante* (1584–5). Both the sources belong to the Valois reign in France, a period that had many similarities in religion and politics with the 1630s in England.[22] Charles and Henrietta were faced with a situation rather like that which faced Catherine de Medici in the 1570s and 1580s, when she had endeavoured to hold a throne that was being threatened by the Catholic League led by the Guises and allied with Spain on the one hand, and by the Huguenots on the other. Catherine, and later her son Henri III, drew around them a party of moderates in religion who would provide a central *bloc*, loyal to the throne, through whom negotiations could be carried on between the court and the extremists on either side. Catherine's ambition was to extend this 'politique' policy to the rest of Europe, bringing an accommodation between the opposed parties at the Council of Trent, and helping to put an end to the Wars of Religion in Europe. One would think that her complete failure to achieve either of these ends might have been sufficient warning to the Stuart court. But Catherine's court, a failure from the point of view of political achievement, had been culturally very influential. In her attempts to bring the two warring sides together and to smooth away differences, Catherine embarked on an elaborate programme of court entertainments and encouragement of the arts. Her programme for religious toleration amounted to a Royalist Counter-Reformation, in which the arts were used in an attempt to soothe the natures of those around her and to influence the course of events, particularly towards an agreement between moderates on the Catholic and Protestant sides.

Catherine's plans for religious reform had included the idea of an alliance through marriage between France and England. The two works on which the English masques were based belonged to a time when she was doing her best to arrange a marriage between one of her sons and Queen Elizabeth. By 1580 the Duc d'Anjou was formally engaged to Elizabeth, and the *Balet comique* (performed in 1581) and other *fêtes* associated with the Joyeuse wedding were held on the eve of his departure for England. A marriage ceremony, in which Sir Philip Sidney acted as one of the principals, was celebrated at Whitehall in the presence of the French ambassadors, and the programme for the marriage tells in a song how Love and Destiny have brought England and France together.[23] When Anjou died a short time later, Catherine put up another candidate, her third surviving son, the Duc d'Alençon, an unsuitable choice which Sidney advised Elizabeth against. For France, the failure of the marriage plan and of

the intended alliance with England meant that Catholic power was likely to return
to Spain, and to its allies the Guises. It was at this point that Giordano Bruno
was sent by Henri III on a mission to England, during which *Lo Spaccio* was
composed, and a dedication written to Sir Philip Sidney. Bruno's purpose may
have been to renew the French offer of friendship to Elizabeth, whom he praises,
to rebuke intransigent Protestants, and to explore the basis for a common attitude
to religion.[24]

Catherine's hopes for peace through marriage failed, but the religious settlement
in France achieved by Henri IV's conversion to Catholicism (which had awakened
in Catholics a hope of some similar settlement when James first came to the
throne) had provided the necessary climate of peace in which flourished the idyllic
pastoral world of *L'Astrée*, and the mystical piety of St François de Sales. Marie
de Medici inherited this world, and during her Regency she made the influence
of love, in bringing about religious agreement, part of the propaganda of her
court festivities.[25] As another Medici, she perhaps saw herself carrying on the
culture of Catherine's court; and, when she was deprived of the power to practise
it in the French court, she may have passed the ambition on to her daughter
in England. Marie's influence certainly followed Henrietta to the English court,
and an entertainment given by the Duke of Buckingham to the King and Queen
in 1626 suggests that it was directed towards the same kind of peaceful religious
settlement through the effects of love that had preoccupied Catherine de Medici.
Salvetti reported that the principal spectacle of the entertainment was 'a mystic
conceit', which showed:

a marine view representing the sea which divides England from France, and above it the
Queen Mother of France, sitting on a regal throne amongst the Gods, beckoning with her
hand to the King and Queen of Spain, the Prince and Princess Palatine, and the Prince and
Princess of Piedmont, to come and unite themselves with her there amongst the Gods, to
put an end to all the discords of Christianity.

(HMC, *Salvetti Correspondence*, pp. 94–5)

Perhaps it was hoped that the seeds of religious concord that Catherine, and
Marie herself, had failed to raise in France would flourish in the more fertile
ground of England. At the Caroline court the marriage between France and England that had been so long deferred had at last become reality, and by 1630
love between the King and Queen had created the atmosphere of peace, moral
fervour, and love of the arts in which it may have been hoped that religious
peace could once more flourish.

In borrowing the sources for the two entertainments, therefore, the Caroline
court may also have been borrowing some of the ideas that lay behind them.
It had been to the culture and civilised manners of Catherine's court that *préciosité*
of the early seventeenth century had looked back for its ideas. Catherine had
surrounded herself with a company of ladies, whom she wished to be 'adorned
like goddesses, but welcoming like mortals' (Yates, *French Academies*, p. 251),
hoping that their grace and beauty, their elegant conversation and manners, would

keep both Protestants and Catholics in allegiance to the King, and put them in love with peace rather than with war. Catherine insisted on a high moral tone in her group, and stated that her aim in this, as in all the arts and entertainments of the court, was 'moderer par quelques doux & gracieux moyens l'aigreur qui est auiourdhuy parmy les Peuples, pour les differends de la Religion' (Yates, p. 200). In her study of these entertainments, Frances Yates commented (p. 235) that what the court sought to contribute to the debate on religion was not so much a policy as an atmosphere, in which concord and agreement did not seem so impossible to achieve as in the world of rational debate. Catherine's court was strongly influenced by Capucinism, and her movement in the arts developed under Capucin influence in the 1580s into a conspicuous form of pietism adopted by Henri III.[26] It took the form of public religious processions led by Henri, or by his Queen, Louise de Lorraine (see figures 7 and 8 above). The processions were accompanied by singing, lights, and music, and were arranged and performed by some of the same people (several of them Capucins) who contributed to court ballets and other entertainments. There is a parallel to be made with the Caroline court, where Henrietta's Platonism had links with her religion and where her Capucin priests instituted public religious processions which she led. The French processions had been penitential in theme, but at the English court the Capucins had in Henrietta a more attractive figure than they had had in the rather pathetic Henri, part of whose religious fervour was directed towards his unsuccessful efforts to produce an heir for the Valois line. This time they had a young and obviously fruitful Queen, whose beauty and virtue echoed the attractive graces of the Virgin; now the theme of their spectacles (for instance in the Queen's chapel) was not penitence and sorrow, but joy and love.

The *Balet comique de la Reine*, on which *Tempe Restored* was based, stated in the Preface that it had a close relation to the times, hiding a fable beneath the story, and Yates's study of the work has shown that it came at a crucial time in the religious policy of the court. It refers both to the efforts Catherine de Medici had been making to conciliate the parties through entertainments and 'all kinds of honest pleasures', and to Henri's new efforts to exorcise evil by religious influence (Yates, *Academies*, pp. 250–3 and 259). It would be interesting to know if any of this had been at the back of the minds of those who chose the text for the Queen's masque: Inigo Jones, for instance, who wrote all the descriptions and designed the scenes, or Aurelian Townshend who wrote the verses. It may be significant that, of the several 'allegories' attached to the *Balet comique*, Jones chose to copy the one by 'Sieur Gordon Escoçois'. Gordon's name would have brought to mind a connection between France and England that was important in James's reign. John Gordon (1544–1619), later Dean of Salisbury, had gone to France under a pension from Queen Mary, and served as Gentleman in Ordinary to Charles IX, Henri III, and Henri IV. He remained a strong Protestant, took part in public disputes on religion with Du Perron, and after 1603 was called to England by James, who valued him as a writer and preacher (see

DNB, under Gordon, John; and D. J. Gordon's notice of him in connection with *Hymenaei* in *Renaissance Imagination*, p. 171). His name in the Allegory of *Tempe Restored* may have vouched for 'Protestant' approval of a French (Catholic) source.

Jones and Townshend worked allusively from the text of the *Balet comique*, but closely enough to suggest the original to those who possessed a copy (Ben Jonson for instance),[27] or who had access to the copy used by Jones. To fit the English masque form, however, they left out the long philosophical speeches of the original, the building up of the plot, and the dramatic climax. In this simplification they somewhat misrepresent the original. The masque opens with the Fugitive Favourite, who has escaped from Circe because of his desire 'to be man again, / Governed by reason, and not ruled by sense', flying to the King for protection (ll. 70–80), and Townshend has him declare 'It is consent that makes a perfect slave ... He finds no help that uses not his own' (ll. 91 and 96). The original, however, makes it clear that reason alone is insufficient to vanquish the passions without the aid of Heaven: Mercury has to counteract Circe's enchantments by sprinkling Moly juice; Minerva (played by the French Queen) has to invoke Jupiter's aid, and Circe has to be vanquished with the gods' assistance in battle, before she is overcome (*Balet comique*, fos. 48r–54v). *Tempe Restored* is much more static. Reason is simply embodied in the King, and the Queen, coming from Heaven, is herself the Divine aid. The Gods are not invoked, and Reason is not shown being assisted by Heaven; the union between reason and divinity is simply accomplished by the union of the King and Queen, and Jupiter and Minerva are only required to preside at the willing surrender of Circe to the virtues of the Royal pair. Moreover the importance of Reason tends to be forgotten in the overwhelming splendour of the scene for the Queen, suggesting that the mere appearance of Divine Beauty is sufficient to attract virtue, free the passions, and bring peace.

In its dependence on scenic splendour and music rather than on poetry or plot, *Tempe Restored* seems to have emphasised another extremely important aspect of the *Balet comique*: the attempt to draw down the good influences of Heaven by a harmony of the arts. The artists who composed the *Balet* believed that, by combining music, poetry, dancing, and choreography in certain ways, they could compose the minds and hearts of the spectators in a harmony that reflected the harmony of the universe. Jones may have shared these ideas, since he followed the views of Renaissance Neoplatonists in regard to the arts. In this view music was the invisible framework of all the arts, the nearest to the divinely created laws and proportions of the universe. For Jones, its harmonies lay behind the spatial relationships of architecture and sculpture, the colours and proportions of painting, and of course behind the measures of poetry and the movement of dance. It was even the basis, as it had been for Plato, of moral behaviour, helping to attune the soul to God.[28] In *Tempe Restored* Jones seems to emphasise these ideas by actually personifying 'Harmony' and the 'Influences', who then introduce the main scene of Divine Beauty. The fourteen Influences of the stars are 'the beams ... of constellations, whose planetic sway, / Though some foresee, all must alike obey' (ll. 158–9), but these are stars 'of a happy constellation' (l. 346), so that, under the conduct of Harmony and the sway of Divine Beauty, the influences they pour down can only be for good. It is possible, therefore, that Jones had in mind the aims of the original artists of the *Balet*: of using a harmony of the arts, with an emphasis on music, as the means of creating harmony in the souls of those who witnessed his scenes for *Tempe Restored*.

Tempe Restored was very much the Queen's masque, demonstrating the power of Divine Beauty to reform the passions and restore the arts. *Coelum Britannicum*, by contrast, is very much the King's: where *Tempe Restored* shows the Queen as the brightest star in a heaven filled with stars, *Coelum Britannicum* ends with a scene in which the King is the brightest star in a constellation of British heroes. It is in fact a *British* Heaven, and the work on which it was based, *Lo Spaccio della bestia trionfante*, was one also concerned with religious reform.[29] Bruno envisaged this taking place within a Catholic framework, but the vices which he expelled from Heaven in *Lo Spaccio* were, in his view, the vices that had become entrenched in a society, and in a version of Christianity (whether Catholic or 'Reformed'), that had become more interested in worldly power than in spiritual purity. His work advocates not only a moral reform, but hints at a reform of religious belief that goes beneath the hypocrisies and postures of both sides; a reformation in which there would be no separation between divine law and civil life, where natural religion, philosophy, the arts and sciences would combine. His vision was of a State, in which 'Magnificence, Generosity, and Dominion ... move about in the areas of Dignity, Power, and Authority' (*Lo Spaccio*, trans. Imerti, p. 83). This was no doubt something of Charles's ideal, and Bruno's ideas are echoed at the end of *Coelum Britannicum*, when 'Concord, Government and Reputation' become the companions of 'Religion, Truth and Wisdom' (ll. 1057 ff.), but this time within an Anglican framework, with 'Eternity' enthroned over Windsor Castle.

While Bruno attacked the vices and luxuries of the Catholic hierarchy, he attacked equally the vices of a rigid Protestantism.[30] He had nothing but contempt for the 'pedantry' and literalism of Reformers that swept away the learning and mystical philosophy of past ages without putting anything in its place, and he despised the barbarity and greed (masquerading as religious zeal) that had destroyed the arts and desecrated the churches. It can easily be seen how Bruno's ideas would appeal to Charles, and it is mainly for its anti-Puritanical tone that Carew drew on *Lo Spaccio*. In Charles's new English 'Reformation' (l. 469), the vices are compared to the 'virulent humours that have been purged from the politic body by the plantations in New England' (l. 390); the arts are praised, and 'Wealth' echoes Bruno's speech on the desecration of the churches (quoted above in chapter 5). The figure of Poverty is used to chide 'some lazy or pedantic virtue' (l. 652) or 'falsely exalted passive fortitude' (l. 663), and the 'low abject brood / That fix their seats in mediocrity' are contrasted with 'Such virtues only as admit excess, / Brave bounteous acts, regal magnificence', magnanimity and heroic virtue (ll. 667–70). On the other hand, the 'Circean charms' of Pleasure, who was 'the author of the first excess / That drew this reformation on the gods' (ll.835–6), are rebuked. The English court of the 1630s is concerned with exorcising the same vices, and extolling the same virtues, as the French court of Henri III for whom Bruno wrote in the 1580s. In *Coelum Britannicum*, however, the reformation of morals that Bruno advocated is represented as having already taken place. It has been accomplished through the example of 'matrimonial union' of the King and Queen, and it only remains for that union to be translated to the 'heavenly' sphere for the Caroline court to achieve complete perfection.

Coelum Britannicum treats several kinds of unity, all of which are intertwined: unity of the three Kingdoms, of the King with his people, and matrimonial union. The masque followed Charles's Coronation in Scotland in the previous year (1633), which had been accompanied by the dissident murmuring of the Scots about 'Popish' ceremonies, and the imposition of the English Liturgy that was to lead later to the signing of the Covenant, and Charles's invasion of Scotland. Thus Charles was concerned to stress the theme of unity in the British Isles, the 'willing knees' and 'melting hearts / That flow with cheerful loyal reverence' (ll. 46–52). Personifications of England, Scotland, and Ireland appear later in the masque (ll. 890–1), and the spiritual unity and kingly power that holds them together is symbolised in the figure of the Genius who sits enthroned above them. Charles, like the Genius, is the 'soul' of the three Kingdoms, and that his sovereignty is a religious (rather than a merely earthly) desire for three crowns is, I think, hinted at by another 'three crowns' that those concerned with the masque would have found in Bruno's text.

At the conclusion of *Lo Spaccio* the gods have to decide the fate of the 'Crown' of stars in Heaven, and for once Jove has no hesitation: 'This', he says, 'is that crown which, not without the lofty disposition of Fate, not without the instinct of divine spirit, and not without very great merit, awaits the most invincible Henri III'.[31] He goes on to explain that Henri, having obtained the crowns of France and Poland, had determined to strengthen the two earthly crowns with another, more eminent and beautiful, in Heaven. Thus he ordered that his emblem should contain three crowns, with this motto: *'Tertia coelo manet'* (the third remains in Heaven). *'Tertia coelo manet'*, adds Jove, is something which this 'most Christian, holy, religious, and pure king can surely say' (p. 270). Bruno goes on to praise Henri in terms that Charles would have been pleased to apply to himself. The heavenly crown is his because he knows it is written:

'Blessed are the meek, blessed are the silent, blessed are the pure in heart, for theirs is the kingdom of heaven.' He loves peace and, as much as it is possible, maintains in tranquillity and devotion his beloved people. He ... loves all acts of justice and blessedness that point out the direct path to the eternal realm.   (*Lo Spaccio*, pp. 270–1)

Similar Biblical sentiments had been built into a court philosophy by James, in his role as 'Rex Pacificus', and inherited by Charles. In his *Declaration to All his Loving Subiects* (1628), for instance, Charles had asked his people to examine in their hearts whether, in respect to 'the great peace and quietnesse which every man enioyeth vnder his own vine and figtree, the happinesse of this Nation can be paralleled by any other of Our neighbour Countreyes ...' (sig. C); whether, indeed, they do not 'liue in a more happy and free estate, then any Subiects in the Christian world' (sig. F3v); similar sentiments are translated into visual form in *Salmacida Spolia* (ll. 158–65). In *Lo Spaccio* Jove had concluded his speech in praise of religious peace by saying 'let the crown remain [in Heaven], awaiting that one who will be worthy of its magnificent possessions. And here also let Victory, Remuneration, Reward, Perfection, Honor, and Glory have their thrones' (p. 271). At the end of *Coelum Britannicum* the King and Queen are ascribed similar virtues and rewards: 'Wisdom, Truth, Pure Adoration, / Concord, Rule, Clear Reputation' (ll. 1106–12), and surely the crown of stars over Windsor Castle is the 'Crown in Heaven' reserved for Charles, who may now fulfil the hopes Bruno had expressed in *Lo Spaccio* for reformation and religious peace (and which, ironically after his death, Charles is represented as attaining in *Eikon Basilike*).

The theme of matrimonial union, easily suggested by Bruno's first *Dialogue* in which Jove rebukes himself for his infidelities and his bad example to others (*Lo Spaccio*, pp. 113–14), becomes in the masque a principal theme. Heaven's reform is complete, even to the point of reciprocation of conjugal affection (ll. 264–5), a particularly welcome sign when the 'lawgiver himself in his own person' observes his own decrees (l. 274). This reformation is entirely due to those 'Bright glorious twins of love and majesty', the King and Queen:

> Your exemplar life
> Hath not alone transfused a jealous heat
> Of imitation through your virtuous court,
> By whose bright blaze your palace is become
> The envied pattern of this underworld,
> But the aspiring flame hath kindled heaven. (ll. 60–5)

Jove has engraven with stars, in capital letters on his ceiling, the word CARLOMARIA, in memory of this 'great example of matrimonial union' (ll. 276–9). In this union the King is the ruling force, but the Queen is his 'twin', his 'royal half' (l. 870), a 'bright deity' (l. 1028) who takes her place by his side. This masque is remarkable for the way it emphasises the Queen's presence as partner to the King. It is the only masque in which both King and Queen are present as audience for all the speeches of the first part, and songs are addressed to the Queen as well as the King when Charles at last appears on the stage, so that her State becomes another stage facing his enthronement in the seat of Honour. When she is praised by the Genius, the Kingdoms, and the Chorus, Carew's words evoke a picture of almost religious splendour:

> see where Glory spreads

> Her glittering wings, where Majesty
> Crowned with sweet smiles shoots from her eye
> Diffusive joy, where good and fair
> United sit in honour's chair.   (ll. 901–5)

Her eyes are brighter than the stars, for

> These shed a nobler influence,
> These by a pure intelligence
> Of more transcendent virtue move;
> These first feel, then kindle love.
> From the bosoms they inspire
> These receive a mutual fire –
> And where the flames impure return,
> These can quench as well as burn.   (ll. 922–9)

It is to this purified beauty and love that the King and his masquers are to be joined.

Matrimonial union from the beginning of the masque is lifted above the personal or merely moral sphere: it very soon expands to become a principle that fills the universe. The prediction of the King and Queen's enthronement takes on cosmic significance when, in the cleansed and vacant rooms of Heaven, the King will first succeed,

> and of the wheeling orb
> In the most eminent and conspicuous point,
> With dazzling beams and spreading magnitude,
> Shine, the bright pole star of this hemisphere.
> Next, by your side, in a triumphant chair,
> And crowned with Ariadne's diadem,
> Sits the fair consort of your heart and throne . . .

> So to the British stars this lower globe
> Shall owe its light, and they alone dispense
> To th' world a pure refined influence.   (ll. 89–95, 99–101)

In this union the King is the dominant masculine and 'British' partner, the 'bright pole star of this hemisphere' whose place is in the 'most eminent and conspicuous point' of the universe, but the Queen is the traditional feminine partner of deity, resplendent with beauty and light. When the King and Queen come together at the end of the masque, the language in which they are addressed raises them to an exalted plane, and the final scene celebrates their union in the most positive terms. The 'old decrepit sphere' is now dark and cold, for

> these bright
> Flames have eclipsed her sullen light;
> This royal pair, for whom Fate will
> Make motion cease and time stand still,
> Since good is here so perfect as no worth
> Is left for after ages to bring forth.   (ll. 1088–93)

The union is praised by all the allegorical figures, including Religion, Truth, and Wisdom, and all the kinds of union set out at the beginning are brought together and connected in the union of the Royal pair:

Eusebia:	Mortality cannot with more
(Religion)	Religious zeal the gods adore.
Alethia:	My truths, from human eyes concealed,
(Truth)	Are naked to their sight revealed.
Sophia:	Nor do their actions from the guide
(Wisdom)	Of my exactest precepts slide.
Homonoia:	And as their own pure souls entwined,
(Concord)	So are their subjects' hearts combined.
Dicearche:	So just, so gentle is their sway,
(Government)	As it seems empire to obey.
Euphemia:	And their fair fame, like incense hurled
(Reputation)	On altars, hath perfumed the world.

(ll. 1094–105)

The exalted language and the overt presence in this final scene of figures like Religion and Eternity seem to make of the King and Queen's marriage an emblem of religious harmony. Charles's is the dominant influence: his is the 'Sun of Intelligence and Light of Reason' that Bruno (*Lo Spaccio*, p. 79) had spoken of as being necessary to spiritual reformation; it is still a 'British Heaven', from the British lion of the King's *impresa* at the beginning (l. 22), to the British tradition of St George and the Garter at the end. But it is perfected by its other 'half', the Queen, who brings with her the 'glittering wings' of Beauty, the purity of Love, the lily of her *impresa* (l. 25) that stands for virtue and fecundity (the emblem both of France and of the Virgin), and the spiritual ardor, 'the nectar of Divine Love' and 'love of beauty' that Bruno (p. 80) had paired with the Light of Reason. The picture given by Eternity lifts the King and Queen to a throne in Heaven that is higher than the heaven of the classical gods with which the masque opened. Pictured 'With wreaths of stars circled about', the couple are enjoined to

> Gild all the spacious firmament,
> And smiling on the panting rout
> That labour in the steep ascent,
> With your resistless influence guide
> Of human change th'incertain tide.

(ll. 1120–5)

Given the heightened tone of the masque, and the background of religious reform that underlay Bruno's work, the harmony of the King and Queen's marriage suggests a pattern for harmony on a universal scale.

Coelum Britannicum stresses the complementary virtues of the King and Queen in a moral setting, as the King's previous masque *Albion's Triumph* had stressed them in a ceremonial setting, each time with the King as the dominant partner.

In the Queen's next masque *The Temple of Love* (1635), love is again raised by the language and imagery to an exalted level, when in the final scene against the background of the Temple two allegorical figures, Sunesis and Thelema, appear and are united. These are heavenly figures, Sunesis a man of noble aspect, richly attired in watchet and gold, a garland on his head 'with a flame of fire issuing from it' (l. 470); Thelema is a young woman, clad in silver and crowned with flowers, 'and at her shoulders were angels' wings' (l. 476). Jones tells us in the Introduction that Sunesis and Thelema intimate 'the understanding and the will' (l. 37), and he had at one time labelled Thelema 'Gnome' (or Divine Will) in his design (see figure 43). These figures could be understood simply in terms of Neoplatonic imagery, the complementary qualities of love that go to make up a perfect whole.[32] But 'Understanding and Will', from the time of St Augustine, had had theological significance as well. St François de Sales used the terms throughout the *Traité de l'amour de Dieu*, quoting from St Augustine, and arguing that reason or understanding is necessary to search out the good, which it then proposes to the will to be loved. Love is the source of all spiritual life, and Sales refers continually to the Canticles for the metaphor of human love and marriage in relation to union with God. The subject was treated again at length by J.-P. Camus in *A Draught of Eternitie* (Doway, 1632), which was dedicated to Lady Anne Arundel as being 'nether vnworthy, nor vnfitt to be presented to the viewes and thoughts of our English Catholikes', since the 'subiect is most soueraigne to remoue contentions, and moue to wholsome thoughts' (sig. *3v). In Camus the Will is the 'Mistrisse' of the Understanding, for he (Understanding) goes before to search out the Good, 'and proposeth it to the *Will* to be loued, who after she hath knowen it, she imbraceth it', and out of this embrace and 'inseparable vnion' with good 'shall flow a floode of continuall ioyes and delightes' (pp. 256–7), leading to 'the vnion or agreement of heartes' in 'Peace and Concord' (pp. 306–7).

The final scene of the masque enacts such a union of Understanding and Will (represented as man and woman respectively, as in Camus) in an image of 'heavenly' love:

Sunesis (Understanding)	Come melt thy soul in mine, that when unite, We may become one virtuous appetite.
Thelema (Will)	First breathe thine into me, thine is the part More heavenly, and doth more adorn the heart.
Both	Thus mixed, our love will ever be discreet, And all our thoughts and actions pure; When perfect will and strengthened reason meet, Then love's created to endure.
Chorus	Were heaven more distant from us we would strive To reach it with prayers to make this union thrive.

From this union comes the figure of Amianteros, the heavenly unity that issues

43 Inigo Jones, Thelema or Divine Will in *The Temple of Love*

from perfected duality; the 'mixture thus made one' is the 'emblem' of his deity. But Amianteros then turns to the King and Queen:

> And now you may in yonder throne
> The pattern of your union see.

So the union of the King and Queen also echoes that of Sunesis and Thelema, the meeting of strengthened reason and perfected will, two faculties of the soul; and from the resulting union issues a deity, Amianteros, who brings more than earthly fruits:

> th' undiscerned increase I bring
> Is of more precious worth than all
> A plenteous summer pays a spring.
>
> The benefit it doth impart
> Will not the barren earth improve,
> But fructify each barren heart
> And give eternal growth to love.   (ll. 503–10)

The King and Queen, like Sunesis and Thelema, present an emblem of love to which both the language and the 'temple' setting lend the overtones of religion: translated to the wider sphere their love could become a 'pattern' for universal peace and understanding.

These masques coincided with the period of friendly discussions with Rome. In the following years the Queen's religion still prospered at court under the influence of the popular agent George Conn, but Charles was under increasing pressure from criticism at home and, with the visit of the Palatine Princes in 1636, for his 'peace' policies abroad. The King's next masque, *Britannia Triumphans* (1638), is accordingly a restatement of Charles's authority, and a reassertion of 'British' values. The figure of Action, labelled *Medio Tutissima* (l. 65), is the spokesman for Reason and Virtue, and the masque attempts to point out the independence of Charles's 'middle way' which alone can save the country from extremes. 'Britanocles' is praised as a saviour, in language that equates him with the sun:

> Break forth thou treasure of our sight
> That art the hopeful morn of every day,
> Whose fair example makes the light
> By which Heroic Virtue finds her way.
>
> O thou our cheerful morning, rise,
> And straight those misty clouds of error clear,
> Which long have overcast our eyes,
> And else will darken all this hemisphere.   (ll. 515–22)

In *Britannia Triumphans* emphasis is all on the King; attention to the Queen does not go beyond a salute to her beauty by the chorus of modern poets (ll. 570–90), and a reference to her role as Charles's wife in the 'Valediction.' Conversely *Luminalia*, as I have suggested, emphasises the interests of the Queen.

In *Salmacida Spolia*, however, the last masque of the reign, the King and Queen came together to present a double masque, and here they seem to change roles: from being the dominant partner the King becomes the passive sufferer, the possessor of 'secret' wisdom, and the Queen now takes the active part. The King had made a defence of his position in *Britannia Triumphans*, but already there was a hint of suffering in the eclipsed 'Sun' image at the end. This note becomes the dominant one in *Salmacida Spolia* (1640), which begins in the darkness that the last speech predicted: 'No glimpse of the sun was seen, as if darkness, confusion, and deformity had possessed the world and driven light to heaven' (ll. 111–13). The King as Philogenes makes his way to the difficult Throne of Honour, whence he dispenses unrequited love to his people:

> O who but he could thus endure
> To live and govern in a sullen age,
> When it is harder far to cure
> The people's folly than resist their rage?   (ll. 196–9)

The King's appearance on the Throne of Honour of course restores calm and peace, and the song that greets him emphasises the Christ-like qualities of 'patience', 'mercy', 'forgiveness'. Kingly patience and mercy outlast and quell the storms and people's rage:

> Nor would your valour, when it might subdue,
> Be hindered of the pleasure to forgive.
> They're worse than overcome, your wisdom knew,
> That needed mercy to have leave to live.   (ll. 372–5)

With the appearance of the Queen the theme of peace and passivity suddenly alters. She is the 'chief heroine', dressed in Amazonian costume, complete with plumed helm, baldric, and antique sword, and accompanied by her martial ladies (ll. 380–96) (figure 44).[33] The colour symbolism of the King's and Queen's costumes is reversed: he wears the 'heavenly' colours of watchet, white, and silver (ll. 350–3) commonly reserved for the Queen; she wears the carnation colours which the King had worn, for example, in *Britannia Triumphans*. Even the Throne of Honour on which the King had sat gradually vanished before the great cloud which descended bearing the Queen, 'as if it gave way to these heavenly graces' (ll. 391–2). If in this masque there is the suggestion of the forgiving Christ, there is in the role of the Queen the suggestion of the Militant Virgin. The Queen was already beginning to seek help abroad, and Charles was being urged by the Catholic powers to join his forces with theirs against dissident elements at home. Against the growing threat of civil war, the Queen's militant appearance seems to complement Charles's willingness still to offer forgiveness and peace. The combination of these two complementary forces leads once more to the scene of harmony between earth and heaven with which the masque ends.

Perhaps it was the overtones of religion in the way the King and Queen were presenting themselves in the masques that led to the elaboration of Charles's role as the suffering Christ in later propaganda (in *Eikon Basilike* for example),

44 Inigo Jones, The Queen in Amazonian costume in *Salmacida Spolia*

and to charges of blasphemy from critics such as Milton.[34] What constituted blasphemy for the seventeenth century was, however, a very mixed question. Ideally, of course, the King and Queen were not intended to be 'gods', but were to be seen as intermediaries between their subjects and God. To stress this inter-mediary function was, it seems to me, the purpose of the spectacular scenes which concluded Jones's masques of the thirties. After the King and Queen have des-cended from the stage and are once more seated in the midst of their court, they too look up to a higher heaven filled not with 'pagan' gods but with abstract figures and angel-like spirits, in a setting which resembles (in *Salmacida Spolia* for example) far more closely the Christian heaven of baroque painters than it does the slopes of Olympus. The classical deities, released from the strictly classical antecedents given them by Jonson, were free to take on again associations with religion that they had never entirely lost; to suggest a Christian hierarchy which was intended to lead through moral virtue from the 'heaven' of the court to a Christian Heaven above. The object of these scenes was not to dazzle the specta-tors with magic show, but to direct the attention, of spectators and Royalty alike, to a higher reality, a Christian power of which the King and Queen were representa-tive on earth.

If, moreover, Charles and Henrietta believed that in the allegorical world of the masques they were representing not simply their court roles, but their respect-ive religions, then praise of their love and harmonious marriage takes on a deeper level of meaning. On their love being reflected at the religious level depended not only the security of the throne and the peace of the country, but the accomplish-ment of a dream that had occupied much of that and the preceding century, the settlement of religious differences through 'love' rather than through war.

Puritan epilogue

Having dealt at such length with the interests of Henrietta Maria, it seems fitting to let the Opposition have the last word, as they did in history. I will end by referring briefly to a satirical print of 1642 that seems to sum up (from the opposite point of view) many of the connections between the Queen's religion and her court entertainments. The print is entitled *Magna Britannia Divisa*, and is in two parts.[35] The first is entitled 'Professio Christiana, or King and Parliament,' the second (figure 45) 'Processio Romana, or King without his Parliament'. Each part is accompanied by a key which refers to letters and numbers on the scenes, and the key is followed by further passages of description and comment. The 'Processio Romana' is by far the more detailed of the two, having no less than ninety numbers attached to the figures, and many pages of references. In this 'Mysterious Procession' (p. 97) are represented the Queen and all the principal members of the Catholic party at court, whose actions are described under the figure of a dance or masque. The Procession starts at the top of the page with a parody of the banners and placards of religious processions, of the type to

45 Hans Vanderpill, *Magna Britannia Divisa* (1642), Pt 2, 'Processio Romana, or King
    without his Parliament' showing the Queen at centre of procession and armed
    Capucin Friars below

be seen in the Capucin processions of Henri III (figure 8 above), followed by
armed bands. The figures carrying them are described as the forerunners that
'caused the first maske of this Procession to be hatched and dansed in Scotland,
anno 1637, 38, and 39' (p. 97). The emblems and descriptions are a skit on processions and masques: the scene is surmounted, for instance, by an ass carrying
a pannier filled with geese, led by a fox; on the fringed banner held aloft by
a monk stands the figure of Religion 'holding a Book in her right hand, a wind
Mil in her left, a knife under her Arme, and a Spit by her side replenisht with
dead Geese' (p. 98). A reverse of fortune is ascribed to 'the horror that holy
mother Church beares on the fore-head, in not having been masked and disguised,
as it behoved in the Figure of the said Banner'.

   Constant play is made on the word 'mask', linking religious deceit or disguise
with court diversions and masque dancing. The Procession shows all the members

of the Catholic party at court, who 'under many subtilities, masks and false vizards' engaged their adherents 'to some diversions among them in favour of this Rebellion, and to the prosecution of the bloudy plot of this Procession and inordinate Maske' (p. 98). Near the head of the Procession is Father O Cony (Conn) 'bearing before him *the Maske of our good Lady*' (the Queen), leading the Recusant Lords (who are named), followed by the Friars 'of sac and corde' (the Capucins). 'Cardinall Barbarino' holds the bridle of a mule, while Pope ('*now or never*') Urban opens 'the spring of the Gregorian Almanacks, Buls, Indulgences, Masques, Dispensations, Chaplets, Reliques, Agnus Dei, and other *excrements of the Mule*' (p. 99). A little further on 'two Almanack sellors after the new stile, sellors of Maskes of Religion and State' precede the Ladies of the 'Congregation beyond-seas' who cry 'Purge not only our purses, but let us make a Peace or Truce between our Husbands and our Sons, which may make them yeeld to the Iesuiticall Roman League' and 'the good Lady transported' (p. 99). The latter is the Queen herself, who, in the company of two other Queens, occupies the central place in the procession (no. 28). She is followed by those of French or Spanish sympathies at court, all of whom are named in the key: Count Olivares, Toby Mathew, Endymion Porter, Windebank, Cottington, Father Philip the Queen's confessor, Bérulle, the Count and Countess of Arundel, Suckling, Henry Jermyn, Kenelm Digby, possibly Davenant,[36] other cavaliers and clergy: all, in fact, whom 'Holy Mother-Church finds means to cause to dance in the great dance of this Mask', which, with 'other sorts of masques and disguisements', make '*a very recreative divertissement or pastime to all the Congregation and most fit to the Propagation of the Jesuitical faith*' (pp. 100–1). These figures are followed by the Frenchified courtiers, and lastly come the Bishops, with the Archbishop of Canterbury, who, 'not being able to assist at this Mask, whose Organs they have been, *ring the bels during this Procession*'. Thus this unholy gathering, which set out to mock the Reformation which the King with his Parliament would have introduced, goes out '*to dance on the Sabath day*, and by pleasant and rash whirlings, no lesse mery than lamentable, go to their *Episcopal down-fall* within the *Abisses*' (p. 102).

The print throws together all those of Catholic sympathies at court and lends support to the idea that the same close links that existed between court entertainments and religious processions at the Valois court under Henri III also existed at the Caroline court under Henrietta Maria. The 'Procession' shown here is no doubt a parody of the Capucin processions in which the Queen took part, and the seditious motives attributed to it are the same as those attributed to Henri's processions after he lost power. The League turned Henri's penitent processions into military associations and used them against him, so that they were later seen as having had a sinister motive from the beginning. In the representation of a Paris procession of 1593 (figure 46), Capucins are shown (as Frances Yates has pointed out) heavily armed, some with their hoods pulled down because they are wearing helmets.[37] A similar group is shown in the English procession,

46 Satirical representation of a procession of the League showing Capucins and other Orders armed

in a central position and just below the Queen. The description identifies the group (nos. 50–5) as the Queen's Almoner, her Confessor (Father Philip), Jesuits 'girt with swords', and Capucins (identified by their hoods) carrying halberds, guns, and pikes (p. 105). The satirist may have had the satirical presentations of Henri's processions in mind when he designed the English scene, especially as the letterpress is printed throughout in French as well as in English. There is nothing derivative about the figures, however, many of whom are recognisable portraits (of, for example, Count Olivares and Father Philip, pp. 104, 105), and the detail of the scenes within the whole procession shows close observation of the English court. The print is another instance of the way in which Puritan satire indirectly provides valuable information on Catholic activities. As Cowley remarked in writing 'The Puritan and the Papist':

> in a *Circle*, who goe contrary,
> Must at the last *meet* of necessity.

The Puritans, with the keen insight of those who hold diametrically opposed beliefs, perhaps understood better than most the way in which Henrietta's social activities and entertainments were linked with her religious life. The difference was that where she saw images of Beauty and Love linking the two, the Puritans more realistically saw bloodshed and war. For a brief period in the 1630s, however, the Queen's view was the one that influenced the life and culture of the court.

In this light, entertainments of the 1630s may be seen not merely as the pastimes of a court that danced while the fires of Civil War began to burn, but as part of the debate on issues that led to that war, opposing one set of values and beliefs with another.

Notes

Full publication details for book titles, and unabbreviated titles for less familiar journals, are given in the References.

Abbreviations used throughout the text and in the notes

CNRS   Centre National de la Recherche Scientifique
CSP   Calendar of State Papers, various series: CSPD (Domestic), CSPI (Italy), CSPV (Venetian)
DNB   *Dictionary of National Biography*
EES   Glynne Wickham, *Early English Stages 1300 to 1660*
HMC   Historical Manuscripts Commission
OED   *Oxford English Dictionary*

Two books frequently used are sometimes referred to by authors' surnames, or by initials for catalogue numbers:

A&R   Anthony F. Allison and David M. Rogers, *A Catalogue of Catholic Books in English Printed Abroad or Secretly in England, 1558–1640*
O&S   Stephen Orgel and Roy Strong, *Inigo Jones: The Theatre of the Stuart Court. Including the complete designs for productions at court ... together with their texts and historical documentation*, 2 vols.

Introduction

1   C. V. Wedgwood, *The King's Peace 1637–1641*, pp. 123–4.
2   Orgel and Strong, I, 64–6 for discussion; II, 537–45 for description.
3   Ben Jonson, *Works*, ed. Herford and Simpson, X, 404–680 for 'Commentary'; G. E. Bentley, *The Jacobean and Caroline Stage*, and Orgel and Strong for references to contemporary opinion cited with masque texts.
4   John Orrell, 'The Agent of Savoy at *The Somerset Masque*', *RES*, 28 (1977), 301–4.
5   For example David Bevington, *Tudor Drama and Politics*, chap. 1; Norbrook, *Poetry and Politics*, 'Introduction'.
6   'Masquing occasions and masque structure', *RORD*, 24 (1981), 7–16.
7   R. Hassel, *Renaissance Drama and the Church Year*, for religious season; also William Hunter, Jr, 'The liturgical context of *Comus*', *ELN*, 10 (1972), 11–15. Brooks-Davies, *The Mercurian Monarch*, gives another view of the 'mystical' dimension of these masques, pp. 99–123.
8   On Jones's religion see *DNB*, and Joseph Gillow, *A Literary and Biographical History*. E. S. de Beer's doubt about Jones's Catholicism ('Notes on Inigo Jones', *N&Q*, 178 (1940), p. 292) was answered by R. Wittkower, 'Puritanissimo fiero', in *Burlington Magazine*, 90 (1948), 50–1. Like the Earl of Arundel and others at Charles's court who shared a Catholic background, his interests were probably humanist and antiquarian rather than specifically religious: see M. Whinney, 'Inigo Jones: a revaluation', *RIBA Journal*, 59 (1952), 286–9; R. Wittkower, 'Inigo Jones, architect and man of letters', *RIBA Journal*, 60 (1953), 83–90.

9   'The French element in Inigo Jones's masque designs', in *The Court Masque*, ed. David Lindley, pp. 149–68.

10 Jean Jacquot, 'Une parodie du *Triumph of Peace*', in *Cahiers Elisabéthains*, 15 (April, 1979), 77–80; Lois Potter, '*The Triumph of Peace* and *The Cruel War*: masque and parody', *N&Q*, 27 (1980), 345–8.

11 Quoted in John Rushworth, *Historical Collections*, II, 280–1.

1   The Queen's fashions

1   J. B. Fletcher, 'Précieuses at the court of King Charles I', *Journ. Comp. Lit.*, I, i (1903), 120–53; reprinted and set in wider context in *The Religion of Beauty in Woman, and Other Essays on Platonic Love in Poetry and Society* (1911).

2   Maurice Magendie, *La Politesse mondaine et les théories de l'honnêteté en France au XVIIe siècle de 1600 à 1660* (1925), pt 1, chap. 9; René Bray, *La Préciosité et les précieux de Thibaut de Champagne à Jean Giraudoux* (1948), pt 2, chap. 1.

3   Odette de Mourgues, *Metaphysical Baroque and Précieux Poetry*, discusses 'Some aspects of précieux poetry,' chap. 8.

4   Accounts of the Hôtel de Rambouillet in René Bray, *La Préciosité*, pt 2; M. Magendie, *La Politesse mondaine*, pt 1, chap. 9; or in most histories of French literature, for example Gustave Lanson, *Histoire de la littérature française*, p. 372 ff.; Antoine Adam, *Histoire de la littérature française au XVIIe siècle*, I, and *Grandeur and Illusion: French Literature and Society 1600–1715*, trans. Herbert Tint; David Maland, *Culture and Society in Seventeenth-Century France*, pp. 45–53.

5   *L'Astrée*, ed. M. Hugues Vaganay, 5 vols. (numbers in brackets following quotations refer to volume and page numbers). For discussion and summary, see Henri Bochet, *L'Astrée: ses origines, son importance dans la formation de la littérature classique*; for its importance in the *salons*, Magendie, *La Politesse*, pp. 166–230.

6   Bochet, chap. 4, 'La théorie de l'amour platonique'; Bray, *La Préciosité*, p. 47 ff, and pt 2, chap. 3: 'L'Amour précieux'. Sister Mary McMahon, *Aesthetics and Art in the Astrée of Honoré d'Urfé*, relates d'Urfé's Neoplatonism to Catholicism, especially chaps. 3 and and 4.

7   Paul Kristeller, *The Philosophy of Marsilio Ficino*, trans. Virginia Conant, especially pp. 256–88; John C. Nelson, *Renaissance Theory of Love: The Context of Giordano Bruno's 'Eroici furori'*, chaps. 1 and 2; John Vyvyan, *Shakespeare and Platonic Beauty*, chaps. 2 and 3.

8   *The Book of the Courtier*, trans. Sir Thomas Hoby, Castiglione, pp. 303–20.

9   See McMahon, *Aesthetics and Art*, chaps. 3, and 4. In the following discussion I use McMahon's translations, but have supplied references to Vaganay's edition, which was not available when she published her study.

10 Compare passage from Ficino's *De Amore*, quoted by Kristeller, *The Philosophy*, p. 266: 'The goodness of all things is the one God Himself, through whom all things are good, but beauty is the ray of God … penetrating all things from that source, first entering the angelic Mind, secondly, the world Soul and the other Souls, thirdly, Nature, fourthly, the Matter of the bodies'.

11 Ian Maclean, *Woman Triumphant: Feminism in French Literature, 1610–1652*, pp. 161–2; Bochet, *L'Astrée*, pp. 63–4, n. 1, for similar view.

12 Critics (for example Magendie, *La Politesse*, pp. 217–22) have drawn attention to the indelicacies and ambiguities of d'Urfé's moral attitudes.

13 Robert Merrill, *Platonism in French Renaissance Poetry*, chaps. 1 and 2; C. S. Lewis, *The Allegory of Love: A Study in Medieval Tradition*, chap. 1 for courtly love.

14 The actual Hôtel was in rue Saint-Thomas du Louvre, but the Marquis' *chateau* at Rambouillet was surrounded by woods in which the company often re-enacted scenes from *L'Astrée* (A. Adam, *Histoire*, p. 265).

15   Plato, *The Symposium*, trans. W. Hamilton, p. 94; Kristeller, *The Philosophy of Marsilio Ficino*, pp. 276 ff.

16   Robert Ellrodt, *Neoplatonism in the Poetry of Spenser*, pp. 27–8, discusses Ficino's inconsistencies on this point.

17   *The French Influence in English Literature: From the Accession of Elizabeth to the Restoration* (1908), especially chap. 7.

18   *The Social Mode of Restoration Comedy* (1926), especially chap. 3.

19   Alfred Harbage, *Cavalier Drama: An Historical and Critical Supplement to the Study of the Elizabethan and Restoration Stage* (1936), especially pt 1, chaps. 1 and 2, and pt 2, chap. 1, which deal with the influence of the court and the Queen on the drama.

20   'Queen Henrietta Maria as patron of the drama', *Studia Neophilologica*, 42 (1970), p. 10. J. S. Harrison, *Platonism in English Poetry*, traced Henrietta's practice back to Marguerite de Navarre's 'licentiousness of conduct' (p. 156), but the movement that influenced Henrietta grew up in reaction to the license of the earlier period: see Louis Clark Keating, *Studies on the Literary Salon in France, 1550–1615*.

21   'Platonic love and the Puritan rebellion', *SP*, 37 (1940), p. 481. For a complete list of Sensabaugh's works, see chap. 2, n. 7.

22   *La Préciosité. Etude historique et linguistique* (1966), 1. Lathuillère, chap. 1, gives a critique of other attempts to define *préciosité*, notably of the broad view of the subject taken by René Bray in *La Préciosité*; de Mourgues discusses 'The question of the term précieux' in *Metaphysical Baroque and Précieux Poetry*, chap. 7.

23   Daniel Mornet, 'La signification et l'évolution de l'idée de préciosité en France au XVIIe siècle', *JHI*, 1 (1940), 225–31.

24   *Histoire littéraire du sentiment religieux en France, depuis la fin des guerres de religion jusqu'à nos jours* (see 1 to III for seventeenth century); I quote from the authorised translation, *A Literary History of Religious Thought in France from the Wars of Religion down to our own Times*, trans. K. L. Montgomery, SPCK, 3 vols. See also *New Catholic Encyclopedia*, VII, under 'Humanism, Devout'.

25   For discussion see Bremond, *A Literary History*, I, pt 1; II and III for details of religious life in Paris; Jean Calvet, *La Littérature religieuse de François de Sales à Fénelon* in *Histoire de la littérature française*, ed. J. Calvet, V, chap. 1; contemporary biography, Jean-Pierre Camus, *The Spirit of St François de Sales*, ed. and trans. C. F. Kelly.

26   Helen White, *English Devotional Literature (Prose) 1600–1640*, pp. 111–13, puts the *Introduction*'s influence in England after c. 1640, but an English translation was available as early as 1613, other editions in 1614, 1617, 1622, 1637: see Allison and Rogers, under Francis, of Sales, Saint; there was a copy in Nicholas Ferrar's community at Little Gidding (John Cosin, *A Collection of Private Devotions*, ed. P. G. Stanwood, Introduction, p. xxix).

27   For the rise of feminism, see Ian Maclean, *Woman Triumphant*, chap. 5; Carolyn C. Lougee, *Le Paradis des femmes: Women, Salons, and Social Stratification in Seventeenth-Century France*; Bronnie Treloar, 'Some feminist views in France in the seventeenth century', *AUMLA*, 10 (1959), 152–9.

28   An English translation by Miles Car, *A Treatise of the Loue of God*, was published at Doway in 1630. For the standard French edition of Sales's work see References. A. F. Allison drew attention to the influence of the *Traité* in 'Crashaw and St François de Sales', *RES*, 24 (1948), 295–302.

29   For a discussion see Henri Lemaire, *Les Images chez saint François de Sales*; Imbrie Buffum, *Studies in the Baroque from Montaigne to Rotrou*, chap. 2, especially pp. 84–5.

30   Bremond, *A Literary History*, I, chap. 10 for discussion; Mary E. Storer, 'Jean-Pierre Camus, Evêque de Belley', *PMLA*, 61 (1946), 711–38; H. C. Lancaster, 'Jean-Pierre Camus', *PMLA*, 62 (1947), 572–3. John Costa, *Le Conflit moral dans l'oeuvre romanes-*

que de Jean-Pierre Camus (1584–1652) includes alphabetical list of titles (pp. 131–42). Magendie, *La Politesse*, analyses some of the plots, pp. 299–304.

31 In *Trente nouvelles choisies et présentées par René Favret*, a series of extracts and discussions. Magendie, *La Politesse*, pt 2, chap. 7, develops the idea that in this period 'La religion est l'auxilaire du roman' (p. 293).

32 Magendie, *La Politesse mondaine*, pt 2, chaps. 8–10 (pp. 305–409), and throughout; for the concept of *honnêteté*, see especially pp. 355–85.

33 I have based my discussion on the 1st edition (Paris, P. Billaine, 1632). The 2nd edition 'reveue corrigée et augmentée par l'autheur' (Paris, Jean Jost, 1633) was translated by N.N. as *The Compleat Woman* (1639); for other editions, see Ian Maclean, *Woman Triumphant*, Bibliography, see under Du Bosc, Jacques (pp. 278–87). According to a note by C. Chesneau, 'Un précurseur de Pascal? Le Franciscain Jacques du Bosc', *XVIIᵉ Siècle*, 15 (1952), 426–48, Du Bosc himself was a 'rather indifferent Franciscan'.

34 A dispute with Puritan John Bastwick belongs to these years (*DNB*). Montague evidently had to change some passages concerning religion: William E. Axon, 'The licensing of Montague's *Miscellanea Spiritualia*', *The Library*, 2nd series, 2 (1901), 269–73.

35 Biographies used: Quentin Bone, *Henrietta Maria: Queen of the Cavaliers* (1972), with a valuable 'Bibliographical Essay' (pp. 253–71) giving sources to information, particularly of a political and historical nature; Elizabeth Hamilton, *Henrietta Maria* (1976) for more personal information; Carola Oman, *Henrietta Maria* (1936). Letters and documents: Charles, Comte de Baillon, *Henriette-Marie de France, Reine d'Angleterre* (1877), including a biographical sketch; Mary Anne Green, *Letters of Queen Henrietta Maria* (1857), translates letters and intersperses explanatory notes; Leveneur, Comte de Tillières, *Mémoires*, ed. M. C. Hippeau (1862).

36 M. A. Green, *Letters* (Introduction); Hamilton, *Henrietta Maria*, pp. 22–30; Jean Jacquot, 'La reine Henriette-Marie et l'influence française dans les spectacles à la cour de Charles Iᵉʳ', pp. 128–30.

37 Henry Lancaster, *A History of French Dramatic Literature in the Seventeenth Century*, I, 272; p. 157 ff. for a description of plays by Racan, d'Amblainville, and other contemporary French dramatists; CSPV and CSPD (1625–8) see under Henrietta Maria, for other references.

38 On anti-feminist pamphlets and replies, see Linda Woodbridge, *Women and the English Renaissance: Literature and the Nature of Womankind 1540–1620* (1984); Katherine Henderson and Barbara McManus, eds., *Half Humankind: Contexts and Texts of the Controversy about Women in England, 1540–1640* (1985) (both books treat feminism, but not from a court point of view); Simon Shepherd, *Amazons and Warrior Women: Varieties of Feminism in Seventeenth-Century Drama* (1981); Robert Brustein, 'The monstrous regiment of women: sources for the satiric view of the court lady in English drama', in *Renaissance and Modern Essays Presented to Vivian de Sola Pinto*, ed. G. R. Hibbard, pp. 35–50. An historical account of anti-feminism is given by Ian Maclean, *Woman Triumphant*, chaps. 1 and 2.

39 Hamilton, *Henrietta Maria*, pp. 17, 27; Bremond, *A Literary History*, II, 211 (chap. 4 for details of Marie's involvement in early development of Devout Humanism).

40 HMC, *Salvetti Correspondence*, 11th report, Appendix, pt 1, to which bracketed page numbers refer.

41 For example, in Henry Ellis, *Original Letters Illustrative of English History*, series 2, III, 260, to the effect that St James is convenient to the King for recreation, 'and the Queene her intertainements and devotions, for which the new-built chappel is decently adorned'.

42 Bone, *Henrietta Maria*, pp. 11–12; her ignorance of Latin led to poets at English

universities writing in English to celebrate Royal occasions: see Alberta Turner, 'Queen Henrietta Maria and the University poets', *N&Q*, 193 (1948), 270–2.

43   Margaret Pickel, *Charles I as Patron of Poetry and Drama*, pp. 27–8.

44   Lucy Hutchinson, *Memoirs of the Life of Colonel Hutchinson*, p. 67.

45   Quoted by Pickel, p. 25, from Thomas Birch, *Court and Times of Charles I*, I, 8.

46   *The Non-Dramatic Works of Sir John Suckling*, p. 30; Suckling's two poems 'Against Fruition' (pp. 37, 38) were answered in dialogue form by Waller, and in another two poems by Henry Bold (all included in *The Non-Dramatic Works*, Appendix A, pp. 181–4). Suckling adopts a respectful attitude to Platonism in his 'Letters' to Aglaura, for which see Hazlitt's edition of *The Poems . . . of Suckling*, II, 173–223; and for discussion see F. O. Henderson, 'Traditions of *précieux* and *libertin* in Suckling's poetry', *ELH*, 4 (1937), 274–98.

47   In French, the ambiguity in the word 'galant' was resolved by word order: 'un *galant homme* marque un homme d'esprit, un homme enjoué, agréable. Mais *homme galant* marque un homme qui a de certaines passions qu'il ne devroit point avoir' (see Lathuillère, *La Préciosité*, pp. 565–78).

48   Carolyn Lougee, *Le Paradis des femmes*, Appendix I (pp. 215–22) lists all identifiable *précieuses* in Parisian *salons*, compiled from Somaize and other sources; no. 30 is 'Madame de Carly' whom Lougee identifies as 'Lucy Percy, married in 1617 to James Hay I, Earl of Carlisle'.

49   Harbage, *Cavalier Drama*, pp. 13–14, and discussion, pp. 36–7, 42–5, 93–5. My references are to the copy printed by Thomas Dring (London, 1629). For correction of the printing date, which is an error for 1659, see W. W. Greg, *A Bibliography of the English Printed Drama*, II, 797.

50   *The Private Memoirs of Sir Kenelm Digby, Gentleman of the Bedchamber to King Charles the First*. For following details see Introductory Memoir, pp. ix, xxi, xxvii.

51   Lancaster, *A History of French Dramatic Literature*, I, 272. My references are to *The Countess of Pembroke's Arcadia (The Old Arcadia)*, ed. Jean Robertson.

52   Josephine A. Roberts, 'Excerpts from *Arcadia* in the manuscript notebook of Lady Katherine Manners', *N&Q*, 28 (1981), 35–6.

53   'The Renaissance artist as plagiarist', *ELH*, 48 (1981), p. 478.

54   Mornet, 'La signification . . . de l'idée de préciosité', p. 228; also Lougee, *Le Paradis*, p. 37 ff. For the contrasting view of Devout Humanists, influenced by St François de Sales, see Maclean, *Woman Triumphant*, p. 91, and chap. 4, 'The Question of marriage'.

2   The tone of court drama

1   Alfred Harbage, *Cavalier Drama* (1936) for a basic discussion, and Martin Butler, *Theatre and Crisis* (1984), especially chaps. 3 and 4. Principal titles to be discussed here are: Lodowick Carlell, *The Deserving Favourite* (1629) and *The Passionate Lovers*, pt I (1635); Thomas Randolph, *Amyntas* (c. 1630; printed 1638) and *The Jealous Lovers* (1632); Joseph Rutter, *The Shepheard's Holyday* (1635); John Fletcher, *The Faithful Shepherdess* (c. 1609; revived 1634); William Davenant, *Love and Honour* (1634), *The Platonic Lovers* (1635), *The Fair Favourite* (1638), and *The Unfortunate Lovers* (1638); William Cartwright, *The Royal Slave* (1636); John Suckling, *Aglaura* (1637); Thomas Goffe, *The Careless Shepherdess* (printed 1656; performed c. 1638); William Berkley, *The Lost Lady* (1639); William Habington, *The Queen of Aragon* (1640); James Shirley, *The Lady of Pleasure* (1637; performed 1635); *Lady Alimony* (anonymously printed 1659). Editions of these plays used for quotations are given in the References. For further information and contemporary comment, see individual entries in Mary Steele, *Plays and Masques at Court*, and G. E. Bentley, *The Jacobean and Caroline Stage*.

2   Printed by Orgel and Strong in *Inigo Jones*, II; for additional information, see Stephen Orgel, '*Florimène* and *The Ante-Masques*', *Ren. Drama*, n.s., 4 (1971), 135–53.

3   G. K. Hunter, 'Italian tragicomedy on the English stage', *Ren. Drama*, n.s., 6 (1973), p. 136; Frank H. Ristine, *English Tragicomedy: Its Origin and History*, pp. 34–7.

4   Douglas Duncan, 'A guide to *The New Inne*', *Essays in Criticism*, 20 (1970), 311–26; Richard Levin, 'The new *New Inne* and the proliferation of good bad drama', *Essays in Criticism*, 22 (1972), 41–7; Anne Barton, '*The New Inne* and the problem of Jonson's late style', *ELR*, 9 (1979), 395–418, and 'Harking back to Elizabeth: Ben Jonson and Caroline nostalgia', *ELH*, 48 (1981), 706–31; Patrick Cheney, 'Jonson's *The New Inne* and Plato's myth of the hermaphrodite', *Ren. Drama*, n.s., 14 (1983), 173–94.

5   *Lodowick Carliell: His Life and a Discussion of his Plays*, ed. Charles Gray, Introduction, pp. 31 ff.; Harbage, *Cavalier Drama*, p. 96.

6   Kenneth Richards, 'Joseph Rutter's *The Shepherd's Holiday* and the *Silvanire* of Jean de Mairet', *Anglia*, 85 (1967), 404–13; Lancaster, *History of French Dramatic Literature*, pp. 157–8.

7   George F. Sensabaugh, 'Love ethics in Platonic court drama 1625–1642', *HLQ*, I (1938), 277–304; 'John Ford and Platonic love in the court', *SP*, 36 (1939), 202–26; 'Platonic love and the Puritan rebellion', *SP*, 37 (1940), 457–81; 'The milieu of *Comus*', *SP*, 41 (1944), 239–49; *The Tragic Muse of John Ford* (1944), chap. 3; 'Platonic love in Shirley's *The Lady of Pleasure*', in *A Tribute to George Coffin Taylor*, ed. Arnold Williams (1952), pp. 168–77.

8   Mark Stavig has a criticism in general terms in *John Ford and the Traditional Moral Order*, pp. 40–3.

9   See 'Love ethics', p. 302 and n. 124, in which Sensabaugh connects 'immoral' attitudes in plays with attitudes at court. Of the two particular cases given by Sensabaugh, however, that of the notorious Lady Frances Howard, Countess of Essex, who married Sir Robert Carr in 1614 after the probable murder of her husband, belongs to James's rather than Charles's reign; Sensabaugh mistakenly identifies her with another Frances Howard, daughter of the Earl of Berkshire (see Orgel and Strong, *Inigo Jones*, index entry), who took part in three of the Queen's masques in the thirties. Sensabaugh's other example is that of Frances Coke, Lady Purbech, who was tried for adultery with Sir Robert Howard in 1627; she, however, had been forced, when still a young girl, to marry Buckingham's brother, the mentally unstable Viscount Purbech, who was declared insane in 1620 (*DNB*, see under Villiers, John). Her case might be regarded by a more enlightened age as an argument against the evils of enforced marriage and its consequences.

10 'The enforcement of marriage in English drama, 1600–1650', *PQ*, 38 (1959). p. 459; also 'Conventions, plot, and structure in *The Broken Heart*', *MP*, 56 (1958), 1–9; for general treatment, F. S. Boas, *An Introduction to Stuart Drama* (1946).

11 See 'The arrangement of marriage', in Lawrence Stone, *The Crisis of the Aristocracy*, pp. 594 ff. Dale B. Randall, *Jonson's Gypsies Unmasked*, pp. 27–8, and pp. 124 ff., discusses examples connected with the Villiers family, including that of Frances Coke.

12 Printed in 1659 (my quotations are from R. Dodsley, XIV, written after 1633 (from references to 'crop-eared histriomastixes', p. 281). Sensabaugh refers to it in 'Love ethics', p. 288, n. 64 and throughout, more extensively in 'Platonic love and the Puritan rebellion', pp. 461–3, and *The Tragic Muse*, pp. 136–40, where he says it 'strips from the coterie [i.e. the Queen's *précieux* group] its mantle of purity and virtue and reveals its beliefs for exactly what they are – an excuse for licentious courtiers and lascivious ladies to follow their individual whims' (*The Tragic Muse*, p. 138).

13 Preface to *The Compleat Woman*, p. 8 (translation by N.N. of Du Bosc's 1633 edition of *L'Honneste Femme*).

14 Ian Maclean, *Woman Triumphant*, chap. 3: 'The new feminism and the *femme forte*, 1630–40'. Shepherd, *Amazons and Warrior Women*, examines 'sexual politics' in plays

mainly earlier in the century, where it focused on the military qualities of Elizabeth as contrasted with the 'soft' qualities of James, a contrast that was placed in a Protestant/Catholic context (chap. 9).

15   'Woman as wonder: a generic figure in Italian and Shakespearean comedy', in *Studies in the Continental Background*, ed. Dale B. Randall, pp. 109–32; see also '*The Virgin Martyr* and the *Tragedia Sacra*', *Ren. Drama*, 7 (1964), 103–26.

16   Butler, pp. 44–9; Anne Barton, 'He that plays the king', in *English Drama: Forms and Development*, eds. M. Axton and R. Williams, pp. 92–3.

3   The Queen's religion

1   John Cosin, *A Collection of Private Devotions*, ed. P. G. Stanwood and Daniel O'Connor, Introduction, p. xxxiv, quoted from John Evelyn's *Diary*. For the book's connections with the Primer, or pre-Reformation book of prayer containing traditional Catholic offices, see Stanwood's *Introduction*, xxiv–xxvii; criticised by Prynne in *A Briefe Survay and Censure of Mr Cozens his Couzening Devotions. Proving both the Forme and Matter . . . to Be Meerely Popish*, and Henry Burton, *A Tryall of Private Devotions* (both 1628).

2   Mary Anne Green, *Letters of Queen Henrietta Maria*, p. 7.

3   'Discours de Marie de Médici à la fille de Henriette-Marie, au moment de son départ pour l'Angleterre', in Leveneur, Comte de Tillières, *Mémoires*, chap. 4, pp. 70–6.

4   Baillon, *Henriette-Marie . . . lettres inédites*, pp. 346–7.

5   *The Holy Court*, trans. T.H., I (Paris, 1626), II (Paris, 1631), both bearing false imprints (see Allison and Rogers, under Caussin, Nicolas, nos. 217, 218). *The Holy Court*, I–III (Rouen, 1634) and IV (Rouen, 1638), both trans. T.H., available in *English Recusant Literature*, facsimile reprints, nos. 367, 368.

6   For Caussin's plays see Ernest Boysse, *Le Théâtre des Jésuites*, pp. 343–6; Pierre Janelle, *The Catholic Reformation*, pp. 151–5. Philip Massinger did in fact base the plot of *The Emperor of the East* (1631) on the story of Theodosius and Athenais in *The Holy Court*, I, bk 4 (entitled 'Of impiety of courts'): see J. E. Gray, 'The source of *The Emperor of the East*', *RES*, n.s., I (1950), 126–35. Massinger addressed a prologue to the King, apparently hoping for a court performance; but considering that the plot concerns an uxorious king who, after his marriage to a beautiful young wife, becomes extravagant and careless in signing petitions, it is not surprising that it failed to gain one. The section following bk. 4 in Caussin is entitled 'Fortunate Piety', and it has been suggested that Massinger alludes to it in his lost play *The Unfortunate Piety* (also 1631): see Peter Phialas, 'The sources of Massinger's *Emperor of the East*', *PMLA*, 65 (1950), p. 476, n. 16. Whatever Massinger's Catholic sympathies (see T. A. Dunn, *Philip Massinger: The Man and the Playwright*, pp. 184–91), we may conclude that he preferred a sturdier brand of Catholicism than that followed by the Queen.

7   Allison and Rogers, see under Camus, Jean-Pierre (nos. 4551–4). *The Spirituall Director Disinteressed* (Roan 1633) quotes the praise given by Caussin to Camus in the passage mentioned above; *A Spirituall Combat* and *A Draught of Eternitie* were both translated in 1632 by Miles Car, Priest. *Admirable Events* (London, 1639) was dedicated to Henrietta (see Storer, 'Jean-Pierre Camus', p. 719).

8   For the following (and for a good general survey of Catholic events at court) see Martin J. Havran, *The Catholics in Caroline England*, chap. 3.

9   Huntington Library, MS HM 120 (4to, 87 leaves) 'Queen Esters Haliluiahs and Hamans Madrigalls Expressed and Illustrated in a Sacred Poem . . . Composed by Fra: Lenton, Gent: the Queenes Poet' (1637). The manuscripts are discussed by Leota (Snider) Willis, 'Francis Lenton, Queen's Poet', Dissertation (1931), pp. 48 ff. Lenton declared to the reader that his intention was not 'to obraide, or whipp, or satirize / This

stubborne world', but in 1649 the title page has the words 'Reflecting on theis Present Tymes' added.

10   Quentin Bone's conclusion in *Henrietta Maria*, Preface, pp. v–vi.

11   *The Memoirs of Gregorio Panzani, giving an Account of his Agency in England in the Years 1634, 1635, 1636*, translation and introduction by Joseph Berington.

12   Albion, throughout, and especially Appendix 1, 'Rome, Charles I, and Art'. Puritans accused Conn of deceiving the King 'with gifts of pictures, antique idols and suchlike trumperies brought from Rome' (quoted by Albion, p. 395).

13   For the following information see entries under individual names in *DNB*; for known Catholics see also Joseph Gillow, *A Literary and Biographical History, or Bibliographical Dictionary, of the English Catholics*, 5 vols.; Brian Magee, *The English Recusants: A Study of the Post-Reformation Catholic Survival*, chap. 7, says that under Charles one-fifth of the Peers were Catholic (he gives a documented list of those who were (a) definitely (b) more doubtfully, Catholic from 1624 on); see also Lawrence Stone, *The Crisis of the Aristocracy*, p. 64. Other basic studies are by David Mathew, *Catholicism in England, 1535–1935*, and 'The Catholic minority' in *The Age of Charles I*; and by John Bossy, *The English Catholic Community, 1570–1850*.

14   *The Private Memoirs of Sir Kenelm Digby*, Introduction, p. xli; Digby was an eccentric, whose real life and courtship of Venetia Stanley, told in romance form in his *Private Memoirs*, is as strange as any of Camus's romances, which in some ways it resembles. His *Conference with a Lady about Choice of Religion* (Paris, 1638) helped convert Lady Frances Howard (Frances Coke) in 1637. He translated Tasso's *Aminta* and Guarini's *Il Pastor fido* (both now lost: see Harbage, *Cavalier Drama*, p. 132).

15   Smuts, 'The Puritan followers of Henrietta Maria', p. 27, says that Jermyn also converted to Catholicism in 1636, but does not cite any evidence; for other names see *DNB*. Important information on the conversions taking place at court in the 1630s is given by Albion, *Charles I*, pp. 200–14. William Prynne, in *Romes Master-Peece*, pp. 23–4, and throughout, names most of the court Catholics mentioned here.

16   See Habington, *Poems*, pp. xxvi–xxix. Habington married Lucy, daughter of William Herbert (cousin of Philip Herbert, Earl of Pembroke).

17   HMC, *Salvetti Correspondence*, p. 85. Buckingham's mother, the Countess, an unwavering Catholic, embarked on a deliberate policy of marrying members of the Villiers family to members of the Stuart court, resulting in many closely interwoven connections (see Randall, *Jonson's Gypsies Unmasked*, pp. 27–8, and throughout).

18   See Odette de Mourgues, *Metaphysical Baroque*, especially pp. 108–16, on the characteristics of *préciosité* discussed below; also René Bray, *La Préciosité*, p. 167.

19   Historical studies: E. N. S. Thompson, *The Controversy between the Puritans and the Stage* (1903); Jonas Barish, *The Antitheatrical Prejudice* (1981). The philosophical grounds of the controversy discussed by Russell Fraser, *The War against Poetry* (1970), and Michael O'Connell, 'The idolatrous eye: iconoclasm, anti-theatricalism, and the image of the Elizabethan theatre', *ELH*, 52 (1985), 279–310. See also P. W. Thomas, 'Two cultures? Court and country under Charles I', chap. 6 in *The Origins of the English Civil War*, especially pp. 172–80. For anti-feminist literature, see n. 38 (chap. 1) above.

20   *The World Turned Upside Down: Radical Ideas during the English Revolution*, especially chap. 15, 'Base impudent kisses', which deals with Puritan attacks on 'free' love practised at the opposite end of the social scale from the court. For other examples see: Alexander J. Denomy, *The Heresy of Courtly Love*; Jeffrey B. Russell, 'Courtly love as religious dissent', *Catholic Historical Review*, 51 (1964–65), 31–44.

21   'Memoirs of the mission in England of the Capuchin Friars ... from the year 1630 to 1669. By Father Cyprien of Gamaches one of the Capuchins belonging to the household of Henrietta Maria'. For a general account see Father Cuthbert (Lawrence

Anthony Hess) OSFC, *The Capuchins: a Contribution to the History of the Counter-Reformation*, II, and Martin Havran, *The Catholics in Caroline England*, chap. 5.

22 Pierre Janelle, *The Catholic Reformation*, p. 237. Father Joseph had been in England previously, took part in many missions, and shared the prefecture of the mission to England (Birch, II, 296). Charles had talked to a Capucin at the Spanish court, Fra Boverio de Saluzzo, who believed Charles needed only to be taught the 'truth Faith' to be converted (Cuthbert, p. 431).

23 Janelle, pp. 196–237.

24 Cuthbert, *The Capuchins*, II, 403–10; Henri Bremond, *A Literary History*, I, pt 2, chap. 14, 'Towards "pure love"'.

25 Cuthbert, II, 410–13. I have been unable to locate a copy of the book, but Cuthbert describes it as exposing the arguments of the *libertins*, and appealing to a fundamental faith in human nature. Zacharie later turned to satire (under the pseudonym Petrus Firmianus) in reaction against the fashionable devotion that had 'turned to insipidity' Sales's saintly teaching (Bremond, I, 256–7).

26 Bremond, I, 396, n. 1.

27 *L'Astrée*, ed. Vaganay, II, 327. Roger Boase, *The Origin and Meaning of Courtly Love*, reviews literature tracing these inter-connections; courtly love is more likely to have influenced Marianism than the reverse (Boase, pp. 83–6), but the two streams seem to have mingled in the thirteenth and fourteenth centuries: see Marina Warner, *Alone of all her Sex: The Myth and the Cult of the Virgin Mary*, chaps. 9–11. Warner gives a history of the cult under headings of Mary as Virgin, Queen, Bride, etc. For a general history see *The New Catholic Encyclopedia*, under Marian Devotion; Mary, Blessed Virgin, and sub-headings.

28 A French description, *Les Royales Cérémonies faites en l'édification d'une chapelle de Capuchins à Londres ...* (Rheims, 1633) stresses the significance of Charles's granting permission for building the chapel (p. 15).

29 *New Catholic Encyclopedia*, see under Sodality: Confraternities and Arch-Confraternities.

30 Wolfgang Lottes, 'Henry Hawkins and *Partheneia Sacra*', *RES*, n.s., 26 (1975), 272. In a note to the Scolar Press edition (1975) of Stephan Luzvic, *The Devout Hart* (trans. Henry Hawkins), Karl Höltgen identifies Lady Anne Arundel (to whom Hawkins dedicated another of his works) as the Patroness of a Marian Society in England.

31 See Herbert's poem 'To All Angels and Saints'; Louis Martz, in *The Poetry of Meditation*, discussed the general relevance of Marian devotion to the Metaphysical poets, pp. 96–112, and the spirit of St François de Sales in the poetry of George Herbert (pp. 249 ff.).

32 Helen White, *English Devotional Literature (Prose) 1600–1640*, especially chap. 6, and also 'Some continuing traditions in English devotional literature', *PMLA*, 57 (1942), 966–80. Catholic books had always been able to enter England with ambassadors: Edward Adair, *The Exterritoriality of Ambassadors in the Sixteenth and Seventeenth Centuries*, p. 186. Allison and Rogers print a list of 'Secret presses operating in England', pp. 184–5. For some of the books devoted to Mary see titles in A&R, nos. 129, 139, 269, 354–6, 433, 557, 648–52, 715, 746, 804.

33 Reprinted by Scolar Press, 1971; described by Rosemary Freeman, *English Emblem Books* (1948), who argues for Henry Hawkins as author (Appendix 3, pp. 243–8). Mario Praz, *Studies in Seventeenth-Century Imagery* (1939 edn.), p. 72, suggested Henry Aston as author, but in revised 2nd edn. (1964) drops his suggestion, p. 154, n. 1.

34 See D. J. Gordon, 'Poet and architect: intellectual setting of the quarrel between Ben Jonson and Inigo Jones', in *The Renaissance Imagination*, pp. 77–101.

35 *DNB*, see under Hawkins, Thomas; Hawkins, Henry and Brooke, Sir Basil; Wolfgang Lottes, 'Henry Hawkins and *Partheneia Sacra*', *RES*, pp. 144–53; Josephine E.

Secker, 'Henry Hawkins, S.J., 1577–1646: A recusant writer and translator of the early seventeenth century', *Recusant History*, 11 (1972), 237–52; and note by Höltgen in the Scolar Press edition of *The Devout Hart*.

36 The pairing of opposite qualities in which 'Beautie should not violate Shamefastnes; grauitie, infringe lowlines; meekenes, grauitie; Simplicitie, Maiestie' ('The Pröem'), is reminiscent of Du Bosc's paired opposites in the section headings of *L'Honneste Femme* (compare chap. 1 above).

37 Praz, *Studies in Seventeenth-Century Imagery*, 2nd edn. (1964), pp. 163–4, suggests the influence of Louis Richeome, whose work I discuss in chapter 5 below. See also Odette de Mourgues, *Metaphysical Baroque*, pp. 80–1, 93–7, and throughout, and Wolfgang Lottes, 'Henry Hawkins and *Partheneia Sacra*', pp. 273–86 for Hawkins's Latin sources.

38 G. F. Sensabaugh, 'Platonic love and the Puritan rebellion' (pp. 479–80), and *The Tragic Muse* (pp. 97–100), gives a list of works connected with the controversy.

39 See my note, 'The authorship of *Maria Triumphans*', *N&Q*, 232 (1987), 313–14, which points out resemblances between the two works.

40 The wording on the two tablets is (as far as I can make out):

King's tablet	*Queen's tablet*
Princesse des Immortels,	Vierge, voicy le cher gage,
Que la splendeur enuironne;	Qu'il vous a pleu m'obtenir;
Je consacre à vos autels	Je vous en fais vn hommage,
Et mon Sceptre et ma Couronne.	Vous l'offrant pour le benir.
Par vostre ayde la Victoire	Vous fustes à sa naissance
M'est acquise contre tous;	Un Astre, pour l'esclairer;
Car je combats pour la gloire	Et c'est par vostre influence,
De vostre Fils et de Vous.	Qu'il doit aussi prosperer.

4 The Queen's masques

1 Stephen Orgel and Roy Strong, *Inigo Jones: The Theatre of the Stuart Court*, especially chap. 4, 'Platonic politics' (pp. 52–8). Subsequent references to masque texts and designs are to this work.

2 Alfred Harbage, *Cavalier Drama*, pt 1, chap. 1; Malcolm Smuts, 'The political failure of Stuart cultural patronage', in *Patronage in the Renaissance*, p. 71; for the court's eager reception of new designs, J. Orrell, 'Inigo Jones and Amerigo Salvetti: a note on the later masque designs', *Theatre Notebook*, 30 (1976), 109–14.

3 Orgel and Strong, p. 52; Strong, *Art and Power*, p. 159.

4 CSP, Italy (1632–36), p. 15.

5 Jonson, *Works* (eds. Herford and Simpson), x, 457 (for Anne); HMC, 'Salvetti Correspondence', pt 1, p. 47 (for Henrietta).

6 Orgel and Strong, chap. 3, especially pp. 36–40.

7 Edward Croft-Murray, *Decorative Painting in England, 1537–1837*, 1, 36–7; for Gentileschi, pp. 201–2, plates 67, 68.

8 Such scenes, described by Orgel and Strong (p. 38) as 'layers of cut-outs, some in moulded relief, standing in front of the back-cloth', are discussed by Richard Southern, *Changeable Scenery: Its Origin and Development in the British Theatre*, pp. 60–3, 75. Some examples are: Jove on an eagle, *Tempe Restored* (figure 14 above); Atlas holding a globe, *Coelum Britannicum* (O&S no. 280); City of Sleep 'placed' on a rainbow (possibly suspended from the fly-gallery), *Luminalia* (O&S, no. 386).

9   Orgel and Strong, p. 18, for discussion of Jones's stage development.

10   Oliver Millar, *Rubens: The Whitehall Ceiling*, pp. 7, and 10–12; Strong, *Britannia Triumphans: Inigo Jones, Rubens, and Whitehall Palace*, pp. 14–15; D. J. Gordon, 'Rubens and the Whitehall ceiling', in *The Renaissance Imagination*, pp. 31–55.

11   Croft-Murray, *Decorative Painting*, I, 34–5.

12   Discussed and illustrated by Gordon, 'Roles and mysteries', in *The Renaissance Imagination*, pp. 3–11.

13   An order for literally hundreds of lights is attached to a drawing for *Albion's Triumph* (O&S, II, 464, no. 193). See chapter on 'Light' in John C. Meagher, *Method and Meaning in Jonson's Masques*.

14   Orgel and Strong, pp. 711–12, nos. 383, 384, and figure 114. For Elsheimer and Rubens, see Kenneth Clark, *Landscape into Art*, pp. 51–2, and plate 60.

15   Frances Yates traced the Tudor origins of the doctrine in *Astraea: The Imperial Theme in the Sixteenth Century*, pp. 38–51, and its connection with Fletcher's revival of Sidneian pastoral romance in *Shakespeare's Last Plays*, pp. 30–70. See also Jonathan Goldberg, *James I*, chap. 1; Graham Parry, *The Golden Age Restor'd*, chap. 10; Roy Strong, *Britannia Triumphans*, p. 28; Orgel and Strong, p. 59.

16   Emile Mâle, *The Gothic Image: Religious Art in France of the Thirteenth Century*, chap. 3 for cult of Virgin; pp. 238–58 for explanations of visual tradition; and Mâle, *L'Art religieux après le concile de Trente*; for illustrations see Robert Hughes, *Heaven and Hell in Western Art*, plate 54 for seventeenth–century example.

17   Albert J. Loomie, S. J. 'King James I's Catholic consort', *HLQ*, 34 (1971), 303–16: Anne's Catholicism, professed in 1601, was not openly practised like Henrietta's.

18   Henri Bremond, *A Literary History of Religious Thought*, I, 253 and throughout; Mario Praz, *Studies in Seventeenth-Century Imagery*; Louis Martz, *The Poetry of Meditation*, chap. 1.

19   Praz, *Studies*, especially chap. 3, 'Profane and sacred love'; Rosemary Freeman, *English Emblem Books*, pp. 116 ff.

20   Bremond, *A Literary History*, I, 27–29; Praz, *Studies*, p. 190.

21   Ed. Oliver Millar, *Walpole Society*, 37 (1958).

22   Jennifer Montagu, 'The painted enigma and French seventeenth-century art', *JWCI*, 31 (1969), 307–35.

23   E. H. Gombrich, 'Botticelli's mythologies: a study in the Neoplatonic symbolism of his circle', *JWCI*, 8 (1945), 7–60; Edgar Wind, *Pagan Mysteries of the Renaissance*, chap. 7.

24   See references in Roland M. Frye, *Milton's Imagery and the Visual Arts*, pp. 230–1 and notes. Milton, who was much influenced by these masques (see John G. Demaray, *Milton and the Masque Tradition* and *Milton's Theatrical Epic*) could well have had the masque as well as the painting in mind.

25   For symbolism of the garden see Robert Hughes, *Heaven and Hell in Western Art*, chap. 2; Terry Comito, 'Renaissance gardens and the discovery of Paradise', *JHI*, 32 (1971), 483–506; and, *The Idea of the Garden in the Renaissance*; Stanley Stewart, *The Enclosed Garden: The Tradition and the Image in Seventeenth-Century Poetry*. The symbolism was of course familiar in literature: see for example C. S. Lewis's discussion in *The Allegory of Love*, pp. 119 ff., in relation to the *Roman de la Rose* and *The Faery Queen*.

26   Brereley, *Virginalia*, Sonnet 15. An allegorical painting by G. Vasari in the Ashmolean Museum, Oxford shows Mary rising from the Tree/Serpent, and paintings of the Annunciation often show Eve simultaneously driven from Paradise.

27   *Le Bréviaire du Cardinal Grimani* (1862) explains the 'Emblèmes symboliques de Marie' (pp. 297–8) in the scene reproduced above (see figure 21): the castle is *Porta Coeli*, 'répondant au titre que l'Eglise donne à Marie dans les Litanies: *Janua Coeli*'; and the tower is *Turris David*, 'symbole sous lequel Marie est souvent désignée

... étant la forteresse imprenable de l'Eglise contre ses ennemis'. See also *Partheneia Sacra* for Hawkins's explanations of each of his emblems.

28   Mary Anne Green, *Letters of Queen Henrietta Maria*, p. 32, quoted from Conn's despatches to Rome; S. R. Gardiner, *History of England*, VIII, 237.

29   Gordon Albion, *Charles I*, p. 148, quoting advice given to Panzani before he set out from Rome in 1634.

30   Enid Welsford, *The Court Masque* (p. 229), noted the name 'Indamor, King of Narsinga' and other similarities in a tourney presented in Florence in 1616, but the plot is closer to 'Une fête équestre à Ferrare: *Il Tempio d'amore* (1565)' described by Irène Mamczarz (*Les Fêtes de la Renaissance*, CNRS, III (1975), 349–72), in which magicians seek to visit the temple of love, are baulked by its disappearance, and in revenge raise false temples, until finally the true temple returns under the influence of the new Queen and her Platonic doctrines of love.

31   *Memoirs of Panzani*, ed. J. Berington, p. 132. Garrard's letter, dated 1 March 1635, reported 'Our French Cavaliers are come home ... on the Eve of the Queen's Mask came the Lord Dunluce and Wat Mountague. Mr Mountague is well received by the King and Queen ...' (Thomas Wentworth, Earl of Strafford, *Letters and Dispatches*, I, 373). Montague announced his conversion to Catholicism soon after.

32   For Father Cyprien's account, see Birch, *Court and Times*, II, 301–6. Jones may have been working on designs from 1623, when chapels both there and at St James were ordered (John Summerson, *Inigo Jones*, p. 76), but nothing definite was done until 1630.

33   *Les Royales Cérémonies faites en l'édification d'une chapelle de Capucins à Londres ...* (Reims, 1633), to which bracketed page nos. refer.

34   Orgel and Strong, I, 40, no. 122 for the Banqueting House; II, no. 334 and Commentary for St Paul's.

35   Burton, *For God, and the King*, quoted for special condemnation the passage in which Stafford (in *The Female Glory*) praised 'the Princes of this our Ile' for erecting Chapels and Temples to the Blessed Virgin (Burton, p. 235).

36   Stephen Orgel, 'Inigo Jones' Persian entertainment', *AARP*, 2 (1972), 59–69, noted the masque's 'allying Caroline reforms with the world of regenerative mysteries and epiphanies' (p. 63); he does not, however, suggest any specific religious occasion.

37   It is of interest for music history that Henrietta brought a strong Oratorian influence to the court: Bérulle and his Oratorian priests in 1625 and Panzani in 1635; Walter Montague, who joined the same Order, used the Papal chapel for his ministry from 1636 (Albion, *Charles I*, p. 145 (n. 2) for Panzani; p. 205 for Montague). At least one noted masque singer, Maturin Mari, belonged to the Queen's chapel (Andrew Sabol, *Four Hundred Songs and Dances from the Stuart Masque*, p. 24), and the music for *Salmacida Spolia* was composed by Lewis Richard, Master of the Queen's music.

38   R. Wittkower, 'Puritanissino fiero', *Burlington Magazine*, 90 (1948), 50–1. The Capucins possibly wanted to reflect credit on themselves by emphasising the difficulties of completing the chapel, but they also concluded that, when finished, the chapel was 'more beautiful, larger and grander than one could ever have hoped for' – hardly the work of a 'Puritan'.

39   S. R. Gardiner, *History of England*, VIII, 130–50 and 238–9; for details of conversions, see Albion, *Charles I*, pp. 196–212; Birch, *Court and Times*, II, 332 ff.

40   For details, see Albion, *Charles I*, pp. 162–4, and plate 4 for an illustration of the interior of the chapel.

41   Albion, pp. 212 and 226; Gardiner, *History of England*, VIII, 239–42.

42   Quoted in the case of The Commons against Laud (1634), in John Rushworth, *Historical Collections*, II, 279.

43   G. F. Sensabaugh gives a summary of the controversy in *The Tragic Muse of John Ford*, pp. 99–100.

44   In Luca Pinelli, *The Societie of the Rosarie*, Mary is hailed as 'Mulier amicta sole / Sub cuius pedibus luna / Quam laudāt astra matutina' (see under *Assumptio* and *Coronatio*).

45   Vicenzo Cartari, *The Fountaine of Ancient Fiction* (London, 1599), describes Aurora (from Homer) as a 'young virgin, hauing her haire disheueled, and hanging loose about her shoulders, being of the colour of the purest gold, and that shee sits in a glorious chaire' (sig. Giv).

46   Mary Villiers, daughter of Buckingham, m. James Stuart, Duke of Lennox (who was regarded as a moderate in religion; see *DNB*).

47   Satire on the public stage seems to confirm this interpretation: Margot Heinemann, *Puritanism and Theatre*, p. 231, quotes two instances in the 1630s of attempts to stop such uses: one, in 1634, was for lending a church robe with the name of Jesus on it to present 'Flamen, a priest of the heathens'; another, in 1639, was for setting up an altar and bowing down before it on the stage, 'and though they allege it was an old play revived, and an altar to the heathen gods, yet it was apparent that this play was revived on purpose in contempt of the ceremonies of the Church' (quoted from CSPD, 1639, pp. 140–1).

5   Religious ceremony and the masques

1   The painting is discussed by Oliver Millar, 'Charles I, Honthorst, and Van Dyck', *Burlington Magazine*, 96 (1954), 36–42. Buckingham purchased Rubens's collection of Venetian Masters in 1626, and Charles the complete collection of the Duke of Mantua in 1628; Arundel's collection specialised in Greek and Roman antiquities.

2   *The Letters* (ed. Petrie), p. 269.

3   For a comprehensive treatment see Roy Strong, *Splendour at Court: Renaissance Spectacle and Illusion* (1973), especially chap. 2; *Art and Power* (1984), pt I.

4   John Symonds, *Renaissance in Italy*, II, 45–75, and throughout. Bonner Mitchell, 'Les intermèdes au service de l'état', *Les Fêtes de la Renaissance*, CNRS, III (1975), 117–31.

5   T. E. Lawrenson, *The French Stage in the XVIIth Century: A Study in the Advent of the Italian Order*, pp. 33–43, and throughout.

6   George Kernodle, *From Art to Theatre: Form and Convention in the Renaissance*, especially pt I, chap. 2 for *tableaux vivants*, and for adaptation of religious to Renaissance art forms in Royal entries and street theatre. See also Glynne Wickham, *Early English Stages 1300–1660* (hereafter referred to as *EES*). Wickham criticises application of Kernodle's theory to the public stage (p. xxxv, Introduction), but Kernodle's argument does seem applicable to court stages. Lawrenson, *The French Stage*, generally supports Kernodle's thesis (he discusses some of its pitfalls in chap. 3) and adds much French material, especially in chap. 2.

7   General studies: Ernest Boysse, *Le Théâtre des Jésuites*; Pierre Janelle, *The Catholic Reformation*, pp. 148–58. Jesuit stages: Kernodle, *From Art to Theatre*, pp. 164–7. For a visual comparison with court stage see M. Baur-Heinhold, *Theater des Barock*, figure 151; also Per Bjurström, 'Baroque theatre and the Jesuits', chapter 6 in *Baroque Art: The Jesuit Contribution*. Some social implications of Jesuit theatre are taken up in *Dramaturgie et Société: rapports entre l'oeuvre théâtrale, son interprétation et son public aux XVIe et XVIIe siècles*, ed. Jean Jacquot, CNRS (Paris, 1968), 2 vols.: in particular see R. P. François de Dainville, S. J., 'Allégorie et actualité sur les tréteaux des Jésuites', II, 433–43, and André Stegmann, 'Le rôle des Jésuites dans la dramaturgie

française au début du XVIIᵉ siècle', II, 445–56; also Margaret McGowan, 'Les Jésuites à Avignon: Les fêtes au service de la propagande politique et religieuse', in *Les Fêtes de la Renaissance*, CNRS, III (1975), 153–71.

8   William McCabe, *An Introduction to Jesuit Theatre*, chap. 11, 'Notes on the St Omers theater'; Suzanne Gossett, 'Drama in the English College, Rome, 1591–1660', *ELR*, 3 (1969), 60–93; Marie-Anne de Kisch, 'Fêtes et représentations au collège anglais de Rome 1612–14' in *Les Fêtes de la Renaissance* CNRS, III, 525–43, describes plays on English subjects presented in the winter of 1612–13; in 1613 Jones was visiting Rome in the company of the Earl of Arundel, the latter at that time still Catholic (*DNB*).

9   Margaret McGowan, *L'Art du ballet de cour en France 1581–1643*, pp. 205 ff.

10   Glynne Wickham, *EES*, I for a detailed history of pre-Reformation forms (pp. 232–4 for examples).

11   For following details see Yates, 'Elizabethan chivalry: the romance of the Accession Day Tilts', *JWCI*, 20 (1957), 4–25; Yates, *Astraea: The Imperial Theme in the Sixteenth Century*, especially pt 2, 'The Tudor Imperial reform'; Strong 'The popular celebration of the Accession Day of Queen Elizabeth I', *JWCI*, 21 (1958), 86–103, and *The Cult of Elizabeth: Elizabethan Portraiture and Pageantry*.

12   Sydney Anglo, 'An early Tudor programme for plays and other demonstrations against the Pope', *JWCI*, 20 (1957), 176–9; Glynne Wickham, *EES*, I, 238–9; II, 28, 181.

13   Described by John Charlton, *The Banqueting House Whitehall*, and discussed by Bentley, *The Jacobean and Caroline Stage*, VI, 255–67. The first hall was approximately 120 feet × 53 feet, the Banqueting House and the additional masquing hall (built after 1635) 110 feet × 55 feet. Jones's use of the basilical model derived from Palladio's research on the Roman basilica: see John Summerson, *Inigo Jones*, pp. 50–5, and his discussion of Jones's work in *Architecture in Britain 1530 to 1830*. Per Palme, in *The Triumph of Peace: A Study of the Whitehall Banqueting House* (1956), commented that the adaptation of church forms to court ceremony made the Banqueting House 'the domain of a secular liturgy' (p. 124).

14   Summerson, *Inigo Jones*, pp. 16–17; Jones's first visit to Italy took place between 1597 and 1603. A description of the Uffizi theatre is given by A. M. Nagler, *Theatre Festivals of the Medici, 1539–1637*, pp. 59–61. For the relation of Jones's architecture and stage design to Italian practice, see Wickham, *EES*, II, chap. 7.

15   *The Elizabethan Stage*, I, 177–8; discussion by Wickham, *EES*, II, (pp. 268 ff. for masque stage).

16   R. Wittkower, *Architectural Principles in the Age of Humanism*, chap. 1 for round churches; Marcia Hall, *Renovation and Counter-Reformation: Vasari and Duke Cosimo in Sta Maria Novella and Sta Croce, 1565–1577* for unified design of altar and nave; James Ackerman, 'The Gesù in the light of contemporary church design', in *Baroque Art: The Jesuit Contribution*, pp. 15–28. For visual similarities between church and stage, Margarete Baur-Heinhold, *Theater des Barock*, various illustrations.

17   Summerson, *Inigo Jones*, pp. 61–5 for St James; Somerset House chapel (pp. 75–8) was destroyed in 1775, but it is known to have been a double cube 60 feet long, the same as the double cube room at Wilton House (p. 60). Jones's 'Protestant' church, St Paul's at Covent Garden, was quite different in style (pp. 86–92).

18   Summerson, *Inigo Jones*, pp. 50–3; Charlton, *The Banqueting House*, p. 18.

19   George Addleshaw and Frederick Etchells, *The Architectural Setting of Anglican Worship*, p. 109; round churches, pp. 22–3, and 32.

20   Addleshaw, p. 137; discussed by Phillips, *Reformation of Images*, pp. 124–8.

21   Addleshaw, p. 139 ff.; Phillips, p. 155 (p. 159, n. 9 for a list of works in the pamphlet war over altars that developed in the 1630s).

22   The controversy can be followed through, for example, Gardiner's *History of England*,

VII and VIII, for the period 1629–39; John Rushworth, *Historical Collections*, I and II, for period to 1640.

23   Addleshaw, *Architectural Setting*, p. 139 for altar; pp. 99–100 for music.

24   William Laud, *The Works*, eds. W. Scott and J. Bliss, VI, 59; discussed by Addleshaw, p. 138.

25   John Pocklington, *Altare Christianum* (London, 1637), pp. 159 and 175.

26   E. N. S. Thompson, *The Controversy between the Puritans and the Stage*, for historical background; Jonas Barish, *The Antitheatrical Prejudice*, especially chap. 6; Barish, 'Exhibitionism and the anti-theatrical prejudice', *ELH*, 36 (1969), 1–29.

27   'A Catholic devotion begun in Italy in the 16th century, in which the Blessed Sacrament was exposed for a period of about 40 hours, fixed as the time Christ's body rested in the tomb' (*Oxford Dictionary of the Christian Church*, ed. Cross, see under Forty Hours' Devotion). For discussion and illustration, Mark S. Weil, 'The devotion of the forty hours and roman baroque illusions', in *JWCI*, 37 (1974), 218–48; Per Bjurström, 'Baroque theatre and the Jesuits', in *Baroque Art*, pp. 104–7. These scenes did not have living figures or dramatic action, but Weil says (p. 220) that 'the *Depositio* and *Elevatio* were often enriched with dramatizations that took place in front of a permanent or temporary monument representing the Holy Sepulchre', and he mentions other semi-theatrical events.

28   Bjurström, p. 105, and plates 55 and 56 for illustration of *quarantore* in the Gesù.

29   Anthony Blunt and H. Lester Cooke, *The Roman Drawings of the XVII & XVIII Centuries in the Collection of Her Majesty the Queen at Windsor Castle*, p. 77, no. 591.

30   My translation, from Italian quoted by Bjurström, 'Baroque theatre', p. 104, n. 21 from O. Pollak, *Die Kunsttätigkeit unter Urban VIII* (Vienna, 1928–1931), I, 163.

31   Dieussart is noticed in Thieme-Becker, *Lexikon der bildenden Künstler*, see under Dusart (Dieussart) François; he was of Flemish birth and, after working at the English court in the 1630s, went to Holland, where he associated with Honthorst and Huygens, and later did work for the Princes of Orange and Charles II.

32   Thomas Wentworth, Earl of Strafford, *Letters and Dispatches*, I, 505. Garrard's letter seems to be misdated, as all other records give December 1636 as the opening.

33   Richard Southern, *Changeable Scenery*, p. 58; also compare Webb's plan for the stage, O&S, no. 400.

34   T. E. Lawrenson, *The French Stage in the XVIIth Century*, from which (pp. 122–3) the following quotations are taken. See also Bjurström, 'Baroque theatre', pp. 102–3, who draws attention to resemblances between Dubreuil's treatise and stage technique at the Hôtel de Bourgogne around 1630 (p. 102, n. 13).

35   Albion, *Charles I*, pp. 205–7; Lytton Sells, *The Paradise of Travellers: The Italian Influence on Englishmen in the Seventeenth Century*, chap. 4 (p. 46 for Montague); Montague was accompanied on this journey by the playwright Thomas Killigrew (Harbage, *Cavalier Drama*, p. 104).

36   Francis Haskell, *Patrons and Painters: A Study in the Relations between Italian Art and Society in the Age of the Baroque*, p. 56. On the Palace and its theatre see Anthony Blunt, 'The Palazzo Barberini', *JWCI*, 21 (1958), 282.

37   Haskell, p. 58; for Bernini's *quarantore* see Mark Weil, pp. 229–30; for Jesuit influence on Bernini see H. Hibbard, *Bernini*, p. 137, note.

38   John W. Stoye, *English Travellers Abroad 1604–1667: Their Influence in English Society and Politics*, p. 180; Milton was entertained there and at the English College in 1639 (Sells, p. 77).

39   Leah S. Marcus, 'Masquing occasions and masque structure', *RORD*, 24 (1981), pp. 10–11. For the complex symbolism of this masque see also D. J. Gordon, '*Hymenaei*: Ben Jonson's masque of union', in *The Renaissance Imagination*, ed. S. Orgel.

40   Leah S. Marcus, 'The occasion of Ben Jonson's *Pleasure Reconciled to Virtue*', *SEL*, 19 (1979), 271–93. On these events, see also Phillips, *Reformation of Images*, p. 141.

41   For discussion see Phillips, *Reformation of Images*, chap. 1; for Anglican attitudes, pp. 152–60.

42   Quoted from Richard Hooker, *The Works* (Oxford, 1890), I, 349–50. Books 1–4 of Hooker's *Laws* were originally published in 1594, book 5 in 1597.

43   William Laud, *The Works*, eds. Scott and Bliss, VI, 16–17; for discussion of the case see Phillips, *Reformation of Images*, pp. 163–4.

44   Quoted from the writings of Bishop Goodman by Phillips, *Reformation of Images*, p. 167. Recent studies seem to support this wider religious context for the debate over word and image: for example Michael O'Connell (extending Jonas Barish's work on *The Antitheatrical Prejudice*) in 'The idolatrous eye: iconoclasm, anti-theatricalism, and the image of the Elizabethan theatre', *ELH*, 52 (1985), 279–310, refers in passing to the quarrel between Jonson and Jones.

45   William Laud, *The Works*, eds. W. Scott and J. Bliss, IV, 11–12.

46   Quoted from Richard Hooker, *The Works*, I, 520.

47   A. M. Nagler, *Theatre Festivals of the Medici, 1539–1637*, pp. 139–40, describes a Medici entertainment of 1628 in which Chloris and Zephyr are united, and Chloris is changed into Flora. The 'plot' is identical with Jonson's: Jupiter announces his decision to endow earth with the counterpart of stars, that is, flowers; Cupid becomes discontented and goes to the underworld for help, as in *Chloridia*.

48   Giorgio Vasari, *Lives of the Most Eminent Painters, Sculptors and Architects*, trans. Gaston du C. de Vere, 'The Author's Preface to the whole work,' I, xxiii ff.

49   John A. Gotch, *Inigo Jones*, Appendix A.

6 Love and religion

1   Albert J. Loomie, 'King James I's Catholic consort', *HLQ*, 34 (1971), 303–16.

2   *Memoirs of Gregorio Panzani*, ed. Berington, p. 216.

3   Smuts, p. 28; Albion, *Charles I*, p. 148; Gardiner, *History of England*, VIII, 237.

4   D. Mathew, *The Age of Charles I*, chap. 14, especially pp. 226–9.

5   Quoted in *Oxford History of England*, ed. G. N. Clark, IX, 202.

6   A. O. Meyer, 'Charles I and Rome', *American Historical Review*, 19 (1913), 13–26.

7   Quoted from Montagu's correspondence with John Cosin in *DNB*, under Montagu, Richard (1577–1641), Bishop of Chichester.

8   A. O. Meyer, 'Charles I and Rome', p. 17.

9   Berington, *Memoirs*, p. 163 (pp. 142–64 for other details of these talks); Albion, *Charles I*, pp. 166–79; S. R. Gardiner, *History of England*, VIII, 130–44.

10   Albion, *Charles I*, pp. 155–6; p. 254 for Oath. Charles showed no inclination to persecute moderate Catholics: Mathew, *The Age of Charles I*, gives the names of Peers granted letters of grace and protection (p. 139, n. 5), and concludes that under Charles 'there were no Catholic lords who were refused this aid'.

11   For this and the following details, see Berington, *Memoirs*, pp. 165–7, 176; Albion, pp. 166 ff. Christopher Davenport (name in religion, Franciscus a Santa Clara) was appointed to the Queen in 1627 and was on good terms with Laud (*DNB*).

12   Martin Butler, 'Entertaining the Palatine Prince', *ELR*, 13 (1983), 319–44. Henrietta's interest in these entertainments seems to me social as much as political.

13   See Orgel and Strong, *Inigo Jones*, I, chap. 3, 'Platonic Politics'; and Roy Strong, *Van Dyck: Charles I on Horseback*.

14   Norbrook, *Poetry and Politics*, throughout; C. A. Patrides, *The Apocalypse in English Renaissance Thought*, pp. 97–109.

15   See Frances Yates, *Astraea: The Imperial Theme in the Sixteenth Century*: the central essay, 'Astraea' was first published 1947 (see especially pp. 76–80 for imagery of Virgin); Yates, 'Elizabethan chivalry: the romance of the Accession Day Tilts', *JWCI*, 20 (1957), 4–25; Louis Adrian Montrose, '"Eliza, Queen of Shepheardes", and the

pastoral of power', *ELR*, 10 (1980), 153–82; Robin Wells, *Spenser's Faerie Queene and the Cult of Elizabeth* (1983), notes Marian imagery throughout.

16   Roy Strong, 'The popular celebration of the Accession Day of Queen Elizabeth I', *JWCI*, 21 (1958), 86–103; Strong, *Portraits of Queen Elizabeth I*, and *The Cult of Elizabeth: Elizabethan Portraiture and Pageantry*, pp. 15–16, 46–70; David Norbrook, *Poetry and Politics*, especially chap. 5.

17   Michael Jaffé, 'Charles I and Rubens', *History To-Day* (January 1951), 67–9; Strong, *Charles I on Horseback*, chap. 4 remarks that Charles epitomises the idea of St George as the chivalrous Knight (p. 61).

18   D. J. Gordon, 'Rubens and the Whitehall ceiling', *The Renaissance Imagination*, especially pp. 28–31.

19   There may have been a tradition of such painting with application to religion: compare R. Wittkower, *Allegory and the Migration of Symbols*, chap. 10 on 'Titian's allegory of *Religion Succoured by Spain*' as a prototype.

20   *New Catholic Encyclopedia* (1967), under Marian Devotion; also E. Wilson, *England's Eliza*, p. 146.

21   G. W. Addleshaw, *Architectural Setting of Anglican Worship*, p. 139, n. 2.

22   Details of the Valois court, its religious policy and its entertainments, based on Frances Yates, *French Academies of the Sixteenth Century*; Yates drew attention to the importance of the French sources for understanding the English masques (*French Academies*, p. 264), but did not relate them to the English religious situation. Additional information on the Valois court (particularly visual) is in Strong, *Art and Power*, pt 2, chap. 3; for historical background, see J. E. Neale, *The Age of Catherine de Medici*.

23   Yates, *The Valois Tapestries*, p. 91; *French Academies*, pp. 263–4.

24   Yates, *Astraea*, pp. 83–7; Daniel Massa, 'Giordano Bruno's ideas in seventeenth-century England', *JHI*, 38 (1977), 227–42; A. D. Weiner, 'Expelling the beast: Bruno's adventures in England', *Modern Philology*, 78 (1980), 1–13.

25   André Stegmann, 'La fête parisienne à la Place Royale en avril 1612', *Les Fêtes de la Renaissance*, III, CNRS (1975), 373–92. Stegmann says that propaganda organised by Marie for the marriage of Louis XIII emphasises a politico-religious accommodation, not only with Protestants but with moderate Catholics and Gallicans, and that her entertainments reinforced this theme (p. 374).

26   Frances Yates, 'Dramatic religious processions in Paris in the late sixteenth century', originally published in 1954 in *Annales musicologiques*, II, 215–60; rpt. as 'Religious processions in Paris, 1583–84', in *Astraea*, pp. 173–207; details of artists, *Astraea*, pp. 179, 183–5.

27   Allan Gilbert, *The Symbolic Persons in the Masques of Ben Jonson*, p. 261. Some of the passages of prose description at the beginning, and with the appearance of Jove at the end, follow the wording of the *Balet*; Jones's 'Argument' translates most of the information delivered at length by the 'Fugitive' in the original.

28   See D. J. Gordon, *The Renaissance Imagination*, p. 100 for Jones's reading of Plato and Plutarch; Per Palme, in *The Triumph of Peace*, pp. 94–5, discussed Jones's ideas, and more recently Malcolm Smuts in 'The Culture of Absolutism' (unpublished doctoral dissertation, 1976, pp. 260–9) has offered additional information on Jones's Neoplatonism.

29   For Carew's use of Bruno's text see Rhodes Dunlap, *The Poems of Thomas Carew with his Masque 'Coelum Britannicum'*, Commentary, pp. 275 ff. My references to *Lo Spaccio* are to the translation by Arthur D. Imerti, *The Expulsion of the Triumphant Beast*. For Bruno's ideas on religion see Imerti, Introduction; Frances Yates, 'Giordano Bruno's conflict with Oxford', *JWCI*, 2 (1939), 227–42; 'The religious policy of Giordano Bruno', *JWCI*, 3 (1940), 181–207; *French Academies*, pp. 225–9; *Giordano Bruno and the Hermetic Tradition*, pp. 178–233.

30   This attack is discussed by Yates, 'The religious policy', *JWCI*, 3, 181–5.

31   *Lo Spaccio*, trans. Imerti, p. 270. Bruno had sympathised with Henri's attempts to bring in a new age by the 'magic' of religious processions and penance; in his reformed Heavens he placed 'Repentance, Purification, Palinode, Reform, and Cleansing' (p. 81), and he himself was hopeful that a new age of religious fervor was about to begin.

32   The paired figures of Eros and Anteros were of course familiar to the court, representing mutual love, or love-in-return, exemplified by the King and Queen (see D. J. Gordon's commentary on Jonson's *Love's Welcome at Bolsover*, in *The Renaissance Imagination*, pp. 99–101; the emblem also appeared in *L'Astrée*, II, bk 5). In *The Temple of Love*, however, the union of the two figures represents a yet higher order of spirituality in the issue of a third figure, Amianteros.

33   The costume has similarities to that in which Rubens painted Marie de Medici, who was present at the masque (l. 305), commemorating her act of generosity in returning Juliers to the Protestants in 1610: see commentary by Claudia Lyn Cahan on the cycle for Marie de Medici, reproduced in *Rubens*, Avenel Art Library, no. xv.

34   The presence of Charles behind Milton's picture of Satan has been felt by many critics, and the subject in relation to court masques has been emphasised by John G. Demaray, *Milton's Theatrical Epic: The Invention and Design of Paradise Lost*, especially pp. 63–5. Roy Strong has repeatedly drawn attention in general terms to the almost blasphemous deification of Charles and Henrietta (for example in *Splendour at Court*, pp. 246–7, and *Charles I on Horseback*, pp. 90–1).

35   *Catalogue of Prints and Drawings in the British Museum*, Division I – Political and Personal Satires, I, no. 143. The print is entitled *MAGNA BRITANNIA DIVISA. La Grande Bretagne divisee. Great Britany divided*. 1642 (Amsterdam, 1642). The Catalogue notes it as extemely rare, and 'remarkably interesting as recording the names of many of the actors in those times' (p. 107). The key is printed on pp. 96–107.

36   In a group of young men who dance, smoke, or drink, while 'one points to his face of which the nose has disappeared' (p. 106).

37   Frances Yates, 'Religious processions in Paris, 1583–4', in *Astraea*, p. 196, plate 40. *The Tragedy of the Cruell Warre* (1643) similarly comments on the blood shed 'since Papists have been entrusted with Armes' (Lois Potter, '*The Triumph of Peace* and *The Cruel War*', p. 348).

References

Listed below are all works referred to directly in the text and notes.

Primary sources and texts

Note Scolar Press facsimile reprints are published in the series *English Recusant Literature 1558–1640*, ed. D. M. Rogers, Menston, Yorkshire.
A Select Collection of Old English Plays, ed. Robert Dodsley, 14 vols., referred to here as Dodsley.

Arch-Confraternity of the Holy Rosary of our Blessed Lady [printed secretly in England], 1636
Anonymous, *Lady Alimony*, London, 1659; rpt. Dodsley, XIV
Baillon, Charles, Comte de, *Henriette-Marie de France, Reine d'Angleterre. Etude historique . . . suivie de ses lettres inédites*, Paris, Didier et Cie, 1877
Bassompierre, François de, *Memoirs of the Embassy of the Marshall de Bassompierre to the Court of England in 1626*, trans. and annot. J. W. Croker, London, John Murray, 1819
Beaujoyeulx, Baltasar de, *Balet comique de la Reine*, Paris, 1582
Berkley [or Barclay], William, *The Lost Lady* (1639); rpt. Dodsley, XII
Birch, Thomas, *The Court and Times of Charles the First*, ed. Robert Folkestone Williams, 2 vols. London, Henry Colburn, 1848
Brereley, John (alias Lawrence Anderton), *Virginalia, or Spiritvall Sonnets in Prayse of the most Glorious Virgin Marie*, Rouen, 1632
Bruno, Giordano, *Lo Spaccio de la bestia trionfante: The Expulsion of the Triumphant Beast*, trans. and ed. Arthur D. Imerti, New Brunswick, NJ, Rutgers University Press, 1964
Burton, Henry, *A Tryall of Private Devotions*, London, 1628
    For God, and the King. The Svmme of Two Sermons Preached on the fifth of November Last in St Matthewes Friday-Streete. 1636 . . . , London, 1636
Camus, Jean-Pierre, Bishop of Belley, *A Dravght of Eternitie written in French . . .* , trans. Miles Car, Doway, 1632; rpt. Scolar Press, 1972
    A Spirituall Combat: A Tryall of a Faithful Soule, or Consolation in Temptation, trans. M[iles] C[ar], Doway, 1632; rpt. Scolar Press, 1974
    The Spirituall Director Disinteressed, According to the Spirit of B. Francis of Sales, trans. A. B., Roan, 1633; rpt. Scolar Press, 1974
    Admirable Events: Selected out of Foure Bookes, trans. S. Du Verger, London, 1639
    The Spirit of St François de Sales (first publ. in 6 vols., 1639–41), ed. and newly trans. C. F. Kelly, London, Longmans, Green and Co., 1953
    Trente nouvelles choisies et présentées par René Favret, in Textes et Documents de la Renaissance, ed. André Stegmann, Paris, Librairie philosophique J. Vrin, 1977
[Capucin chapel], *Les Royales Cérémonies faites en l'édification d'une chapelle à Londres en Angleterre, dans le Palais de la Royne*, Rheims, Nicholas Constant, 1633
Carew, Thomas, *The Poems . . . with his Masque 'Coelum Britannicum'*, ed. Rhodes Dunlap, Oxford, Clarendon, 1949
Carey, Patrick, *Trivial Poems and Triolets, written . . . 1651*, ed. Sir W. Scott, London, John Murray, 1820

Carlell [or Carliell], Lodovick, *The Deserving Favourite* (reprinted from the original ed. of 1629) in Charles H. Gray, *Lodowick Carliell: His Life and a Discussion of his Plays*, Chicago, University of Chicago Press, 1905
> *The Passionate Lovers*, pt 1, London, 1635

Cartari, Vicenzo, *The Fountaine of Ancient Fiction*, trans. Richard Linche Gent., London, 1599

Cartwright, William, *The Plays and Poems*, ed. G. Blakemore Evans, Madison, University of Wisconsin Press, 1951

Castiglione, Baldassare, *The Book of the Courtier*, trans. Sir Thomas Hoby, 1561; with introd. J. H. Whitfield, London, Dent, 1974

Catalogue of Prints and Drawings in the British Museum, Division 1 – Political and Personal Satires, I, (1320–1689), London, Chiswick Press, 1870

Caussin, Nicolas, *The Holy Court*, I, trans. T[homas] H[awkins] with dedication to Henrietta Maria, Paris, 1626; II, Paris, 1631
> *The Holy Court*, I–III, Rouen, 1634; IV, Rouen, 1638, both trans. Thomas Hawkins; rpt. Scolar Press, 1977
> *The Christian Diurnal, Reviewed, and much Augmented*, trans. Thomas Hawkins, Rouen, 1640; rpt. Scolar Press, 1973
> *The Penitent, or Entertainments for Lent*, trans. B[asil] B[rooke], London, 1643

Chambers, John David, *Divine Worship in England*, London, B. M. Pickering, 1877

Chambers, Sabine, *The Garden of our B. Lady, or A Devout Manner How to Serve her in her Rosary*, St Omer, 1619

Charles I, *His Majesties Declaration ... respecting the XXXIX Articles of Religion*, London, 1628
> *His Majesties Declaration to All his Loving Subjects. Of the Causes Which Moued him to Dissolve the Last Parliament*, London, 1629
> *Eikon Basilike. The Portraiture of His Sacred Majesty in his Solitudes and Sufferings* (1649), ed. Philip A. Knachel, New York, Cornell University Press, 1965
> *The Letters, Speeches, and Proclamations of King Charles I*, ed. Charles Petrie, London, Cassell, 1935

Chillingworth, William, *Works* (includes *The Religion of Protestants*, 1638), Oxford, Oxford University Press, 1838; rpt. New York, AMS Press, 1972

Cosin, John, *A Collection of Private Devotions* (1627), ed. and introd. P. G. Stanwood, with assistance of Daniel O'Connor, Oxford, Clarendon, 1967

Coton [or Cotton], Pierre, *The Interiour Occupation of the Soule ... Composed in French ... and translated into English by C. A. for the benefit of all our Nation*, Doway, 1618; printed secretly in England

Crashaw, Richard, *The Poems*, ed. L. C. Martin, 2nd edn., Oxford, Clarendon, 1966

Daniel, Samuel, *Vision of the Twelve Goddesses* (1604); rpt. Herbert A. Evans, *English Masques*, London, Blackie and Son, 1897

Davenant, Sir William, *The Dramatic Works*, with prefatory Memoir and notes by J. Maidment and W. H. Logan, 5 vols., 1872–4; rpt. New York, Russell and Russell, 1964
> *The Shorter Poems and Songs from the Plays and Masques*, ed. A. M. Gibbs, Oxford, Clarendon, 1972

Davenport, Christopher [Franciscus a Santa Clara], *Deus, natura, gratia ... Ubi ad frutinam fidei Catholicae examinatur confessio Anglicana*, Lyons, 1634

Digby, Sir Kenelm, *A Conference with a Lady about Choice of Religion*, Paris, 1638; rpt. Scolar Press, 1969
> *Private Memoirs of Sir Kenelm Digby, Gentleman of the Bedchamber to King Charles the First*, with an introductory Memoir, London, Saunders and Otley, 1827

Du Bosc, Jacques, *L'Honneste Femme*, pt 1, Paris, P. Billaine, 1632
> *L'Honneste Femme*, 2nd revised edn., Paris, Jean Jost, 1633
> *The Compleat Woman ...* , trans. of *L'Honneste Femme* (1633 edn.) by N. N., London, Thomas Harper and Richard Hodgkinson, 1639; rpt. New York, Da Capo Press, 1968

The Accomplish'd Woman, trans. of *L'Honneste Femme* (1632 edn.) by Walter Montague, London, Gabriel Bedell and Tho. Collins, 1656

Ellis, Henry, *Original Letters Illustrative of English History*, series 2, III, 1827; rpt. New York, AMS Press, 1970

Falconer, John, *The Mirrour of Created Perfection, or The Life of the Most Blessed Virgin Mary Mother of God*, St Omer, 1632; rpt. Scolar Press, 1971

Faret, Nicolas, *L'Honneste Homme, ou l'art de plaire à la cour* (1630), ed. M. Magendie, Paris, 1925; rpt. Geneva, Slatkine, 1970

The Honest Man, or The Art to Please in Court, trans. E[dward] G[rimstone], London, 1632

Ficino, Marsilio, *Commentary on Plato's Symposium*, trans. Sears Jayne, University of Missouri Studies, 19, Columbia, Columbia University Press, 1944

Fletcher, John, *The Faithful Shepherdess*, in *The Dramatic Works in the Beaumont and Fletcher Canon*, gen. ed. Fredson Bowers, III, Cambridge, Cambridge University Press, 1976

Gamaches, F. Cyprien de, 'Memoirs of the mission in England of the Capuchin Friars ... from the year 1630 to 1669', in Thomas Birch, *Court and Times of Charles the First*, ed. Robert Folkestone Williams, II, London, Henry Colborn, 1848

Gardiner, Samuel R. *History of England from the Accession of James I to the Outbreak of the Civil War 1603–1642*, 10 vols., 1884; rpt. New York, AMS Press, 1965

Goffe, Thomas, *The Careless Shepherdess: A Pastorall Tragi-Comedy* (performed in 1638), London, Rogers and Ley, 1656

Green, Mary Anne E., *Letters of Queen Henrietta Maria, Including her Private Correspondence with Charles I ...* , London, Richard Bentley, 1857

Grimani Breviary, *Le Bréviaire du Cardinal Grimani*, facs., rpt. of the seventeenth-century illuminated MS in Biblioteca Marciana, Venice, with French commentary, Venice, 1862

Habington, William, *The Queen of Aragon* (1640); rpt. Dodsley, XIII

The Poems, ed. Kenneth Allott, Liverpool, Hodder and Stoughton, 1948

Hawkins, Henry, *Partheneia Sacra, or The Mysterious and Delicious Garden of the Sacred Parthenes*, Rouen, John Cousturier, 1633; rpt. Scolar Press, 1971

The Devout Hart (transl. of *Le Coeur dévot* by Stephan Luzvic, 1627), Rouen, 1634; rpt. with introd. note on Hawkins by Karl Josef Höltgen, Scolar Press, 1975

Historical Manuscripts Commission, *Salvetti Correspondence*, 11th Report, Appendix, pt 1, London, HM Stationery Office, 1887

Hooker, Richard, *Works*, ed. J. Keble, 2 vols., Oxford, Clarendon, 1890

Howell, James, *Epistolae Ho-Elianae: The Familiar Letters of James Howell*, ed. Joseph Jacobs, 2 vols., London, 1892

Hutchinson, Lucy, *Memoirs of the Life of Colonel Hutchinson* (first publ. 1806), introd. Margaret Bottrall, London, J. M. Dent, 1968

Jones, Inigo, [For complete descriptive catalogue of masque designs, see Stephen Orgel and Roy Strong, *Inigo Jones: The Theatre of the Stuart Court*, 1973]

Jonson, Ben, *Works*, ed. C. H. Herford, Percy and Evelyn Simpson, 11 vols., Oxford, Clarendon, 1925–52

Laud, William, *The Works*, ed. W. Scott and J. Bliss, 9 vols., Oxford, John Henry Parker, 1847–60

Lenton, Francis, 'Queene Esters Haliluiahs and Hamans Madrigalls expressed and illustrated in a Sacred Poeme ... composed by Fra: Lenton, Gent: the Queenes Poet' (1637), Huntington Library MS HM 120 (4to, 87 leaves)

Great Britains Beauties, or The Female Glory ... Encomiastick anagrams and acrostiches upon the highly honoured names of the Queenes most gracious Majestie, and the gallant Lady-Masquers in her Graces glorious Grand-Masque [i.e. *Luminalia*], London, 1638

Les Royales Cérémonies, see Capucin chapel

Leveneur, Tanneguy, Comte de Tillières et de Carrouges, *Mémoires inédits du Comte Leveneur ...* , *Ambassadeur en Angleterre, sur le cour de Charles Ier, et son mariage avec Henriette* *de France, recueillis, mis en ordre et précedés d'une introduction par M. C. Hippeau*, Paris, Paulet-Malassis, 1862

Loarte, Gaspar, *Instrvctions and Advertisements, How to Meditate the Misteries of the Rosarie of the Most Holy Virgin Mary . . . , newly translated into English*, Rouen? 1600?

Lvminalia, or The Festivall of Light . . . Shrovetuesday Night, 1637, London, 1638

Luzvic, Stephan, *The Devout Hart, see* Hawkins, Henry

Marcelline, George, *Epithalamium Gallo-Britannicum, or, Great-Britaines . . . Ioy, for the most happy Vnion of Charles Prince of Wales and the Lady Henriette Maria. Presaging the Destruction and Ruine of Antichrist*, London, 1625

Marmion, Shakerley, *Dramatic Works*, in *Dramatists of the Restoration*, ed. J. Maidment and W. H. Logan, Edinburgh, William Paterson, 1875

Massinger, Philip, *The Plays and Poems*, ed. Philip Edwards and Colin Gibson, Oxford, Clarendon, 1976

Mendoza, Andres A., *Two Royall Entertainments Lately Given to Charles, Prince of Great Britaine, by Philip IV of Spaine*, trans. from Spanish, London, 1623; rpt. as *The English Experience*, Norwood Johnson, 1977

Montague, Walter, The Copy of a Letter sent from France by Mr W. Montagu to his father the Lord Privy Seale [giving his reasons for embracing the Roman Catholic religion] with an answer thereunto, London, 1641

Miscellanea Spiritualia, or Devout Essaies (with dedication to Henrietta Maria), pt 1, London, 1648

The Accomplish'd Woman, London, Gabriel Bedell and Tho. Collins, 1656

The Shepherd's Paradise (performed in Jan. 1633), London, Thomas Dring, 1629 [i.e. 1659]

Montfaucon, Bernard de, *Monumens de la monarchie françoise*, 5 vols., Paris, Gandouin et Giffart, 1729–33

N.N., *Maria Triumphans, A discourse, Wherein (by way of a Dialogue) the B. Virgin Mary, Mother of God, is Defended, and Vindicated* (with dedication to Henrietta Maria), St Omer, 1635

Panzani, G., *The Memoirs of Gregorio Panzani, giving an Account of his Agency in England in the Years 1634, 1635, 1636*, trans. from Italian and introd. Joseph Berington, Birmingham, Swinney and Walker, 1793

Pinelli, Luca (attrib.), *The Societie of the Rosarie . . . together with the Life of the Glorious Virgin Marie*, trans. from Italian, St Omer, 1624 (also catalogued under Garnet, Henry)

Plato, *The Symposium*, trans W. Hamilton, Penguin Classics, Harmondsworth, 1951

Pocklington, John, *Altare Christianum*, London, 1637

Primer, *The Primer, or Office of the Blessed Virgin Marie*, St Omer, 1631

Prynne, William, *A Briefe Survay and Censure of Mr Cozens his Couzening Devotions. Proving both the Forme and Matter . . . to Be Meerely Popish*, London, 1628

Histrio-Mastix. The Players Scourge, or Actors Tragoedie, Divided into Two Parts. Wherein it is largely evidenced by divers arguments . . . that popular stage-playes . . . are sinfull, heathenish, lewde, ungodly spectacles, London, 1633

The Popish Royall Favourite, or A Full Discovery of his Majesties Extraordinary Favours to and Protections of Notorious Papists, Priests, Jesuits . . ., London, 1643

Romes Master-peece, or The Grand Conspiracy of the Pope and his Jesuited Instruments, to Extirpate the Protestant Religion, Re-establish Popery, etc., London, 1643

Quarles, Francis, *Divine Fancies: Digested into Epigrammes, Meditations, and Observations*, London, 1632

Randolph, Thomas, *The Poetical and Dramatic Works of Thomas Randolph* (for *The Jealous Lovers* (1632), and *Amyntas* (1638)), ed. W. C. Hazlitt, London, Reeves and Turner, 1875

Ribadeneira, Pedro de, *The Lives of the Saints* (incorporated in *Flos Sanctorum* by Alfonso de Villegas), trans. W[illiam] P[etre], St Omers, 1669

Richeome, Louis, *Peinture spirituelle, ou l'art d'admirer, aimer et louer Dieu en toutes ses oeuvres et tirer de toutes profit salutaire*, Lyons, 1611
 Holy Pictures of the Mysticall Figures of the most Holy Sacrifice and Sacrament of the Eucharist, trans. C.A., printed secretly in England, 1619

Ridpath, John, *The Stage Condemn'd*, 1698; rpt. New York, Garland Publishing Co., 1972

Ripa, Cesare, *Iconologia*, Padua, 1611; rpt. New York, Garland Publishing Co., 1976

Rushworth, John, *Historical Collections of Private Passages of State*, 8 vols., London, D. Browne, 1721–22 (see I and II for period to 1640)

Rutter, Joseph, *The Shepheard's Holyday* (1635); rpt. Dodsley, XII

Sales, François de, Saint, *Introduction à la vie dévote*, first published in 1609; authorised edition, Dom B. Mackey, ed., *Oeuvres*, III
 Introduction to a Devovte Life, trans. I[ohn] Y[akesley], 3rd edn., Rouen, 1614
 Introduction to the Devout Life, trans. Michael Day, London, Dent, 1972
 Le Traité de l'amour de Dieu, first published in 1616; authorised edition, Dom B. Mackey, ed., *Oeuvres*, IV–V
 A Treatise of the Loue of God, trans. Miles Car, Douai, 1630
 The Love of God: A Treatise, trans. Vincent Kerns, London, Burns and Oates, 1962
 Oeuvres. Édition complète . . . , ed. Dom B. Mackey, 26 vols., Annecy, J. Niérat, 1892–1932

Salo, Alexis de, *An Admirable Method to Love, Serve, and Honour the B. Virgin Mary . . .* , trans. R.F., Rouen, 1639

Salvetti, *Correspondence*, *see* Historical Manuscripts Commission

Shirley, James, *The Lady of Pleasure* (printed in 1637); rpt. Scolar Press, 1973
 The Dramatic Works and Poems, ed. W. Gifford and A. Dyce, 6 vols., London, John Murray, 1833

Sidney, Sir Philip, *The Countess of Pembroke's Arcadia* (*The Old Arcadia*), ed. Jean Robertson, Oxford, Clarendon, 1973

Smart, Peter, *The Downe-fall and Vanitie of Popish Ceremonies*, Edinburgh, 1628; rpt. Norwood Johnson, 1977

Spenser, Edmund, *The Shepheardes Calendar*, 1579 edn.; facsimile edn., Scolar Press, 1968
 The Faerie Queene, 1596 edn.; introd. Graham Hough, 2 vols., Scolar Press, 1976

Stafford, Anthony, *The Female Glory, or The Life and Death of Our Blessed Lady, the Holy Virgin Mary*, London, 1635

Strafford, Earl of, *see* Wentworth, Thomas

Suckling, Sir John, *The Poems, Plays, and other Remains of Sir John Suckling*, ed. W. C. Hazlitt, 2 vols., London, Reeves and Turner, 1892 (*Aglaura*, the play, I; *Letters*, incl. those to 'Aglaura', II, 173–223)
 The Non-Dramatic Works of Sir John Suckling, ed. Thomas Clayton, Oxford, Clarendon, 1971

Thorn Drury, George, *A Little Ark, Containing Sundry Pieces of Seventeenth-Century Verse*, London, Dobell, 1921

Tillières, Comte de, *see* Leveneur, Tanneguy

Townshend, Aurelian, *Aurelian Townshend's Poems and Masks*, ed. E. K. Chambers, Oxford, Clarendon, 1912

Urfé, Honoré d', *L'Astrée* (1607–27), ed. M. Hugues Vaganay, 5 vols., Lyons, Pierre Masson, 1925–8; rpt. Slatkine, 1966

Van der Doort, Abraham, 'Abraham Van der Doort's catalogue of the collections of Charles I', ed. Oliver Millar, *Walpole Society*, 37 (1958–60)

Vasari, Giorgio, *Lives of the Most Eminent Painters Sculptors and Architects*, trans. Gaston Du C. de Vere, 10 vols., London, Macmillan and Co., 1912–14

Vitruvius, Pollio, *Vitruvius, On Architecture . . .* , ed. and trans. Frank Granger, 2 vols., London, 1931–4

Waller, Edmund, *The Poems*, ed. G. Thorn Drury, Muses Library, 2 vols., London, Routledge and Sons, 1893

Ware, Isaac, *Designs of Inigo Jones and Others, publ. by I. Ware*, London, 1735
Wentworth, Thomas, Earl of Strafford, *Letters and Dispatches*, comp. William Knowler, LL.D., I, Dublin, R. Reilly, 1711

Secondary Sources

Note Titles of periodicals are abbreviated according to the Master List in *MLA International Bibliography Annual*, but unfamiliar titles are given in full. The CNRS series *Les Fêtes de la Renaissance*, ed. Jean Jacquot, published in three volumes, is referred to here as *Fêtes* I (1956), *Fêtes* II (1960), *Fêtes* III (1975).

Ackerman, James S., 'The Gesù in the light of contemporary church design', in *Baroque Art*, ed. R. Wittkower, pp. 15–28

Adair, Edward R., *The Exterritoriality of Ambassadors in the Sixteenth and Seventeenth Centuries*, London, Longmans, 1929

Adam, Antoine, *Histoire de la littérature française au XVIIᵉ siècle*, I, Paris, del Duca, 1962
    Grandeur and Illusion: French Literature and Society 1600–1715, trans. Herbert Tint, London, Weidenfeld and Nicolson, 1972

Addleshaw, G(eorge) and Frederick Etchells, *The Architectural Setting of Anglican Worship: An Inquiry into the Arrangements for Public Worship in the Church of England from the Reformation to the Present*, London, Faber and Faber, 1958

Albion, Gordon, *Charles I and the Court of Rome: a Study in Seventeenth-Century Diplomacy*, London, Burns, Oates and Washbourne, 1935

Allison, Anthony F., 'Crashaw and St François de Sales', *RES*, 24 (1948), 295–302

Allison, Anthony F. and David M. Rogers, *A Catalogue of Catholic Books in English Printed Abroad or Secretly in England, 1558–1640*, 2 parts, Bognor Regis, The Arundel Press, 1956; rpt. London, Wm. Dawson and Sons, 1964

Anglo, Sydney, 'An early Tudor programme for plays and other demonstrations against the Pope', *JWCI*, 20 (1957), 176–9

Axon, William E. 'The licensing of Montague's *Miscellanea Spiritualia*', *The Library*, 2nd series, 2 (1901), 269–73

Axton, Marie and Raymond Williams, eds., *English Drama: Forms and Development*, Cambridge, Cambridge University Press, 1977

Barish, Jonas A., 'Exhibitionism and the antitheatrical prejudice', *ELH*, 36 (1969), 1–29
    The Antitheatrical Prejudice, Berkeley and L.A., University of California Press, 1981

Barton, Anne, 'He that plays the King', in M. Axton and R. Williams, eds., *English Drama: Forms and Development*, pp. 69–93, Cambridge, Cambridge University Press, 1977
    '*The New Inn* and the problem of Jonson's late style', *ELR*, 9 (1979), 395–418
    'Harking back to Elizabeth: Ben Jonson and Caroline nostalgia', *ELH*, 48 (1981), 706–31

Baur-Heinhold, Margarete, *Theater des Barock: Festliches Bühnenspiel im 17. und 18. Jahrhundert*, München, Verlag Georg D. W. Callwey, 1966

Beer, E. S. de, 'Notes on Inigo Jones', *N&Q*, 178 (1940), 290–2

Beeverell, James, *The Pleasures of London*, trans. and annot. W. H. Quarrell, London, Witherby and Co., 1940 (contains a 'History of the entry of Marie Medici' to London, 1638)

Bentley, Gerald E., *The Jacobean and Caroline Stage*, 7 vols., Oxford, Oxford University Press, 1941–1968

Bergquist, G. William, ed., *Three Centuries of English and American Plays: A Checklist* [England, 1500–1800], New York, Readex Microprint Corporation [refers to plays available on microfiche]

Berington, Joseph, ed. *The Memoirs of Gregorio Panzani. Giving an Account of his Agency in England, in the years* 1634, 1635, 1636, trans. and introd. Joseph Berington, Birmingham, Swinney and Walker, 1793

Bevington, David, *Tudor Drama and Politics: A Critical Approach to Topical Meaning*, Cambridge, Mass., Harvard University Press, 1968

Bjurström, Per, 'Baroque theatre and the Jesuits', in *Baroque Art: The Jesuit Contribution*, eds. R. Wittkower and Irma Jaffé, chap. 6, pp. 99–110, New York, Fordham University Press, 1972

Blaney, Glenn, 'Conventions, plot, and structure in *The Broken Heart*', *MP*, 56 (1958), 1–9

'The enforcement of marriage in English drama, 1600–1650', *PQ*, 38 (1959), 459–72

Blunt, Anthony, 'The Palazzo Barberini', *JWCI*, 21 (1958), 256–87

Blunt, Anthony and Hereward Lester Cooke, *The Roman Drawings of the XVII and XVIII Centuries in the Collection of Her Majesty the Queen at Windsor Castle*, London, Phaidon Press, 1960

Boas, Frederick S., *An Introduction to Stuart Drama*, London, Oxford University Press, 1946; rpt. 1964

Boase, Roger, *The Origin and Meaning of Courtly Love: A Critical Study of European Scholarship*, Manchester, Rowman and Littlefield, 1977

Bochet, Henri, *L'Astrée: ses origines, son importance dans la formation de la littérature classique*, 1923; rpt. Geneva, Slatkine, 1967

Bone, Quentin, *Henrietta Maria: Queen of the Cavaliers*, London, Peter Owen, 1972

Bossy, John, *The English Catholic Community, 1570–1850*, London, Darton, Longman and Todd, 1975

Boysse, Ernest, *Le Théâtre des Jésuites*, Paris, 1880; rpt. Geneva, Slatkine, 1970

Bray, René, *La Préciosité et les précieux de Thibaut de Champagne à Jean Giraudoux*, Paris, Editions Albin Michel, 1948

Bremond, Henri, *Histoire littéraire du sentiment religieux en France, depuis la fin des guerres de religion jusqu'à nos jours*, 11 vols. and index (1916–59); rpt. Paris, Librairie Armand Colin, 1967

A Literary History of Religious Thought in France from the Wars of Religion down to our own Times, trans. K. L. Montgomery, SPCK, 3 vols., London, Macmillan, 1928–36

Brooks-Davies, Douglas, *The Mercurian Monarch: Magical Politics from Spenser to Pope*, Manchester, Manchester University Press, 1983

Brustein, Robert, 'The monstrous regiment of women: sources for the satiric view of the court lady in English drama', in *Renaissance and Modern Essays Presented to Vivian de Sola Pinto*, ed. G. R. Hibbard, London, Routledge and Kegan Paul, 1966, pp. 35–50

Buffum, Imbrie, *Studies in the Baroque from Montaigne to Rotrou*, Yale Romantic Studies, 2nd series, no. 4, New Haven, Yale University Press., 1957

Butler, Martin, 'Entertaining the Palatine Prince: Plays on foreign affairs 1635–1637', *ELR*, 13 (1983), 319–44

Theatre and Crisis 1632–1642, Cambridge, Cambridge University Press, 1984

Cahan, Claudia Lyn, *Rubens* (reproductions include the Marie de Medici cycle), Avenel Art Library, Milan, Fabbri Editori, 1980

Calvet, Jean, *La Littérature religieuse de François de Sales à Fénelon*, in *Histoire de la littérature française*, ed. J. Calvet, v, Paris, del Duca, 1956

Chambers, Edmund K., *The Elizabethan Stage*, I, Oxford, Clarendon, 1923

Charlton, John, *The Banqueting House Whitehall*, London, HMSO, 1964

Cheney, Patrick, 'Jonson's *The New Inn* and Plato's myth of the hermaphrodite', *Ren. Drama*, n.s., 14 (1983), 173–94

Chesneau, C., 'Un précurseur de Pascal? Le Franciscain Jacques du Bosc', *XVIIᵉ Siècle*, 15 (1952), 426–48 (catalogued under *Dix-Septième Siecle*)

Clark, Kenneth, *Landscape into Art*, London, John Murray, 1949

Clements, Robert J., *Picta Poesis. Literary and Humanistic Theory in Renaissance Emblem Books*, Roma, Edizioni di Storia e Letteratura, 1960

Clifton, Robin, 'Fear of Popery', in *The Origins of the English Civil War*, ed. C. Russell, pp. 144–67, London, Macmillan, 1973

Clubb, Louise George, '*The Virgin Martyr* and the *Tragedia Sacra*', *Ren. Drama*, 7 (1964), 103–26
 'Woman as wonder: A generic figure in Italian and Shakespearean comedy', in *Studies in the Continental Background of Renaissance English Literature*, ed. Dale B. Randall, pp. 109–32, Durham, NC, Duke University Press, 1977

Comito, Terry, 'Renaissance gardens and the discovery of Paradise', *JHI*, 32 (1971), 483–506.
 The Idea of the Garden in the Renaissance, New Brunswick, NJ, Rutgers University Press, 1978

Costa, John, *Le Conflit moral dans l'oeuvre romanesque de Jean-Pierre Camus (1584–1652)*, New York, Burt Franklin and Co., 1974

Council, Norman, 'Ben Jonson, Inigo Jones, and the transformation of Tudor chivalry', *ELH*, 47 (1980), 259–75

Coulton, George, *Art and the Reformation*, Cambridge, Cambridge University Press, 1953

Croft-Murray, Edward, *Decorative Painting in England, 1537–1837*, 2 vols., London, Country Life Ltd., 1962

Cruikshank, John, ed., *French Literature and its Background*, II, Oxford, Oxford University Press, 1969

Cuthbert, Father, OSFC [Lawrence Anthony Hess], *The Capuchins: A Contribution to the History of the Counter Reformation*, 2 vols., 1928; rpt. London, Kennikat Press, 1971

Dainville, R. P. François de, S. J., 'Allégorie et actualité sur les tréteaux des Jésuites', in *Dramaturgie et Société*, ed. J. Jacquot, II, 433–43

Daniel-Rops, Henry, *The Catholic Reformation*, trans. John Warrington, London, Dent, 1968

Davis, Walter R., 'A map of Arcadia: Sidney's romance in its tradition', in *Sydney's Arcadia*, Yale University Studies in English, 158, New Haven, Yale University Press, 1965

Demaray, John G., 'Milton's *Comus*: The sequel to a masque of Circe', *HLQ*, 29 (1966), 245–54
 Milton and the Masque Tradition: The Early Poems, 'Arcades', and 'Comus', Cambridge, Mass., Harvard University Press, 1968
 Milton's Theatrical Epic: The Invention and Design of Paradise Lost, Cambridge, Mass., Harvard University Press, 1980

Denomy, Alexander J., *The Heresy of Courtly Love*, 1947; rpt. Gloucester, Mass., P. Smith, 1965

Dickens, A. G., ed., *The Courts of Europe: Politics, Patronage, and Royalty 1400–1800*, London, Thames and Hudson, 1977

Dodsley, Robert, ed., *A Select Collection of Old English Plays*, 4th edn., revised and enlarged by W. Carew Hazlitt, 14 vols., London, Reeves and Turner, 1875

Duncan, Douglas, 'A guide to *The New Inne*', *Essays in Criticism*, 20 (1970), 311–26

Dunn, Thomas A., *Philip Massinger: The Man and the Playwright*, London, Thomas Nelson and Sons, 1957

Ellrodt, Robert, *Neoplatonism in the Poetry of Spenser*, Geneva, Librairie E. Droz, 1960; rpt. Folcroft Library Editions, 1978

Fletcher, Jefferson B. 'Précieuses at the court of King Charles I', *Journ. Comp. Lit.*, I (1903), 120–53
 The Religion of Beauty in Woman, and Other Essays on Platonic Love in Poetry and Society, 1911; rpt. New York, Haskell House, 1966

Fordyce, Rachel, *Caroline Drama: A Bibliographical History of Criticism*, Boston, Mass., G. K. Hall, 1978

Fraser, Russell, *The War against Poetry*, Princeton, NJ, Princeton University Press, 1970

Freeman, Rosemary, *English Emblem Books*, 1948; rpt. New York, Octagon Books, 1966

Frye, Roland Mushat, *Milton's Imagery and the Visual Arts: Iconographic Tradition in the Epic Poems*, Princeton, NJ, Princeton University Press, 1978

Gethner, Perry J., 'Jean de Mairet and poetic justice: a definition of tragicomedy', *Ren. Drama*, n.s., 11 (1980), 171–87

Gilbert, Allan H., *The Symbolic Persons in the Masques of Ben Jonson*, Durham, NC, Duke University Press, 1948

Gillow, Joseph, *A Literary and Biographical History, or Bibliographical Dictionary, of the English Catholics*, 5 vols., London, Burns and Oates, 1885–1902

Goldberg, Jonathan, 'The politics of Renaissance literature: A review essay', *ELH*, 49 (1982), 514–42

    James I and the Politics of Literature: Jonson, Shakespeare, Donne and their Contemporaries, Baltimore and London, Johns Hopkins University Press, 1983

Gombrich, Ernst H., 'Botticelli's mythologies: A study in the neoplatonic symbolism of his circle', *JWCI*, 8 (1945), 7–60

Gordon, D. J. *The Renaissance Imagination: Essays and Lectures by D. J. Gordon*, ed. Stephen Orgel, Berkeley and Los Angeles, University of California Press, 1975

Gossett, Suzanne, 'Drama in the English College, Rome, 1591–1660', *ELR*. 3 (1969), 60–93

Gotch, John Alfred, *Inigo Jones*, 1928; rpt. New York, Benjamin Blom, 1968

Gray, Charles H., *Lodowick Carliell: His Life and a Discussion of his Plays*, Chicago, University of Chicago Press, 1905

Gray, J. E., 'The source of *The Emperor of the East*', *RES*, n.s., 1 (1950), 126–35

Greg, Walter W., *A Bibliography of the English Printed Drama to the Restoration*, 2 vols., Oxford, Oxford University Press, 1951

Guilday, Peter, *The English Catholic Refugees on the Continent, 1558–1795*, London, Longmans, Green Co., 1914

Hall, Marcia B. *Renovation and Counter-Reformation: Vasari and Duke Cosimo in Sta Maria Novella and Sta Croce, 1565–1577*, Oxford-Warburg Studies, Oxford, Clarendon, 1979

Haller, William and Malleville, 'The Puritan art of love', *HLQ*, 5 (1942), 235–72

Hamilton, Elizabeth, *Henrietta Maria*, London, Hamish Hamilton, 1976

Harbage, Alfred, *Cavalier Drama: An Historical and Critical Supplement to the Study of the Elizabethan and Restoration Stage*, 1936; rpt. New York, Russell and Russell, 1964

Harris, John, Stephen Orgel, and Roy Strong, *The King's Arcadia: Inigo Jones and the Stuart Court*, an illustrated catalogue of an exhibition held at the Banqueting House, Whitehall, 1973, Arts Council of Great Britain, 1973

Harrison, J[ohn] S[mith], *Platonism in English Poetry of the Sixteenth and Seventeenth Centuries*, 1903; rpt. New York, Columbia College, 1930

Haskell, Francis, *Patrons and Painters: A Study in the Relations between Italian Art and Society in the Age of the Baroque*, London, Chatto and Windus, 1963

Hassel, Rudolph Chris, Jr., *Renaissance Drama and the Church Year*, Lincoln and London, University of Nebraska Press, 1979

Havran, Martin J., *The Catholics in Caroline England*, California, Stanford University Press, 1962

Heinemann, Margot, *Puritanism and Theatre: Thomas Middleton and Opposition Drama under the Early Stuarts*, Cambridge, Cambridge University Press, 1980

Held, Julius S., *The Oil Sketches of Peter Paul Rubens*, Princeton, Princeton University Press, 1980

Henderson, Fletcher O., 'Traditions of *précieux* and *libertin* in Suckling's poetry', *ELH*, 4 (1937), 274–98

Henderson, Katherine Usher and Barbara F. McManus eds., *Half Humankind: Contexts and Texts of the Controversy about Women in England, 1540–1640*, Urbana and Chicago, University of Illinois Press, 1985

Herrick, Marvin T., *Tragicomedy: Its Origin and Development in Italy, France, and England*, Urbana, University of Illinois Press, 1955

Hibbard, H., *Bernini*, Harmondsworth, Penguin Books, 1965

Hill, Christopher, *The World Turned Upside Down: Radical Ideas during the English Revolution*, London, Temple Smith, 1972

Hocking, George Drew D'Arcy, *A Study of the Tragoediae Sacrae of N. Caussin (1583–1651)*, Baltimore, Md., Johns Hopkins Press, 1943

Höltgen, Karl Josef, *see* Primary sources under Hawkins, Henry, *The Devout Hart*

Hughes, Robert, *Heaven and Hell in Western Art*, London, Weidenfeld and Nicolson, 1968

Hume, Martin, *The Courtships of Queen Elizabeth: a History of the Various Negotiations for her Marriage*, London, T. F. Unwin, 1898

Hunter, G. K. 'Italian tragicomedy on the English stage', *Ren. Drama*, n.s., 6 (1973), 123–48

Hunter, William B., Jr., 'The liturgical context of *Comus*', *ELN*, 10 (1972), 11–15

Jacquot, Jean, 'La reine Henriette-Marie et l'influence française dans les spectacles à la cour de Charles Ier', 9e *Cahier de l'association international des études françaises*, Paris, Société d'éditions 'Les Belles Lettres' (1957), 128–60

'Une parodie du *Triumph of Peace*', *Cahiers Elisabéthains*, 15 (1979), 77–80

Jacquot, Jean, ed., *Dramaturgie et société: rapports entre l'oeuvre théâtrale, son interpretation et son public aux XVIe et XVIIe siècles*, 2 vols., Paris, Editions du CNRS, 1968

ed., *Le Lieu théâtral à la Renaissance*, Paris, Editions du CNRS, 1968

Jaffé, Michael, 'Charles I and Rubens', *History To-Day* (1951), 61–73

Rubens and Italy, Ithaca, Cornell University Press, 1977

Janelle, Pierre, *The Catholic Reformation*, 1963; rpt. London, Collier-Macmillan, 1975

Keating, Louis Clark, *Studies on the Literary Salon in France, 1550–1615*, Harvard Studies in Romance Languages, 16, Cambridge, Mass., Harvard University Press, 1941

Kernan, Alvin B., 'The theatre of ritual and the theatre of politics', *Yale Review*, 63 (1974), 434–9

Kernodle, George R., *From Art to Theatre: Form and Convention in the Renaissance*, Chicago, Chicago University Press, 1944

Kisch, Marie-Anne, de, 'Fêtes et représentations au Collège anglais de Rome 1612–14', in *Fêtes* III (1975), 525–43

Kristeller, Paul O., *The Philosophy of Marsilio Ficino*, trans. Virginia Conant, New York, Columbia University Press, 1943

Lamont, William and S. Oldfield, eds., *Politics, Religion, and Literature in the Seventeenth Century*, London, Dent, 1975

Lancaster, Henry C., *A History of French Dramatic Literature in the Seventeenth Century (1610–34)*, 2 vols, Baltimore, Md., Johns Hopkins Press, 1929

'Jean-Pierre Camus', *PMLA*, 62 (1947), 572–3

Lanson, Gustav, *Histoire de la littérature française*, Paris, Librairie Hachette, n.d.

Lathuillère, Roger, *La Préciosité. Etude historique et linguistique*, 1, Publications romanes et françaises, 87, Geneva, Librairie Droz, 1966

Lawrenson, T. E. *The French Stage in the XVIIth Century: A Study in the Advent of the Italian Order*, Manchester, Manchester University Press, 1957

Lemaire, Henri, *Les Images chez saint François de Sales*, Paris, Nizet, 1962

Levin, Richard, '*The New Inne* and the proliferation of good bad drama', *Essays in Criticism*, 22 (1972), 41–7

Lewis, C. S., *The Allegory of Love: A Study in Medieval Tradition*, 1936; rpt. Oxford, Oxford University Press, 1967

Lindley, David, ed., *The Court Masque* (with Bibliography to 1984, pp. 185–94), Manchester, Manchester University Press, 1984

Logan, Terence P. and Denzell S. Smith, eds., *The Later Jacobean and Caroline Dramatists: A Survey of Recent Scholarship and Criticism*, Lincoln, Nebraska University Press, 1978

Loomie, Albert J., S.J., 'King James I's Catholic Consort', *HLQ*, 34 (1971), 303–16

Lottes, Wolfgang, 'Henry Hawkins and *Partheneia Sacra*', *RES*, n.s., 26 (1975), 144–53, 271–86

Lougee, Carolyn C., *Le Paradis des femmes: Women, Salons, and Social Stratification in Seventeenth-Century France*, Princeton, NJ, Princeton University Press, 1976

Lynch, Kathleen, *The Social Mode of Restoration Comedy*, 1926; rpt. New York, Frank Cass, 1967

McCabe, William H., 'The play-list of the English College of St Omers 1597–1762', *Revue de Littérature Comparée*, 17 (1937), 355–75

'Notes on the St Omers College theatre', *PQ*, 17 (1938), 225–39

'Music and dance on a seventeenth-century college stage', *The Musical Quarterly*, 24 (1938), 313–22

An Introduction to Jesuit Theatre, ed. Louis J. Oldant, St Louis, Institute of Jesuit Sources, 1983

McGowan, Margaret, *L'Art du ballet de cour en France 1581–1643*, Paris, Editions du CNRS, 1963

'Les Jésuites à Avignon: les fêtes au service de la propagande politique et religieuse', *Fêtes* III (1975), 153–71

McGuire, Maryann Cale, *Milton's Puritan Masque*, Athens, University of Georgia Press, 1983.

Maclean, Ian, *Woman Triumphant: Feminism in French Literature 1610–1652*, Oxford, Clarendon, 1977

McMahon, Sister Mary C., *Aesthetics and Art in the Astrée of Honoré d'Urfé*, Catholic University of America Studies in Romance Languages and Literature 1, Washington, DC, 1925

Magee, Brian, *The English Recusants: A Study of the Post-Reformation Catholic Survival and the Operation of the Recusancy Laws*, London, Burns, Oates and Washbourne, 1938

Magendie, Maurice, *La Politesse mondaine et les théories de l'honnêteté en France au XVIIe siècle de 1600 à 1660*, Paris, 1925; rpt. Geneva, Slatkine, 1970

Maland, David, *Culture and Society in Seventeenth-century France*, Studies in Cultural History series, London, B. T. Batsford Ltd., 1970

Mâle, Emile, *The Gothic Image: Religious Art in France of the Thirteenth Century*, trans. of 3rd French edn. by Dora Nussey, 1913; rpt. Icon Editions, New York, Harper and Row, 1972

L'Art religieux après le concile de Trente, Paris, Librairie Armand Colin, 1932

Mamczarz, Irène, 'Une fête équestre à Ferrare: Il Tempio d'amore (1565)', *Fêtes*, III (1975), 349–72

Marcus, Leah Sinanoglou, 'Present occasion and the shaping of Ben Jonson's masques', *ELH*, 45 (1978), 201–25

'The occasion of Ben Jonson's *Pleasure Reconciled to Virtue*', *SEL*, 19 (1979), 271–93

'Masquing occasions and masque structure', *Research Opportunities in Renaissance Drama*, 24 (1981), 7–16

Martz, Louis, *The Poetry of Meditation. A Study in English Religious Literature of the Seventeenth Century*, 2nd rev. edn., New Haven, Yale University Press, 1962

Massa, Daniel, 'Giordano Bruno's ideas in seventeenth-century England', *JHI*, 38 (1977), 227–42

Mathew, David, *Catholicism in England, 1535–1935. Portrait of a Minority, Its Culture and Tradition*, London, Longmans, 1936

The Age of Charles I, London, Eyre and Spottiswoode, 1951; rpt. 1977

Meagher, John C., *Method and Meaning in Jonson's Masques* London, University of Notre Dame Press, 1966

Merrill, Robert V., 'Eros and Anteros', *Speculum*, 19 (1944), 265–84

Merrill, Robert V., with Robert J. Clements, *Platonism in French Renaissance Poetry*, New York, New York University Press, 1957

Meyer, Arnold Oskar, 'Charles I and Rome', *American Historical Review*, 19 (October 1913), 13–26

Millar, Oliver, 'Charles I, Honthorst, and Van Dyck', *Burlington Magazine*, 96 (1954), 36–42

Rubens: The Whitehall Ceiling, London, Oxford University Press, 1958 ed., 'Abraham Van der Doort's catalogue of the collections of Charles I', *The Walpole Society*, 37 (1958–60)

Mitchell, Bonner, 'Les intermèdes au service de l'état', *Fêtes* III (1975), 117–31

Montagu, Jennifer, 'The painted enigma and French seventeenth-century art', *JWCI*, 31 (1969), 307–35

Montrose, Louis Adrian, '"Eliza, Queene of Shepheardes", and the pastoral of power', *ELR*, 10 (1980), 153–82

Mornet, Daniel, 'La signification et l'évolution de l'idée de préciosité en France au XVIIe siècle', *JHI*, 1 (1940), 225–31

Mourgues, Odette de, *Metaphysical Baroque and Précieux Poetry*, Oxford, Clarendon, 1953

Nagler, Alois Maria, *Theatre Festivals of the Medici, 1539–1637*, trans. G. Hickenlooper, New Haven, Yale University Press, 1964

Neale, J[ohn] E. *The Age of Catherine de Medici, and Essays in Elizabethan History*, London, Jonathan Cape, 1943; rpt. 1970

Nelson, John Charles, *Renaissance Theory of Love: The Context of Giordano Bruno's 'Eroici furori'*, New York, Columbia University Press, 1958

New Catholic Encyclopedia, ed. Staff of Catholic University, 15 vols., New York, McGraw-Hill, 1967

Norbrook, David, *Poetry and Politics in the English Renaissance*, London, Routledge and Kegan Paul, 1984

O'Connell, Michael, 'The idolatrous eye: iconoclasm, anti-theatricalism, and the image of the Elizabethan theatre', *ELH*, 52 (1985), 279–310

Oman, Carola Lenanton, *Henrietta Maria*, London, Hodder and Stoughton, 1936

Orgel, Stephen, *The Jonsonian Masque*, Cambridge, Mass., Harvard University Press, 1965
  'Florimène and The Ante-Masques', *Ren. Drama*, n.s., 4 (1971), 135–53
  'Inigo Jones' Persian entertainment [i.e. *The Temple of Love]*, in *Art and Archaeology Research Papers [AARP]*, 2 (1972), 59–69
  The Illusion of Power: Political Theatre in the English Renaissance, Berkeley, University of California Press, 1975
  'The Renaissance artist as plagiarist', *ELH*, 48 (1981), 476–95

Orgel, Stephen and Roy Strong, *Inigo Jones: The Theatre of the Stuart Court. Including the Complete Designs for Productions at Court . . . together with their Texts and Historical Documentation*, 2 vols., London, Sothebey Parke Bernet, and Berkeley, University of California Press, 1973

Orrell, John, 'Inigo Jones and Amerigo Salvetti: a note on the later masque designs', *Theatre Notebook*, 30 (1976), 109–14
  'The Agent of Savoy at *The Somerset Masque*', *RES*, 28 (1977), 301–4

Oxford History of England, ed. G. N. Clark, IX, Oxford, Clarendon, 1949

Palme, Per, *Triumph of Peace: A Study of the Whitehall Banqueting House*, Stockholm, Almqvist and Wiksell, 1956

Parry, Graham, *The Golden Age Restor'd: The Culture of the Stuart Court, 1603–42*, Manchester, Manchester University Press, 1981

Patrides, C. A. and Joseph M. Wittreich, eds., *The Apocalypse in English Renaissance Thought and Literature*, Manchester, Manchester University Press, 1984

Patterson, Annabel M., *Censorship and Interpretation: The Conditions of Writing and Reading in Early Modern England*, Madison, University of Wisconsin Press, 1985

Peacock, John, 'The French element in Inigo Jones's masque designs', in *The Court Masque*, ed. David Lindley, pp. 149–68 (with 24 illustrations), Manchester, Manchester University Press, 1984

Phialas, Peter G., 'The sources of Massinger's *Emperor of the East*', *PMLA*, 65 (1950), 473–82

Phillips, James Emerson, *Images of a Queen: Mary Stuart in Seventeenth-Century Literature*, Berkeley, University of California Press, 1965

Phillips, John, *The Reformation of Images: Destruction of Art in England, 1535–1660*, Berkeley, University of California Press, 1973

Pickel, Margaret B., *Charles I as Patron of Poetry and Drama*, London, Frederick Muller, 1936

Plowden, Alison, *Marriage with my Kingdom: the Courtships of Elizabeth I*, New York, Stein and Day, 1977

Potter, Lois, 'The Triumph of Peace and The Cruel War: masque and parody', *N&Q*, 27 (1980), 345–8

Praz, Mario, *Studies in Seventeenth-Century Imagery*, 2nd edn., Michigan, Scholarly Press, 1964

Randall, Dale B. J., *Jonson's Gypsies Unmasked: Background and Theme of The Gypsies Metamorphos'd*, Durham, NC, Duke University Press, 1975

Randall, Dale B. J. and George W. Williams, eds., *Studies in the Continental Background of Renaissance English Literature: Essays presented to John L. Lievsay*, Durham, NC, Duke University Press, 1977

Richards, Kenneth, 'Joseph Rutter's *The Shepherd's Holiday* and the *Silvanire* of Jean de Mairet', *Anglia*, 85 (1967), 404–13

'Queen Henrietta Maria as patron of the drama', *Studia Neophilologica*, 42 (1970), 9–24

Richmond, Hugh M., *The School of Love: The Evolution of the Stuart Love Lyric*, Princeton, NJ, Princeton University Press, 1964

Ristine, Frank Humphrey, *English Tragicomedy: Its Origin and History*, New York, Columbia University Press, 1910

Roberts, Josephine A., 'Excerpts from *Acadia* in the manuscript notebook of Lady Katherine Manners', *N&Q*, 28 (1981), 35–6

Russell, Conrad, ed., *The Origins of the English Civil War*, London, Macmillan, 1973

Russell, Jeffrey B., 'Courtly love as religious dissent', *Catholic Historical Review*, 51 (1964–5), 31–44

Sabol, Andrew J., 'New documents on Shirley's masque *The Triumph of Peace*', *Music and Letters*, 47 (1966), 10–26

Four Hundred Songs and Dances from the Stuart Masque, Providence, RI, Brown University Press, 1978

Secker, Josephine E., 'Henry Hawkins, S. J., 1577–1646: A recusant writer and translator of the early seventeenth century', *Recusant History*, 11 (1972), 237–52

Sells, A. Lytton, *The Paradise of Travellers: The Italian Influence on Englishmen in the Seventeenth Century*, London, George Allen and Unwin, 1964

Sensabaugh, George F., 'Love ethics in Platonic court drama 1625–42', *HLQ*, 1 (1938), 277–304

'John Ford and Platonic love in the court', *SP*, 36 (1939), 202–26

'Platonic love and the Puritan rebellion', *SP*, 37 (1940), 457–81.

'The milieu of *Comus*, *SP*, 41 (1944), 239–49

The Tragic Muse of John Ford, New York, Benjamin Blom, 1944

'Platonic love in Shirley's *The Lady of Pleasure*', in *A Tribute to George Coffin Taylor*, ed. Arnold Williams, pp. 168–77, Chapel Hill, University of North Carolina Press, 1952

Shepherd, Simon, *Amazons and Warrior Women: Varieties of Feminism in Seventeenth Century Drama*, Brighton, Harvester Press, 1981

Smuts, R. Malcolm, 'The Culture of Absolutism at the Court of Charles I', unpublished doctoral dissertation, Princeton University, 1976 [Microfilm]

'The Puritan followers of Henrietta Maria in the 1630s', *EHR*, 93 (1978), 26–45

'The political failure of Stuart cultural patronage', in *Patronage in the Renaissance*, eds. Guy Fitch Lytle and Stephen Orgel, Princeton, NJ, Princeton University Press, 1981

Southern, Richard, *Changeable Scenery: Its Origin and Development in the British Theatre*, London, Faber and Faber, 1952

Stavig, Mark, *John Ford and the Traditional Moral Order*, Madison and London, University of Wisconsin Press, 1968

Steele, Mary Susan, *Plays and Masques at Court during the Reigns of Elizabeth, James, and Charles (1558–1642)*, Cornell University Press, 1926; reissued New York, Russell and Russell, 1968

Stegmann, André, 'Le rôle des Jésuites dans la dramaturgie française au début du XVIIᵉ siècle', in *Dramaturgie et Société*, ed. J. Jacquot, II, 445–56

'La fête parisienne á la Place Royale en avril 1612', *Fêtes* III (1975), 373–92

Stewart, Stanley, *The Enclosed Garden: The Tradition and the Image in Seventeenth-Century Poetry*, Madison, University of Wisconsin Press, 1966

Stone, Lawrence, *The Crisis of the Aristocracy*, Oxford, Clarendon, 1967

Storer, Mary E., 'Jeane-Pierre Camus, Evêque de Belley', *PMLA*, 61 (1946), 711–38

Stoye, John W., *English Travellers Abroad 1604–1667: Their Influence in English Society and Politics*, London, Jonathan Cape, 1952

Strong, Roy C., 'The popular celebration of the Accession Day of Queen Elizabeth I', *JWCI*, 21 (1958), 86–103

'Festivals for the Garter Embassy at the court of Henry III', *JWCI*, 22 (1959) 60–70

Portraits of Queen Elizabeth I, Oxford, Clarendon, 1963

Van Dyck: Charles I on Horseback, Art in Context series, London, Penguin, 1972

Splendour at Court: Renaissance Spectacle and Illusion, London, Weidenfeld and Nicolson, 1973

The Cult of Elizabeth: Elizabethan Portraiture and Pageantry, London, Thames and Hudson, 1977

Britannia Triumphans: Inigo Jones, Rubens, and Whitehall Palace [12th Walter Neurath Memorial Lecture], Hampshire, Thames and Hudson, 1980

Art and Power: Renaissance Festivals 1450–1650 (revision and expansion of *Splendour at Court*), Berkeley, University of California Press, 1984

Summerson, John, *Architecture in Britain*, 1530–1830, 4th rev. and enl. edn., Pelican History of Art, Harmondsworth, Penguin Books, 1963

Inigo Jones, Pelican *Architect and Society* series, Harmondsworth, Penguin Books, 1966

Symonds, John Addington, *Renaissance in Italy*, 5 vols., London, 1875–1886; rpt. New York, Modern Library Edition, 1935

Thieme, Ulrich, and Felix Becker, *Allgemeines Lexikon der bildenden Künstler von der Antike bis zur Gegenwart*, Leipzig, 1907

Thomas, P. W., 'Two cultures? Court and country under Charles I', in *The Origins of the English Civil War*, ed. Conrad Russell, chap. 6, pp. 168–93, London, Macmillan, 1973

Thompson, E[lbert] N. S., *The Controversy between the Puritans and the Stage*, Yale Studies in English, 20, New York, Henry Holt and Co., 1903

Treloar, Bronnie, 'Some feminist views in France in the seventeenth century', *AUMLA (Journal of Australasian Universities Language and Literature Association)*, 10 (1959), 152–9

Turner, Alberta, 'Queen Henrietta Maria and the University poets', *N&Q*, 193 (1948), 270–2

Upham, Alfred Horatio, *The French Influence in English Literature: From the Accession of Elizabeth to the Restoration*, 1908; rpt. New York, Octagon Books, 1965

Veevers, Erica, 'The source of Walter Montague's *The Accomplish'd Woman*', *N&Q*, 30 (1983), 439–40

'The authorship of *Maria Triumphans*', *N&Q*, 34 (1987), 313–14

Vyvyan, John, *Shakespeare and Platonic Beauty*, London, Chatto and Windus, 1961

Warner, Marina, *Alone of all her Sex: The Myth and the Cult of the Virgin Mary*, New York, Alfred A. Knopf, 1976

Wedgwood, C. V., *The King's Peace 1637–1641*, London, Collins, 1955

'Rubens and King Charles I', *History To-Day*, 10 (1960), 809–20

Poetry and Politics under the Stuarts, Cambridge, Cambridge University Press, 1960

Weil, Mark S., 'The devotion of the forty hours and Roman baroque illusions', *JWCI*, 37 (1974), 218–48

Weiner, A. D., 'Expelling the beast: Bruno's adventures in England', *Modern Philology*, 78 (1980), 1–13

Wells, Robin H., *Spenser's Faerie Queene and the Cult of Elizabeth*, London, Croom Helm, 1983

Welsford, Enid, *The Court Masque: A Study in the Relationship Between Poetry and the Revels*, Cambridge, Cambridge University Press, 1927

Whinney, Margaret, 'Inigo Jones: a revaluation', *Royal Institute British Architects Journal*, 3rd series, 59 (1952), 286–9

White, Helen C., *English Devotional Literature (Prose) 1600–1640*, University of Wisconsin Studies in Language and Literature, no. 29, 1930; rpt. New York, Haskell House, 1966
  'Some continuing traditions in English devotional literature', *PMLA*, 57 (1942), 966–80

Wickham, Glynne, *Early English Stages 1300 to 1660*, I and II, London, Routledge and Kegan Paul, 1963

Willis, Leota (Snider), 'Francis Lenton, Queen's Poet', unpublished doctoral dissertation, Philadelphia, 1931 (held at Henry E. Huntington Library)

Wilson, Elkin Calhoun, *England's Eliza*, Harvard Studies in English, 20 (1939); rpt. New York, Octagon Books, 1966

Wind, Edgar, *Pagan Mysteries in the Renaissance* (chaps. 7 and 8 on Botticelli), New Haven, Yale University Press, 1958

Wittkower, Rudolf, 'Puritanissimo fiero', *Burlington Magazine*, 90 (1948), 50–1
  Architectural Principles in the Age of Humanism, 1949; 3rd rev. edn., London, Alec Tiranti, 1962
  'Inigo Jones, architect and man of letters', *RIBA Journal*, 60 (1953), 83–90
  Allegory and the Migration of Symbols, London, Thames and Hudson, 1977

Wittkower, Rudolf and Irma B. Jaffé, eds., *Baroque Art: The Jesuit Contribution*, New York, Fordham University Press, 1972

Woodbridge, Linda, *Women and the English Renaissance: Literature and the Nature of Womankind 1540–1620*, Urbana, University of Illinois Press, 1984

Yates, Frances A., 'Giordano Bruno's conflict with Oxford', *JWCI*, 2 (1939) 227–42
  'The religious policy of Giordano Bruno', *JWCI*, 3 (1940), 181–207
  The French Academies of the Sixteenth Century, Studies of the Warburg Institute, 15, London, 1947; rpt. Nendeln, Liechtenstein, Kraus Reprint, 1968
  'Poésie et musique dans les "Magnificences" au mariage du Duc de Joyeuse, Paris, 1581', in *Musique et Poésie au XVIe Siècle*, Paris, CNRS, 1954, pp. 241–64
  'Elizabethan chivalry: the romance of the Accession Day Tilts', *JWCI*, 20 (1957), 4–25
  The Valois Tapestries, London, Warburg Institute, 1959
  Giordano Bruno and the Hermetic Tradition, London, Routledge and Kegan Paul, 1964
  Shakespeare's Last Plays: A New Approach, London, Routledge and Kegan Paul, 1975
  Astraea: The Imperial Theme in the Sixteenth Century, London, Routledge and Kegan Paul, 1975

Index